Existentialist Criminology

Existentialist Criminology captures an emerging interest in the value of existentialist thought and concepts for criminological work on crime, deviance, crime control, and criminal justice.

This emerging interest chimes with recent social and cultural developments – as well as shifts in their theoretical consideration – that are oriented around contingency and unpredictability. But whilst these conditions have largely been described and analysed through the lens of complexity theory, post-structuralist theory and postmodernism, their exploration by critical criminologists in existentialist terms offers a richer and more productive approach to the social and cultural dimensions of crime, deviance, crime control and, more broadly, of regulation and governance. Covering a range of topics that lend themselves quite naturally to existentialist analysis – crime and deviance as becoming and will, the existential openness of symbolic exchange, the internal conversations that take place within criminal justice practices, and the contingent and finite character of resistance – the contributions to this volume set out to explore a largely untapped reservoir of critical potential.

Ronnie Lippens is Professor of Criminology at Keele University. **Don Crewe** is Lecturer in Criminology at Roehampton University.

Existentialist Criminology

Edited by Ronnie Lippens
and Don Crewe

Routledge·Cavendish
Taylor & Francis Group
a GlassHouse book
LONDON AND NEW YORK

Fifth published 2009
by Routledge-Cavendish
2 Park Square, Milton Park, Abingdon, Oxon OX14 4RN

Simultaneously published in the USA and Canada
by Routledge-Cavendish
270 Madison Ave, New York, NY 10016

a GlassHouse book

Routledge-Cavendish is an imprint of the Taylor & Francis Group, an informa business

Typeset in Sabon by Wearset Ltd, Boldon, Tyne and Wear
Printed and bound in Great Britain by TJI Digital, Padstow, Cornwall

British Library Cataloguing in Publication Data
A catalogue record for this book is available from the British Library

Library of Congress Cataloging in Publication Data
Existentialist criminology / Ronnie Lippens and Don Crewe (eds.).
p. cm.
1. Criminology. 2. Critical criminology. 3. Existentialism.
I. Lippens, Ronnie. II. Crewe, Don.
HV6025.E83 2009
364.01–dc22   2008030160

ISBN10: 0-415-46771-3 (hbk)
ISBN13: 978-0-415-46771-1 (hbk)

ISBN10: 0-203-88265-2 (ebk)
ISBN13: 978-0-203-88265-8 (ebk)

Contents

List of contributors   vii

Introduction: Existentialism – freedom, being and crime   1
DON CREWE AND RONNIE LIPPENS

1 Will to self-consummation, and will to crime: a study in
   criminal motivation   12
   DON CREWE

2 Being accused, becoming criminal   51
   GEORGE PAVLICH

3 Biaphobia, state violence and the definition of violence   70
   WILLEM SCHINKEL

4 Existentialism, edgework, and the contingent body:
   exploring the criminological implications of Ultimate
   Fighting   94
   STEPHEN LYNG, RICK MATTHEWS, AND WILLIAM J. MILLER

5 Scrounging: time, space, and being   127
   JEFF FERRELL

6 White-collar offenders after the fall from grace: stigma,
   blocked paths and resettlement   145
   BEN HUNTER

7 'We just live day-to-day': a case study of life after release
   following wrongful conviction   169

   STEPHEN FARRALL

8 The seductions of conformity: the criminological
   importance of a phenomenology of exchange   197

   SIMON MACKENZIE

9 Existentialism and the criminology of the shadow   222

   BRUCE ARRIGO AND CHRISTOPHER WILLIAMS

10 Towards existential hybridization? A contemplation on
   the *Being and Nothingness* of critical criminology   249

   RONNIE LIPPENS

   Index   291

Contributors

Bruce Arrigo, Professor, Department of Criminal Justice, University of North Carolina at Charlotte, USA.

Don Crewe, Lecturer (Assistant Professor), School of Business and Social Sciences, Roehampton University, London, UK.

Stephen Farrall, Reader (Associate Professor), Centre for Criminological Research, Sheffield University, UK.

Jeff Ferrell, Professor, Texas Christian University, USA.

Ben Hunter, PhD Candidate, Research Institute for Law, Politics, and Justice, Keele University, UK.

Ronnie Lippens, Professor, School of Criminology and Sociology, Keele University, UK.

Stephen Lyng, Professor, Department of Sociology, Carthage College, USA.

Simon Mackenzie, Senior Research Fellow, Scottish Centre for Crime and Justice Research, University of Glasgow, UK.

Rick Matthews, Associate Professor, Department of Sociology, Carthage College, USA.

William J. Miller, Associate Professor, Department of Sociology, Carthage College, USA.

George Pavlich, Professor, Department of Sociology, University of Alberta, Canada.

Willem Schinkel, Hoofddocent (Associate Professor), Faculty of Social Sciences, Erasmus University Rotterdam, the Netherlands.

Christopher Williams, Associate Professor, Department of Sociology and Criminology, University of West Georgia, USA.

Introduction

Existentialism – freedom, being and crime

Don Crewe and Ronnie Lippens

Existentialism

The term existentialism has come to apply to a disparate range of human endeavour in the past half-century. Works of cinema such as Bergman's *The Seventh Seal* (1957) or of literature, such as the work of Kerouac[1] (*On the Road* 1957) or Borroughs[2] (*The Naked Lunch* 1959) were contemporary with the flowering of existentialism in philosophy. The term has also been applied to works such as Kundera's[3] *The Unbearable Lightness of Being* (1984), in that it deals with the apparent insignificance, lightness, nothingness of human 'being'.[4] Historically some have suggested that existentialism has been with us since the ancient Greeks, suggesting that Socrates was the first existentialist for his belief that his life was what he made it. We might suggest that Nietzsche's 'death of God' is rooted in the birth of modernity and Copernican heliocentrism, in that man, and not God, has become the measure of Man, or a similar idea expressed in Kant. Certainly there are strong traces of existentialist-like thought in Blaise Pascal's nihilist sentiments. Moreover, far from existentialist thought having become a minor backwater, many recent writers make use of existentialist ideas.

However, in recent times the term has also come to apply to any work that expresses profound nihilism – particularly contemporarily in the face of the end of the benign Holocene – the hopelessness of the human condition, or indeed, merely ennui. This dissipation of the precision of the term has lead some to suggest that existentialism is no more than a historical cultural affectation. A similar kind of affectation was fashionable in the seventeenth century when melancholy was a privileged emotion in the arts and in 'cultured' discourse – *'Semper Dowland Semper Dolens'*.[5] Indeed, it is suggested by some that both are cultural sentiments whose time is past.

The view that existentialism may be such a dissipated term stands in stark contrast to the claim that Sartre and only Sartre should be considered existentialist. This claim suggests that there is no place within the scope of existentialism for the merely literary (Dostoevsky, de Beauvoir or Camus, for example), that Heidegger rejected the term, and that those said to be the progenitors of the field, Kierkegaard and Nietzsche, were working before the term was coined. Neither position is tenable as a description of the nature of existentialism. In essence, existentialism is a field of human enquiry that has at its root a philosophical position that says that neither scientific nor moral inquiry are adequate to reveal questions concerning the nature of human being. Existentialism is that form of inquiry about the nature of human being that locates the essential quality of being human in the notions of freedom and authenticity. In the face of the impossibility of absolute reason, in the face of the impossibility of a universal morality, the traditional philosophical questions concerning, for example, how we should live must be found in the 'authentic' behaviour of the individual human: in the choices made about an individual life project. This is bound up with the question of human freedom; not merely to ask what is 'the nature of human freedom, but to experience freedom and to practise it ... to learn that ... the sense of freedom which we have is justified; and moreover that, in some sense, causation is an illusion'.[6]

The most fundamental theme addressed by existentialism is the question of being. Whilst Heidegger rejected the label 'existentialist', it is within his work that this theme receives its most telling exploration: the establishment of the idea that existence precedes essence. For Heidegger, earlier philosophers haven't really been asking about being at all, or have dismissed the question of being – what it is for humans to have being or to be – as meaningless (see Crewe, this volume); thus, he famously begins by renaming this aspect of humanity 'Dasein' or 'there-being'. For Heidegger, Dasein is being-in-the-world, an idea which is at odds with Cartesian dualism. The foundation for Dasein's engagement with the world, Heidegger claimed, lay with Husserl's phenomenological account of intentionality – we possess states of mind that are directed to some object which we represent to ourselves – that is, we are conscious of the objects in the world towards which our states of mind are directed, and we are able to experience having those states of mind 'phenomenally'. This, for Heidegger, means that we are that creature who, uniquely, can inquire into the nature of his own being. Furthermore, since phenomenological inquiry is into the constitution of the meaning of things, inquiry into our being must be into the constitution of the meaning of being for us: what it means for me to be. When we make this inquiry, we are capable of seeing ourselves as being in a world of others like us.

For both Nietzsche and Kierkegaard, the true meaningfulness of life is revealed in one's relationship with God – for Nietzsche when there is no God, and for Kierkegaard when we reject God's moral codes. For both, this reveals the necessity for an individual voluntaristic search for one's own ethic. For Heidegger, drawing on both these ideas, finding ourselves in a world of like others reveals to us the necessity to transcend other-driven inauthentic behaviour to find the authentic individual life project. The problem arises, however, that if we are to seek an individual ethic 'beyond good and evil', then what standard have we by which we may judge the meaningful and good life? For Kierkegaard in *Fear and Trembling*, Abraham's abrogation of his ethical duty to his son is not an instinctive, unthinking (libidinal) act, indeed, it is his ethical conscience – to care for his son, and which he overrides – that is his instinctive desire. Kierkegaard claims that conventional philosophies cannot comprehend this and thus are led to condemn Abraham's behaviour as being unethical. Kierkegaard claims that because of the unethical command that He gave to Abraham, God's law cannot be seen as a universal law governing all people. Instead, it must be seen as addressing Abraham as an isolated individual. What this means for Kierkegaard is that if Abraham's life is to have meaning, then it must mean that the individual is greater than the universal: that individual freedom can transcend, ethically, the limitations of a universal morality. Thus, for Kierkegaard, life has meaning when we truly 'know' ourselves and act with passion and freedom to be that person that truly lies within us as individuals.

In contrast to Kierkegaard, who, as a devout Christian, articulated his thought through the relationship of man and his faith in God, Nietzsche, in *On the Genealogy of Morals*, responding to the growing natural sciences and particularly to Darwinism, asks the question: where does our ethic come from in the face of 'the death of God' that it was thought at the time Darwinism brought about? Nietzsche sees in Christianity a stultifying life-denying morality: a 'herd morality' that penalises genuinely life-affirming freedom in humans. As in Kierkegaard, where 'the crowd is untruth', the herd morality in Christianity represents the resentment felt by the weak towards the strong: it represents the weak's 'will to power' and their inability to possess it in the life-affirming way that the powerful do. Any universal morality is no more than the merely normal. In contrast to this, as in Kierkegaard, Nietzsche finds the root of human truth in individual freedom, in an individual ethic, rather than universal morals. As science shows its truth that there can be no God, so the universal morality of Christianity evaporates. In the face of this realisation, the weak falls into despair at his realisation that life has no meaning. That is, should we agree with Hegel that a human's life is made meaningful by adherence to universal laws, 'the death of God' removes the possibility for a life to have any intrinsic meaning. However, for the strong, this *tragedy* gives them freedom and therefore the opportunity to take responsibility for their own actions. This person, then, is the *Übermensch*, the person who has realised that any ethic arises in the understanding that this very tragedy is the death of morals and the birth of the life-affirming potential of an autonomous ethic.

For some the only true existentialist, Sartre drew heavily on these themes, particularly on Nietzsche, but also on Heidegger. The relevant Heideggerian ideas are dealt with in Don Crewe's contribution to this book, so we won't rehearse them here. However, the significant point for this brief discussion has to do with history – *Being and Time*. For Heidegger, acting is always acting in a world of others, and in a world with a past. The *facticity* of this past and present (its throwness) permits our authentic choices, which we 'project' into the future. However, whereas in Heidegger, and Nietzsche, we are *called*, normatively, to be free, for Sartre, we cannot choose to be free, we are 'condemned to be free'. First, for Sartre, there are no real things in the world; there are only our perceptions. The appearance of an object is absolute; the 'noumenon' – the thing itself – simply isn't there. This is important because it has ramifications for the way in which humans perceive themselves (for want of a better term). For Sartre, it is necessary to distinguish between 'being-in-itself' and 'being-for-itself'. Being-in-itself is concrete, unchanging and unaware; being-for-itself is conscious of its own consciousness. Because, as in Heidegger, existence precedes essence, the for-itself must generate *its* own essence from nothingness, by engagement in the world. Sartre next asserts that the for-itself is only given meaning through its engagement with the future; that is, it is not what it is essentially now but what it will become. Actually, man has no essence at all because everything that he has been, is and will become is the result of contingency and choice. This absence of essence apprehended through the difference between the in-itself and the for-itself, where the for-itself is conscious that it is not itself as represented by the in-itself, shows the for-itself that it is a nothingness, *tabula rasa*, on which it must create its own being. Thus, the for-itself is defined by its realisation that it is axiomatically separated from the in-itself, and we know this because the for-itself can perceive the in-itself and can see that it is different – it is present-to the in-itself, not identical to it. Following from this, Sartre believes that the nature of intersubjectivity stems from the 'look' of the other that defines me in terms of his difference from me. That is, I am taken away from that state of being that is meaningful for *me* (the subject-position) and cast as that which is meaningful for the *other*: I am objectified. As Sartre puts it, he is cast as French through the loathing of a German, or as Jewish through another's anti-Semitism. This means that whereas the phenomenological position of Heidegger, say, from Husserl, has it that we have self-identity – we are that entity that can represent itself to itself as an object; for Sartre, the capacity to take a perspective on ourselves, or however others might objectify us, means that we are different to ourselves. That is, we are free precisely because we are not selves but are a presence-to-self – the nihilation of self. We are thus free, as we are free of ourselves and our situation. Freedom is the very nature of man: we have no choice other than to be free.

The power to appropriate the 'subject-position' lay, for Sartre, not only in intersubjective relations but in our relations with institutions or social structures. This idea, it may be said, derives from his engagement with the proto-existentialist Marxism of Alexandre Kojève. Indeed, Sartre considered existentialism a mere moment within Marxism. Such inequalities as racism or poverty, created through the appropriation of the 'subject-position', are restricting of freedom, and thus engagement with the idea of freedom is political.

For Sartre, history represented the facticity out of which the project of self-making occurs. This led him to abandon the project of establishing the nature of human freedom through transcendental argument and to claim instead that the writer should always *engage* on the side of freedom, imagining paths to overturn injustice. Thus, philosophy must be made material through engagement: ivory tower theorising is otiose. This of course presupposes the freedom of the reader to respond, establishing through the praxis of political engagement the ultimate value: freedom as self-making.

This insistence on existence preceding essence and on freedom (normative and ontological) in existentialism has resonated strongly in the social sciences more recently, providing tools for critical engagement with the ideas that Tiryakian[7] has called 'sociologism' – the idea that freedom is unimportant in the face of *sui generis* social reality. More recently, Douglas and Johnson[8] have stressed the relative freedom of social actors, emphasising interpretation, social construction, will and emotion for the determining of social behaviour. Empirical studies by Espeland,[9] Johnson and Ferraro,[10] Ebaugh,[11] Kotarba and Bentley,[12] or Messinger and Warren[13] have concentrated very much on the existential freedom of humans to construct their own identities and life projects within social structures. Furthermore, forms of writing or expressing existential ideas have continued to make use of literary or poetic forms, performances, films or essays, leaving existentialist engagement in the social sciences as an engagement with freedom and, as Nisbet would have it 'an expression of movement, of becoming, and, in short, life'.[14]

Existentialism and criminology

No systematic attempt has hitherto been made, within the broader criminological community, to apply existential thought to problems of crime and crime control, or to put it to use in the expansion or further development of criminological theory. An existentialist thinker such as Sartre himself was quick to take the insights which he had developed in his massive *Being and Nothingness* (1942) into the criminological domain with his follow-up book *Saint Genet* (1952), an existentialist biographical analysis of the extraordinary self-creative life of Jean Genet: foundling, thief, prostitute, poet, novelist and journalist. In *Saint Genet*

Sartre applied the more fundamental insights from *Being and Nothingness* to a painstaking and minute analysis of Genet's multiple re-inventions of self. Whilst existentialist thought *did* have some impact on psychiatry and forensic psychiatry, most criminological literature remained largely unaffected by this emerging strand of theory. Certainly, authors such as David Matza did refer to, and indeed were inspired by, Sartre's *Saint Genet*. In his ground-breaking *Becoming Deviant*, published in 1969, Matza made a conscious effort to tap into Sartre's existentialist thought. However, the book seems to have appeared too late for it to be able to generate much momentum at a time when French structuralism had, in Europe at least, managed to capture academic audiences, including criminological ones. Across the Atlantic, symbolic interactionism had emerged and was already to a quite considerable extent structuring research agendas. There are many connexions to be made between interactionism, George Herbert Mead's in particular, and, for example, Sartre's existentialist thought. Both, for example, focus on the dialogical self and its internal deliberations and conversations. But such overlap never led to any systematic exploration of and application of existentialism within the criminological community, apart, that is, from Matza's undertaking. This is all the more surprising in view of the fact that the late 1960s might perhaps be looked upon as an 'existential' moment in history, i.e. an age when critical self-reflexivity was at its peak. A certain 'scientistic' bent in criminology has furthermore tended to close off meaningful engagement with notions of freedom, self constitution, morality, and authenticity – all experiences of 'human being' addressed very much by existentialists. In sociology more generally, existentialism re-surfaced – albeit not all too conspicuously – around the early 1980s, at another one of those historical existential moments, i.e. the onset of what later would become known as hyper-reflexive, indeterminate, indeed chaotic post-modernity. A small number of essay collections have since appeared, the most important of which, arguably, are those by Joseph Kotarba.[15] However, such work did not focus primarily on issues and problems of crime, deviance, and crime control.

But having said that, we should of course acknowledge a number of strands within current criminological scholarship which it might be argued have some connexions with the broader existential domain. First, there is the strand of peacemaking criminology which can be related to the work of writers such as Richard Quinney, Hal Pepinsky, Kevin Anderson, Gregg Barak, Bruce Arrigo, Larry Tifft and Dennis Sullivan, and others. This work however does not always engage extensively with existentialism proper (by that we mean the ideas and concepts expounded in works by authors such as Kierkegaard, Nietzsche, Heidegger, Sartre, and others), although the impact of related sources of inspiration (e.g. Erich Fromm's work) is notable.

Second, there is also the strand of scholarship which has become known as 'existential criminology', or the criminology of transgression or transgressive *becoming*. Here the work of researchers and scholars such as Jack Katz, Jeff Ferrell, Stephen Lyng, Dragan Milovanovic, Bruce Arrigo, Willem Schinkel, and others, should be noted. This work focuses on what Jack Katz, in his 1988 book *Seductions of Crime*, has called the 'foreground' factors, and on the situational contingencies therein, of 'criminal' events and what others have called 'edgework'. Although many of these highly interesting works are certainly relevant to our problematic – e.g. some of this work really does make a significant effort to analyse processes of constitution of the self or the creative *becoming* of self in view of legal and moral norms and pressures – few have done so through a sustained engagement with existentialism.

Finally, there's the more recent strand of what we now know as 'cultural criminology'. Here the work of writers such as Jeff Ferrell, Mike Presdee, Keith Hayward and Jock Young, and others, should come to mind. Whilst this work focuses on the contingencies on which often quite reflexive and inventive movements of (urban) resistance thrive, again we would stress that much of this effort is done largely without a sustained critical engagement with existentialism.

This then is where we hope to be able to somehow redress the situation a little. More than two decades into this post-modern hyper-reflexive age of ours, one cannot help but notice how existentialism is now gradually being rediscovered, including by criminologists. There has been in recent years an unmistakable resurgence of existentialist thought and concepts in criminological work on crime, deviance, crime control, and criminal justice. Much, if not most, of this work has appeared in single book chapters or journal articles and/or essays.[16] Emerging scholars are beginning to explore work by earlier existentialists (e.g. Kierkegaard, Nietzsche, Heidegger, Sartre, etc.) in doctoral theses.[17] This emerging interest in existentialist thought, one could argue, is no mere coincidence. It chimes quite harmoniously with recent and current social and cultural developments (as well as shifts in the theoretical reflection on these developments) that can be characterised as contingent, unpredictable, open to change, de-traditionalising, indeed chaotically 'becoming', to use an existentialist phrase. In a way, these conditions are quite similar to those in the immediate post-war era, when existentialism itself came to full fruition. Today's conditions of existential contingency, however, have largely been analysed, within the community of critical scholars and criminological researchers, through the lens of complexity theory, post-structuralist theory, or 'post-modernism'. There is an argument to be made for the exploration and application, by critical criminologists, of existentialism, and of existentialist concepts, when trying to get to grips with current social and cultural dimensions of issues and problems of crime, deviance, crime control and, more broadly, regulation and governance. As mentioned above, some scholars and researchers within criminology have made a start with such work. Now, we believe, is the time to build on this emerging awareness of the importance of existentialism.

There are a number of topics that lend themselves quite naturally to existentialist analysis, such as: crime and deviance as will and becoming (see, in this volume: Crewe, Pavlich, Lyng *et al.*, Ferrell); the existential openness of symbolic exchange and interaction, and in internal conversations and deliberations that take place within or around criminal justice practices (in this volume: Ferrell, Hunter, Farrall, Mackenzie); the potential for alternatives to conventional criminal-justice policies and practices that open up in the space of such existential self-reflexivity (Pavlich, Schinkel, Arrigo and Williams, Lippens); or the ineradicably contingent and finite character of *willed* critical resistance and attempts at justice (Pavlich, Schinkel, Lippens). The contributions in this volume all set out to explore such issues in quite some depth. In doing so, they connect into a hitherto largely untapped neo-Nietzschean reservoir of critical potential. Indeed, most existentialist concepts and ideas have, to some extent, roots in Nietzsche's work. This tapping into the 'existential Nietzsche', the Nietzsche of *becoming*, of potential and of change, of creative affirmation, is, in itself, already a worthwhile exercise. It is at this point, then, in trying to address this relative lack of existentialism-inspired criminological work, where we hope to be able to contribute in some measure, however small.

The contributions[18]

In his chapter on the 'will to self-consummation', Don Crewe engages with the work of Heidegger and with notions of becoming to establish how humans come to view themselves as objects of the future. In so doing, he develops and subsequently applies his notion of *will to self-consummation* to a critique of David Matza's concept, 'The will to crime', and concludes that such a will is not possible, but that problematic behaviour may result from a *will* to transgress.

George Pavlich shows how Nietzsche's thought enables us to grasp criminality not as essential being, but as complex becoming. For Nietzsche, description and evaluation are not distinct; rather the will, the choice, to classify being in this way is already an ethical statement, and one to which we are always responsible, despite evasive, 'bad faith', 'inauthentic' attempts to suppress this. Pavlich asks the question of how, in light of Nietzsche's contributions to existential thought, responsibility is implied by the all-too-common events that create criminals as objective elements against which to define a given order.

Based on Husserl's phenomenology and Heidegger's ontology, Willem Schinkel fleshes out an ontological definition of violence as reduction of being. Reduction of being is an ontological process that always happens the moment persons enter into interaction. Violence is hence a productive reduction of an ontological horizon grounding the conventional legitimate order. Seen from this perspective, aprioristic negative attitudes towards violence could then be called a form of biaphobia, which is a negation of the active force of life which Nietzsche called 'denial of life'. Schinkel shows how the dominant, biaphobic notion of violence procures the difference between legitimate violence (as *potestas*) and illegitimate violence (*violentia*) that founds the modern state, avoiding questions of legitimation in the process. Abandoning commonsensical and biaphobic conceptions of violence for an ontological one, Schinkel opens up space for a reflexive critique of moral and legal order.

Illustrating their thesis with empirical evidence on Ultimate Fighting, Stephen Lyng, Rick Matthews, and William Miller examine the intersections between existentialist thought and the 'edgework' approach to risk agency. The examination of Ultimate Fighting allows them to explore the critical connections between discipline, domination, the contingent body, and experiential transcendence in violent encounters that are both non-criminal and criminal in nature. Demonstrating the relevance of existentialist ideas to the increasing structural uncertainty and reflexivity of the risk society and the emergence of edgework as an expression of risk agency in this social context, Lyng and his colleagues also underline the importance of incorporating the body into the existentialist analysis of risk structure and agency.

In his contribution, Jeff Ferrell recounts his own experiences as a scrounger. Inspired by Situationism, he develops what he calls an 'existential ethnography' whereby he describes how the experience of marginal time (Zen time) and marginal space (the spaces of the scrounger) does not just write and invent an illicit map of the city, but also transforms the latter, as well as the self as it roams and meanders at a slowed-down pace, in the everyday at the margins. This urban experience of *detournement* and *derive* in back alleys and abandoned urban spaces, and the existential freedom that goes with it, Ferrell argues, are ultimately about creative revaluation and creative (self-)transformation.

Ben Hunter draws upon existential literature to provide an understanding of the reactions of white-collar offenders to their treatment at the hands of the criminal justice system and their resettlement in the wake of punishment. Data was gathered from published autobiographical accounts whereby white-collar offenders discuss their offences and punishment. The concerns that white-collar offenders have speak to an awareness of how one is situated within the world and the threat that one's sense of self may be subjected to by their offending. Detection of their offences puts what may have been a previously assumed future in jeopardy. The aftermath of punishment is likely to represent a search to determine who they are in the 'legitimate' world, a world they used to be part of but must now renegotiate their place within.

Stephen Farrall similarly analyses existential reflexivity. His chapter seeks to analyse resettlement experiences of those who, wrongfully convicted, are then released. He focuses upon the existential aspects of the experiences of one such released prisoner, Angela Cannings, in particular. The loss of their 'assumptive world', as well as other existential dilemmas faced by the wrongfully convicted inevitably raise issues which mainstream work on resettlement has overlooked, but which Farrall seeks here to explore.

In his chapter, Simon Mackenzie considers a phenomenology of exchange, as it may be relevant for the production of civility and the prevention of criminality and anti-social behaviour. Building on a philosophy of social contribution and social reciprocity Mackenzie contemplates ways which would satisfy the crime-reductive desires of the current political interest in community activation. It is here, he argues, that a phenomenology of exchange might really come into its own: as a means to understand certain elements of social engagement and its breakdown as experiential aspects of being in the world encountered by wrongdoers.

In their contribution, Bruce Arrigo and Christopher Williams build on a number of critical theories, including Erich Fromm's work on negative freedom, displaced spontaneity, and mechanisms of escape, in order to critically examine the contours of what they call the 'criminology of the shadow'. Adding a critique of evidence-based criminal justice, actuarial penology, and the policing of risk (which all work to eradicate the distinction between the subject *of* crime, i.e. transgression, and the subject *in* crime, i.e. transgressors), Arrigo and Williams go on to specify the existentialist dilemma for sustaining a criminology of the stranger.

And finally, Ronnie Lippens introduces and expands on the thesis that critical criminology may be able to re-invent itself through Sartre's existentialism. Beginning with an extensive analysis of critical criminology's postwar history, Lippens goes on to offer new 'guiding images' (most notably, existential hybridization) which, it is suggested, might be able to provide critical criminology with a renewed sense of purpose.

Notes

1 J. Kerouac, *On the Road*, London: Penguin, 1991.
2 W.S. Burroughs, *The Naked Lunch*, London: Flamingo, 1993.
3 M. Kundera, *The Unbearable Lightness of Being*, trans. M.H. Heim, London: Faber & Faber, 1985.
4 See F. Nietzsche, *The Gay Science*, trans. J. Nauckhoff, Cambridge: Cambridge University Press, 2001 §341.
5 The title of a collection of lute music by seventeenth-century English composer John Dowland.

6 M. Warnock, *Existentialism*, Oxford: Oxford University Press,1970.
7 E. Tiryakian, *Sociologism and Existentialism*, Englewood Cliffs, NJ: Prentice Hall, 1962.
8 J. Douglas, and M. Johnson, *Existential Sociology*, New York: Cambridge, 1977.
9 W. Espeland, 'Blood and Money: Exploring the Embodied Self', in J. Kotarba and A. Fontana, eds, *The Existential Self in Society*, Chicago: University of Chicago Press, 1984.
10 J. Johnson, and K. Ferraro, 'The Victimised Self: The Case of Battered Women', in J. Kotarba and A. Fontana, eds, *The Existential Self in Society*, Chicago: University of Chicago Press, 1984.
11 H. Ebaugh, 'Leaving the Convent: The Experiences of Role Exit and Self-Transformation', J. Kotarba and A. Fontana, eds, *The Existential Self in Society*, Chicago: University of Chicago Press, 1984.
12 J. Kotarba and P. Bentley, 'Workplace Wellbeing and the Existential Self', *Social Science and Medicine*, 1988, 26/5: 551–558.
13 S. Messinger and C. Warren, 'The Homosexual Self and the Organization of Experience: The Case of Kate White', in J. Kotarba and A. Fontana, eds, *The Existential Self in Society*, Chicago: University of Chicago Press, 1984.
14 R. Nisbet, *Sociology as an Art Form*, New York: Oxford University Press, p. 94. Cited in J. Kotarba and J. Johnson, eds, *Postmodern Existential Sociology*, Walnut Creek: Rowman & Littlefield, p. 9.
15 J. Kotarba and A. Fontana, eds, *The Existential Self in Society*. Chicago: Chicago University Press, 1984; and later, after decades of 'postmodernism': J. Kotarba and J. Johnson, eds, *Postmodern Existential Sociology*, Walnut Creek: Altamira, 2002.
16 W. Morrison, 'Crime and the Existentialist Dilemma', in *Theoretical Criminology: From Modernity to Post-Modernism*, London: Cavendish, 1995, pp. 349–382; B. Arrigo, 'Critical Criminology, Existential Humanism, and Social Justice: Exploring the Contours of Conceptual Integration', *Critical Criminology*, 2001, 2, 83–95; S. Farrall, 'On the Existential Aspects of Desistance from Crime', *Symbolic Interaction*, 2005, 3, 367–386; S. Mackenzie, 'Situationally Edited Empathy: An Effect of Socio-Economic Structure on Individual Choice', *Critical Criminology*, 2006, 3, 365–385; C. Williams 'Engaging Freedom: Toward an Ethics of Crime and Deviance', in B. Arrigo and C. Williams, eds, *Philosophy, Crime, and Criminology*, Chicago: University of Illinois Press, 2006, pp. 167–196; R. Lippens, 'Whither Critical Criminology? A Contemplation on Existential Hybridization', *Critical Criminology*, 2008, 2, 145–156.
17 W. Schinkel, *Aspects of Violence*, Rotterdam: Erasmus University, 2005; D. Crewe, *Will, Power, Constraint & Change: Prologomena to a Study of Self and the Emergence of Structure in a Young Offender Institution*, Keele: Keele University, 2007.
18 The editors are grateful to all contributors.

Chapter 1

Will to self-consummation, and will to crime

A study in criminal motivation

Don Crewe

Introduction

When people ask me 'What is criminology?' – people I might meet in the pub, friends, family, spouse – I suspect the reply they expect is that it seeks to answer the question: 'Why do people commit crime?' Within the criminological community, we tend to lose track of the simplicity of the implications of this question. We think, 'Well, we can't answer that question until we answer the question: "What is crime?"' We tend to ask a subtly different question: 'What causes crime?' The answer to that question gives rise to answers that tend to fit on a continuum between 'criminals cause crime', and 'societies cause crime'. This is the distinction we teach to undergraduates, between classicist criminology and positivist criminology, and we know that the ramifications of adherence to one or another of these positions are immense. Fundamentally, the classicist position says that humans have free will, and therefore can be held responsible for their actions; the positivist position, similarly fundamentally, insists that humans are caused to behave in certain ways, through genetics, social learning, psychopathology, or the rigours of the free-market society (amongst other things), and therefore cannot be held responsible for their actions. This dichotomy is represented in the broader sociological world by the conflict that sets the concept 'agency' over against the concept 'structure'. The classical position states that we have agency, the positivist tradition states that we are determined by the power of structure. We might say that the older position that humans are free, which grew out of the enlightenment, was overtaken by the structuralist positions of writers like Marx or Parsons (amongst others) for whom social structure was the determining force in human behaviour. The apparent failure of Marxist or Weberian structuralism, brought about in part by Western perceptions of Stalinism, and the failure of meta-narratives in general after the Second World War[1] (amongst other things), led sociological writers to attempt to find ways of steering a course between the two traditions, and thus structuration theories were developed. Giddens' structuration theory,[2] for example, suggests that agency and structures emerge simultaneously from our repetitive or ritual behaviour.

The point that I wish to stress here is that the two sides of the balance, agency and structure, one asserting itself at the expense of the other, are central to most contemporary sociological thinking. Even Foucault uses the ideas, and indeed, suggests that certain structures are capable of robbing the human being of all agency, producing what he calls 'docile bodies'.[3] This is also true of criminology. Some criminologists are of the belief that structure does not limit people's agency but that they are rationally calculating 'free' agents: they choose freely to commit crimes (some varieties of control theory – rational choice theory, for example). Others are of the belief that crimes are driven by social conditions and that, dependent upon those conditions, a person is more or less 'caused' to commit crimes: they are in some way determined by social structures to do so (early conflict criminologies, for example). Now we live in a sociological world where pure classicism or pure structuralism are unthinkable; most positions, at whatever point along the continuum between freedom or determination, rely upon the concepts of agency and structure: they exist in a zero-sum relationship with one another (that is, outside structuration theories).

There are, however, certain problems associated with the concept of agency. Furthermore, while we hang on to the notion of agency – because we can only talk about it in terms of the absence of its antithesis, structure – we cannot get off the continuum that lies between the classical view and the positivist view. If we are to talk meaningfully about criminal motivation – about 'why people commit crime' – we have to move away from the crude 'he was free to choose, *ergo* he must be wicked', 'he was caused to do it, it's not his fault', tit-for-tat arguments. We have to do this if we are genuinely to understand criminal motivation.

In this chapter I am going to talk about the agency part of the above dichotomy, and what I am going to do first is to say why I think that agency is not a particularly good concept for making sense of criminal motivation. So, what I'm going to do is to talk about an older concept, that of will, and suggest that it is a better tool for looking at criminal motivation. In other words, I suggest that we might conceive of human behaviour as being the product of constrained will. To do this, I'm going to examine what will is. I will found my examination of will on the nature of human being, and I do this for two reasons: first, because it allows me to suggest that my conception of will is useful in understanding human behaviour because it is a *fundamental* part of being human; and second, because it allows me to view will as a part of the way in which humans change. The latter I will do by dealing with ideas that have to do not just with being – being complete, being what we are, and being here – but with ideas that say that the necessary parts that make us what we are, whilst necessary, are not sufficient to make us what we will become. When someone commits a crime, they *become* someone who has committed that crime – they do something new.[4] Furthermore, they didn't just do it by accident (usually), they chose to do it: they had a will to do it. Of course, we know that we can have a will to do things and be unable to do them: I would like to be on holiday by the sea all summer, but I can't because I haven't got the money or the time. These are constraints on my will. Sometimes we are *caused* to do things that are against our will. This is the positivist, structuralist side of the balance. I'm not going to talk about that in this chapter, although I will make allusion to some ideas concerning the nature of constraints upon our will.

Those familiar with the work of David Matza[5] will know that he was particularly interested in the idea of will, and will probably be wondering why I should feel the need to revisit the idea. So, before I look at the nature of will in the abstract, I'm going to look at Matza's conception of the 'will to crime' in order that we may have some idea of how the concept 'will' has been treated criminologically. I shall then explore the concept of will and postulate a new expression that I will term 'the will to self consummation'. I shall return to Matza's 'will to crime' and show that it needs to be reassessed in view of what I have proposed, leaving 'will' in the criminological sense merely the 'will to transgress' situationally negotiated norms. I shall begin, however, by looking at a particular problem with regard to the concept of 'agency' that leads me to abandon the conventional 'agency'/'structure' dualism in favour of the conception of human behaviour being emergent from constrained 'will'.

Agency

The concept 'agency' is usually set over against the term 'structure'. In this dualism, agency represents an attempt to capture the freedom from determinism that writers have claimed is inherent in human behaviour. That is, that the agent is free to act in ways that conceptions reifying structure do not permit. In some accounts, agency is a mere synonym for action, yet in others agency is bound up with notions of free will. In either case, the conception is reliant upon completed actions as evidence of its existence – if one is taken to be unable to do a thing, one is taken not to have agency in that regard. This is not to say that this is untrue; clearly, if agency is that concept that speaks of concerns regarding the failure of structures to constrain us, then should those structures constrain us we are not possessed of that quality which expresses our freedom from such constraint. However, the most significant problem with the concept of agency arises not when we consider what it means to be constrained and therefore not in possession of it, but when we consider what it means to say that we *are* in possession of it.

For Giddens, agency equates to action[6] and thus is a 'stream of ... causal interventions of corporeal beings in the ongoing process of events-in-the-world'.[7] We are possessed of agency when we act in a way that exhibits the capacity to have acted otherwise,[8] either through positive intervention or through forbearance.[9] In other words, we are possessed of agency when we are not the subject of coercion or constraint. In sociological terms, the notions of coercion and constraint equate to elements of determination. This locution – 'could have done otherwise' – presents us with a serious problem. To suggest that someone could have done otherwise is to suggest that they could have *chosen* to do otherwise; that is, their choice was in no way constrained or coerced (determined) and thus, conventionally, the agent has free will. For most people, in commonsense language, I suspect, the idea of having free will means that they 'to all intents and purposes' are free to choose; that is, they do not *perceive* any constraints that there might actually be upon their choices.

In common parlance, criminals are frequently said to be evil because they *chose* to commit a crime. Because they chose to commit a crime, they are fully responsible for their actions and thus are not entitled to the same claims to liberty or welfare as other people who have no choice. This (amongst other things) is taken to be the basis of our right to punish as a society. It is particularly the case where the doctrine of less eligibility is concerned.[10] Poor people are taken, for example, to be poor through no fault of their own – they are determined, it is claimed; criminals, however, are seen to be able to choose freely to be criminals.

The public and policy-makers might feel that the criminal (for want of a better word) is perfectly free to choose between committing a crime or, for example, going peacefully to the football match. However, it is far from clear what we might be saying if, having chosen to commit a crime, we say that the criminal *could* have chosen to go to the football match. The phrase 'could have done otherwise' is problematic because it suggests free will means having the ability to choose without constraint or determination. When we think of constraint, the matter is moderately straightforward. I can think of many physical constraints upon my choice to commit a crime or go to the football match – there may be no tickets left, or they may be too expensive; the house I was intending to burgle has an alarm or is occupied or has a high wall – all the things that rational-choice theorists tell us deter me from committing a burglary – and those constraints may be absent. However, when we speak of the absence of determination, the matter is somewhat more difficult. If we say we are free to choose, I suspect what we really mean is that 'to all intents and purposes' we *feel* free to choose. However, the requirement of the technical concept 'agency' is that we exhibit free will in the technical sense – the common sense usage won't do – technically, we must be free to choose in an environment where we *could have done otherwise*; that is, the choices must be ours, and we must be free of *any* determination, or constraint, and that means *all* determination or constraint. This presents us with a problem, because if the choices are ours (agent causation[11]) '[t]he cause of the volition is the man that willed it'.[12] That is, it didn't 'just happen', I caused the choice – I determined it. If it had just happened, then, of course, my choice to burgle the house would be inexplicable, and it would be unclear how I could speak of the choice being mine. However, if I choose to burgle the house, it is also unclear how such a choice might be free, since it is I who determines it, and freedom must be free of all and any determination. Thus, the idea that we might be 'free to choose' seems to show us that the locution 'free will' is an oxymoron since choice is a kind of determination and freedom cannot be determined. This has led several writers to believe that the notion of freedom in 'free will' is incoherent,[13] incompatible with realities that we take to be true of this world,[14] or that we simply cannot speak in any meaningful way about free will or free choice.[15] Indeed, agency, expressed in the above way, looks more like a description of 'power' than 'free will'. The problem lies with agency's reliance on the notion of freedom. If we remove the requirement for freedom and concentrate not on 'free will' but merely upon 'will', then we are able to situate motivations, including motivations to commit crimes, within the greater world of people's pasts, presents and futures in a way that agency cannot do: we can locate human behaviour as an emergent property of constrained will. Before giving an account of will, I shall outline a significant criminological account of will from David Matza. Matza is also concerned to situate criminal motivation away from the dichotomies of determinism and freedom, and within the complex world of histories and futures. He does this by engaging with the notion of will. However, Matza has a particular take on the conception of will with which I will later take issue.

The will to crime

In the first chapter of *Delinquency and Drift* Matza lays out the social–ontological dichotomies that I have outlined above. Matza is at pains to critique the conventional view of positive criminology – consistent, says Matza, with Schopenhauer – that humans 'can absolutely never do anything else than just what at that moment [they] do'.[16] Schopenhauer goes on to say, 'Accordingly, the whole course of a man's life,... is as necessarily predetermined as the course of a clock'. According to Matza, such views have permitted social scientists from Lombroso and Ferri, through behaviourists like Watson, the psychological determinism of Freud, and the operant conditioning of Skinner, to believe that sociological investigation can be undertaken in exactly the same way as that of natural science. Hence, it became a philosophical and methodological necessity, says Matza, to eradicate all notions of the capacity for reason and freedom. Methodologically this was so, following from Ferri's claim to have demonstrated that statistics prove the non-existence of free choice.[17] This move was also philosophically necessary since, paradoxically, as expressed in another passage from Ferri, the possession of the capacity of reason permitted the un-reason of the capacity for the metaphysicality of moral liberty.[18,19] This view yielded the conclusion that criminals were not so by virtue of reason or through failure of judgement of moral licence, but were criminal because they were in some way – biologically, psychologically or socially – determined so to be.

Matza goes on to point out that it would be naive to assume that social scientists are all divisible into these two extremes, and lays out in defence of this position a belief in what he terms 'soft determinism'. Soft determinism is a position that subscribes to the view that mankind exhibits freedom, but also experiences determination. The position is put succinctly by McIver:

> According to [soft determinism] there is ... no contradiction whatsoever between determinism and the proposition that human beings are sometimes free agents. When we call an action 'free' we mean that the agent was not compelled or constrained to perform it. Sometimes people act in a certain way because of threats or because they have been drugged or because of posthypnotic suggestion or because of an irrational overpowering urge that makes a kleptomaniac steal something he does not really need. On such occasions human beings are not free agents. But on other occasions they act in certain ways because of their own desires, because of their unimpeded efforts, because they have chosen to act in these ways. On those occasions they are free agents although their actions are just as much caused as actions that are deemed free. In distinguishing between free and unfree actions we do not try to mark the presence and absence of causes but attempt to indicate the *kind* of causes that are present.[20]

From this Matza draws the conclusion that '[t]he fundamental assertion of soft determinism is that human actions are not deprived of freedom because they are causally determined'.

Matza's concern is with a particular aspect of the interaction between positive and classical criminology, and that is the notion that the reason that most people do not commit crime is because there are in place most of the time controls to which we submit. Matza observes that criminologists subscribing to control theories suggest that these controls are formed by allegiance – to others through desire or compulsion to maintain bonds, or to norms and laws through common beliefs – or by rational calculation of the risk and cost of being caught. Both, however, require the conception that such acts, deemed criminal, are the default behaviour of humans – that is, humans are predisposed to commit crime – and this is a key issue in *Delinquency and Drift*.

The primary thesis of *Delinquency and Drift* is that

> [n]orms may be violated without surrendering allegiance to them. The directives to action implicit in norms may be avoided intermittently rather than frontally assaulted. They may be evaded rather than radically rejected. Norms, especially legal norms, may be neutralized. Criminal law is especially susceptible of neutralisation because the conditions of applicability, and thus inapplicability, are explicitly stated. Most if not all norms in society are conditional. Rarely, if ever, are they categorically imperative.... Because in law the conditions are specified, neutralization is not only possible, it is invited. The criminal law, more so than any other system of norms acknowledges and states the principal grounds under which an actor may claim exemption.[21]

Thus 'the moral bind between the actor and legal norms [the mode of control], is neutralised'[22] and a substantial portion of the text is given to explicating the ways in which these neutralisations take place, producing the now-famous five techniques of neutralisation. However, possession of the capacity to neutralise the 'moral bind between the actor and legal norms' is insufficient as an explanation for the commission of the delinquent act; 'the moral vacuum implicit in the removal of cultural restraints is not sufficient to explain the occurrence of delinquency.'[23] What Matza wishes to suggest is that 'the missing element which provides the thrust or impetus by which the delinquent act is realised is *will*'[24] not any fundamental predisposition of all humans to indulge in any *bellum omnium contra omnes*. Nonetheless, Matza wishes to know why there should be a will to commit delinquent acts, and spends the last chapter of *Delinquency and Drift* exploring how the actor develops what he terms a 'Will to Crime'.[25] Matza recognises that the notion of will is the aetiological motor of classical theory, but suggests that the reason that classical conceptions of will were rejected were metaphysical.

> Nowadays, our rejection of a conception of will would be on fundamentally different grounds. We would immediately, and perhaps condescendingly grant that no such thing as will exists. Will, like any other concept – say, decision making – is an abstraction by which we hopefully make sense of concrete happenings. We no longer care whether will exists, only whether it enlightens.[26]

However, the abstraction that Matza puts forward as his conception of will is the 'will to crime', and there are some fundamental problems with this conception, which I will return to having made an examination of, and a new expression of, the concept of 'will'.

Will

This leaves us in what appears to be a very difficult situation. We appear not to be able to talk about criminal motivation, or a person's choice to commit a crime, if we rely on the concept of agency. If we are entirely free to choose, then we cannot speak of having choice, because choosing is a form of determination and therefore not free. The locution 'free choice' is seen to be an oxymoron. So, what we need to do is to get rid of the notion of freedom. If we do this then we have to situate our choices, or the choices of criminals, within their complex pasts, presents and futures, and the concept that permits us to do this is the concept of 'will'. We can speak of people having will without having to talk about freedom at all, because we know that we can have will to do something and still not be free to do it, whereas we cannot have agency and be constrained from fulfilling it. So, what we might say in place of the idea that structure constrains agency is that human behaviour is a property emergent from constrained will. We can readily imagine that our will can be constrained after we have it, but it can also be constrained before we have it, in that it is not possible for us simply to will anything for ourselves. What we will for ourselves must be limited by our imagination, and our imagination can be limited in many different ways. A habitual burglar may not be able, for example, to imagine becoming a chemical bomber because he or she has no knowledge of what a chemical bomb is. I will look at some mechanisms that limit our will towards ourselves later in the chapter.

What I want to do is to talk about having will towards ourselves as being a part of the nature of Human Being. When we talk about *being* as a person, we usually talk about being here, that is, we say that we are self present. We talk about being me – self identity – that is, we talk about being that person who is me. We talk about being human, that is, we say that I satisfy all the requirements (I am in possession of all the necessary predicates) of being human – when we do this, we also suggest that being means being complete. However, none of these ideas answers the question: 'What is Being?' This is the question addressed by Heidegger in *Being and Time*[27] I'm going to take a look at this work now, because I want to begin to establish how being human and having will are related, and Heidegger lays out firm ground for us to do that. So, even if this seems, at times, a little tangential, this is the way Heidegger approaches the task, and the relevance of what he has to say will become evident later in the chapter.

Being and time

Defining the question

The first thing that Heidegger attempts to do in *Being and Time* is to establish the object of his study, and he begins this task by criticising the way that philosophers have conventionally conceived of the question of Being. Initially, he suggests that there are three ways in which philosophers have attempted to show that Being is an unworthy object of study. Philosophers of the past, claims Heidegger, have taken the question of being to be universal to all things and therefore to have no specificity, and therefore tell us nothing that we don't already know about something by virtue of its existence. Kant, for example, says 'the real contains no more than the merely possible. A hundred thalers do not contain the least coin more than one hundred possible thalers.'[28] Second, because it has no specificity, they have taken it to have no definitional content and therefore to be indefinable. And, finally, they have taken it to be self-evident and therefore unworthy of study. Heidegger suggests that because, as Aristotle points out, the being of real objects appears to be different to that of imaginary objects like unicorns or numbers, for example, 'Being' cannot be a universal concept. Next, to suggest that 'Being' is indefinable because it lacks specificity is to suggest that it is an entity; definition is a tool that only applies to entities, and since 'Being' is not an entity in itself, but only *of* entities, definition is not an appropriate tool for examining 'Being'. Finally, the notion that 'Being' is a self-evident concept – found in locutions like the tree *is* green – Heidegger claims is flawed. Such locutions, he claims, are evidence of 'an average kind of intelligibility which merely demonstrates that it is unintelligible'.[29] Thus, the standard reasons for dismissing the questions concerning being, that they are unanswerable, or that they are self-evident, are refuted by Heidegger. It is this that leaves Heidegger in the position where he has to reformulate the question concerning Being, such that it is no longer a question of the relationship between the human of substance and his rational mind – the *cogito*: the possibility of 'distinct perceptions'[30] – but what it is to have access to entities and to 'make sense of making sense'.[31] Heidegger wants to uncover the nature of Being itself. Heidegger's final correction to the nature of the *question concerning* Being involves the call to phenomenology. He adopts the exhortation of his mentor, Husserl, to get back to the things themselves,[32] to be free from metaphysical preconceptions; however, he feels that Husserl has misinterpreted the call. Heidegger's concern is not merely for things to be allowed to present themselves to the enquirer in some kind of simplistic empiricism, but since things show themselves to us – and this includes other humans – it is with us that our inquiry into their Being must begin. Since we interpret that presentation in various ways, the nature of the understanding must be hermeneutic, and to fathom this hermeneutic, we must first be concerned with the nature of Being of the interpreter. In other words, we must inquire first into the nature Being of that being (us) who perceives (and is therefore perceived by) others like them in the world.

Being-in-the-world (of others) and inauthenticity

Whatever the nature of our enquiry, whatever we wish to know, our investigation is possessed of some object: any enquiry is about something. The problem that we have in this regard is that our enquiry is about the meaning of being. We are not in a position to use the word 'being' in our question since it is the very term at issue and therefore we cannot know to what the term refers (axiomatically). We can have no presuppositionless origin for our question, we must supply some more or less – we hope less – arbitrary referent from which to begin our enquiry, and then own responsibility for it. Thus Heidegger adopts the term Dasein as the object of his enquiry.

In everyday German, Dasein means the 'everyday essence of human existence' or 'human being'. It therefore means an individual as well as that which is universal to all humans. We should be wary, however, when we think of Dasein in the singular, of thinking that this refers to a conscious subject. He writes, 'One of our first tasks will be to prove that if we posit an "I" or subject as that which is [primarily][33] given, we shall completely miss the phenomenal content of Dasein'.[34] Consciousness is not a fundamental property but a property emergent from the fundamental nature of Dasein: '[t]he intentionality of "consciousness" is grounded in the ecstatical temporality of Dasein.'[35]

What Heidegger is saying here is that the fundamental essence of Dasein is phenomenological; it emerges from our experience, that is, from our experience of ourselves and of others in the world. Hence, Dasein is not an individual human, but that property of *individuals* in virtue of their Being that is *universal* in humans. What is fundamental to us is in our experience of ourselves and others in the world: 'Being-with is an existential constituent of being-in-the-world.... So far as Dasein *is* at all, it has Being-with-one-another as its kind of being.'[36]

In one of its forms, Heidegger deals with Being-with-one-another as *everyday* Being-with-one-another, or being with in the mode of das *Man* – 'the they', 'the one': 'The "who" is not this one, not that one, not oneself, not some people, and not the sum of them all. The 'who' is the neuter, the "*they*".'[37] Heidegger's claim, then, is that we deal with others, first and foremost, in the form of what we might call 'the one'.[38]

> By 'Others' we do not mean everyone else but me – those over against whom the 'I' stands out. They are rather those from whom, for the

most part, one does *not* distinguish oneself – those among whom one is too. This Being-there-too ... is something of the character of Dasein; the 'too' means a sameness of Being as circumspectively concernful Being-in-the-world'.[39]

That is, we conceive of ourselves in relation to others in terms of what *one* ordinarily does in situations that confront us. Before we think about what we would choose (exhibit will), we understand the world in terms that the others around us in the world have introduced to us. All acts therefore are social and take place within a pre-existing context.[40] Even resistance is resistance to an existing state of affairs. Thus the question is no longer, 'How can I know that there are others and that they have experiences?' But, instead, 'How can I know who *I* am, since it appears that all that I am is pre-existent in the world of "the one"?' This act of *recognition* of the 'nothingness' (the nihilism) of being – its boundedness by the norms of others – Heidegger describes as distancing, or 'distantiality' in the Macquarrie and Robinson translation.

> [T]his distantiality which belongs to Being-with, is such that Dasein, as everyday Being-with-one-another, stands in *subjection* to Others. It itself is not; its being has been taken away by Others to dispose of as they please. These others moreover are not *definite* Others. On the contrary, any Other can represent them.... One belongs to the Others oneself.[41]

According to Heidegger, therefore, all that we (conventionally) do has its origin in the pre-existing dispositions of others. That is not to say, however, that we can posit any individual who makes decisions for us. On the contrary, we may be able to trace the origin of certain beliefs or practices, but ultimately no *one* can be responsible for their cultural dominance, just as I cannot ultimately (or originally) be responsible for *my* choices, even my choice to commit crimes.

By organising our world, conformity provides the foundation upon which we make important decisions (however grounded in the presence of others they may be). When we resist conformity, it is necessary that we take stock of our difference – 'distantiality' – from others. This 'distantiality', says Heidegger, tends to level down our practices; it is the classic example of the origin of dumbing-down: we modify our behaviour to a level where it is acceptable to the majority of our fellow humans. This 'distantiality' also has the effect of 'disburdening' us with the responsibility for our judgements. The result is that no one ever really decides how things should be done.[42] The danger is that we so thoroughly disburden ourselves that we can no longer claim to be *ourselves*; we can no longer claim to be 'authentic'.

The Self of the everyday Dasein is the *they-self*, which we distinguish from the *authentic self* – that is, from the self which has been taken hold of in its own way. As they-self, the particular Dasein has been *dispersed* into the 'they', and must first find itself. This dispersal characterises the subject of that kind of Being which we know as concernful absorption in the world we encounter.[43]

The question therefore remains, 'What is the authentic self, and, since we exist in the world, how can we have any form of being for which we have sole responsibility whilst still being in-the-world?' Thus, Heidegger becomes concerned with the way in which we can be responsible for our *own* actions, for bringing meaning to our *individual* lives, for choosing for *ourselves* a fulfilling and ethical path: choices concerning not the satisfactory or sufficient, but the genuinely authentic and eudaimon life. This is where we break, in criminological terms, with positivism. If we are merely inauthentic beings (in Heidegger's terms) we could never apportion criminal responsibility. This would be a view of people as so bound by their phenomenological engagement with the norms of others that the idea of people *choosing* to commit crime would be nonsense. This is unadulterated positivism: the criminal as the determined subject of social structures. It is the position that founds biological and psychological positivist theories; it is the root of the social disorganisation theories of the Chicago school. It is the root of Mertonian anomie theories and of subculture theories. It is the position that grounds other social-learning theories such as those of Sutherland, and is the foundation of deviance and labelling theories. As criminologists, we are aware that simple social positivism, or untrammelled determinism, provides only a partial account of criminal etiological processes. External influences are not the be-all and end-all of causes of crime: motivation is also involved. Heidegger next talks about how we can be motivated to bring meaning to our lives as authentic individuals. These are the authentic individuals who also *choose* to commit criminal acts or indulge in problematic behaviour that is subsequently criminalised. Criminal acts are motivated internally and externally by behaviour to norms and by the will to transgress them: by decisions and non-decisions alike.

Authenticity and death

Thus far we have seen that Heidegger claims that we conventionally merely behave in a way that doesn't disturb cultural norms: he says we are inauthentic. In criminological terms, this simply gives us problematic behaviour that is caused by following the behaviour of others in a way that has been outlined by social learning theorists. (Actually, most behaviour deemed to be problematic, most behaviour studied by criminologists wouldn't fall into this category as it would not be deviant. However, problematic behaviour generated as a result of adherence *to* (sub)cultural norms, like certain forms of corporate crime or crimes associated with gang membership, for example, would be related to inauthentic behaviour). Heidegger's account, thus far, does not allow us to talk about how people might choose to behave in a certain way, how they might choose to *become* criminal. *Choosing* is authentic behaviour and, for Heidegger, to be authentic is the source of Dasein's greatest dignity: this is achieved by stripping away self-deception. A further belief held in common with the existentialists is that it is through fearless engagement with the idea of our own death that we can face up to our responsibility for achieving our own meaningful life:

> He who is resolute knows no fear; but he understands the possibility of anxiety[44] as the possibility of the very mood which neither inhibits nor bewilders him. Anxiety liberates him *from* possibilities which 'count for nothing', and lets him become free *for* those which are authentic.[45]

Indeed, death is that which makes us the beings that we are: death is our 'ownmost possibility'.[46] We are finite beings. For Heidegger, it is necessary to separate two aspects of death: the physical processes of death – often thought of in terms of causes – and the existential aspects of death. The existential aspects of death include no longer being part of our world, no longer able to do things, no longer capable of striving, particularly towards our *eudaimon* life. Death is defined by Heidegger as 'the possibility of the impossibility of every way of comporting oneself towards anything, of every way of existing'.[47] The key here is that death is a 'possibility' – it matters not that it is a certainty, that we cease to exist when death is actual is irrelevant – it is a possibility and as such it is able to shape our experience of the world since we *do* exist when death is possible. Because it is the possibility of the impossibility of ever being anything any more, we are made aware of the *possibilities* of being that will cease. Death is meaningful to us in life. Thus, since at some point I will cease to be, no manner of living can achieve the fulfilling, meaningful life, since no way of living will permit me to continue in the world. This, contends Heidegger, should shatter any illusion that mere norm-following might be the right way to live. Thus, in the face of our inevitable death we are brought to reject our reliance on cultural norms as the *eudaimon* way to be, and to take responsibility for our own selves. In anticipating death I reject 'the they' and take responsibility for myself: I become authentic. The knowledge that our lives will end brings with it the joy of the realisation that our choices about our way of being matter.

We may now summarise our characterisation of authentic Being-towards-death as we have projected it existentially: *anticipation reveals to Dasein its lostness in the they-self, and brings it face to face with the possibility of being itself, primarily supported by concernful solicitude, but of being itself, rather, in an impassioned* freedom towards death – *a freedom which has been released from the illusions of the 'they', and which is factical,*[48] *certain of itself, and anxious.*[49]

Thus our concern with death introduces to us anxiousness (angst) concerning the way we live our lives, with the result that we begin to make decisions that are our own, not merely following the herd.

Being-in-time

It will be evident from the foregoing that Heidegger's conception of our Being-towards-death opens the possibility of our having will and, indeed, places the choice-making that flows from the possession of will towards ourselves in a normatively positive light. Furthermore, it is evident from the use of words like 'anticipation' that such choice-making has temporal qualities – we have will towards ourselves as objects of the *future*. This will towards ourselves as objects of the future is a key element of the new concept 'The will to self-consummation' that I shall propose later in the chapter.

The radical nature of Heidegger's work, and one that has profound implications for the present project, is that Heidegger renders Being (*Dasein* – there-being) not only as Being-in-the-world – the comportment of oneself in recognition of others and oneself as objects in the world – but as Being-in-time. The relevance of this conjunction to the current enterprise is that it permits us to have intentions towards ourselves as objects of the future: aspirations, hopes, desires. It is my contention that when we choose to behave in problematic ways, we do so because we view ourselves as being a particular way in the future; we have will towards ourselves as objects of the future. A particular person may see himself as *becoming* a tough street-gang warrior, and thus attempt to buy a gun. A person may see themselves as *becoming* a resident of a luxury mansion and thus attempt to defraud a company's shareholders. We have moved into the realm where I can choose to commit a crime, and I do so because I see myself as becoming something that I currently am not. However small, there is a gap between what I am now and what I want to become. It is thus appropriate that we consider how we come to have the desires that we do.

In the face of certain issues concerning the resolution of problems of authenticity at the end of Division I in his book, Heidegger introduces the term 'care'. Following from the claim, consistent with existentialists, that the fundamental human value is Angst, and that that angst may be at the knowledge of the ultimate tragedy of the human race – its ultimate inability ever to *become* complete or whole (I will later use the term 'consummate'), it follows from our being-in-the-world with others and our awareness of the ultimate tragedy of *their* lives, that we experience the value of care towards others. Since Dasein is always occupied with the objects it encounters in the world, the world and everything that is in it cannot fail to matter to it: '[T]he being of Dasein means ahead-of-itself-Being-already-in(-the-world) as Being-alongside (entities encountered within-the-world). This Being fills in the signification of the term "*care*".'[50]

The point is made clearly, not that there cannot be failures of sympathy, not that Dasein is always concerned, but that Dasein cannot fail to be engaged with the fate (as it were) of every other.

As we have seen in the foregoing, authenticity presupposes our openness to temporal aspects of our being, it provides for the disposition of ourselves towards the future state of our being as we will it to be. Such 'projection' – such colonisation of the future, as it has elsewhere been termed[51] – requires that we grasp the essential nature of Dasein as 'Being-guilty'.[52] For Heidegger, this means engaging with oneself as past – what one has been – as an indelible aspect of what one is, present. That is, since authenticity 'discloses'[53] the current moment as a situation of choice towards action – towards the future – it requires that we are open to responsibilities for all others in the world with us; this is the nature of care – of concern for or commitment to others in the world – and of the condition of 'Being-guilty'.

Heidegger refers to the structure of care as ahead-of-itself-already-being-in (-the-world) or Being-alongside (others in the world). This arises out of Dasein's existence as 'thrown projection', an expression that suggests that we are neither determined nor free, or that we are simultaneously both. Where authenticity and resoluteness against the angst concerned with the possibility of death provide for anticipation of the future, 'thrown projection' represents our active colonisation of that future: it therefore implicitly recognises an openness to the temporality of existence. 'Ahead-of-itself' refers to Dasein's awareness through anticipation of that property of the future, that it has 'possibilities', Already-Being-in recognises the capacity of Dasein to relate to the past, and Being-alongside represents the being in the world with all those others, for whom we have responsibility – for whom we are 'circumspectively concernful' – in the present. Thus the three aspects of our relationship to time are interrelated, but Heidegger's ordering of his definition reveals the primacy of existence as future; existence is a matter of projecting (will towards the future) thrownness (the nature of our determining past) into the future through present choices. As authenticity is consummated in anticipation, so existence is consummated through colonisation of the future.[54]

I necessarily do violence to Heidegger in the above rendering of his account, through inadequate attention to the subtleties of his thought. Nonetheless, I achieve my aim in showing how Heidegger opens up for us the concept that we can have future-oriented concerns. Nonetheless, Heidegger's account is inadequate. It is flawed inasmuch as it relies on our presupposed disposition towards our death. Even though Rousseau tells us, 'I can certainly say that I never began to live until I looked upon myself as a dead man',[55] I think it would be relatively uncontroversial to suggest that most people do not go about making choices about their future in the light of their possibility of not-being; nor because they are made aware of the possibility of making choices through an understanding of the impossibility of their being able to consummate themselves because they will inevitably at some point cease to be. Indeed, we witness, especially among the young, a degree of disengagement from concerns about their own eventual demise that gives rise to dangerous – reckless – behaviour; paradoxically, in some circumstances hastening the possibility of their departure from the world. And yet, these people make decisions concerning their own future – they have will towards themselves as objects of the future – their hopes and desires, their aspirations and ambitions, and thus upon the way that they project themselves into the future. They make choices about going to university or getting a job or career or a family. More mundanely, they make choices about what to wear on Friday night when they go clubbing, what drink to have, whether to cross the road here or at the crossing, whether to look in the shop window, and some make choices about whether or not to commit crimes. All of which they do without recourse to understandings of the possibilities of life, of which the possibility of their death, Heidegger maintains, makes them aware. Furthermore, they make choices unconsciously or semi-consciously in social situations. They decide when it is appropriate to laugh or smile, when to pass condolence, when to frown, when not to cough. All of these decisions are decisions about the future. They are oriented towards the expected interpretation of another which is yet to come: favourable or unfavourable. It is simply impossible for such a response to be contemporary with its origin – its stimulus – no matter how soon after the event it is: it is *after*. Thus *all* decisions are oriented towards the future as much as they are rooted in the past. Very few, if any, require us to engage with the possibility of our own death for them to be thought, willed or realised. Furthermore, whilst it may be laudable to initiate a call for authenticity – not to be as the herd – this is a merely normative call. Hence, if we take it from Heidegger that we have the capacity to orient ourselves towards our future and yet reject that this stems from a particular disposition towards our own death, we need to enquire what form that orientation takes. It will be the contention of this chapter that the form of this orientation is that of constant movement towards an unachievable completion – consummation. I therefore introduce at this point the work of a writer who challenges notions that we are already somehow complete – which notion is embedded in static concepts of being – permitting a conception of ourselves as constantly in a process of becoming.

Being and self-presence – being complete

Derrida and supplementation

Derrida's primary concerns are with the nature of communication, and it is therefore unsurprising that he is not frequently the first port of call for criminologists in their search for a solution to their problems. Nonetheless, Derrida's method of deconstruction, and his critique of authority based upon logocentrism[56] – the archaic view of the privilege of speech over writing – and notions of self-presence, present criminologists with a critical tool of significant utility, particularly in relation to the law, but indeed with regard to any topoi of authority or plenitude.

Derrida claims that logocentrism is the form of all philosophy to date, and indeed is the common ground that permits philosophies to privilege notions of presence and presence's axiomatic counterpart, completeness. It is this notion of completeness that I wish to challenge through Derrida's work so that I can talk about ideas such as becoming and, from that, 'consummation'. So, for Derrida, all philosophy has been a 'metaphysics of *presence*':[57]

> We already have a foreboding that phonocentricism merges with the historical determination of the meaning of being in general as *presence*, with all the subdeterminations which depend on this general form and which organize within it their system and their historical sequence (presence of the thing to the sight as *eidos*,[58] presence as substance/essence/existence (*ousia*), temporal presence as point (*stigme*) of the now or of the moment (*nun*), the self-presence of the cogito, consciousness, subjectivity, the co-presence of the other and of the self, intersubjectivity as the intentional phenomenon of the ego, and so forth). Logocentrism would thus support the determination of the being of the entity as presence.[59]

These concepts, Culler points out, are indissolubly related to those of centring or grounding.[60] Furthermore Lee, in his argument concerning what we might term an 'ontology of childhood',[61] takes such notions to be indicative of authority founded in notions of the 'completed' adult, a point to which I will return shortly.

Further engagement with the pervasiveness of logocentrism is undertaken by Derrida in a critique of Rousseau's *Essay on the Origin of Lan-*

guages. This particular turn is of significance to the current project in that it deals with Rousseau's notion of the supplement, and I wish to introduce the idea of becoming or 'consummation' being achieved by the adoption of supplements. For Rousseau, writing is a supplement to speech. Derrida has already (in a section of *Of Grammatology* that I do not discuss here) revealed the 'classical' distinction between pure and innocent nature, and the impure imposition of culture present in the work of Levi-Strauss,[62] where Strauss equates the imposition of culture with the deleterious effects of the imposition of writing over the pure nature of speech:[63] 'Thus we are led back to Rousseau. The ideal profoundly underlying this philosophy of writing is therefore the image of a community immediately present to itself, without difference, a community of speech where all the members are in earshot.'[64] In Rousseau, however, writing is not merely violence, but necessary: it is a necessary supplement. The question arises, 'What is this writing a supplement to?' The answer that Rousseau provides is that it restores the presence of the writer. Derrida, however, maintains that this is a supplement fulfilling some *lack* in nature:[65] the adoption of the supplement makes visible an original deficiency. '[T]here is *lack* in Nature and that *because of that very fact* something is *added* to it ... the supplement comes *naturally* to put itself in Nature's place.'[66] Thus writing is *'required'* by nature and must therefore be considered as 'inscribed in the origin of language *as such*'.[67] What this means for our current project is that, in the face of notions of the correlation between absence and alterity,[68] the failure of notions of presence founded in logocentrism present us with the impossibility of the possibility of completeness of self-presence. That is, faced with the knowledge of the infinite regression of 'mediation' – of signifiers of signifiers – inscribed in intersubjective communities, we are all originarily communal: we are all in need of supplementation – presence itself depends upon supplementation.

Lee: the paradox of power and completion

In his work concerning an ontology of childhood, Nick Lee[69] engages with the above constellation of ideas present in Derrida to outline a deconstruction of notions of self-sufficiency claimed for adults as against the conventionally incomplete child. In so doing he takes the associated metaphors for self-presence – centeredness, groundedness, that we found earlier in Culler[70] – and places them at the centre of our natural associations with authority. For Derrida, says Lee, the equation between central control and stability at the heart of the Fordist Marshall plan for Europe

did not necessarily hold good, yet he was well aware that this equation had long informed the distribution of power within western culture. Only those deemed capable of controlling themselves from their own 'centres' have enjoyed the benefits of being thought stable and reliable.[71]

One concomitant of this is that powerless groups are frequently deemed to be justly so because of some perceived lack or deficiency, in particular in the case of women, and less so in the case of children and slaves, unable to moderate themselves from their own centres. That is, they have frequently been seen as ir-*rational*[72] in a society that values the logocentric product of rationality – 'truth'. Rationality is the product of Cartesian self-presence and, thus, those who are powerful are seen to be those who exhibit self-presence. The notion of self-presence in this context involves connotations of economic self-ownership – and indeed the ownership of others such as slaves, wives and children; it involves connotations with consistency and trustworthiness. For Derrida, observes Lee, the most interesting manifestation of self-presence is the ownership of one's voice. Self-present persons are seen to be well-moderated, in that they are seen as capable of controlling their own utterances such that they always intend to say what they say: of directing their meanings from the centre of their self-awareness. The opinions of the self-present can be taken seriously because, in being in control of their utterances, they are less likely to declare that they did not mean what they said. Self-presence, for Derrida, claims Lee,[73] is another way of saying 'human being'. Communities of the self-present can generate and 'other' those who are deemed not to own themselves. The voices of women, children and slaves have historically been muted, partly because they were not deemed to have voices of their own that were worth listening to – we may call to mind the oft-repeated phrase 'children should be seen and not heard'.

Derrida's concerns, however, are not primarily with the normative aspects of such inequalities, but with the claim of self-presence upon which these inequalities are based. As we saw above, the quality of self-presence has been taken to be constitutive of a person's power: the possession of direct control over their own voice and the connotations that has with presence bound up in speech. However, should that powerful person wish to assert power over distance or time, then they are in need of some kind of mediation.[74] They must historically commit their words to a messenger or other mediation. It will immediately be apparent that in so doing they absent themselves from their own voice. Such supplementation destroys their self-presence. Thus it may be seen that the more powerful a person is perceived to be in virtue of their self-presence, the less self-present they are, and the more dependent upon the agency of others they are seen to be: '[T]he power and self-possession of the powerful is never complete. As soon as their spoken word is conveyed, they are distanced from themselves, dispossessed of themselves in the moment that self-possession is broken.'[75]

The exercise of their power axiomatically cuts them off from the source of their power. Thus notions of adults as being in a completed self-sufficient state of *being* – as over against children, men as over against women, owners as over against slaves – is shown to be an unfounded proposition. In the face of this persistent state of incompleteness we must view humans as being in a constant state of becoming, of having intentions towards ourselves with regard to the future: intentions towards what we might become – criminal or law-abiding. The nature of those intentions is the subject of the next section of this chapter.

Intentionality

Whilst adherents of the analytical tradition have their own concerns regarding intentionality, in order to further coherence with the ideas I have drawn from Heidegger, it is to the expression of this concept amongst phenomenologists that I wish to confine my exposition. Intentionality is that quality of mental states or events that means that they are *about* or *of* things, as in 'I am thinking about this object' or 'I am thinking of that occasion' and so forth. That is to say, intentionality refers to the *directed-ness* of mind or a state of mind *towards* things – objects, events, etc. To have hopes or beliefs, those hopes and beliefs must be about something; when we have will, that will is towards something. If we have aspirations and ambitions, they are aspirations and ambitions concerning our selves because we can have states of mind that are directed towards ourselves: our ambitions are *about* us, we have will towards ourselves. It will be evident from this depiction that it is indivisibly bound up with notions of consciousness and of phenomenology: we are conscious of the objects in the world towards which our states of mind are directed, and we are able to *experience having* those states of mind 'phenomenally'. That is, our experiences of our directedness are states of mind in which it seems that we are having 'something like'[76] the experience of being aware of our directedness towards a particular object. What is of import to our current project is that we are capable of states of mind that are directed towards ourselves and that those states of mind are representative of the world as it is, relative to our view of ourselves in it futurally: we have the *innate* capacity to view ourselves as part of the world of the future, but that the experience of those objects is not representative of an 'objective' reality but of our relationship to them.

The social conditioning of objects

It has been suggested that phenomenal experience and intentional acts are socially interrelated; that is, our own objects are conditioned by the know-ledge of the nature of the objects of others (what we might call positive conditioning, which we might find in the process of typification, to which I shall return shortly) or disjuncture in our knowledge of the objects of others and our subsequent *relative* interpretations of claims or ascriptions of commitment to those objects – what we might call negative conditioning. This is illustrated admirably by Robert Brandom in his book *Making it Explicit: Reasoning, Representing, and Discursive Commitment.*[77] In this book, Brandom argues that ambiguities between *de dicto* and *de re* ascriptions of belief about objects are not reconcilable outside a degree of common social knowledge between those giving or receiving reasons for those beliefs:[78]

> [W]hat is expressed by *de re* specifications of the contents of the beliefs of others are crucial to *communication*. Being able to understand what others are saying, in the sense that makes remarks available for use as premises in one's own inferences, depends precisely on being able to specify those contents *de re*, and not merely *de dicto* terms. If the only way I can specify the content of the shaman's belief is by a *de dicto* ascription
>
>> He believes malaria can be prevented by drinking the liquor distilled from the bark of that kind of tree,
>
> I may not be in a position to assess the truth of his claim. It is otherwise if I can specify that content in the *de re* ascription
>
>> He believes of quinine that malaria can be prevented by drinking it,
>
> for quinine is a term with rich inferential connections to others I know how to employ. If he says that the seventh sun god has just risen, I may not know what to make of his remark. Clearly he will take it to have consequences that I could not endorse, so nothing in my mouth could ever *mean* just what his remark does. But if I am told that the seventh god is the sun then I can specify the content of his report in a more useful form
>
>> He claims of the sun that it has just risen,
>
> which I can extract *information* from, that is, can use to generate premises that I can reason with.[79]

The ambiguity inherent in such ascriptions or claims of commitment cannot be resolved without mastery of 'the *social* dimension of their inferential articulation'.[80] That is, the situation as defined by the previously acquired social-context-knowledge of all the other actors – in Brandom's terms, the state of play in the game of giving and asking for reasons. The social dimension cannot be avoided because the inferential significance of a claim cannot be established outside a background of other commitments that are available as plausible other reasons for action or belief present in the repertoire of the other actors in the situation. Thus our own objects are conditioned by the disjuncture in our knowledge of the objects of others and our subsequent *relative* interpretations of claims or ascriptions of commitment to those objects.

The social conditioning of being and becoming

Thus far my argument has followed this trajectory: (1) The Heideggerian perspective takes humankind from the merely "knowing" creatures of Cartesian accounts to ones who exhibits an active role in their own self-constitution, in a world of which they are integral parts. This view further projects humankind as having the capacity to comport itself towards itself as an object of the future. (2) Traditional, historical, conventional accounts have treated merely of humans as static completed creatures. Rousseau, Derrida and Lee place this account under considerable strain and present humans as becomings, not beings. (3) Studies of the directed nature of mental states – their aboutness – have provided for an account of the social contingency of our expressions concerning our objects, and thus the social contingency of the *possibilities* of the content of our intentional states – and thus the social contingency of the possibilities of our own view of our selves as objects directed towards the future. That is, we have mental states that are directed towards ourselves as objects of the future, the possible nature of which objects is socially conditioned.[81] In Foucauldian language, we might say that there exists, with regard to our will towards ourselves as objects of the future, a 'historical *a priori*'[82] limiting the repertoire of objects that we can conceive of ourselves as being: there exists a 'historical *a priori*' limiting the freedom of will, that simultaneously removes from us any possibility of knowledge of that limitation. Thus *free* will must be seen to be an illusion.

The further trajectory of the current argument is that we make socially conditioned (constrained or enabled) choices about *goals* towards our selves as objects that are constituted by the *conception* of our selves as objects of the future. It is appropriate that I should now turn to examine the sociological nature of the conditioning of those objects; in other words, how do we come to have the aspirations concerning ourselves that we do? I shall proceed by outlining the concept from the interactionist tradition of Typification and then briefly discuss its near relation, reference group theory. I shall then suggest that the notion of performativity gives us an insight of what it means to 'be' – we are what we perform. I shall then return to Rousseau's notion of the supplement to introduce the notion that making choices involves the adoption of supplements (extensions) and will conclude with the introduction of a new concept, 'The Will to Self-Consummation', that draws together all the above strands.

Typification

For interactionists, typification is one of the most important forms of social knowledge (Schütz, A., *On Phenomenology and Social Relations*, ed. H.R. Wagner, Chicago: Chicago University Press, 1970, pp. 111–22). Whilst the notion is quite straightforward, its ramifications are significant. Furthermore, it will become apparent that the concept is entirely in keeping with the Husserlian phenomenology of the account from Heidegger outlined above. Our knowledge of what to expect from a particular situation relies upon certain assumptions that we make concerning the roles of various others in that situation. We know that different people in different roles behave in recognisable ways in specific circumstances. A doctor behaves like a doctor in a doctor's surgery, for example. Our typification of a doctor consists in a set of assumptions concerning what doctors conventionally do in that situation. As long as the doctor conforms to that 'knowledge', and that the behaviour is in the appropriate situation – i.e. the doctor is not at the opera for example – so the identity 'doctor' and the definition of the situation are not in need of challenge (mostly). Should the doctor go about the opera house placing his stethoscope in the cleavage of the female singers he will find himself spending a night in chokey, whereas such behaviour might be normal of a doctor when in his surgery. Typification, then, is that image of a person, role or situation that organises their knowledge of it. Such typification takes place on the basis of visual and auditory cues: we observe and respond to others' words and deeds. We also respond to appearance; that is, we respond to their dress and demeanour – their physical features – as well as what they do and say. Every aspect of these observations form cues in establishing a typification.[83]

Remarkably little about people is visible to observers: appearance constituted in physical features of body or face, dress, mannerisms, posture. In addition, we have a restricted, socially conditioned repertoire of formal linguistic expressions concerning the representation of our objects. These are all that we have to draw upon when we encounter others. Their motives, beliefs, capacities or histories remain relatively hidden in most circumstances. And yet, all these things serve as clues upon which we found a whole set of assumptions for which we have little, or no, concrete evidence. These attributes are all that we have upon which to base considerable inferences concerning the identity of the person concerned, and to place him or her in a collection of typical categories that help us to make sense of the world and the people in it. For example, we typify the doctor *qua* doctor, on the grounds that he is sitting in a doctor's surgery and wearing a bow tie and a velvet waistcoat (perhaps), and because he invites us to sit down, saying, 'And what seems to be the problem Dr Crewe?' (or Andrews or whatever). Actually, it is probable that we typify him as a doctor *merely* because he is sitting in a doctor's surgery. Indeed, if we saw the doctor at the opera house, placing his stethoscope in the ample cleavages of the female singers, we would not typify him as a doctor at all, but as someone with challenging behaviour problems.

'Appearance is important not only because it provides us with the cues we need to typify someone initially, but also because it assists us in maintaining and refining that typification as interaction proceeds.'[84] We typify a bank manager on the grounds that they are wearing a pin-striped suit and sitting in an office in a bank, but we continue to refine that typification by listening to ever-more subtle clues like tone of voice, so that we can typify them as being cold, arrogant, courteous, charming, brusque, etc. Because we have relatively little information, we can never know what people are really like. Certainly we can never predict with certainty what they may or may not do, but the more information we have the closer we can get to an accurate assessment. We consequently are capable of refining our prediction of what people are really like by gathering more, and more detailed, information: we can say (more or less) that people will behave in certain ways because we can draw upon a stock of this social knowledge that we call 'typifications'.

The process of taking roles relies on just such typifications. People can assume knowledge of the way that others view them because they can typify *their own* acts and they can know that if they themselves typify people, they themselves will be typified by others and the roles in which they are typified shapes their situated identity. Thus, role *taking* is a process in which we attend to others' typifications of us and role *making* a process in which we comport ourselves in a manner likely to generate certain desirable typifications of ourselves in others. On the strength of our awareness of this stock of social knowledge, we observe others and may choose to adopt certain behaviours that encourage others to redefine the situation in accordance with our choices of the typification that we wish to adopt: our choice concerning what we wish to become.

The major problem here is that people appear to choose behaviours that result in negative typifications; that is, in the criminological sense, shame is insufficient to alter behaviour: people steal, 'knowing' that they will be typified as a thief.

It is a long-established notion that humans act in accordance with conventions of groups with which they are associated. Nonetheless, as the example of the thief's failure to respond to favourable typifications shows, the notion is not universally without difficulty. Some of the difficulties concerning failure of behaviour to be shaped by membership of particular groups – such as the Conservative-voting working class, for example, or social-reforming aristocrats – begins to be addressed by reference group theory.[85]

Numerous expressions of reference group theory have spawned a similar number of attempts to show universal explanations of the selection of normative groups. Some argue that adoption of a particular reference depends upon the ease with which contacts are made, others that reference is made to self-status image. Further accounts stress the degree to which interdependence is established, and yet others emphasise the social-functional value of the individual to the referent group. The most significant *consequence* identified in seminal papers by Stouffer[86] and by Runciman,[87] is that of relative deprivation. However, significant problems exist with operationalisation of such studies in that tautology is difficult to avoid; that is, reference to a particular group is both the *explicandum* and part of the *explanans* of the investigation. From the point of the current project, reference group theory fails in that it does not exhibit sufficient *understanding* of the *processes* of reference to any particular group or individual, merely the empirical observation that certain references have been made. Any actor may have any number of opportunities for reference to a huge array of referents, especially in this globally mediated age. Indeed, reference group theory has a tendency to suggest a wholesale adoption of sets of attitudes and behaviours as a kind of complete, one off, 'do-it-all' kit approach to self-constitution.

However, actors do not – by-and-large – simply choose a reference group – individual or collectivity – and decide to be like that reference group; but, rather, adopt a whole sequence of separate self-completing extensions that will come from many sources, but that may come predominantly from the reference group, such that attitudes and behaviours approach more nearly those of the reference group. This is necessarily so; if it were not, all those for whom David Beckham constitutes a reference would turn out pretty much like David Beckham. Of course, the meaning that 'David Beckham' has is different for different people. For some he represents a particular kind of successful masculinity through his sporting prowess, for others a different kind of masculinity through his marriage. Others may simply like his clothes or his haircut, but those close to him might adopt a particular speech pattern or even more intimately a way of holding his mouth or raising an eyebrow. The lines of these miniscule choices are etched in the faces of every human being; they are heard in the inflections of every individual's speech. They are manifested in their walk, they are inscribed upon and in their bodies, they are embedded in their religion, they inform their political views, they transform the way they eat spaghetti, or hold a cigarette. Only in the most generalised view of these choices can a reference group – individual or collective – be identified as forming behaviour, but every single conscious or unconscious decision at the most miniscule level represents choice about becoming, and contributes towards the manifestation of the 'will to self consummation'. The question is therefore not, 'Why do individuals make the choices that they do?', but, rather, 'What are the constraints that mean that only some choices are successful?' The answer to this question is that our choices have a tendency to conform to those suitable to 'the situation', and that some people have more power than others to define what that situation is and what behaviours – performances – are appropriate. Thus, some more-or-less powerful people define the situation and those others in the situation are thus more-or-less constrained to bring to it only those behaviours drawn from referents that are compatible with that definition. Those who bring performances to the situation that are deemed inappropriate are cast as deviant. The objects that we are capable of seeing our selves as futurally are conditioned by our social environment.

Performance

At the beginning of my argument concerning being and becoming, I addressed certain conceptualisations that relied upon a more-or-less static conception of the nature of being, in that it was related to the notion of presence or absence, and to ideas related to plenitude, sufficiency and completion. These conceptions were brought under considerable strain through engagement with the accounts of Heidegger and Derrida in particular, in an attempt to establish a view of the human as a process of becoming, or that *what it is to be* human is *to partake in* a process of becoming. Without undermining this conception one iota, I wish to return now to the nature of being in the way that we might ask the question, 'What am I?' and answer, 'I am a burglar' (or a criminologist or a concert pianist). I wish to establish the idea that *alongside* any consideration of what we are becoming is the question of what one is now. The period of the present is equal to $1/\infty$ seconds.[88] This is the period of the now – of what we *are* – and what we are is our current performance.

Perhaps the most enduring account of performance in the social context is to be found in the work of Erving Goffman. For Goffman, the most central sociological idea is that the self is a social product. It will be evident in so saying that we have taken a turn from Mead's essential definition of the self as that which is an object to itself and are now in the realm of concepts of self that bleed into ideas of identity and constructivist representationalist views of identification and prepared subject positions. Goffman is far less precise when he uses the word 'self' than Mead is or than I would like to be. Consequently, I should like to offer a suggestion of what it is that I think Goffman is talking about. When Mead speaks of self he speaks of that which we can see when we look at ourselves. For Goffman the concept is more nebulous, not least because, for Goffman, the self can be that which other people see. This raises the problems associated with authentic performances. When we watch a play or a film[89] we might suggest that we are watching some one *being* something they *are not*. How can we simultaneously be and not be that which we are? The answer lies in saying what the person is *now*: they are an actor *playing Bottom*; and in saying that, we say something about what they are not *now*: they are not merely an actor, and they are not 'Wopsle Waldengarver, celebrated thespian'.[90] This leads us to suggest that we *are* only our current performance (and we can of course perform to ourselves) and the repository of knowledge that in part led to that performance.

In Goffman, we see two seemingly contradictory expressions of what the self is. First, he suggests on the one hand that the self is purely socially generated with no essential foundation. On the other he suggests a dualistic view in which there is an unsocialised component that drives the individual to social interaction or isolation, and may promote deviant behaviour. Second, there is the suggestion that individuals are not fully determined by society, but are able to manipulate situations through performances rather in the way that actors do on stage. On the other hand again, Goffman suggests that we are not entirely free to choose which images of self we present. We would take each of these views as consistent with the current view presented here. The reason that they appear contradictory in Goffman is because he does not present them in a coherent scheme, but disperses them through several works. Furthermore, they are seen as contradictory in the light of the kind of dualism mentioned at the start of this chapter, concerning agency and structure; in this case choice and constraint. That is, choice is conditioned by its social environment providing an illusion of free will; expression of that choice is constrained by social structures. Goffman does not tell us how these things come about in a systematic, internally consistent, coherent account that relates the different elements and levels of his analysis.

The foundations of Goffman's ideas about self emerge in the early paper, 'On Cooling the Mark Out',[91] in which he discusses performances of self in terms of more-or-less successful self-claims. That is, to give a performance of self is to make a claim about oneself that is either sustainable or not. In some cases, as in the case where the 'mark' or proposed victim of a 'sting' or 'con trick' can no longer sustain his performances of self once it is known that he is the 'mark', we need to make adjustments to our performance of self to reflect the fact that our self claims can no longer be sustained. The degree to which such claims can be sustained is socially contingent. The mark's claims may only be valid claims within the criminal community, and as such will only cease to be sustainable in that community; he may need to make no other adjustments to his performances to his (unknowing) wife, for example. The process of 'cooling the mark out' is the process whereby the community eases the changes that the person needs to make to his unsustainable performances.

In 'On Face Work',[92] Goffman's dualism of self is clearly evident:

So far I have implicitly been using a double definition of self: the self as an image pieced together from the expressive implications of the full flow of events in an undertaking; and the self as a kind of player in a ritual game who copes honourably or dishonourably... with the judgemental contingencies of the situation.

In other words, the self is the performance – which is socially constrained – and the performer, who chooses which performance to enact. In 'The Presentation of Self in Everyday Life', a similar dualism persists in the distinction between the 'all-too-human self' and the 'socialized self'.[93] The 'all-too-human self' is the embodiment of moods and emotions and energies, but it is also the preparer of performances. Thus the performer is not solely a social being but the harbour of imagination, dreams and desires, and the bearer of shame and pride.[94] Such considerations, in conjunction with the socialising forces over sustainable self-claims, produce the socialised self. This entity conforms to the character being performed as over against the performer, and it is this socialised self, or self-as-character, that for Goffman represents our unique humanity. Paradoxically, this means that, for Goffman, our 'true' self is the self that is performed outwardly in the situation, not that which we might assume most people would take to be our 'real' self – our inner, motivational self.[95]

A correctly staged and performed character leads the audience to impute a self to a performed character, but this imputation – this self – is a *product* of a scene that comes off, and is not a *cause* of it. The self, then, as performed character is not an organic thing that has a specific location, whose fundamental fate is to be born, to mature, and to die; it is a dramatic effect arising diffusely from a scene that is presented, and the characteristic issue, the crucial concern, is whether it will be credited or discredited.[96]

Whilst it is important here to stress that Goffman distances himself from the suggestion that the situationally defined role is *all* that the self is,[97] it is crucial that we take on board that what any person is in the moment of *now* is their performance and that all of our social acts are performances.

Extension

The importance of the foregoing to our present project is this. The objects that we see ourselves as being are performances; when we view ourselves as objects in the world we view ourselves as performances. The choices concerning what those objects look like are socially conditioned by our reflexive engagement with our own biography and by our engagement with the presentation of the selves and biographies[98] of others, either within social interaction or, importantly contemporaneously, via various mediations. Performances, thus, are statements of self. When we view ourselves as objects of the future, we view future statements. It will be apparent that we make different statements in different situations. This confirms the fact that our statements are not congruent with one another but change from situation to situation. Furthermore, because this is true for everyone, situations also change; even where superficially situations are the same – the same office, the same pub, the same holiday accommodation – it will be apparent that they also are constantly in flux. It follows therefore that we are never the same person twice: we never repeat a performance. Each performance, each statement, is different. Each statement represents an expression of the nature of the object that we hold ourselves to be *now*, and each performance is the consummate statement of that self; it leaves nothing out and it requires nothing to complete it; there is no remainder and there is no deficit in the performance of the self of *now*. However, since we are never the same person twice, what we will be (however near that future) must be different to the self of *now*. If this is so, then there must be some *thing* that is different about us then and us in the future – some deficit or some remainder revealed by the difference between us then and future. We recall Derrida when he says that the supplement *reveals* the deficit. If we were complete in that *now* past, and are now somehow different, we must have adopted a supplement, an extension, to that completeness, some addition, that permitted us to become the self of *this* moment, and since we will change again, we will adopt other extensions, other supplements to our simultaneously completed and incomplete selves, for we are complete in this moment and we will adopt supplements to complete ourselves again in the next.

Earlier I indicated that this notion of supplementation stretches back to Rousseau, and forms a central part of Derrida's argument in *Of Grammatology*.[99] Derrida's concern is with writing, and in particular with deconstructing the notion that writing is somehow a supplement to speech or presence. We observed that, for Rousseau, writing was a 'dangerous supplement'; it represented a product of necessity born of an ever-increasing growth of impersonal human networks. Writing was necessary as a supplement to mediate speech across social distances that were too large for presence and unmediated voice alone to bridge. Writing, for Rousseau, is the supplement adopted by the powerful, lawgivers, priests, as the ultimate tool of social control and of the perpetuation of inequality. It is the disruptor of a state of communal grace where communities would exist on a scale commensurate with unmediated self-presence.[100] A similar conception is evident in Rousseau when he speaks of the origins of music. For Rousseau, the high-baroque contrapuntal style of his contemporary and countryman Rameau is the result of the application of the supplement of melody to rhythm, of harmony to melody, and of counterpoint to harmony. Rousseau is concerned to show how the music of his age has departed from an elysian ideal in which musical communication is achieved by self-present humans in a community of equals. The adoption of the series of supplements separates musical expression from some, since not all possess the skills of harmony or counterpoint. Thus supplementation for Rousseau is a producer and reproducer of inequality. It is not important to this portion of the current argument that Derrida brings these notions under significant critical scrutiny, but it is important that Rousseau brings to our attention the idea that portions of apparently taken-for-granted wholes are in fact supplements to an earlier whole.

We spoke above of agency as that concept which frees us from structural determination. Another way of saying this is to say that agency is that concept which permits change in that it allows us to resist convention. It exhibits significant utility in this form in that it permits pre-existent social injustice to be changed; it permits the undermining of power. If one is an agent, one has the self-possessed capacity for independence from the constraints of structure.[101] The question arises, however, of where this self-possession comes from. An answer to this question of significant interest to the current argument is to be found in the Sociology of Translation, sometimes referred to as Actor Network Theory, significant statements of which are to be found in Latour[102], Law[103] and Callon.[104] The Sociology of Translation suggests that the more a person appears to be self-present and possessed of agency in terms of the apparent power to achieve certain actions, or to be self-possessed of their identity, the more that person is reliant upon a network of extensions or supplements to that self.[105] Perhaps the most straightforward account of this type is to be found in Latour's account of the work of Louis Pasteur.[106] Pasteur is thought of as being an independent scientist and thinker who single-handedly developed the processes that made milk safe to drink. However, when one examines this conception, it becomes evident that Pasteur was reliant upon a network of other actors, politicians, researchers, bacteria, education and so on. Indeed, Pasteur himself is but one small element of the assemblage[107] of extensions that imbues him with the *appearance* of agency. This assemblage now includes the vast majority of milk farmers in the western world. Hence, for Translation theorists, agency does not rely on completedness and self-possession but is dependent upon a network of supplements or extensions. The more complete the powerful self-present appears, the more that appearance of completeness is reliant upon a network of other actors and of mediation that reveals the incompleteness of that person. The supplement reveals the deficit.

The will to self-consummation

If agency can be seen as dependency, then self and identity can be seen as merely partial. Self in this view becomes an open-ended *process* of becoming – a process of producing self by the adoption of extensions to the existing self. As Garfinkel has put it, life is an 'endless ongoing accomplishment'.[108] Of course we can never be complete except at the point of death, and then we are only completed because there can be no more process of becoming. I wish now to begin to conclude this chapter by introducing a new concept that refers to the process of becoming in human beings and relates it to our will.

I opened this chapter by separating two aspects of agency: will, and the overcoming of constraint upon the execution of that will. Through engagement with Heidegger, I have shown that we are capable of viewing ourselves as objects of our own cognition and that we are further capable of viewing that object as a projection into the future. I have conceptualised the movement from self present to self future in terms of the adoption of supplements or extensions to the existing self in order to complete the self of *this* moment. We have further noted that such a process of 'completion' is never finally accomplished but that we continually 'complete' ourselves; we are in a never-ending process of 'self consummation'. Our desires concerning our future selves are reflected in us having will towards ourselves as objects of the future; that is, desires and aspirations concerning future performances. Such will is manifest in the choices that we make concerning extensions to our existing selves that temporarily complete us in our current performance. Our will towards ourselves as objects of the future relies upon a repertoire of objects that we may view ourselves as being in the future that is conditioned by social circumstance and biography; that is, by the playing out of the biographies of our own and other selves in social situations. The choices that we make concerning our temporary consummation are constrained by processes of structuration. This constrained will towards ourselves as objects of the future I thus term 'The Will to Self-Consummation'.

The 'will to crime' revisited

We are now in a position to return to Matza's conception of 'will'. The problem with Matza's conception is not whether determinism deprives us of freedom but a false conception of the notion of freedom and determinism, and the relationship between them in human experience. If we change the language a little, the notion becomes clearer. If we say we are *constrained*, we can say we are not free. This is because freedom is set against constraint not against cause or determination. Hence, to say that we are constrained is not the same thing as saying that we have no will. We can choose anything that we can imagine, even though we cannot always *exercise* that choice. This is because will is *emergent* from a human's capacity for reflexivity: the capacity for will is *emergent from* human's awareness of the complexity of their history and the complexity of their situated self; it is not *reducible* to either or even to both. Will is not a whole, reducible to its subvening causes, will is an emergent capacity that is greater than the sum of its parts: our will has causes; however, those causes, whilst necessary, are insufficient.

In common with many other control theorists, and other theorists of the time, Matza accepts unproblematically a conception of law as an expression of societal consensus.[109] This is evident in his casting of delinquent behaviour as sub-cultural.[110] Indeed, the conception of a will to crime presupposes an ontological reality to crime that we would today reject.[111] If we accept the ontological non-existence of crime, then there is no object upon which a 'will to crime' may focus. This is crucial because, as I have shown in this chapter, will is intentional; that is, it is a state of mind that is directed towards some object. In the case of human beings, I have shown that the object to which that state of mind is directed is the self as an object of the future. In Matza's case, the object towards which the state of mind is directed must be crime, but if, as many criminologists now accept, crime has no ontological reality, there is nothing in Matza's conception towards which the state of mind, 'will', *can* be directed. However, this is not to say that delinquent acts may not be wilful; to be sure, a delinquent may choose an act because it is transgressive – and, indeed, Matza suggests that such choices may be made. But here, again, there is confusion between a 'will to crime' and choice, or any kind of general will. If crime has no ontological reality, then it is not possible to have will towards that abstract, 'crime'. However, it is perfectly possible to choose to do something because it is transgressive. Amongst the influences upon the imagination – whose limitations limit the capacity to imagine – is some possible knowledge of what is transgressive in a particular situation; however, there cannot be knowledge of *crime* in any sense other than its *legally* transgressive form. (A will to crime would surely require a proper knowledge of the law.) Thus, a will to transgress presupposes in the delinquent knowledge of what constitutes transgressive behaviour in *that situation*. We know, of course, that what is transgressive in any particular situation is highly contingent, even where – as Matza himself illustrates[112] in his account of an exchange between a drunken teenager and a policeman – the offices of the law are involved. I have argued elsewhere[113] that what constitutes transgressive behaviour in any situation is negotiated in that situation in interaction with others who possess will, and who exhibit differentially distributed power to constrain or enable that will. Will to act in a way that is deemed inappropriate through negotiation of what *is* appropriate in the situation is, if enacted, transgressive. Thus, what I suggest is that all will is merely the motor of becoming. It is the intentional state of mind that is directed to the self as an object of the future: as *any possible* object of the future that the individual can imagine. The actual *choice* of mode of becoming is only limited by the imagination, which itself emerges from the complex reflective awareness of history and circumstance. The exercise of that choice is differentially constrained such that some behaviours *become* delinquent – emerge as delinquent – from the negotiations of norms of acceptable behaviour in any given situation. Thus, it may be possible that a will to transgression may *emerge* in a particular situation, where that transgression is an act of becoming. Thus we may not postulate a general will to crime, but merely a situated will to transgress.

Notes

* I should like to thank Ronnie Lippens for considerable support, both intellectual and 'psychological', as a friend and mentor, in the writing of this chapter.
1 E. Tavor Bannet, *Structuralism and the Logic of Dissent: Barthes, Derrida, Foucault, Lacan*, London: Macmillan, 1989.
2 A. Giddens, *The Constitution of Society: Outline of the Theory of Structuration*, Berkley: University of California Press, 1986 [1984], and *Central Problems in Social Theory*, London: Macmillan Press, 1979.
3 M. Foucault, *Discipline and Punish: The Birth of the Prison*, trans. A. Sheridan, Harmondsworth: Penguin, 1991 [1975].
4 All events and states are new [novel] at the time they occur, because they have all previous events and states in their past, and nothing that is prior to the current event can have *all* the events in its past that the current event has. Tuesday has Monday and Sunday in its past, Monday only has Sunday. As Bergson says, 'no two moments are identical in a conscious being' (H. Bergson, *The Creative Mind*, trans. M. Andison, New York: The Citadel Press, 164). Heidegger discusses this point in M. Heidegger, *The Metaphysical Foundations of Logic*, trans. M. Heim, Bloomington: Indiana University Press, 1984.
5 In particular D. Matza, *Delinquency and Drift*, London: John Wiley, 1964.
6 A. Giddens, *The Constitution of Society: Outline of the Theory of Structuration*, Berkley: University of California Press, 1986 [1984], 55.
7 Ibid.
8 Ibid. 56.
9 This has significant ramifications when considering criminal will or responsibility.
10 See R. Sparks, 'Penal austerity: the doctrine of less eligibility reborn?', in P. Francis and R. Matthews (eds), *Prisons 2000*, London: Macmillan, 1996, 74–93.
11 See R. Chisholm, *Person and Object*, London: Allen & Unwin, 1976; T. O'Connor, *Persons and Causes: The Metaphysics of Free Will*, New York: Oxford University Press, 2000; or R. Clarke, *Libertarian Accounts of Free Will*, Oxford: Oxford University Press, 2003, for example.
12 T. Reid, *Essays on the Active Powers of the Human Mind*, ed. B. Brody, Cambridge: MIT Press, 1969, 88.
13 G. Strawson, *Freedom and Belief*, Oxford: Clarendon Press, 1986.
14 D. Pereboom, *Living Without Free Will*, Cambridge: Cambridge University Press, 2001.
15 This position is particularly clearly put by Thomas Nagel in *What Does it All Mean? A Very Short Introduction to Philosophy*, Oxford: Oxford University Press, 1987.
16 A. Schopenhauer, *The Essays of Arthur Schopenhauer: On Human Nature*, trans. T. Bailey, London: Swan Sonnenschein, 1902; cited in Matza, op. cit.

17 Matza, op. cit.
18 See E. Ferri, *Criminal Sociology*, trans. J. Kelly and J. Lisle, ed. W. Smithers, Boston: Little, Brown & Company, 1917, 303–4 & 297–8.
19 See Ferri, op. cit. 297–8.
20 R. McIver, *Social Causation*, Boston: Ginn, 1942; cited in Matza, op. cit. 8–9.
21 Matza, op. cit. 60–1.
22 Ibid. 101.
23 Ibid. 181.
24 Ibid.
25 Ibid. 181–91.
26 Ibid. 183.
27 M. Heidegger, *Being and Time*, trans. J. Macquarrie and E. Robinson, Oxford: Blackwell, 1996 [1926].
28 I. Kant, *The Critique of Pure Reason*, ed. P. Vasilis, London: Dent, 1993, BII ChIII, section 4.
29 Heidegger, op. cit. 23.
30 R. Descartes, *Meditations on First Philosophy with Selections from the Objections and Replies*, trans. J. Cottingham, Cambridge: Cambridge University Press, 1996 [1641].
31 H.L. Dreyfus, *Being-in-the-World: A Commentary on Heidegger's Being and Time, Division I*, Cambridge: MIT Press, 1997.
32 This comes from William James ('Essays in radical empiricism', *Essays in Radical Empiricism & A Pluralistic Universe*, Gloucester: Peter Smith, 1967 [1912]) via Husserl (*Ideas: General Introduction to Pure Phenomenology*, London: George Allen & Unwin, 1976 [1913]) who was Heidegger's mentor. James summarised his view thus: 'To be radical, an empiricism must neither admit into its constructions any element that is not directly experienced, nor exclude from them any element that is directly experienced' (James, op. cit. 42).
33 Macquarrie and Robinson (Heidegger, op. cit. 72) render 'proximally' here.
34 Heidegger, op. cit. 72.
35 Ibid. 498.
36 Ibid. 163.
37 Ibid. 154.
38 'das Man'. In German, *Man* is an indefinite pronoun, it renders in English as 'they' or 'one', thus we would find it in phrases such as 'they do x' or 'they say y' but also as in 'one does x' or 'one says y'; however, in the Macquarrie and Robinson translation, we have rendered only 'the they'. When we use 'one does x' in English it carries an implied presumption; there is an implicit 'should'. Further, that presumption is impersonal: no one in particular has made that presumption. When we use the form '*they* do x' we lose both the presumption and its impersonal nature: 'they' means specifically, those other than myself. I choose to make *explicit* the distinction absent in Macquarrie and Robinson between 'one' and 'they' where the distinction is *implicit* in their translation. Justification, I believe, is evident in Heidegger, as outlined above.
39 Ibid.
40 See also Brandom (*Making it Explicit: Reasoning, Representing, and Discursive Commitment*, Cambridge: Harvard, 1994, outlined below.
41 Heidegger, op. cit.
42 It will be evident that this has resonances with Giddens' 'Practical Consciousness'; people have inherent knowledge about what it is to 'go on' in everyday

existence without recourse to cognitive or discursive states of mind – they do not make 'decisions'.

43 Ibid. 167.

44 Angst – anxiety, anguish, suffering – is the existentialist value par excellence. It arises from the recognition of the impossibility of human fulfilment. This cannot come through the stoic's rejection of the world (to be human is to be-in-the-world); through the 'ordinary man's' search for a life of physical pleasure (we cannot be fulfilled except through use of all our capacities, including the capacity to question our fulfilment); or through the philosophers' call to reason (we deny our humanity by separating it from the desires of ordinary humans). The essential value is that of Angst, the fundamental distress at the knowledge that all that is may not be. It is rendered in some accounts (like Nietzsche, for example) as the will to strive. There can be no freedom without anguish, since every choice involves it.

> In sum, existentialist values have a common source, a common function, and a common identifying characteristic. Their common source is acute awareness of the tragedy inherent in the human condition. Their common function is to liberate us from the fears and frustrations of everyday life or the tedium of philosophical dreaming. Their identifying characteristic is intensity.
>
> (R.G. Olson, *Introduction to Existentialism*, New York: Dover, 1962)

45 Heidegger, op. cit. 395.

46 Ibid. 302.

47 Ibid. 307.

48 IN fact.

49 Ibid. 307.

50 Ibid. 273.

51 A. Giddens, *Modernity and Self Identity*, London: Polity, 1991, 125.

52 'Guilt' is not used in its common usage but in the sense used by Dostoevsky in *The Brothers Karamazov* about which Levinas has this to say:

> I am responsible for the Other without waiting for his reciprocity.... Reciprocity is his affair.... It is I who support all, [... as in] that sentence in Dostoevsky: 'We are all guilty of all and for all men before all, and I more than the others.' This is not owing to such or such a guilt which is really mine, or to offences that I would have committed; but because I am responsible for a total responsibility, which answers for all the others and for all in the others, even for their responsibility. I always have one responsibility more than the others.
>
> (See V. Vinokurov, 'Levinas's Dostoevsky: A Response to "Dostoevsky is Derrida"', *Common Knowledge*, 2003, 9/2: 318–40)

53 Disclosedness – hence disclosure – *revealing* of truth. Stripping away self-deception (see Heidegger, 1996, op. cit. 167).

54 Heidegger's understanding of the nature of time is explored throughout Division II and, indeed, its relation to the everyday was to be fully expanded in an unwritten Division III. This conception of time is so far removed from our everyday conception of time that it is of little interest to our project here. Fundamentally it involves an inversion of the conventionally accepted notion of time being a framework within which events take place, to one where events are the framework within which – for humans in their way of being – time takes place.

55 Cited in J. Derrida, *Of Grammatology*, trans. G.C. Spivak, Baltimore: Johns Hopkins University Press, 1976 [1967], 143.

56
> the effective presence of an origin in an historical development..., the transumption of thesis and antithesis in a dialectical synthesis, the presence in speech of logical and grammatical structure, truth as what subsists behind appearances, and the effective presence of a goal in the steps that lead to it, the *authority of presence*. ... The notions of 'making clear', 'grasping', demonstrating, 'revealing', and showing what is the case, all invoke presence...
>
> (J. Culler, *On Deconstruction: Theory and Criticism after Structuralism*, London" Routledge, 1993, 93–4; my emphasis)

Interestingly, in Christianity, the 'logos' of John's gospel (John 1:1) is Christ – the word made *present* (to us) in flesh.

57 J. Derrida, *Writing and Difference*, trans. A. Bass, Chicago: University of Chicago Press, 1978, 279; my emphasis.

58 Form.

59 Derrida, 1976, op. cit. 12.

60 Culler, op. cit. 93.

61 N. Lee, *Childhood and Society*, Buckingham: Open University Press, 2001.

62 Particularly 'Structural Anthropology'.

63 Derrida shows that Levi-Strauss' study is significantly flawed and guilty of ethnocentrism.

64 Derrida, 1976, op. cit. 136.

65 Ibid. 146–7.

66 Ibid. 149.

67 Smith, op. cit. 42.

68 He who is not self-present with me is not me: he is 'other' than me. He who is not co-present with me is a stranger or is 'other' than 'us' (those who are co-present with me).

69 Lee, op. cit.

70 Culler, op. cit. 93–4.

71 Lee, op. cit. 108.

72 See discussions of hysteria in T. Szasz, *The Manufacture of Madness*, London: Routledge and Kegan Paul, 1971, and *The Myth of Mental Illness*, St Albans: Paladin, 1972 [1962], or M. Foucault, *Madness and Civilisation: A History of Insanity in the Age of Reason*, trans. R. Howard, London: Tavistock, 1971 [1961], for example. Historically, madness was considered a female problem: women were considered inherently unstable. It was believed that the uterus moved around the body, during menstruation it came to rest in the brain causing 'hysteria' – Gr. *Hysterikos*, womb.

73 Lee, op. cit. 108.

74 Here Nick Lee embarks on a favourite method of reading of Derrida's own. We might suggest that Lee is 'reading across the grain' in his use of writing as supplement. In Lee's account, writing is used in the sense of Rousseau's dangerous supplement rather than in Derrida's originary sense, to deconstruct Derridean fashion, the possibility of power based on self-presence. Reading across the grain is Derrida's method of very careful 'misreading' of the texts of canonical philosophers to render subtle, imaginative and meaningful interpretations of their work. The whole section in Lee's book that deals with Derridean themes may be read as just such an interpretation.

75 Lee, op. cit. 110.

76 This is, in essence, the phenomenological account of perception. Its origins in this form are founded on Nagel's statement that

> the fact that an organism has conscious experience *at all* means, basically, that there is something it is like to *be* that organism ... an organism has conscious mental states if and only if there is something that it is to *be* that organism – something it is like *for* the organism.
> ('What is it Like to be a Bat?' *Philosophical Review*, LXXXIII, 1974: 435–50)

So we might ask, 'What is it like to be the Queen?', answer, "It is like X to be the Queen'. Thus we would say, there is something, 'X', it is like to be the Queen. To extend this, we might ask, 'What is it like to perceive a car?' Well, there is something, 'Y', it is like to perceive a car, and we experience that something when we see a car.

77 Brandom, op. cit.

78 *De re* ascriptions provide the words 'of' and 'about' the intentional directedness towards the thing (*res*) that the sentence is about, whereas ascriptions *de dicto* pertain to a belief in some saying (*dictum*). Brandom asks us to consider the following: 'The President of the United States will be black by the year 2000.' Read *de dicto*, this means the utterance 'The President of the United States *is* black' will be true by the year 2000. Read *de re* it means that the *res* of the ascription (the thing) the President, i.e. (at that time) Bill Clinton, will be black by the year 2000. In this case, certain understandings concerning the permanence of skin colour disambiguate these two claims.

79 Brandom, op. cit. 518.

80 Ibid.

81 I use the phrase 'socially conditioned' where 'socially contingent' might be more conventional. I use the word 'conditioned' to indicate ennablement *or* constraint and reject 'contingent' since it has residual structural deterministic connotations. Conditioning is softer.

82 Foucault, 1970, op. cit. (see note xlii).

83 G.P. Stone, 'Appearance and the Self: A Slightly Revised Version', *Social Psychology Through Symbolic Interaction*, 2nd edn, ed. G.P. Stone and H.A. Farberman, New York: Wiley, 1981, 121–47.

84 J.P. Hewitt, *Self and Society: A Symbolic Interactionist Social Psychology*, 7th edn, Boston: Allyn and Bacon, 1997 [1976].

85 H. Hyman and E. Singer, eds, *Readings in Reference Group Theory and Research*, New York: Free Press, 1968.

86 S.A. Stouffer, *The American Soldier: Adjustment During Army Life*, Vol. I, Princeton: Princeton University Press, 1949.

87 W.G. Runciman, *Relative Deprivation and Social Justice*, Harmondsworth: Pelican, 1972.

88 The temporal value of the present must be viewed as an asymptote, which value is diminished by considering the proximity of the future and of the past. Thus the temporal value of the present is $1/\infty$ seconds (minutes, or hours, it matters not).

89 Less so in film because we are not looking at a discrete complete performance but an edited-together collection of different performances.

90 Dickens, '*Great Expectations*'.

91 E. Goffman, 'On Cooling the Mark Out', *Psychiatry*, 1952, 15/4: 451–63.

92 E. Goffman, 'On Face-Work', 1955; reprinted in E. Goffman, *Interaction Ritual*, Chicago: Aldine, 1974, 5–46.

93 E. Goffman, *The Presentation of Self in Everyday Life*, London: Penguin, 1990 [1956].

94 Ibid. 252–4.

95 In her study of the effects of the media on the construction of masculine identities in prison, Yvonne Jewkes (Y. Jewkes, *Captive Audience: Media, Masculinity and Power in Prisons*, Cullompton: Willan, 2002) inverts this dualism and places the *echt* self in a private domain and the *ersatz* in public view. She suggests that the private self is the place to which we retire when we are tired of our public performances. This view fosters the medicalised notion that the private 'self' is somehow *echt* and 'healthy' (ibid. 40) and the public *ersatz*, and represents a misunderstanding of the role of the private and the public in the act of self-constitution. Supporters of Jewkes' position might argue that we all know people who pretend to be something that they are not; that is, that their performances of self are somehow fake. It is conceded that there are those who fabricate identities for themselves to evade the law, for example, or who pretend to be policemen or doctors, for example, in order to dupe people. But to assume that these people are exhibiting a *false* aspect of themselves is to fall into the trap of Bourdieu's 'biographical illusion' (P. Bourdieu, 'The Biographical Illusion', 1987, in P. DuGay, J. Evans and P. Redman (eds) *Identity: A Reader*, London: Sage, 2002, 297). These people notwithstanding, we are left with 'Walter Mitty' characters, and those whose behaviour simply seems out of place. The Walter Mittys of this world fantasise about being something that they are not – we experience a disjuncture between the performance that we perceive and the performance that they think they are giving; others more subtly misread the constraints of the discourses of their milieu, they exhibit what we often describe as affectation. In either case, it is a mistake to assume that what these people produce as performances of self is somehow false. The performance that they make is as much a part of the interplay between their private selves and social reality as any other aspect of their, or any other person's, performance of self. Bourdieu frequently speaks of people as virtuosi in dealing with the social world; perhaps it would be more realistic to suggest that we all exhibit varying degrees of competence in our performances of self and that some people's performances leave more to be desired than others.

96 Goffman, 1990, op. cit. 252–3.

97 See E. Goffman, *Frame Analysis: An Essay in the Organisation of Experience*, Harmondsworth: Penguin, 1975, where Goffman deals with the biographical continuity of self. For the purposes of this study I take such biographical continuity of self to be constituted in persisting recursive practices and states of mind; that is, memory and habit which, when they become the reflexive object, help to inform the view of ourselves as objects of the future.

98 All representations of ourselves or others are, of necessity, biographical since the present is past in a microscopic instant and thus all reflections are reflections of things past – it is impossible for us to reflect upon the present. The temporal value of the present is as close as it is possible to be to non-existence.

99 J. Derrida, *Of Grammatology*, trans G.C. Spivak, Baltimore: Johns Hopkins University Press, 1976 [1967].

100 Ibid. 137.

101 This is further evidence that when we speak of agency we are in fact really talking about power.

102 B. Latour, *The Pasteurisation of France*, Cambridge: Harvard, 1988.

103 J. Law, 'Power, Discretion and Strategy', in J. Law (ed.) *A Sociology of Monsters: Essays on Power, Technology and Domination*, London: Routledge, 1991.

104 M. Callon, 'Some Elements in a Sociology of Translation: Domestication of the Scallop and Fishermen of St. Brieuc Bay', in J. Law (ed.) *Power, Action and Belief*, London: Routledge and Kegan Paul, 1986; and M. Callon, 'The Sociology of an Actor-Network: The Case of the Electric Vehicle', in M. Callon, J. Law and A. Rip (eds) *Mapping the Dynamics of Science and Technology*, London: Macmillan, 1986.

105 Lee, 1998, op. cit.

106 Latour, 1988, op. cit.

107 See G. Deleuze and F. Guattari, *Thousand Plateaus: Capitalism and Schizophrenia*, trans. B. Massumi, Minnesota: University of Minnesota Press, 1987, 71, 88–91, 323–37, 399, 503–5.

108 H. Garfinkel, *Studies in Ethnomethodology*, Englewood Cliffs: Prentice Hall, 1967.

109 W. Einstadter and S. Henry, *Criminological Theory: An Analysis of its Underlying Assumptions*, Fort Worth: Harcourt & Brace, 1995.

110 'Subcultural delinquents hold implicit views on the legitimacy of a variety of offenses' (Matza, op. cit. 161). The norms of the delinquent are not the norms of society as a whole, as expressed in the law, but are the norms of a subculture.

111 Becker's conception of crime as a socially constructed label in 'Outsiders' was published just one year before *Delinquency and Drift* in 1963. Hulsman's crucial statement concerning the lack of ontological reality in the concept of 'crime' was more than 20 years away (L. Hulsman, 'Critical Criminology and the Concept of Crime', *Contemporary Crises*, 1986, 10/1: 63–80, 71).

112 Matza, op. cit. 163–4.

113 D. Crewe, *Will, Power, Constraint and Change: Prolegomena to a Study of Self and the Emergence of Structure in Young Offender Institutions*, Keele: Keele University, 2007, unpublished PhD thesis.

Chapter 2

Being accused, becoming criminal

George Pavlich

He who fights with monsters should be careful lest he thereby become a monster. And if thou gaze long into an abyss, the abyss will also gaze into thee.[1]

Introduction

Along with Kierkegaard, Nietzsche is frequently described as the philosopher who cleared the intellectual ground for that somewhat diverse group of writers known as 'the existentialists'. Mary Warnock helpfully sketches existential philosophers as broadly interested in human freedom, but more significantly with human freedom as 'a practical problem'.[2] She continues:

> They aim to show people *that they are free*, to open their eyes to something which has always been true, but which for one reason or another may not always have been recognized, namely that men are free to choose, not only what to do on a specific occasion, but what to value and how to live.

Their point was not simply to discuss in abstract terms what it is to be free, but to grapple with the complexities of the very experience of freedom. Such complexities are worked through in various genres: fictional texts (e.g. Sartre's *Nausea*, Camus' *The Plague*), plays (e.g. Sartre's Nietzschean-inspired *The Flies*) and philosophical treatises (e.g. Sartre's *Being and Nothingness*, Heidegger's *Being and Time*). All grapple with the paradoxical, anxiety-provoking experience of having to ascribe meaning and value to an ultimately meaningless and undetermined existence.

To be sure, echoes of Nietzschean thinking resonate in even this brief allusion to existential texts, but not without ambiguity, contrast or contradiction. Although much needs to be said on this particular topic, the following chapter is specifically concerned with this question: what does Nietzsche's work contribute to an analysis of crime, criminals and criminology, especially in light of existential thinking? My responses to this question will not repeat the usual tendency within criminology to align phenomenological or existential approaches with subjectivist approaches to crime, mostly as a counterweight to the structuralist fervours of 1970s critical criminology.[3] Without denying aspects of that claim, I will interpret Nietzsche's scattered statements on crime, criminals and punishment within the broader context of several (existential) themes in his work. By so doing, one is better able to flesh out the somewhat banal – and potentially misleading – subjectivist approach ascribed to Nietzschean and existential thinking. At the same time, the intention is to offer a more developed sense of the contributions, ambiguities and problems that Nietzsche's aphorisms hold for discourses on crime.

Of course, such exalted ambitions in the context of a chapter threaten to collapse under their own weight. But, to avoid this, and to address the wider remit of this collection, I focus on only two vital themes within Nietzsche's work – the will to power and the genealogy of morality. Aside from their later expression in existential thought,[4] these themes provide some context against which to understand his references to crime, criminals and punishment.

Theme 1: the will to power and the experience of freedom

In posthumously published notes, collected by Walter Kaufmann under the title of *The Will to Power*, Nietzsche offers several descriptions of an instinctive 'will' that defines what it is to be a *living* organism. At base, this will involves mastering, interpreting and shaping the environment around it.[5] As 'an insatiable desire to manifest power' that exercises 'power as a creative drive',[6] this will to power

> can manifest itself only against resistances; therefore it seeks that which resists it – this is the primeval tendency of the protoplasm when it extends its pseudopodia and feels about. Appropriation and assimilation are above all a desire to overwhelm, a forming, shaping and reshaping, until at length that which has been overwhelmed has entirely gone over into the power domain of the aggressor and has increased the same.[7]

The resulting force – which Foucault elaborates upon in his analyses of power–knowledge relations[8] – comes to be only through its exercise. There may well be echoes of Nietzsche in the 'facticity'[9] that Sartre posited as the substrate around which human freedom moves.[10] However, one should be weary of a direct connection – Nietzsche's will to power is expressly formulated as an *'instinct for freedom'*.[11] The paradox is easy to miss, but

Nietzsche enunciates it as 'the innermost essence of being'[12] a radically indecipherable, never pre-given, will to power that is nominal[13] and only experienced through its effects.[14]

I leave open whether this foregrounds Sartre's 'existence precedes essence' adage; but it does suggest that we experience our basic constitution through performance and possibly effect. That is, the will to power is not merely a feature of a predetermined, pre-given subject – it surrounds relational complexes that fabricate historical subjects. A being that emerges as 'human' becomes so by imposing itself on the world in ways that are not inherently determined, except perhaps by the contingent operation of other wills that constitute a given historical moment. Equally, the modern political and legal subject who appears as an *a priori*, free-willing, rational being is, for Nietzsche, a creature of given force relations.

As such, he rejects the idea that freedom is a function of individual volition because, 'there is no such thing as "will"'.[15] His concept of the will to power contests psychological conceptions of will as a predicate of a pre-existing, free individual.[16] The 'instinct for freedom' is an unconditional one that exceeds given conditional formulations in history. Moreover, as he sees it, power is not antithetical to freedom, but the means of the latter's historical expression. To be sure, this sort of challenge to the liberal subject and its freedom has far-reaching moral and political implications. It also suggests particular images of law, crime, criminals and punishment.

Nietzsche: criminal law, criminals and the will to power

When turning expressly to law and crime, Nietzsche notes that the making and enforcing of laws (i.e. legislation) is the chief instrument through which a modern will to power (incarnated in the 'state') revolves. His theory of law, and especially criminal law,[17] provides a framework for understanding crime as the outcome of force relations that use concepts of duty, guilt or innocence to produce compliant legal subjects. Like moral subjects, or the subject of grammar, the criminal subject is created out of subjections – in this case historical processes that institute criminal law.

Indeed, for him, the 'most decisive act' performed by a 'supreme power' as soon as it is 'strong enough to do so – is the institution of the *law*'.[18] This involves,

> the imperative declaration of what in general counts as permitted, as just, in its eyes, and what counts as forbidden, as unjust: once it has instituted the law, it treats violence and capricious acts on the part of individuals or entire groups as offences against the law, as rebellion against the supreme power itself...[19]

If the state thus defines the forbidden, it also appropriates conflicts from subjects and disallows injured parties from pursuing private revenge.

In this historical expression of its will to power, a relational complex (nominally, the 'state') claims an exclusive right to define criminal action through its legislation of criminal law. In that process, it interprets the 'criminal' – relying on Christian moral precepts of good and evil – as a 'guilty subject' who has freely chosen to violate the law, and who is punished in the name of 'deterrence'. Against this classical formulation – well known in criminology via Bentham and Beccaria – Nietzsche conceptualises crime as the outcome of complex struggles. Criminals are created from shifting strategic alliances whereby the state legislates through criminal law and produces subjects of its will to power. Here, concepts like 'just' and 'unjust' exist, 'only after the institution of the law'.[20]

With specific reference to the will to power, one detects different images of crime in his work. First, crime is in some places described as belonging 'to the concept of "revolt against the social order"';[21] punishment then involves a 'suppression of a revolt' or 'security measures against the suppressed'.[22] Legislating crime and creating punishable criminal subjects takes place in a complex of force relations, involving local battles over what is, or is not, to be deemed criminal. Also, there are conflicts over the identities of criminals, in which 'every society has the tendency to reduce its opponents to caricatures – at least in imagination – and, as it were, to starve them'.[23] For their part, criminals respond to this complex in one of two ways. We shall return to this in more detail later, but suffice here to note his distinction between a 'pale criminal' who feels remorse over the act (and so reinforces the state's morality) and the 'great criminal' whose actions open out onto new ways of being.[24]

Nietzsche understands the first as a 'wretched' being, 'a miscarried type of criminal',[25] whose instinct for freedom is 'internalized' as a form of 'bad conscience' and who feels 'guilty' for pursuing a state-prohibited act.[26] It should be noted that he rejects life-destroying acts of the 'miserable criminal', but not the (new) life-affirming 'great man' of history. But is this romanticised conception of the criminal as rebel compelling if taken at face value? One is here reminded of the often-trifling debates between orthodox and neo-Marxist versions of critical criminology in which the former's romanticised visions of the rebellious criminal were justifiably ousted.[27] Regardless, Nietzsche seeks to differentiate – without relying on modern moral or legal categories – criminalised subjects who destroy life from those who affirm new life beyond modern political, legal and moral arenas.

Second, this orientation leads him to downplay differences between law-abiding subjects and the 'great criminal'. Nietzsche asserts that all 'men' are potentially criminal: 'if men like us have no crime, e.g. murder, on our conscience – why is it? Because a few opportune circumstances were lacking.'[28] Or, indeed, our actions have escaped the state's legislative prohibitions in a given instance. Criminal law is here the pivot for generating law-abiding and criminal subjects, always in the interest of the modern state's changing political forces. The very category of 'criminal' is predicated on the state's changing need to create pliable subject identities. Law-abiding subjects, for Nietzsche, only become stable when required ways of thinking and acting are 'burned' into 'memory' through violence – hence the political significance, initially at least, of cruel and harsh punishments. But, 'As its power increases, a community ceases to take the individual's transgressions so seriously, because they can no longer be considered as dangerous and destructive to the whole as they were formerly.'[29] Thus, the changing patterns of crime and punishment are directly related to complex power relations of a historical will to power.

Third, the juridical form of the will to power paradoxically creates the very identities that potentially transgress a given order. For example, 'punishment isolates even more than the crime', and that 'one emerges from punishment as an *enemy* of society. From then on, it has one more enemy.'[30] This sows the seeds of transgression, and invites the state's bid to neutralise enemies by subtly emerging as neutral arbiter: it manages 'universal anger' directed to the criminal, and makes great efforts to 'localize the affair and to prevent it from causing any further, let alone a general, disturbance'.[31] This gives the appearance that a given criminal event is 'dischargeable'; i.e. that crime is a local problem for which there is a finite solution.

In each example, Nietzsche views the becoming of criminal subjects as part of changing forms within a given will to power, such that, 'with every real growth in the whole, the "meaning" of the individual organs also changes'.[32] Almost as an aside, he suggests that decriminalisation (restorative justice?) does not necessarily overcome the state's legislation by empowering individual subjects, because 'in certain circumstances their partial destruction, a reduction in their numbers (for example, through the disappearance of intermediary members) can be a sign of increasing strength and perfection'.[33]

Theme 2: genealogy, morality and politics

Another prominent theme in Nietzsche's work focuses on the 'lowly beginnings' of western morality, politics and its beings. His overall assumption is this:

> More strictly: one must admit nothing that has being – because then Becoming would lose its value and actually appear meaningless and superfluous. Consequently one must ask how the illusion of being could have arisen (was bound to arise); likewise: how all value judgements that rest on the hypothesis that there are beings are disvalued.[34]

From this vantage, Nietzsche emphasises historical processes of becoming over fixed conceptions of being, and views any ontological statement as a simultaneous expression of value. Hence, he offers a 'genealogy' of the way in which a modern subject's psychology has developed into a moral and political being.

Forged over centuries, this being emerges as a pliant entity for modern state legislations through historical processes of 'moralization'. Against the (Aristotelean) idea that human beings are by nature political (or moral) animals, or the sense that individuals are naturally capable of making promises (Hobbes, Rousseau) that bind them, he argues that modern political subjects are historically produced beings. They have 'evolved' (note: not progressed![35]) from a 'pre-moral period of man'[36] into moral and political beings capable of projecting promises into the future, making social contracts and being held responsible for their actions. His 'genealogy' of this evolution chronicles the becoming of human psychology – from a non-moral being to one whose moral sensibilities are coupled with modern political subjections. For Nietzsche, the modern 'sovereign' individual is thus imbued with a free will, a capacity to make promises (contracts) and a duty of obligation as a political being. This being is further developed as a 'legal subject' through appropriations of Christian moral concepts like innocence, duty, guilt, justice, obligation and right.

But while such concepts developed modern political and moral subjects, they have (for him) outlived their ability to respond to the altered circumstances of our current predicament. They are also unable to usher in new ways of becoming. Therefore, he calls for new kinds of knowledge capable of confronting an incomprehensibly transformed situation resulting from a cataclysmic event: 'God is dead,' declares the madman of *The Gay Science* and worse, '*We have killed him* – you and I! We are his murderers.'[37] If modern knowledge is unable to grasp, let alone respond to, this formidable deed, the effects of which continue to reverberate through the foundations of our collective being, Nietzsche did have at least three related responses.[38] All of these involved creating 'deific substitutes' that Fitzpatrick nicely summarises as the rise of new idols (e.g. the state, liberalism, etc.), attempts to create new forms of unity (e.g. a remaining faith in grammar) and a prescient foreboding of a sort of totalitarian politics that threatened twentieth-century Europe. At the same time, however, Nietzsche detects a hunger for an exhilarating overcoming of prevailing life, the anticipation of radically new forms of life that open out onto horizons not yet available to modern eyes.[39]

In such an ethos, overcoming the responses of liberal politics, disciplinary grammars and totalitarian conquests conditions the very possibilities of a new politics. This realisation has conditioned the work of more recent theorists – including Foucault,[40] Derrida[41] and Agamben[42] – indicating the still far-reaching implications of his legal and political theory. Of course, this is quite aside from discussions that ponder whether his work actually licensed the appropriations of Nazi *Volk* politics, or whether he predicted (and condemned) the rise and fall of Nazi (and indeed communist) politics.[43] No doubt, readings of selected aphorisms can be variously appropriated, but Kaufmann wisely cautions that Nietzsche's political and legal theory must be 'considered in the context of his philosophy and against the background of his total literary output'.[44] As such, and germane to our current interests, one might ponder how to imagine the current criminal justice terrain without simply accepting the concepts, grammars and forms of knowledge that founded modern criminal law and its subjects.

If the first essay of the *Genealogy* focuses on the evolution of a moral 'self', the second focuses more specifically on how notions of law and justice emerged historically. As might be inferred, he rejects the idea that law incarnates a consensual 'social contract' between naturally free individuals. Rather, he argues that the 'state' and its law came into being by laying 'its terrible claws upon a populace perhaps tremendously superior in numbers but still formless and nomad'.[45] Rejecting the 'sentimentalism' of 'contract theorists', he notes that,

> One does not reckon with such natures; they come like fate, without reason, consideration, or pretext; they appear as lightning appears, too terrible, too sudden, too convincing, too 'different' even to be hated. Their work is an instinctive creation and imposition of forms.[46]

And in that lightning violence, the minds of pliant legal subjects are shaped. Such subjects arise from pre-moral contexts where action was interpreted through custom, authority and tradition. Interestingly, here, the very idea of individuality, of singularity, was considered a form of punishment.[47] Yet, the preparations for creating a modern 'political animal' lie in custom – it introduced modern politics by training political and legal subjects as beings who possess a free will and who become dependable, predictable and disciplined. The preparatory work involves cruel and highly coercive punishments that etch a 'memory' to fashion moral and legal subjects. As he puts it, 'if something is to stay in the memory it must be burned in: only that which never ceases to *hurt* stays in the memory.'[48] But once established, this creature represents a 'creative' evolutionary leap that serves as the basic unit of modern politics. Paradoxically, custom prepares the way for the emergence of the subsequent political and moral subject, just as that entity makes possible new ways to explore an autonomous political life beyond modern political and legal precepts. Nietzsche's later fragments of writing allude to the philosopher as a 'legislator of evaluation'[49] as the linchpin of a post-moral politics in the evaluation of the 'abnormal' in ways that do not rely on concepts of good and evil.[50] In this respect, Nietzsche appears to endorse a certain biopolitics (not quite of the sort that Foucault and Agamben review) as a preface to the 'great politics' that he envisages. How does this all assist us to grasp his not always unambiguous conceptions of crime and criminals?

A genealogy of crime?

As suggested above, Nietzsche's work calls for a discussion of crime that examines its genealogy alongside the development of: a modern political subject, the moralisation of custom and the violence by which the modern state legislates its 'being' and legitimacy. The formation and development of criminal law, as well as its changing practices and conceptions of crime, could then be seen as an integral part of the state's will to power. Nietzsche's analysis turns attention away from questions about the intrinsic or essential character of crime, criminal law or criminals, to one that provides a history of the development of crime creation as part of a general politico-moral ethos. As noted before, when the supreme power institutes the law, it declares what is permitted or what is forbidden and unjust – once it has successfully instituted such a law, however, 'the eye is trained to an ever more *impersonal* evaluation of the deed'.[51] Interestingly, Nietzsche argues that this shift provides a prerequisite for considering post-moral political subjects and new forms of legislation through evaluation.[52]

This basic formulation allows him to conceptualise criminal law and its concept of punishment as an outgrowth of bartering relations of earlier societies in which people evaluated and measured to exchange or trade goods with one another. The modern subject of law, who recognises personal obligations to others, is an offshoot that developed with 'fundamental forms of buying, selling, barter, trade, and traffic'.[53] For instance, images of debt, payment, owing, duty, etc., were grafted onto moral concepts and appear in law through concepts like guilt, punishment, evil, injustice, and so on. Moreover, these exchange relations provided a vocabulary for crime and punishment that later appeared as 'obvious', 'natural' and even 'unavoidable'; namely, 'the criminal deserves punishment because he could have acted differently'.[54]

But, Nietzsche insists, not only does this classical formulation 'misunderstand' earlier trade relationships, it also forgets that 'a high degree of humanity had to be attained before the animal "man" began even to make the much more primitive distinctions between "intentional," "negligent," "accidental," "accountable," and their opposites and to take them into account when determining punishments.'[55] Indeed, he notes, for 'the greater part of human history', punishment did not target the offender as 'responsible for his deed' – the idea that punishment should be directed to the 'guilty' is a later invention; before that, it rested on 'anger at some harm or injury, vented on the one who caused it'.[56] In modern criminal law, and no doubt 'classical criminology', such anger is contained through the idea that 'every injury has its equivalent and can actually be paid back, only through the pain of the culprit'.[57] Here, as noted, the process isolates a given criminal event and construes it as 'dischargeable' once punishment has been exacted.[58] As the 'power of the community' increases, so the need for spectacularly harsh punishments for specific criminal acts decreases, just as the attitude of a rich trader can be more accommodating of debtors. In this ethos, more subtle forms of regulation take root.

For instance, the criminal deed becomes separated from the criminal; morality is thereby 'denaturalised' alongside a belief that 'there are actions that are good or bad in themselves'. Nietzsche's critique of this belief is unequivocal: 'an action in itself is perfectly devoid of value: it depends on *who* performs it. One and the same "crime" can be in one case the greatest privilege, in another stigma.'[59] As such, he also challenges the classical criminological view that posits punishment as a way 'to prevent further damage' or 'to deter'. He adds that 'both of these so different elements of revenge are actually tied together in punishment' and this generates a 'conceptual confusion' in which 'the individual who revenges himself usually does not know what he really wants'.[60] However, this 'primeval, deeply rooted, perhaps by now ineradicable idea' derives from 'the contractual relationship between creditor and debtor',[61] providing a line of descent for the emergence of modern conceptions of crime, punishment and justice.

From this genealogical vantage, the state's criminal law legislates a power that welded 'a hitherto unchecked and shapeless populace into a firm form'; we have noted that this was 'carried to its conclusion by nothing but acts of violence' giving 'the oldest state' the appearance of 'a fearful tyranny, as an oppressive and remorseless machine' which 'went on working until this raw material of people and semi-animals was at last not only thoroughly kneaded and pliant but also formed'.[62] Moral conceptions of just and unjust emerged out of such legislations, as part of the 'new things' created by the living state that rules in a coordinated and delimited fashion.[63] The criminal, who is deemed to have a free will to choose, is created out of this political and moral ethos. Nietzsche rejects the 'presupposition' that an offence became punishable when an offender 'intentionally acted contrary to his intelligence – it is precisely this presupposition which is annulled by the assumption of "free will"'.[64] That is, he regards punishment inflicted against our instinct for freedom as a cruel element of modern morality.

This is perhaps why he wants to 'naturalise' crime and to reverse the 'denaturalisation' in which criminal and criminal event are distinguished. In a sense, Nietzsche's discussion of crime seems to echo a rising tide of criminal anthropology that brings nature to the forefront of its discussions of crime. However, that comparison is misleading for – as noted – Nietzsche understands 'nature' and its relation to 'life' in a unique way. Balke usefully describes how Nietzsche's understanding of the will to power implies Foucault's concept of 'biopower' that – especially in his later work – vacillates between concepts of 'cultivation' and 'breeding'.[65] Although beyond the scope of this particular chapter, it is important at least to understand that Nietzsche's engagement with concepts of biopower do not in any way seek to: isolate the natural causes of crime, predict who will become criminal, or try to govern criminal lives or populations. Instead, against precepts of criminological positivism, Nietzsche's conception of biopower involves a 'will to power' in which shifting norms take precedence over morally based law, and where a historically malleable 'instinct for freedom' deposits particular sorts of subjects. His conception of what it is to 'live' is not in accord with the arbitrary formulations of nature by 'self-deceivers': 'To live – is not that just endeavouring to be otherwise than nature?'[66] We see here that Nietzsche's formulation of 'life' was never meant to capture a static being, but alludes to an endless becoming evinced through changing instances of the will to power.

Within this contingently understood 'biopower', Nietzsche distinguishes – as alluded to above – between the weak or 'pale criminal' and the 'great criminal' who acts out of strength. He is contemptuous of the 'weak' criminal who destroys life and does not challenge the moral categories against which his/her action offended. Of these subjects he says:

> the criminals, the anarchists – these are not the oppressed classes but the scum of previous society of all classes. Realising that all our classes are permeated by these elements, we understand that modern society is no 'society', no 'body', but a sick conglomerate of chandalas – a society that no longer has the strength to *excrete*.[67]

He is especially critical of the 'pale criminal' who becomes remorseful of criminal deeds – as this implies for Nietzsche a version of bad conscience in which the subject internalises an externally imposed guilt. This 'miscarried type of criminal' mistrusts him or herself, and belittles offending deeds.[68] As well, he forcefully derides those criminals who he deems to be part of the 'criminal race' – he tells us, for instance, that a criminal should be allowed to make peace with society:

> provided he does not belong to the race of criminals. In that case one should make war on him even before he has committed any hostile act (first operation as soon as one has him in one's power: his castration).[69]

This extraordinary, and no doubt early eugenic, formulation suggests Nietzsche's failure to take seriously the complexity of criminality in favour of an analysis that conforms to his overall critique of modernity and which draws on the 'science' of his day. Yet, at the same time, Nietzsche declares that punishing on the basis of an individual will, and even of a past, is highly problematic. Logically, he says, it is not appropriate to punish 'a man's past' because if we go further back you will have to punish

> the cause of his past – I mean parents, teachers, society. In many instances we shall then find the *judges* somehow or other sharing in the guilt. It is arbitrary to stop at the criminal himself when we punish his past.[70]

On the other hand, Nietzsche considers the 'great criminal' to be a courageous being. Although he certainly does not endorse the view that all 'crime belongs to greatness', or that 'all great human beings have been criminals', Nietzsche does consider the 'grand' as opposed to the 'miserable' criminal to be a courageous identity capable of affirming life and standing up to modern orders.[71] One might suppose his exemplar of the strongest type would include someone like Nelson Mandela, who with strength and deliberation stood up to the apartheid political ethos, and actively – courageously – strove for an unspecifiable future that was yet to come. There was no remorse for his acts that led him to the Rivonia treason trials from where he was sentenced to life on Robben Island.[72] Of the concept of the 'great criminal', Nietzsche's latter work offers scattered claims that such a 'great man' incarnates a new sort of political subject who fully embraces life by revaluing particular values of the day, even working beyond existing moral concepts of good and evil, and – although this would not apply to Mandela – moral images of law. This 'great criminal' is allied to Nietzsche's great philosopher, and forms part of his quest to grapple with who exactly might be the agent for bringing into being a new non-moral political ethos.

As Balke points out,[73] this new subject is a strong being who replaces moral concepts of good and evil with images of 'healthy–pathological' or 'normal–abnormal'. This being operates within a new will to power that legislates not through morally inspired laws, but ushers in a new 'great politics' based on strength and weakness that 'legislates' through evaluation.[74] Such great politics involve judging abnormality through the perspective of whether particular forms of abnormality contribute to the life force of a new dawn, a new post-state (but neither anarchic nor socialist) political ethos beyond good, evil and law-based visions of the just. Perhaps the aspiration to this new dawn is captured in the following:

> But some day, in a stronger age than this decaying, self-doubting present, he must yet come to us, the redeeming man of great love and contempt, the creative spirit whose compelling strength will not let

him rest in any aloofness or any beyond, whose isolation is misunderstood by the people as if it were flight from reality.[75]

If Nietzsche places emphasis on the great individual – rather than the all-too-common 'insanity ... in groups, parties, nations, and epochs'[76] – to redeem history, he also insists on the strength of character required to relentlessly embrace the unconditional by opening the patterned conditions of an age. We might view this aspiration as consistent with Nietzsche's overall conception of democracy:

> I speak of democracy as of a thing to come. What at present goes by
> that name is distinguished from older forms of government only by the
> fact that it drives with new horses; the roads and the wheels are the
> same as of yore.[77]

Concluding reflections: Nietzsche and criminology

Nietzsche's insights on crime are at times disturbing and not always consistent – especially for those who stand on this side of the 'great' politics that have marred the twentieth century in genocidal tragedies, often dictated by men who conceived of themselves as having sovereign strength. Is it really the case that those with inordinate strength of character should be taken to be the 'highest specimens' of human life? And should such high specimens be entrusted with the task of conveying a non-moral philosophy of life? Why is his biopolitical vision, with its aggregated elevation of (even if a gay) 'science' and residues of modern morality, not merely a new ethical discourse? Is it even possible – let alone desirable – fully to overcome the achievements and sacrifices of past politics? Should one conceptualise criminal law as a moral form of legislating a will to power, or does modern legality provide – as Fitzpatrick would suggest – a way of understanding the paradoxical contradictions between the permanent decision-making and aspirations to something more eternal (e.g. the 'deific substitutes' in the absence of a God)? And what of then-rising eugenic ideas which are readable in Nietzsche's aphorisms, and which would have brought so much misery to so many people? Does Nietzsche not too quickly overlook the achievements of modern morality and its political expressions? (To be sure there are moments when he too affirms the paradoxical value of morality in modern politics for the very overcoming that he seeks.)

These sorts of questions should alert us to using Nietzsche's work not as a prescriptive set of guidelines for how to live, but as a conceptual resource that provides flashes of brilliance for discussions of crime, criminals and punishment. Kazantzakis expresses his unease thus: "In its negative aspect, Nietzsche's work was indiscriminate and rather facile, animated as it was by its destructive impetus."[78] At the same time, he also notes the affirmative value, the sheer honesty and quest to move beyond what is ordinarily taken for granted at a given moment in time. So, it is with a measure of trepidation that one might reflect on what Nietzsche's work on crime could mean for criminology. In what remains, I suggest two key implications drawn from Nietzsche's work. The first is an attempt to understand the *crimen* to which criminology might address itself. The second concerns the overall orientation – the *logos* – of such a discourse.

Crimen as becoming

First, against conventional formulations that posit criminology as the scientific study of crime, Nietzsche's aphorisms indicate crime as a 'being' in any absolute sense does not exist – therefore there is no such being for science to discover. As noted, he challenges classical criminologists who saw criminal action as the appropriate domain of criminology, and punishment as the best means of specifically and generally deterring rational subjects from engaging in criminal acts. Indeed, he rejects almost all aspects of this utilitarian approach: a free-willed subject, the possibility of separating a criminal from an act, the idea that an act is intrinsically good or bad, the prospect of calculating pleasures and pains across individuals, and even the redemptive or deterrent role of punishment.

At the same time, Nietzsche for the most part challenges criminal anthropology's (and, later, positivist criminology's) focus on the supposedly distinctive biological or psychological make-up of criminal subjects. Even if he was to envisage prospects for a version of science (philosophy?) to overcome notions of good and evil in the context of crime, Nietzsche's work does not endorse criminological positivism's quest to establish the natural (biological/psychological) causes for crime and the generation of criminals; as we have seen, his notion of biopower is very much a function of what he terms the 'instinct for freedom' that conditions his highly malleable (evolutionary?) conception of nature, fashioned through specific legislations of the will to power. While he may also question the idea and legitimacy of punishment in such circumstances, he certainly rejects the determinist view of criminals or their acts embedded in positivist criminology.

Given his emphasis on the will to power, some might be tempted to regard Nietzsche's approach as more consistent with critical criminology's focus on fundamental conflicts that generate criminogenic social structures. By implication, to overthrow crime one needs to revolutionise social, political and economic structures. To some extent, elements of this approach may be recovered from Nietzsche's aphorisms, but he also emphasised an individual instinct for freedom against socialist versions of critical criminology that target social, political and economic structures. He also expressly rejected anarchism of any shade. His will to power may align more with Weber's analysis of the power that shapes social action, or Foucault's work on the ways in which power–knowledge relations constitute contingent forms of social being. I read his quest to transcend modern politics as opening up to the possibility of thinking beyond categorisations of criminal law bound to moral notions of guilt and innocence, or free-willed subjects. Perhaps a Nietzschean-inspired discourse on crime might also be consistent with a cultural criminology directed towards the processes by which contested cultural meanings settle as 'representations' of complex designations of crime, criminal and punishment.[79]

Although there are various ways of interpreting Nietzsche, it is clear that neither 'crime' nor 'criminals' can be the 'objects' of analysis – these only emerge as contingent 'beings' through ongoing patterns of 'becoming' as a consequence of complex power formations. Elsewhere, I have noted the value of returning to the etymology of criminology, to uncover the idea that *crimen* may be associated with practices of criminal accusation rather than crime.[80] If this is so, then the proper object of criminology begins with moments of accusation when ordinary everyday events are arrested and socially sanctioned declarations of criminality asserted. This discourse would focus on the complex power–knowledge relations that create criminal identities. Although societal reaction theories are relevant here, suffice to note that the contested power–knowledge relations spawned by a particular accusatorial context could constitute an appropriate target of a Nietzschean-inspired *logos* of *crimen*.

Orientation

What orientation could such a discourse – directed to the contingent processes that create crime – adopt? Nietzsche's *Genealogy* of modern morality offers suggestions on how to orientate a *logos* focused on the becoming of a criminal identity. To begin with, his analytical gesture always returns to complex lines of descent, out of which moments experienced as being emerge. As with his analyses of law, crime, criminal, the modern political subject, morality, etc., Nietzsche understands identities as transient and changing effects of complex (and unstable) strategic situations, while his foundational analysis charts how beings are brought into existence – from 'lowly beginnings' – recognising that there is nothing absolute about their current form. At the same time, although Nietzsche tends to reverse common ideas, he rejects the nihilist sense that without absolute certainty we are doomed to stasis. On the contrary, he senses in this denial of essence the opportunity to always open up to what might be, fashioning new 'life' and politics (his 'biopolitics'?) by relentlessly overcoming what current instances of the will to power have produced. Our undetermined 'instinct of freedom' suggests that we have no option but to be free (as per Sartre's 'condemned to be free').

From this vantage, one could recover a version of analysis that turns its attention to generating a new politics and legality of crime. No doubt, it implies a *critical* discourse that does not cling to modern 'grammars' of critique. That is, one need not define the practice of critique, or critical analysis, as *necessarily* involving judgements of given social contexts based on criteria derived from Kantian reason, communicative reason, or Marxist praxis to guide social forms to a higher, advanced or progressive state. I have elsewhere described in some detail such modern grammars of critique, noting their flailing legitimacy in a governmentalised crime-creating ethos contoured by obdurate 'uncertainty'.[81] Whatever else this might mean, it does not bode well for a *critical* criminology that continues to cling to declining critical grammars. Hence one might note the growing value of developing new *grammars of critique*, taking seriously Nietzsche's, and later Foucault's, call to distinguish critical judgement and the practice of 'separating out' (as implied by the etymological root of critique, *krinein*). One could, for example, develop such a grammar around Derridean decon-struction, or Foucault's sense of governmental critique as a limit attitude that permanently considers this: 'how not to be thus.'[82] In each case, one senses an *experience* that aligns with Nietzsche's call for a relentless over-coming of existing 'life' by revaluing the sign-constellations, and power for-mations, that erect the historically specific limits of a criminal 'being'.

Perhaps we could bring this discussion to a close by pondering just how this Nietzschean-inspired approach to a new politic and legal ethos could help to set terms for approaching an existential criminology. Here, we might remind ourselves of Nietzsche's call for a 'man of the future' who stridently redeems us,

> not only from the hitherto reigning ideal but also from that which was bound to grow out of it, the great nausea, the will to nothingness, nihilism; this bell-stroke of ... the great decision that liberates the will again ... this victor over God and nothingness – he must come one day.[83]

And in this call, it is difficult to miss his prescient enunciation of what would later inspire existential philosophers; some might even read them-selves as the very 'man'! However, one cannot help but think that Niet-zsche's madman would rise up again to proclaim the arrival of a new imposter, only to declare the death of all 'deific substitutes', including exis-tential criminology, in whose name this collection is gathered.

Notes

1 F. Nietzsche, *Beyond Good and Evil: Prelude to a Philosophy of the Future*, New York: The Macmillan Company, 1911 (volume 12 of *The Complete Works of Friedrich Nietzsche*, trans. Helen Zimmern) 146 – hereafter BGE.

2 M. Warnock, *Existentialism*, Oxford: Oxford University Press, 1979, p. 1.
3 For example, see W.B. Groves and M.J. Lynch, 'Reconciling Structural and Subjective Approaches to the Study of Crime', *Journal of Research in Crime and Delinquency*, 1990, 27, 4, 348–375.
4 For example, M. Warnock, op. cit., pp. 15–22, and J. Reynolds, *Understanding Existentialism*, Chesham: Acumen Books, 2006, pp. 7–11.
5 My exegesis of Nietzsche's work has been aided here, as elsewhere, by the collected essays in: K.A. Pearson (ed.), *A Companion to Nietzsche*, London: Blackwell Publishing, 2006.
6 F. Nietzsche, *The Will to Power*, New York: Vintage Books (trans. Walter Kaufmann and R.J. Hollingdale), at 619 – hereafter WP.
7 WP, 656.
8 For instance, M. Foucault, *Power-Knowledge: Selected Interviews and Other Writings, 1972–1977*, New York: Pantheon Books, 1980.
9 See Crewe, this volume, note 49.
10 J.-P. Sartre, *Being and Nothingness*, London: Methuen and Co., 1981, pp. 79–84.
11 F. Nietzsche, *On the Genealogy of Morals* and *Ecce Homo*, New York: Vintage Books (trans. Walter Kaufmann) ,1969, II, 18, p. 87 – hereafter GM.
12 WP, 692.
13 See W. Kaufmann, *Nietzsche: Philosopher, Psychologist, Antichrist*, New York: Meridian Books, 1959, pp. 152–181.
14 WP, 620–621.
15 WP, 671.
16 WP, 692.
17 See M. Valverde, 'Pain, Memory, and the Creation of the Liberal Legal Subject: Nietzsche on the Criminal Law', in P. Goodrich and M. Valverde (eds), *Nietzsche and Legal Theory: Half-written Laws*, London: Routledge, 2005, pp. 67–88.
18 GM, II, 11, p. 75.
19 GM, II, 11, pp. 75–76.
20 GM, II, 11. He adds too that

> To speak of just or unjust *in itself* is quite senseless; *in itself*, of course, no injury, assault, exploitation, destruction can be 'unjust', since life operates *essentially*, that is in its basic functions, through injury, assault, exploitation, destruction and simply cannot be thought of at all with out this character.

21 WP, 740.
22 WP, 740: here he adds:

> one does not 'punish' a rebel; one *suppresses* him. A rebel can be a miserable and contemptible man; but there is nothing contemptible in a revolt as such – and to be a rebel in view of contemporary society does not in itself lower the value of a man. There are even cases in which one might have to honour a rebel, because he finds something in our society against which war ought to be waged – he awakens us from our slumber.

23 WP, 374.
24 WP, 736.
25 Ibid.
26 'All instincts that do not discharge themselves outwardly turn inward – this is what I call the internalization [*Verinnerlichung*] of man: thus it was that man

first developed what was later called his "soul" ' (GM, II, 16). It is this internal-isation that breeds 'bad conscience'.

27 I. Taylor, P. Walton and J. Young (eds), *Critical Criminology*, London: Rout-ledge and Kegan Paul, 1975.

28 WP, 740.

29 The general precept is this: 'As the power and self-confidence of a community increase, the penal law always becomes more moderate; every weakening or imperilling of the former brings with it a restoration of the harsher forms of the latter' (GM, II, 10).

30 WP, 742.

31 GM, II, 10.

32 GM, II, 12.

33 Ibid.

34 WP, 708.

35 That is,

> The 'evolution' of a thing, a custom, an organ is thus by no means its *progressus* toward a goal, even less a logical *progressus* by the shortest route and with the smallest expenditure of force – but a succession of more or less profound, more or less mutually independent processes of subduing, plus the resistances they encounter, the attempts at trans-formation for the purpose of defense and reaction, and the results of suc-cessful counteractions.
>
> (GM, II, 12)

36 BGE, 32.

37 F. Nietzsche, *The Gay Science: with a Prelude in German Rhymes and an Appendix of Songs*, New York: Cambridge University Press, 2001, 120 – here-after GS.

38 P. Fitzpatrick, ' "What Are the Gods to Us Now?": Secular Theology and the Modernity of Law', *Theoretical Inquiries in Law*, 2006, 8, 161–190.

39 Intriguingly, Fitzpatrick grafts his conception of the law onto Nietzsche's vague reference: 'No matter how constrained, how seemingly settled, law may be, what remains somehow intrinsic to it is an always unsettling, restless appetency for what is illimitable beyond its existent realisation' (op. cit., p. 188).

40 M. Foucault, *Security, Territory, Population: Lectures at the Collège de France, 1977–78*, New York: Palgrave Macmillan, 2007.

41 J. Derrida, *Politics of Friendship*, New York: Verso, 1997.

42 G. Agamben, *Homo Sacer: Sovereign Power and Bare Life*, Stanford: Stanford University Press, 1998.

43 See Kaufmann, op. cit.

44 Kaufmann, op. cit., p. 20.

45 GM, II, 17, at 86.

46 Ibid.

47 GS, 117. Specifically, he says:

> But during the longest period of the human past nothing was more terrible than to feel that one stood by oneself. To be alone, to experience things by oneself, neither to obey nor to rule, to be an individual – that was not a pleasure but a punishment; one was sentenced to 'individ-uality.' Freedom of thought was considered discomfort itself. While we experience law and submission as compulsion and loss, it was egoism that was formerly experienced as something painful and as real misery.

48 GM, II, 3.
49 WP, 972.
50 See F. Balke, 'From a Biopolitical Point of View: Nietzsche's Philosophy of Crime', *Cardozo Law Review*, 2002–2003, 24, 705–722.
51 GM, II, 11.
52 As he puts it:

> If we place ourselves at the end of this tremendous process ... society and the morality of custom at last reveal what they have simply been the means to: then we discover that the ripest fruit is the *sovereign individual*, like only to himself, liberated again from morality of custom, autonomous and supramoral (for 'autonomous' and 'moral' are mutually exclusive).
>
> (GM, II, 2; see also WP, 972)

53 GM, II, 4.
54 Ibid.
55 Ibid.
56 Ibid.
57 Ibid.
58 GM, II, 10.
59 WP, 292.
60 HH, 33.
61 GM, II, 4.
62 GM, II, 17.
63 GM, II, 14.
64 F. Nietzsche, *Human All – Too – Human: a Book for Free Spirits*, Part II, 'The Wanderer and his Shadow', New York: Russell and Russell, 1964, p. 23 – hereafter HH. Following this quotation he adds: 'You adherents of the theory of "free will" have no right to punish, your own principles deny you that right!'
65 F. Balke, op. cit., p. 706.
66 BGE, 9, p. 13.
67 WP, 50.
68 WP, 736.
69 WP, 740.
70 HH, 28, p. 208.
71 WP, 736.
72 One thinks here of Nietzsche's claim that, 'Our highest insights must – and should! – sound like follies and in some circumstances like crimes when they are heard without permission by those who are not predisposed and predestined for them' (BGE, 30).
73 F. Balke, op. cit., p. 715 ff.
74 WP, 972.
75 GM, II, 12.
76 BGE, 156.
77 HH, 293.
78 N. Kazantzakis, *Friedrich Nietzsche on the Philosophy of Right and the State*, New York: State University of New York Press, 2006, p. 57.
79 J. Ferrell. *Cultural Criminology Unleashed*, London: GlassHouse, 2004.
80 See G. Pavlich. 'The Lore of Criminal Accusation', *Criminal Law and Philosophy*, 2007, 1, 1, 79–97, and 'Forget Crime: Governance, Accusation and Criminology', *The Australian and New Zealand Journal of Criminology*, 2000, 33, 2, 136–152.

81 G. Pavlich, *Critique and Radical Discourses on Crime*, Aldershot: Ashgate, 2000.
82 See G. Pavlich, 'Nietzsche, Critique and the Promise of Not Being Thus...,' *International Journal for the Semiotics of Law*, 2001, 13, 357–375.
83 GM, II, 12.

Chapter 3

Biaphobia, state violence and the definition of violence

Willem Schinkel

Problems of definition

There is a long-standing debate in the social science of violence concerning the definition of its research-object. There are those who hold that violence is an 'essentially contested concept', and who feel that a definition of violence is unattainable, or even undesirable. One proponent of this idea is Zygmunt Bauman, who has commented on the attempt to (not) define violence that:

> Virtually all writers attempting to come to grips with the phenomenon of violence find the concept either under-, or over-defined, or both. They also report in other writers (if they not display it themselves) an amazing reluctance, or ineptitude, to resolve the confusion and put things straight. Above all, they find in the texts they read plenty of understatements and half-truths, a lot of embarrassed silence, and other signs of shamefacedness.[1]

On the other hand, there are many who do define violence, or who take it to be a self-evident truth that violence equates to something along the lines of 'intentional physical harm'. In fact, as a review of sociological and criminological journals quickly reveals,[2] most research on violence hardly bothers to define it, let alone conceptually analyse it. These two attitudes towards the concept of violence remain unsatisfactory for those occupying a third position in this debate. This position is that there is a need for an 'extended definition' of violence, and that neither the methodologically safe and common-sense definition of violence as intentional physical harm, give or take a few further qualifications, nor the paradoxical position of an essentially undefinable essence of violence will do. In this chapter, I scrutinize a conceptualization of violence based on this view. I will explicate a definition of violence, based on the work of Husserl and Heidegger, after which I illustrate how this ontological definition of violence allows us a more 'defamiliarizing' perspective on the relationship between violence and the state.

The discussion between proponents of an 'extended definition' and those in favour of a 'restricted definition' usually boils down to the point that the former feel that the latter define too much, while the latter are convinced the former define too little. Proponents of an extended definition are accused of blurring the concept, and even of being 'politically unhelpful'.[3] In response they state that underlying the restricted definition is an ideology that aligns social science with common sense and that is therefore too political in legitimating existing social constructions of violence. Mary Jackman has therefore suggested that 'we must analyze the ideology of violence, to try to assess how and why various acts of violence are repudiated, ignored, denied, praised, or glorified'.[4] Johan Galtung concluded decades ago that 'an extended concept of violence is indispensable'.[5] In consequence, he coined the well-known concept of 'structural violence'.[6] Similar problems arise when considering the position of the essential contestedness of the concept of violence. Apart from it being, as noted, somewhat paradoxical, it denies social science the possibility of critically analysing the results of popular contestations of the meaning of 'violence'. In other words, social science loses its ability to be more than just another voice in the choir. The sociology of violence would, in that case, come up with first-order observations instead of second-order observations, i.e. observations of observations.[7] From the perspective of a sociology of sociology, one might conclude from all of this, and from the evident lack of consensus on definitions of violence, that the concept of violence indeed remains a black box. But a lack of consensus about a certain definition does not logically imply that any definition is as good as any other. Or, one might conclude, as Niklas Luhmann has stated, that matters of definition serve less the accurate description of phenomena than they do the distinguishment thereof.[8] But still, that does require giving substance to concepts. It is therefore my firm conviction that it is heuristically useful to propose a definition of violence, and to then see what it can make intelligible that would otherwise remain relatively little understood. What follows is a proposal to see connections that remain unobserved without or with another concept of violence. Rather than triggering a debate on the essence or 'natural kind' of violence, I wish to show how a critical social science can gain in its analysis of the state from a specific kind of 'extended' concept of violence.

Violence defined as reduction of being

I define violence ontologically as a reduction of being. This definition is inspired by Heidegger's ontological difference, but also on Husserl's phenomenology. In order to gain insight in what violence as 'reduction of being' is, I first pick up some elements from Husserl's phenomenological analysis of the perception of spatial objects. Next, I discuss the relevance of Heidegger's ontological difference for a definition of violence.

Elements of a definition of violence: Husserlian phenomenology

Starting from phenomenology's basic tenet, the idea that consciousness is intentional, Husserl describes, by way of transcendental reduction, the perception of spatial objects in the natural attitude. Noesis, the intentional act(s), gives a noematic structure of an object that is never a unity in itself, but which consists of parts, of aspects in different experiences. Husserl gives the example of a table.[9] The perception of a table continuously changes, and yet the table is perceived as a continuity itself. Let's say, for simplicity's sake, that in the case of a table only visual perception is relevant. I see a table. Then I close my eyes. When I open them again, I see that same table again. I do not, however, have the same perception of it. I have, so to speak, a 'new' perception of the table. The perception of the table can be repeated many times, but it is never the same. Although repeated perception gives me the assurance that the table is what it is and will be when I close my eyes, my perceptions are part of what is for Husserl a flow of consciousness in which temporal perceptions are interconnected. In order to experience the table as what it is, consciousness has to transcend itself. Each experience of the table in fact consists of more than one perception; other perceptions are always already included in a single act of consciousness. For the perception of the table 'now' immediately flows into a 'just-now' perception, a perception of the past, whilst a new 'now' becomes actual.[10] These different perceptions are, by means of retention and, concerning expectations towards the future, protention, included in any intentional act of consciousness, which is therefore transcendent.

Husserl makes a distinction between aspects (*Bestimmtheiten*) of objects and profiles (*Abschattungen*) of these aspects.[11] An aspect is a continuous characteristic of the object. Such an aspect is experienced by means of a perceptual adumbration: successive perceptions that are part of the *Abschattungssystem* of an aspect. Take, for example, the colour of an object. The same colour appears, according to Husserl, in a multifariousness of profiles.[12] Each time I perceive the colour of an object, I perceive a profile of the aspect 'colour' of the object. Continuous perception gives me many profiles of such continuously present aspects. Husserl gives the example of the colour of a tree.[13] While the position of the eyes continuously changes and the gaze moves from trunk to twig, while we take a closer look or step back, we bring different perceptions into flow. Yet each profile points at the same aspect – in this case the colour of the tree – and out of a multifariousness, unity is experienced.[14] I can perceive an object because it adumbrates or variegates itself ('es sich "abschattet"')[15] according to its aspects. Consciousness does not only transcend the immediate perception of the object because of past or possible future perceptions. It also extrapolates on aspects of the object I am not readily able to experience, such as the fact that a table has a reverse side, or that it has several legs while I might not even see one. I don't have to check if a tree has a reverse, I know this a priori and, as such, my conscious experience of the tree transcends any temporal perception I may have of it. At any time, my conscious experience of an object incorporates things that are not present at hand, perceptions that I do not have at that moment. That is so, not only because I need past perceptions in conscious experience, but also because I need complementary 'views' of the object, which I am not able to have all at once, or perhaps not at all.[16] This is the case when I assume that the Earth is spatially extended in many directions beyond my room without being able to verify that perceptually. Any object can, in principle, only be given in a one-sided fashion.[17] But with each one-sided givenness of the object, other possible sides or ways of perceiving it are included (mitgegeben). Those remain at hand in what Husserl calls a horizon or background of an act of consciousness.[18] As such, there are always many different 'possible pluralities of perception, which, continually flowing over into each other, contract to form the unity of a perception, in which the continuously existing thing shows ... ever new (or returning old) sides'.[19] Perception of a spatial object is therefore based on a being ready at hand of several complementary profiles of different aspects that are stored in a horizon of an act of consciousness and that can each be actualized in experience. At each time a certain selection out of that horizon becomes actualized.[20]

Applying this to human beings means speaking of an ontological horizon of a person. This horizon is necessarily reduced, since selection of aspect is necessary in social life. Sociologists have formulated this, for instance, in terms of roles. In any one situation, one cannot show all of one's faces, Goffman might have said.

Elements of a definition of violence: Heideggerian ontology

As I said, I wish to define violence ontologically. The difference between an ontological level and an empirical level is best explicated in Heidegger's terms, as the difference between the ontological and the ontic. This difference, which goes by the name of the 'ontological difference', is the basis of the ontology of Sein und Zeit. It is my intention to interpret the same ontological difference as a way of analysing what 'happens' ontologically before we can speak of empirical events that we normally classify as 'violence', which always involve a selection of aspects in their realization and in their subsequent observation. Heidegger introduces the ontological difference in order to distance himself from a Western metaphysical tradition (roughly starting with Parmenides, Plato and Aristotle; culminating in Descartes, Kant and Nietzsche) that has sought to think of Being in terms of being(s), or that has reduced Being to a 'highest being', a 'first mover'.

According to Heidegger, what has thereby been forgotten is Being itself (*Seinsvergessenheit*). In terms of Parmenides: 'what is, is, and what is not, is not.' But, as Heidegger says, there is something more, although this really 'is' not a 'something'. What has been forgotten is that it actually is the being of ontic beings that should be the focus of thought. This being of beings, which Heidegger writes as 'Being', is what an ontology is concerned with. What *is* this Being? It '*is*' not, since that would make it a being in the ontic, or 'empirical', sense:

> Das Sein des Seienden 'ist' nicht selbst ein Seiendes. Der erste ... Schritt im Verständnis des Seinsproblems besteht darin, ... Seiendes als Seiendes nicht durch Rückführung auf ein anderes Seiendes in seiner Herkunft zu bestimmen, gleich als hätte Sein den Charakter eines möglichen Seienden.[21]

Being is always the Being of (a) being. There 'is' no such 'thing' as Being, independent (in a non-ontic sense) of beings. For Being is to be seen as the Being of beings, the naked 'that' of the Being of a being. Or, it might be termed the *happening* or *process* of being, the unfolding of being, when all these terms are not themselves taken to refer to ontic beings of some sort. A flawed analogy would be to say that when I am walking, there is me, moving, walking, but there is also the walking itself; or, in another example, there is me, violating, but there is also the violence itself, which, though it can only be distinguished ontologically, 'is' not factually. I am a being, and therefore I can speak of the Being of me as a being. This being, which we ourselves are, Heidegger refers to as *Dasein*.[22] Man, as a being, is Dasein. Before he realizes himself in real, ontic states of affairs, he always already *is* a being. His 'Being' refers to this always already being a being. Next to speaking of man as an ontic being, for instance as a man, a farmer, a father of children, one can say that that being is a being. Then, one can speak of his Being in the ontological sense. Heidegger's *Sein und Zeit* is mainly concerned with the ontological structure of man as a being, of Dasein. As such, his project can be compared to Kant's in that he tries to find (transcendental) conditions of possibility of the ontic (empirical). *That* a person looks towards the future is possible because he or she, ontologically, is thrown into a world in which he or she has past, present and future.

A similar ontological a priori is what my definition of violence as 'reduction of being' is meant to be. Whatever ontic shape violence assumes, it always 'is' a reduction of being. I have hereby given a preliminary sketch of only the nature of my definition of violence. In order to further explain it, I draw more on the work of Heidegger and (other) phenomenologists. First, what has been said there, rather eclectically combined with certain ideas of Wittgenstein, was the basis for the

epistemological outlook I have termed 'fractured realism'. Every observation, I argued, consists of a necessary selection of certain aspects of reality,
which are highlighted and make up what is seen, at the equally necessary
cost of excluding other aspects. Unselected aspects remain in a back-
grounding horizon, awaiting possible future observational selection. The
premise here is that reality is infinitely rich and complex. Finite beings
necessarily have to come to what Luhmann calls a 'reduction of complexity', which at the same time does not do away with complexity, since it
saves a horizon of alternative aspects that would, if selected, constitute a
different reduction of complexity. Every observation therefore has its blind
spot, and no observation captures the whole of reality (if only because of
Russell's paradox of the impossibility of observing one's own observation
in that observation). What Husserl in the end calls 'world' (*Welt*) cannot
be observed as a whole. Reality is rich and cluttered: opaque. I now want
to apply these premises to (inter)action. It immediately needs to be stressed
that this does not concern an incorporation of Husserlian phenomenology
in the analysis of violence. The Husserlian model of aspects in acts of
consciousness, as briefly outlined above, can be taken as a model for social
action in which actions towards others are said to highlight aspects of the
being of those others.[23] Actions, too, are reductions of complexity in the
sense that the actually performed action is but one contingent possibility
out of a horizon of possibilities. The object of action, or that space of
reality that is affected or changed by it, thereby gets equally reduced; it is
reduced to 'something to do so and so with...', whereas it 'contains' many
alternative ways of dealing with. Any action reduces the other to but one
aspect of his or her being, and this selection of aspect allows the other to
be in social practice. At the same time, this selection is co-constitutive of
the selection in light of which the social practice as a whole unfolds. That
is to say that if I violate another person, that person is not only reduced to
what he or she at that time is in the social situation in which he or she
exists, but social practice itself now stands in a certain relational light.
This means that the whole practice of reducing the other reduces the situation to but one possible aspect, since it could have been a different situation. Consciousness is not a prerequisite for this social process in which
any action is always also a reduction. That is why the Husserlian theory of
aspects is only used as a model. In the end, first-order observers may
reduce another person, i.e. exert violence, without consciously being
aware of this. And in the end, only from the sociological second-order
perspective can the observation 'violence' be made on the basis of a meta-
theory of what the substance of violence is – if only for the reason that
first-order observers, immersed in social life, do not operate by means of
such a meta-theory.

Violence, ontologically defined as reduction of being, thus pertains to
the reduction which has always already taken place prior to any ontic state

of affairs between people. This definition can be further developed by putting forward two claims, which are elaborated upon below: (1) violence is that aspect of the social which consists of a reduction of the ontological aspect-horizon of a being; (2) violence is an aspect of the social that is always at work in a more or less highlighted sense. That is, it is an aspect that is, qua, aspect, always present (in a non-ontic sense!), but the degree to which this aspect is actualized as effective in practice differs. Ontically, violence therefore is a sliding scale.

Changing the aspect of, and in, violence

Every human being (Dasein) can be ontologically characterized by possibility: 'Dasein *ist* je seine Möglichkeit.'[24] That is to say that before any ontic realization of a being, that being 'is' the sum total of unrealized possibilities. Furthermore, being-in-the-world is always already a being-together.[25] If we see a person (Dasein) as a being that is ontologically characterized by possibility, each ontic realization of ontological possibilities constitutes a reduction of complexity. It is possible to reintroduce as a characterization of Dasein Husserl's concept of a *horizon* here, when that is in no way regarded too technically, that is in the sense of a limited set of well-defined alternatives. Nonetheless, ontologically, that person can be regarded as a horizon of alternative ontic states of being (not unlike the way Hume speaks of a 'bundle' of impressions). This horizon is to be seen as an ontological a priori without beginning or end. Ontologically, a person is always, in Levinas' terms, an infinite Other. This person, like any person, is a being-together with other persons (*Mitdasein*). Although Heidegger clearly recognizes this, he soon falls back into a story of a Fall (*Verfall*) into 'das Man' against an 'authenticity' (*Eigentlichkeit*) of Dasein, which turns ontology into deontology. Heidegger then states that Dasein first and foremost listens to public opinion, does what everybody else does, etc. Although he explicitly says he does not undervalue this inauthentic being, his tone and concepts betray a preconceptual dislike (in his terms: a certain *Vorgriff*).[26] However, we are here concerned with an ontological definition of violence that is as 'neutral' as possible. It will not do to change concepts the moment one doesn't like what one sees from an ontological point of view. The essence of his social ontology is nonetheless contained in those few pages of *Sein und Zeit* that may guide us here. Man, fundamentally understood as being-social, as being-with, being-together or being-with-others, always exists in relation to other beings. As such, he is constantly exposed to others, and their influence shapes his being. In part, this is what sociology has termed 'socialization'. This way of being-in-relation is not solely an existence of (ontological) freedom. Precisely when ontology adequately incorporates the social, the simultaneous effects of freedom and constraint that the encounter with the other entails are highlighted. Every influence Dasein undergoes reduces his being in the sense that he is not free to be whatever he could want to be, but he is that which the coming together of the influence of others on him and his influence on them allows him to be. A subject is precisely this: Dasein in sociality, always already under the influence of others. I therefore use the concept of 'subject' in a literal sense (the Latin, not the Greek): a subject is sub-ject, always subjected to others.[27] At the same time, however, a subject always subjects others. This reciprocal subjection, or reduction, is crucial to the understanding of violence as reduction of being. To be a subject is to be reduced *to* a subject. That is to say, a subject is an ontic being whose ontological horizon has been reduced to certain aspects that are highlighted in his being-subject. As soon as there is existence of an ontic being, a reduction of being to the being that that being is at that moment has taken place. At any time, a selection has been made of certain aspects out of a horizon of possible ways of being, while other aspects remain unactualized. *Violence is precisely that aspect of human interaction which consists of a reduction of being, of selection of ontological aspects and non-selection of others.* Precisely because a being is potentially many things (a 'becoming', as Nietzsche or Deleuze might have said), any way of being necessarily means a reduction of being. The question of violence now hinges on the potential to realize potential, i.e. on *the possibility of changing the aspect of the other*. The aspect of the social that entails the reduction of being in any social interaction can only be identified within a second-order observation. To the first-order observer, this aspect has always already been highlighted, albeit not necessarily in a subjectively experienced way, since the subject itself is already a product of a reduction of being.

That any interaction entails a selection of some aspects of being of those involved in interaction and non-selection of other aspects, i.e. that any interaction involves a reciprocal reduction of the ontological horizon of those involved in interaction, can be illuminated by the example of an interaction between professor and student, or between a father and a son. The professor is a professor to a student. He is not, at least in most cases he is not, a friend, lover or neighbour of the student. In their interaction, the student reduces the other to a professor, whereas the professor is much more than that. In order to interact, however, a selection that is relevant to the situation of interaction needs to be effectuated. This involves, as Parsons would say, a choice on various pattern variables that determine the actor's orientation towards the other.[28] The other is thereby necessarily reduced to less than he or she is. For the professor likewise reduces the student to a student, and cannot at the same time regard the student as a friend, a lover, etc. The same goes for the interaction between father and son. In the end, they are constrained by the need to regard the other as father and son, and this causes some things to be banned from interaction.

What needs to be emphasized immediately is that the ontological negation present in social interaction is not purely a negativity. For two things become apparent when violence is considered in this way. First, *violence is an aspect of all (human) being and (inter)acting*. Second, *violence is not a priori to be regarded as negative, as solely constraining*.

If the only way to be is to have always already been reduced to but a few of many possible aspects of being, this reduction of being is necessary for anyone to be. Therefore, violence is an aspect of every situation. It is positive in that it is constitutive of sociality, since only the reduction of being that violence is, lets beings be what they are, while they 'are', in the ontological sense, always much more. If this is what 'violence' amounts to, then how does this have anything to do with the way violence is predominantly conceptualized? To explain this, I return to the concept of the ontological horizon. That horizon may be more or less reduced in the sense that in any selection of aspects, a host of alternative aspects is kept ready at hand. This reduction, violence, can therefore be seen as a sliding scale. This should be a premise that clears the conceptual mist that may exist relative to common notions of violence in the social sciences to a certain degree. While all interaction necessarily involves a certain violence, since a reduction of being is necessary for such interaction to exist, there are grave differences between this everyday reduction of being and the reduction of being that takes place in cases where the more commonsensical notion of violence applies. Consider again the example of the professor and his student. The student reduces the professor to 'a professor', since he cannot interact with him while acknowledging the whole potentiality of the professor's being. He has to 'deal with' the professor in a certain manner that conforms to behaviour appropriate to professor–student interaction, and as a result, many aspects of the professor's being remain unselected. The student does not interact with the professor primarily in light of the aspect that the professor is a man, or in light of his being someone's lover, etc. Likewise, the professor reduces the student to 'a student'. The only way to consistently conceive of violence is to regard this elementary reduction of being as violence too. But although the violence of the professor and the student is a certain violence, it is not a violence that is 'grave' in the sense that it strikes one as being particularly violent in the commonsensical negative or destructive sense of the term. In other words, the aspect of violence hardly becomes highlighted in this professor–student interaction, although it is always highlighted, i.e. actualized as a situational precondition, to a certain degree. What is this 'certain degree'? What is the difference between this violence and the violence that is highlighted to such a degree that it becomes the dominant aspect of interaction, that it, in other words, becomes that in light of which the situation unfolds itself? This difference might be said to be located in the extent to which the ontological horizon of alternative aspects of being is allowed to co-constitute the interaction. A horizon of negated, unselected aspects is not merely cast aside, forgotten, but it remains at hand, and co-constitutes the interaction together with the aspects that are selected. So the professor treats his student primarily as a student, but co-constitutive of this are the non-selected aspects of the student being a man, someone's friend, someone's lover, a son, with a certain life-experience, etc. Although at any time it is not possible to see the student in light of all these aspects – since the list is infinite – many are co-constitutive of the interaction between professor and student. It is crucial, however, that this is not yet what determines the level of violence in interaction. It would be mistaken to say that the aspect of violence is highlighted to the extent to which the ontological horizon of the other is co-constitutive of interaction. For a student might kill his professor precisely because of 'all' the things that the professor is. The ontological horizon of the professor is then co-constitutive of the interaction between professor and student, yet violence is present to an extreme extent. So the crucial question really is whether or not the ontological horizon is kept at hand in the sense that, as Wittgenstein says, a *change of aspect* is allowed to occur.

The scale of violence

There is an inverted symmetrical relationship between the extent to which the aspect 'violence' is highlighted in interaction and the extent to which the ontological horizon of the other in interaction is kept at hand in the interaction and a different selection is possible, along with the aspect(s) that are selected. In yet other words, one can say that violence is relatively little present in interaction so long as the interacting actors are prepared to 'change the aspect' of the other. Professor and student are in most cases prepared to do that, to change the aspect of the other when interaction requires this, to see the other in a different light. They then retain the richness of the other's being. When they do so to a lesser degree, a more severe reduction of being takes place. The further the ontological horizon of the other is reduced, the more violently the other is treated. In the extreme case of the student killing the professor, the ontological horizon, the infinite array of aspects of being of the professor, is shrunk to only one aspect: the professor is now merely an object, he is reduced to his pure material being, to mere *res extensa*. No other aspects of his being are highlighted or are allowed to become highlighted. Out of his ontological horizon, nothing can be selected any more; the student intent on killing the professor in the end will not change the aspect of the professor. Although it is highly likely that the ontological horizon of the professor is still co-constitutive of this reduction of his being to but one unchangeable aspect, since in most cases someone is killed because of certain aspects of his or her being the killer would rather not see, this horizon is not kept at hand and a change of aspect does not take place when the professor, in our example, is indeed killed. One advantage of defining violence ontologically as reduction of being is that *violence can now be seen as a sliding scale*. It is now possible to distinguish between more and less severe forms of violence based on a substantial criterion, instead of an arbitrary one. It has never been a matter of doubt that killing a person constitutes a more severe form of violence than bullying a person does, but the difference has been primarily based either on intuitive classification, or on relatively arbitrary hierarchies, often juridical in origin, that lacked a precise conceptualization of when and why violence takes a more serious shape. In the terminology put forward here, the question becomes: 'to what extent does the ever present aspect of violence in interaction become highlighted?' The answer lies in the extent to which the other is reduced in his being. One of the most drastic reductions is that to pure matter. This is an aspect that is always co-constitutive of (inter)action, since the other would not be that other if he weren't always also a material thing.[29] Yet he or she is always more than that. Any (inter)action that fails to display the readiness to acknowledge this 'surplus of being', to allow the other to be seen in a different light, that is in light of other aspects, can be characterized as severely violent.

Another advantage this definition has concerns the 'when' of violence. When do we ordinarily speak of violence? Existing empirical definitions have great problems here, since if violence is, for example, seen as intentional physical hurt, then when does 'violence' actually occur? When does it set in? The moment A hits B? But what *is* that moment? Has it set in as soon as A raises his hand, or does it not set in until his hand forcefully hits B's face? And does it only last as long as the contact lasts? Or is 'violence' the label we pin upon the whole social situation in which such events take place? Does it, as the ethnomethodologists say, define the situation? But what would then be the 'beginning' of this situation? And its end? And is there, within this situation, no difference in the degree of violence before A hits B, and during this action? If 'violence' is the definition of a situation, then does it make sense to even speak of levels or degrees of violence? Does it make sense to differentiate, within a violent situation, between more and less violent moments? When violence is regarded as reduction of being, the answer to such questions would be that there is a certain degree of violence in every situation to begin with. In a 'violent situation', then, the reduction of being is an aspect of the situation that becomes strongly highlighted or 'urgently present' in the foreground of (the horizon of) the situation (it then becomes plausible to say that violence starts to 'define the situation'). It remains highlighted to that 'violent' degree for as long as A or B, or both, act in relative oblivion of their respective ontological horizons, in the sense that these may be co-constitutive of the aspect(s) that are selected and are thus constitutive of the situation, but can only to a limited degree be changed for another selection of aspect(s). The limit, or extreme case of violence is reached when no such change of aspect is allowed for. As soon as A and B are prepared to change the aspect of the other the fight ends, and violence no longer is an aspect that is highlighted, brought to the foreground, of the situational horizon. In the 'afterwards I felt sorry'-argument,[30] which perpetrators of violence often make,[31] it becomes apparent that they are able to see their former opponent in light of more than their mere status of 'enemy', which is the only thing they could see them as in the heat of the situation.

The productivity of violence – on biaphobia

Durkheim has said that 'a very intense social life always does a sort of violence to the organism, as well as to the individual consciousness, which interferes with its normal functioning'[32]. While I agree with the recognition that there always is 'a sort of violence', I would add that this is endemic to *all* social life, and that this violence is always a part of and a necessary condition of the 'normal functioning' (whatever that is exactly) of a person. To paraphrase Nietzsche's Zarathustra, it comes down to not seeing only one face to Dasein.[33] The *productivity* of violence has to be acknowledged. Or, in other words, we must change the aspect in thinking about violence in such a way that a consistent conceptualization becomes at hand according to which violence is not seen as a destructive negativity a priori. A comparison is in order here with the question of whether freedom can exist alongside rules that regulate behaviour. The answer is of course yes, since the rules are constitutive of freedom. Only the rules of chess provide the freedom to play chess, they are a necessary precondition for it. Violence is productive in a similar fashion: it is an ontological precondition of ontic being. Violence is thus the very subjectification and objectification that precedes the situational existence or appearance of a sub-ject. *Before one can speak of a subject, there has been violence.* Violence is, so to speak, the 'end' or 'point of contact' of the relation between subjects. *Violence is the shape of the surface of the subject, which touches the relational between of subjects-in-interaction.* Only when the aspect of violence becomes highlighted in a one-sided fashion, i.e. where other aspects of interaction are, in a practical sense, undervalued, is it possible to say that violence becomes a negativity in the sense that it destroys instead of produces (this is of course irrespective of the normative 'positivity' or 'negativity' of both productive and destructive violence). Similarly, only when a regulatory frenzy exists and rules grow rampant can there be a conflict between rules and freedom.

The productivity of violence is a forgotten aspect of violence. Especially in the humanistic tradition, violence has been one-sidedly seen in light of its destructive aspect. Even though Seneca says that the wise person is not surprised at the omnipresence of aggression, 'since he has examined thoroughly the circumstances of human life (*conditio humanae vitae*)',[34] this wisdom only pertains to the idea that 'shit' quite simply just happens, and that there is little one can do about it but withstand the negativity of it.[35] In more 'idealistic' versions of humanism, from Erasmus to Condorcet, Turgot and Comte, through to Galtung, Ricoeur and Habermas, one finds the attempt to therefore eradicate all violence.[36] Two recent extended definitions of violence, subsequently brought forward by Henry and Barak, suffer from the same ill. Barak defines violence as 'any action or structural arrangement that results in physical or nonphysical harm to one or more persons'.[37] Henry defines it as 'the use of power to harm another, whatever form that takes'.[38] While being extended vis-à-vis the dominant legalistic definitions, these definitions share with such commonsensical definitions a one-sided focus on harm; destructiveness is said to be a defining characteristic of violence. Yet this humanism can be critiqued on the grounds that it has not been humanistic enough. It has misrecognized the *conditio humanae* by a priori excluding from it something it misrecognized as being purely destructive. I will call this view of violence as a pure negativity and as being solely destructive *biaphobia*. It is a specifically scholastic and intellectualistic fallacy found in much humanist and Enlightenment thought, which today finds its most explicit expression in peace movements and other organizations promoting 'non-violence', often inspired by Gandhi and Martin Luther King, who spoke of 'violence' exclusively as 'physical violence'. A critique of this humanism that highlights both its relevant insight into the nature of violence and its biaphobic moment allows for a further clarification of the definition of violence.

That violence, in all its manifestations, is a counterforce that disturbs human community is a tenacious prejudice. The very formation of the concept of *humanitas* (in the second century BC) grew out of dissatisfaction with the rather militaristic notion of *homo romanus*, which became *homo humanus*, a concept popularized greatly by Cicero.[39] The ideal of the *homo humanus* was furthermore opposed to *inhumanus*, which replaced the no longer usable notion of *barbarian*. Violence was associated with the latter *inhumanus*, virtue with the *homo humanus*. With Roman humanism the notion of *vir*, the true man, is stripped of its more forceful connotations in favour of its moral overtones. It would remain as such until Machiavelli, who lived in a time of Italian revitalization of Roman (historiographic) humanism, recombined the two. The separation between violence and true humanity is of course also a basic dogma in the thought of the Enlightenment. Yet at the perimeters of that thought, Freud too opposes *Lebenstrieb* and *Destruktionstrieb* – not insignificantly first elaborated upon in *Zeitgemässes über Krieg und Tod* – analogous to Eros and death. But why place the destructive instinct on the side of death (in the sense of being opposed to life)? It is being human and human life that is characterized by it as much as it is under the influence of the opposite urge. The fact that violence and sociality are not diametrically opposed not only holds with respect to the necessary everyday reduction of being of which I have argued that it would be consistent to include it in the conceptualization of violence. It also refers to situations in which the aspect of violence is much more brought to the fore – situations, therefore, to which the commonsensical notion of violence applies. Social science has often seen violence in light of a certain moral aspect, though there is at the same time a wide consensus within social science that that is not the aspect it is supposed to select as an object of research. Only when the social is a priori seen as a harmonious *and* (these are not opposites) non-violent realm of human being-together, can violence be biaphobically conceptualized as something that runs counter to that being-together. But when this implicit social scientific morality is cast off, it becomes necessary to say that even extreme forms of violence establish a connection, a relation. Violence most of the time *brings people together.* When the simplified situation of A and B fighting is considered once more, violence is to be seen as the dominantly highlighted aspect of the togetherness of A and B. They could be together working or playing, and they can be together in violence – since these are always only aspects of a social situation, the only difference is the degree to which such aspects are actualized or highlighted. Strictly speaking, the first social scientific observation, which is always a second-order observation, can, with respect to violence, only be that it is a form of sociality, of human being-together. This may be a truism, but this axiom seems to be rarely remembered in the study of violence. Now, it is very well possible that violence bring people together in a 'positive' or constructive way. Reports from war mention the special bond that enemy-soldiers develop when dug into opposing trenches, for instance during the First World War.[40] On a more 'abstract' level, it is relevant to point out that the very basis of whatever 'order' is said to exist within the societal system is based on a reservoir of violence, a threat, that is called the state's 'monopoly of legitimate violence' (or, as this may be reformulated in accordance with the dominant semantics of violence: the state's legitimate monopoly of violence). Constitutive of the *polis* is the *polemos.* Added to this is the idea in social theory that the 'constitution of society' (Giddens) is based on the exclusion of an alterity, therefore on a certain violence, which is said to be a 'normal' social fact.[41] It shows indeed the normality of violence as constitutive of sociality. There is nothing inherent to 'violence' in general that opposes it to a relatively homeostatic social system; it is an integral part of social life that has a basic constitutive function in that life. Heidegger demonstrates how the *polis* refers not only to the 'city' or 'state', but to the place of being in general.[42] The constitutive connection between *polis* and *polemos* thus similarly exists at all levels of the social. If violence is defined as reduction of being, there is no reason at all to limit violence to interpersonal or private violence, although my examples above are examples of interpersonal violence. To conclude, I therefore discuss the consequences of this definition of violence for the relationship between violence and the state. It is here that it becomes clear that an ontological definition of violence as reduction of being allows for a more defamiliarizing perspective on violence, a perspective that moves beyond the ideological acceptance of violence as private physical violence, which tends to only legitimate the state as a machine of legitimate (as Max Weber has said: 'that is, legitimated') violence.

The biaphobic legitimation of the state

It has been the gradual autonomization of the state that necessitated first of all a view of the urgency of the problematic of physical violence, and second of all an attempt to eradicate it from the newly born civil society. The taken-for-grantedness of violence as physical violence is no doubt connected to the taken-for-grantedness of the 'monopoly of legitimate violence' of the state, which is nothing other than a monopoly of *physical* violence. Physical violence has not always been the obsession of the predecessors of the state. In ancient Germanic law, *Gewalt* did not serve as a juridical concept. In ancient Germanic tribes, crime in general was often punished not by corporal punishment of the perpetrator, but by retribution in terms of money or property, and by reconciliation of victim and perpetrator. Only the severe cases of murder and treason were punished by exile, in which case the perpetrator was outlawed. *Gewalt*, however, was deemed part of the freedom the law did not pertain to.[43] '*Gewalt*' remains an ambiguous concept even today, since it became translated both as *potestas* and as *violentia* in the Middle Ages. This difference already marks the autonomization of the state and its appropriation of legitimate violence. While, in scholastic thought, divine power was equally translated as *Gottesgewalt* and as *violentia spiritualis*, the connotation of 'power' was gradually transferred to *potestas* – *potesta* being, in medieval law from the twelfth century on, magistrates to whom conflicting parties turned for mediation.[44] This difference exists equally in the semantic history of 'violence', and is pressed, for instance, by Hobbes, who equates *vis* or *violentia* to the violence of the state of nature and *potestas* to the (legitimate) violence of the sovereign state. A similar difference is denoted by the French *pouvoir* and *force* (*violence*). By the eighteenth century, the opposition between legitimate and illegitimate force had driven a wedge between the concepts of 'power' and 'violence', two concepts originally hard to distinguish. One might thus write a genealogy of violence and focus on the differentiation between *potestas* and *violentia*. A condition of possibility for the modern sovereign state is the differentiation between these, and the recoding of *potestas* as legitimate and reactive violence against the illegitimate and reactive violence that *violentia* signifies. This means that the state operates on the basis of a usurpation of violence not recognized as such.

That violence is at the core of the state's origin is expressed in many theories of the origin of the state, whether in a positive or negative sense.[45] Machiavelli praises Romulus for killing his brother, which enabled Rome to be founded and become a great state. Bodin, Hobbes, Kant and the English empiricists in the end see the state as the way out of the violent situation of the natural state. Other historically minded political theorists[46] such as Voegelin stress the fact that centralized states often appear as a consequence of war, which forces feudal fiefs to combine. The Marxian theory of the state sees in the state a perpetual violence in the form of a legitimization and juridification of bourgeois interests. And as Sorel spoke of *'l'idéologie de l'état'*,[47] peace-researchers may see in the violence of the state 'the real substratum which give (*sic*) the myths of consensus reality'.[48] Either way, violence is of foundational relevance for the state. Looking at the state in light of the aspect of violence, then, the state always has the character of a Leviathan, spreading its arms wider with each new regulation and procedure, and with each regulation providing for the exceptions to each regulation.

The modern Western state has an immanent tendency to become an autonomous force directed towards self-preservation. Wolfgang Sofsky sees in this development a final act in the history of violence,[49] wherein the people find a common ground in their absolute equality before the autonomous law. After the inaugural violence of the state, the state has become a usurper of violence against people whose power has been diffused in an ever-expanding network of representation. For Sofsky, as for Walter Benjamin,[50] the inaugural violence of the state withers on in the present as a 'certain, inescapable threat'.[51] A similar, though perhaps more sophisticated, analysis can be found in the work of Michel Foucault, who relates the state's 'institutions of subjugation'[52] to a subjectification of the people to the smallest detail, from the measurement of holiday-time to the measurement of the normal body and mind. In a totalizing movement of inclusion, the prison, the school, hospital and workshop[53] all take on their role in the atonement of the subject in accordance with juridical and anthropological forms, which became entirely appropriated by state power during the Middle Ages, according to Foucault.[54] His study on the prison shows how the disciplinary apparatus moulds the criminal into the desired shape – that of the epitome of the socialized subject, the *homme aimable* – by meticulously parcelling both space and time in prison.[55] With Foucault, one can say that the violence of the state can be experienced everywhere as the fabrication of *subjects* according to a juridico-anthropological form (which, especially in Foucault's earlier work – among which his work on the prison can be counted – is seen in a Marxian perspective of discipline of the worker in the workshop, according to capitalist logic). An alternative perspective is that of Elias, which stresses an all-pervasive movement of civilization and a disappearance of violence from society. With Elias, one reads history in light of another aspect. The disappearance of corporal punishment in the eighteenth and nineteenth centuries, in Elias' perspective, does not point towards a more refined violent movement of, to a large degree, external subjectification of the subject, but rather indicates a near disappearance of physical forms of violence altogether, and a substitution of *Fremdzwange* by *Selbstzwange*.[56] This seems to bear a resemblance to Hobbes' idea that the obligation *in foro interno*, the compliance with the natural laws 'to a desire they should take place' is stronger than the obligation *in foro externo*.[57] Elias' *Selbstzwange* could be seen as the empirical realization of Hobbes' idea of the obligation *in foro interno*. But the reverse can also be claimed: that Hobbes' theory of such an internal obligation to compliance with those (internal) natural laws is a consequence, or a symptom, of a historical development towards *Selbstzwange*. And then, Foucault's analyses seem to have the advantage of indeed also positing a *Selbstzwange*, but whilst at the same time explaining that will of the prudent as being a result of a historical creation of subjects that are, as subjects, subjected to a certain *episteme*, a dispositive and a discourse in which they can be what they are: subjected beings. But subjected beings with the possibility of being within epistemico-ontological parameters, and at the same time, in that possibility, being subjected to the power of discourse, itself a product of a historical interplay of forces that arbitrarily combine to the configuration in which the modern subject could appear. Foucault is able to show how *Selbstzwange* and a theory such as Hobbes' are the products of the ontological embeddedness of the 'empirico-transcendental subject'[58] in power–knowledge structures, in which *Selbstzwange* is the mere product of a quite literal incorporation (in Foucault's work, the body-politic becomes partly decentralized as biopolitics) of anthropological forms that are meticulously adjusted to juridical forms. With respect to the biopower inherent in the sexual dispositive, Foucault states: 'Irony of this dispositive: it makes us believe it concerns our "liberation".'[59] But the irony is rather in the paradox: for, as Foucault stresses the productive force of power, so too must the subject of this dispositive be seen as the product of a certain violence in the sense of a reduction of being.

With respect to the violence of the state, Foucault's work seems convincing enough to reject the counterfactual notion of the state arising out of a 'natural state' by covenant or contract. Rather, a centralization of violence was at stake – a redistribution of violence, according to Zygmunt Bauman[60] – together with a widening of control that was not without a certain initial violence. Paradoxically, the state has become both the most potentially 'violent' modern institution, and the most frustrated victim, as in modern times a violent crime first and foremost offends not God or king, but the state. Moreover, the subject of what used to be regicide is no longer a king that apparently fell out of grace with God or the gods; it is the 'innocent victim' of the political individual, and his or her death is first of all punished because it is unlawful, because it offends the state, like any murder.[61] A more problematic paradox is that all violence cannot be legitimate. In other words, the state cannot succeed in gaining a true monopoly of violence, eradicating all private violence, since then it would become obsolete. Legitimate violence therefore exists by virtue of the existence of non-legitimate private violence. One might therefore say that, without private violence, the state would lose its core-function, and that the practice of the state would imply explicitly working towards its own destruction, at least in so far as it is based on the intended dissolving of all private violence.

Both these paradoxes are deparadoxized by means of a normativity that exists in the modern semantics of violence. According to this 'ethic of violence', the state's violence, which is legitimate, is deemed 'good', whereas private, illegitimate violence, is 'bad', 'evil' even. This leads to the almost exclusive reservation of the term 'violence' for cases of private violence. As Bauman has said:

> one category of coercion is called 'enforcement of law and order', while the nasty word 'violence' is reserved only for the second. What the verbal distinction hides, though, is that the condemned 'violence' is also about certain ordering, certain laws to be enforced – only those are not the order and the laws which the makers of the distinction had in mind.[62]

By only speaking of violence in the case of private physical violence, the state thus legitimizes itself – or at the very least it avoids questions of legitimation. But only with the use of an ontological definition of violence – a definition which departs with commonsensical and biaphobic conceptions that only legitimate the (violence of the) state – can one be able to observe this.

The violent tautology of state and society

The inaugural violence of the state and its continuous reproduction are immanent to the state and cannot, therefore, be said to be based on the state's guardian-like function of merely reacting against private forms of transgression of the order the state is said to preserve. Important here is that it is crucial for the preservation of the legitimate, or, as Weber says, allegedly legitimate basis of its violence, that the state is able to suppress the visibility of its initiative in the execution of violence. The situation in which the state derives its self-observation from the difference between its active and reactive forms of violence can exist as a consequence of the state's ability to keep that difference itself undisputed.[63] A paradox is at work in the definition of the state and its monopoly of legitimate violence. The state survives only by overcoming the paradox of acting violently upon violence. In other words, this situation can exist because of the political semantics whereby the state's violence is actually 'the people's' reactive violence against not properly subjectified persons. From this point of view, state violence is, in the end, a reduction of such subjects to legitimate subjects. The paradox of state violence as legitimate because it is opposed to something illegitimate which is nonetheless violence as well is resolved by *turning the paradox into a tautology, which then in turn needs to be detautologized.* The apparatus of state control functions under the sole premise that the self-image of the state is functionally adjusted to the self-image of the society from which the state differentiates itself by claiming a central position in the *communis civilis* – as opposed to peripheral parts thereof – or by claiming a position at its 'head' – in the language of the hierarchy of the body (from *logos* to 'lower parts') that, since Plato, has been an exemplary model of the state and the 'body-politic'. Only this 'ideological' self-image of state and society facilitates the overt subjection of people acting in violation of the legitimate order. But it also facilitates the subjectification of 'normal' subjects within the social system, since only by virtue of the differentiation of 'state' and 'society' is it possible to speak of 'subjects of the state'. With respect to the violation of persons violating the legitimate order, the most obvious example is the reduction of being of the inmate, who is subjected to fit the wall and bars of the institution, and also to fit the parameters of the larger legitimate order within what is legitimately called 'society' by means of programs of 'resocialization' or 'reintegration'. The very separation of the society of 'integrated' subjects and an 'outside' of maladjusted is indicative of the difference that is constitutive of the self-definition of state and society.

Functionally, these self-observations are mechanisms of social control. The self-observation of the social system as a whole is facilitated, first of all, by a differentiation of state and society, wherein the state is observed as the means that society deploys in order to secure itself against threats. Such threats may be internal or external, but the concern is here mainly with internal threats to the unity of the self-defining distinction between state and society. The definition and subsequently the existence of crime in general, and more specifically of private violence, makes the existence of the state as a societal subsystem functionally plausible. So next to the state–society differentiation, a second differentiation exists between 'society' and a general category that is placed outside it, as a hostile environment. Mead, for instance, defines the criminal as a person living in a small community outside the larger community, who then makes depredations against that larger community.[64] But the performative speech-acts in which society is separated from an illegitimate outside are scattered throughout social science and popular discourse. In the popular media, such statements can be heard each day, each day realizing what they supposedly depict, and each day fulfilling their integrative function for the social system as a whole. In this outside, crime and private violence (sometimes structural violence as well) are situated. The discursive exorcism of the criminal from society cleanses society itself from illegitimate elements – a secularized form of 'deliverance from evil' – and of blame for the illegitimacy of the criminal, thus ensuring that a society of properly subjectified subjects remains a *communitas perfecta*. As soon as subversive elements appear, these are excommunicated as existing 'outside society'.[65] This leads to a tautological self-definition of the social system by means of a state–society differentiation: it is what it is, because it is not what it is not. Precisely the tautological nature of this self-definition needs to be negated. It is an a priori of the self-observation of society that persons that resort to violence thereby actually betray the fact that they really *are not* a part of that society, since society consists of socialized subjects that do not resort to violence. Here, society's self-observation clearly takes on a tautological form, as Luhmann says it will necessarily have to do.[66] Yet the ideological and moral legitimization that facilitates this is a necessary de-tautologization. The exorcism of the violent person (in any case, a criminal) is therefore a *functional a priori of the undisputed functioning of the differential unity that underlies the self-definitions of state and society*. State violence then becomes an integrative tool to 'get the violent person back into society', to 'reintegrate' him or her. It is not surprising that Kant condemned resocialization efforts as violating a subject's autonomy. But it needs to be said oppositely that the autonomy of law-abiding subjects is facilitated by an autopoietic form of state violence as well. Only, here, it is willed. In society, autonomy presupposes heteronomy. This sociological adagio, which has existed at least since Durkheim, has hardly ever been regarded in light of the aspect of violence. When this is done, it appears that even the quiet state at the head of utopia itself functions on the basis of an ever-present differentiation of active and reactive violence. Crucial for the future existence of this 'contract' is the negation of its violent origin – the negation of the inaugural violence of the state. Pascal has said that 'il faut ... en cacher le commencement'.[67] For, in the beginning, there is violence. This is the *secret* (Foucault) that the state rests upon. Where reactive violence is absent – where, in other words, the subjects of the state are perfectly 'integrated', having abandoned the resort to physical forms of private violence – there still remains an autopoiesis of active reduction of being of those subjects *to* sub-jects, on behalf of the state. This autopoiesis is indeed a functional prerequisite of the distinction, or difference, that facilitates it. In functionalist terms, the violent subsystems within the state have an 'integrative primacy' within the social system, since they facilitate the reproduction of the social system as a whole. In the same sense in which the tautology is always true, the tautological process by which the social system defines itself through a state–society differentiation as opposed to an environment, an 'outside', if undisputed – that is, if ideologically legitimized and thereby de-tautologized – always works.

Notes

1 Z. Bauman, *Life in Fragments: Essays in Postmodern Morality*, Oxford: Blackwell, 1995, p. 139.
2 A review of, for instance, the *British Journal of Criminology*, *Crime and Delinquency*, *Aggression and Violent Behavior*, *Aggressive Behavior*, *Journal of Adolescence*, *Journal of Interpersonal Violence*, or also the *American Sociological Review* and the *American Journal of Sociology*, quickly illustrates that when violence is the topic of research, it is mostly private violence which is focused on.
3 *Routledge Encyclopedia of Philosophy*, 1998, Vol. 9, p. 616.
4 M.R. Jackman, 'Violence in Social Life', *Annual Review of Sociology*, 28, 2002, 387–415 (p. 408).
5 J. Galtung, 'Violence, Peace, and Peace Research', *Journal of Peace Research*, 6(4), 1968, 167–191 (p. 168).
6 See also G. Barak, *Violence and Nonviolence: Pathways to Understanding*, London: Sage, 2003.
7 See N. Luhmann, *Soziale Systeme: Grundriß einer allgemeinen Theorie*, Frankfurt/M.: Suhrkamp, 1984.
8 N. Luhmann, *Soziologie des Risikos*, Berlin: de Gruyter, 1991, p. 16.
9 E. Husserl, *Ideen zu einer reinen Phänomenologie und Phänomenologische Philosophie*, Bd. III Husserliana, Den Haag: Martinus Nijhoff, Bd. I, 1976, pp. 73–74.
10 Ibid., pp. 74, 164–165.
11 See, for the translation into 'aspects' and 'profiles', R. Sokolowski, *Introduction to Phenomenology*, Cambridge: Cambridge University Press, 2000, p. 19.
12 Husserl, op. cit., Bd. I, pp. 74, 202–204.
13 Ibid., Bd. I, pp. 202–203.
14 Husserl summarizes this point as follows:

> In Wesensnotwendigkeit gehört zu einem 'allseitigen', kontinuierlich einheitlich sich in sich selbst bestätigenden Erfahrungsbewußtsein vom selben Ding ein vielfältiges System von kontinuierlichen Erscheinungs- und Abschattungsmannigfaltigkeiten, in denen alle in die Wahrnehmung mit dem Charakter der leibhaften Selbstgegebenheit fallenden gegenständlichen Momente sich in bestimmten Kontinuitäten abschatten. Jede Bestimmtheit hat ihr Abschattungssystem, und für jede gilt, daß sie für das erfassende, Erinnerung und neue Wahrnehmung synthetisch vereinende Bewußtsein als dieselbe dasteht trotz einer Unterbrechung im Ablauf der Kontinuität aktueller Wahrnehmung.
>
> (Ibid., Bd. I, pp. 74–75)

15 Ibid., Bd. I, p. 77.
16 'danach hat ein Erlebnis … seinen Horizont nichterblickter Erlebnisse' (ibid., Bd. I, p. 166).

17 Ibid., Bd. 1, p. 81.
18 Ibid, Bd. 1, p. 167n: ' "Horizont" gilt hier also soviel wie in § 35, S. 62, die Rede von einem "Hof" und "Hintergrund".' I will henceforth use the term 'horizon' to refer to such a background of alternative profiles of aspects which are ready at hand to be experienced.
19 Ibid., Bd. 1, p. 81.
20 Compare, on the idea of a *selection* out of a Husserlian horizon of contingent alternatives: N. Luhmann, 'Sinn als Grundbegriff der Soziologie', in N. Luhmann and J. Habermas, *Theorie der Gesellschaft oder Sozialtechnologie. Was leistet die Systemforschung?* Frankfurt/M.: Suhrkamp, 1971.
21 M. Heidegger, *Sein und Zeit*, Tübingen: Max Niemeyer, 1993, p. 6.
22 Ibid., pp. 7, 11.
23 Compare, for an analogous sociological use of Husserlian phenomenology, N. Luhmann, 1971, op. cit.
24 Ibid., p. 42.
25 Ibid., p. 118: 'Die Welt des Daseins ist *Mitwelt*. Das In-Sein ist *Mitsein* mit Anderen. Das innerweltliche Ansichsein dieser ist *Mitdasein*.'
26 A more consistent elaboration of the Being of Dasein as Mitsein has been rendered by Jean-Luc Nancy. See, for instance, J.-L. Nancy, *La Communauté Désœuvrée*, Christian Bourgeois Éditeur, 1986; J.-L. Nancy, *Être singulier pluriel*, Paris: Galilée, 1996.
27 Heidegger's *Geworfenheit* therefore always already means: *Unterworfenheit*.
28 See, for instance, T. Parsons and E.A. Shils, (eds), *Toward a General Theory of Action*, New York: The Free Press, 1962, p. 77.
29 When a person is predominantly seen in light of their biological being, they are reduced to this material aspect. That this aspect is, however, always co-constitutive of interaction, is expressed in the notion of *structurally coupled* systems (Maturana), by which Luhmann expresses the fact that the biological and the psychological system of a person are preconditions for each other's operational closure.
30 Robert de Niro in the movie *Jackie Brown*.
31 See, for instance, L. Presser, 'Remorse and Neutralization Among Violent Male Offenders', *Justice Quarterly*, 20(4), 2003, pp. 801–825.
32 E. Durkheim, *The Elementary Forms of the Religious Life*, London: George Allen & Unwin, 1915, p. 227.
33 F. Nietzsche, *Werke* II, Frankfurt/M.: Ullstein, 1979, p. 310.
34 Quoted in M. Nussbaum, 'Equity and Mercy', *Philosophy and Public Affairs*, 22(2), 1993, 83–125 (p. 100).
35 I realize that the 'aggression' Seneca mentions is not quite the same as violence – I will define 'aggression' as a predisposition to extreme forms of private violence – but there is no doubt that his view on violence was of similar 'humanist' content. This view is characterized by the knowledge-through-*Weltschmerz* that Sloterdijk ascribes to the cynic: P. Sloterdijk, *Kritik der zynischen Vernunft*, Frankfurt/M.: Suhrkamp, 1980.
36 The Leitmotiv here is summarized by Erasmus' statement that only to man 'nature' has given 'the use of speech and deliberation, both pre-eminently suitable to nurture and nourish benevolence, so that not in man too, all would be accomplished solely by physical force' (my translation). D. Erasmus, *Oorlog (Dulce bellum inexpertis)*, Amsterdam/Antwerpen: Wereldbibliotheek-Vereniging, 1969, p. 14. This of course also reverberates in current discourse on deliberative democracy.
37 Barak, op. cit., p. 26.

38 Henry, op. cit., p. 19. See especially pp. 19–20 with respect to the concept of 'harm' in the definition of violence.
39 For a discussion of the concept of *humanitas*, see, for instance, M. Landmann, *Philosophische Anthropologie. Menschliche Selbstdarstellung in Geschichte und Gegenwart*, Berlin & New York: de Gruyter, 1982, p. 22.
40 As mentioned in J. Derrida, *The Gift of Death*, Chicago: University of Chicago Press, 1995, pp. 17–18.
41 See, of course, E. Durkheim, *Les règles de la méthode sociologique*, Paris: PUF, 1937. As a contemporary source: E. Laclau and C. Mouffe, *Hegemony and Socialist Strategy: Towards a Radical Democratic Politics*, London: Verso, 1985.
42 M. Heidegger, *Einführung in die Metaphysik*, Tübingen: Max Niemeyer, 1953, p. 117.
43 J. Ritter, (ed.), *Historisches Wörterbuch der Philosophie*, Darmstadt: Wissenschaftliche Buchgesellschaft, 1974, p. 562.
44 R. Sprandel, *Verfassung und Gesellschaft im Mittelalter*, Paderborn: Schöningh (UTB), 1975, p. 112ff.
45 As Martin Albrow says, at least since Machiavelli, violence or force and coercion – both externally as internally against the people within the nation state – have been characterized as the defining properties of the nation state: M. Albrow, *Abschied vom Nationalstaat. Staat und Gesellschaft im Globalen Zeitalter*, Frankfurt/M.: Suhrkamp, 1998, p. 101.
46 Since it can hardly be said that Machiavelli was not a historian. For the writings on Rome I refer to: N. Machiavelli, *The Discourses*, London: Penguin, 2003.
47 G. Sorel, *Réflections sur la violence*, Paris: Rivière, 1919, p. 29.
48 H.L. Nieburg, 'Uses of Violence', *The Journal of Conflict Resolution*, 7(1), 1963, pp. 43–54 (pp. 43, 54).
49 W. Sofsky, *Traktat über die Gewalt*, Frankfurt/M.: Fischer, 1996, p. 25.
50 Benjamin, op. cit., p. 42: 'die rechserhaltende Gewalt ist eine drohende.'
51 Sofsky, op. cit., p. 13.
52 M. Foucault, *Power*, London: Penguin, 1994, p. 81.
53 Ibid., p. 77.
54 Ibid., p. 43. This thesis is of course contestable, but it remains a historical matter. One might perhaps sooner attribute the appropriation of juridical forms by state power to the Enlightenment, or at least locate it after or in conjunction with the development of the Western European sovereign states. Either way, the important issue in the end is this appropriation by state power.
55 See M. Foucault, *Surveiller et punir: Naissance de la prison*, Paris: Gallimard, 1975.
56 N. Elias, *Über den Prozeß der Zivilisation. Soziogenetische und psychogenetische Untersuchungen* (1 & 2), Frankfurt/M.: Suhrkamp, 1980.
57 Hobbes, op. cit., p. 166.
58 See M. Foucault, *Les mots et les choses: Une archéologie des sciences humaines*, Paris: Gallimard, 1966, p. 329.
59 M. Foucault, *Histoire de la sexualité I: La volonté de savoir*, Paris: Gallimard, 1976, p. 211.
60 Bauman, op. cit., p. 141.
61 See, for an analysis of the change in semantics from 'regicide' to 'political murder', T. Scheffler, 'Vom Königsmord zum Attentat. Zur Kulturmorphologie des politischen Mordes', in T. von Trotha (ed.), *Soziologie der Gewalt. Sonder-*

heft Kölner Zeitschrift für Soziologie und Sozialpsychologie, Opladen: Westdeutscher Verlag, 1997, pp. 183–199.

62 Bauman, op. cit., p. 141. See also Thomas Lindenberger and Alf Lüdtke, 'Daraus entwickelt sich eine Dialektik in sich widersprüchlicher Gewalt-Diskurse: Wer gegenwärtige Herrschaft legitimieren will, redet nur dann von "Gewalt", wenn sie das staatliche Gewaltmonopol durchbricht und illegal ist; das ist dort, wo der moderne Zentralstaat sich erfolgreich – und das schließt auch immer ein: gewaltsam – etabliert hat, in der Tat seltener der Fall als früher', in T. Lindenberger and A. Lüdtke, *Physische Gewalt. Studien zur Geschichte der Neuzeit*, Frankfurt/M.: Suhrkamp, 1995, p. 20.

63 As soon as the difference constitutive of the state's self-observation (seen in light of the aspect of violence) does become a topic of observation itself, or when, in other words, the state's negation of the difference between active and reactive state violence is uncovered and exposed as being a negation, the question of the legitimization of this negation and hence of the state itself arises. Such events, or even such times, are what the term 'legitimation crisis' refers to.

64 G.H. Mead, *Mind, Self & Society from the Standpoint of a Social Behaviorist*, Chicago: Chicago University Press, 1962, p. 265.

65 See, for a discussion of this discourse and the functional role of the social sciences herein, especially of current criminology, W. Schinkel, 'The Modernist Myth in Criminology', *Theoretical Criminology*, 6(2), 2000, pp. 123–144. See also W. Schinkel, *Denken in een tijd van sociale hypochondrie. Aanzet tot een theorie voorbij de maatschappij*, Kampen: Klement, 2007.

66 Actually, Luhmann emphasizes the fact that society's self-description either takes a paradoxical or a tautological form. N. Luhmann, 'Tautology and Paradox in the Self-Descriptions of Modern Society', *Sociological Theory*, 6(1), 1988, 21–37.

67 B. Pascal, *Pensées*, Mercure de France, II, 1976, § 94, p. 64.

Chapter 4

Existentialism, edgework, and the contingent body

Exploring the criminological implications of Ultimate Fighting

Stephen Lyng, Rick Matthews, and William J. Miller

> You aren't alive anywhere like you're alive at fight club. When it's you and one other guy under that one light in the middle of all those watching. Fight club isn't about winning or losing fights. Fight club isn't about words. You see a guy come to fight club for the first time, and his ass is a loaf of white bread. You see this same guy here six months later, and he looks carved out of wood. This guy trusts himself to handle anything.
>
> (Chuck Palahniuk, *Fight Club*)

Introduction

Chuck Palahniuk's book, *Fight Club*,[1] and its film adaptation by director David Fincher,[2] has generated a sizable and highly divided body of commentary on its significance as a critical examination of social life in the age of neoliberal capitalism. While some critics applaud Palahniuk for exposing the tragicomic dimensions of individual and group adaptations to the empty consumerism and market-driven ethos of our time, others have expressed disgust at what they regard as a veiled attempt to valorize hyper-masculinity and fascism. The polarized character of these critical responses to the book and film suggest that this fictional work may offer insight into the decentring personal consequences of living with the complex and contradictory currents of late modern society.

The stir caused by *Fight Club* among book and film critics and the reading and viewing public at large parallels recent reactions to a real-life subculture of unconventional fighting that has emerged in the last two decades in many Western countries. As one of the most recently evolved "extreme sports," Mixed Martial Arts, Ultimate Fighting or No Holds Barred Fighting (NHB), has moved from "fight club" obscurity to international media prominence in a very short period of time while also generating criticism and concern among some public officials and cultural commentators. The rapid rise of Ultimate Fighting as a sport and the growing popularity of extreme sports in general suggests that these new lifestyle and leisure projects may harmonize with some of the central structural imperatives of the contemporary social order.

A key assertion of this chapter is that Ultimate Fighting and other extreme sports, along with a wide range of other social practices seemingly unrelated to sport and leisure, reflect the growing importance of risk and uncertainty at the levels of both social structure and agency in the late modern era. In this chapter, we examine the intersections between existentialist thought and the "edgework" approach to risk agency and illustrate these ideas with empirical evidence on Ultimate Fighting. Although it is possible to draw on a wide range of risk-taking activities to empirically illustrate our existentialist analysis of risk, we have chosen to analyze Ultimate Fighting because it offers an opportunity for a deep engagement with themes that are critical to the general focus of the present volume – exploring possibilities for an existential criminology. An examination of Ultimate Fighting will allow us explore the critical connections between discipline, domination, the contingent body, and experiential transcendence in violent encounters that are both non-criminal and criminal in nature. In this sense, our chapter parallels Palahniuk's novelistic effort to use of his 'fight club' narrative to explore problems of identity, self-creation, and agency in late modernity.

The present study pursues four interrelated goals. First, we will demonstrate the relevance of existentialist ideas to the increasing structural uncertainty and reflexivity of the risk society, and the emergence of edgework as an expression of risk agency in this social context. Second, we demonstrate the importance of incorporating the body into our existentialist analysis of risk structure and agency. Third, we illustrate these theoretical ideas by applying the framework to our field data on Ultimate Fighters. Finally, we conclude by considering the implications of this existentialist–edgework analysis of Ultimate Fighting for understanding violent street crime.

Existentialism, risk society, and edgework

In recognizing the timeliness of an edited collection of essays and empirical studies devoted to exploring the intersection between existentialism and criminology, the contributors to this volume share an awareness of the increasing uncertainties of social living in the twenty-first century. The conditions of social life in the developed and developing world today share a basic similarity with the global context in which existentialist thought first emerged as a formal theoretical system. With the publication of key works in the 1940s and 1950s, existentialist thinkers were responding, in part, to a situation of enormous global uncertainty not unlike that which exists today. While philosophers, theorists, and other cultural observers in the immediate post-war period were struggling to make sense of the international realignments, genocidal campaigns, and the technologies of past and future mass killing made possible by global war, the social and cultural transformations taking place today are being driven primarily by global cultural and economic forces (which many observers see as also impelling another important source of global uncertainty – international terrorism). Despite the differences in the steering currents at work in each era, both periods can be characterized as times of unprecedented change that have stimulated new ways of thinking about the conditions of our collective existence. In a view shared by other contributors to this book, we believe that existentialist ideas have acquired special significance in the contemporary social context.

Although there has been a growing appreciation for the contemporary relevance of existentialist concepts among some sociologists and criminologists, little agreement exists within these groups about the most useful approach for theorizing the changes in structure and agency that are behind the revival of existentialism. In order for existentialism to yield useful insights about sociological or criminological problems, it must be linked to a framework for conceptualizing the social and cultural environment within which existential themes can be addressed – i.e. issues of authenticity, morality, self-constitution, and freedom. A range of theoretical frameworks can be employed for this purpose, but we have chosen to orient our discussion of existentialist themes to a perspective that highlights the rise of reflexive risk culture and risk agency in the late modern context. At present, this approach consists of a set of sensitizing concepts drawn from a preliminary effort to connect elements of the "risk society and culture"[3] perspective and the "edgework"[4] model of voluntary risk taking. While this approach does not constitute a fully formulated theoretical perspective at this point, it does offer a useful standpoint for exploring the existentialist dimensions of risk and uncertainty in the contemporary social order.

From the "death of God" to the "death of the social"

The link between existentialist thought and the social conditions of uncertainty can be traced to the rise of the modern Western worldview beginning in the sixteenth and seventeenth centuries. A common concern among the progenitors of twentieth-century existentialism was the irrevocable shift in human self-reflection that accompanied the breakdown of traditional ways of living. With the growth of science and the new "attitude of skepticism" that marked the shift to the modern era, the accepted truths and moral certainties of the traditional world were brought into question. For Nietzsche, this marked the beginning of a historical epoch in which all absolutes would be cast aside, a movement of critical annihilation of the ultimate foundations for values and beliefs that he referred to as the "death of God." Nietzsche's use of this dramatic phrase covered not only the collapse of religious absolutes but also all other transcendent foundations of meaning and value. As Guignon and Pereboom write,[5] "the madman's" statement that "God is dead" in Nietzsche's *The Gay Science* applies to the full pantheon of transcendental concepts appearing in the last several centuries:

> God, Reason, the cosmos, providence, divine rights, the noumenal realm, *Geist*, Humanity, History – all these conceptions of the ultimate foundation for our beliefs and practices have been shown up for what they are: human constructs, expressions of our own thinking and acting.

Had Nietzsche been able to see the latest historical turn in the project of modernity, he may have been surprised by his own prescience. The successive collapse of absolutes has been a key trajectory of the modernization process over the last several centuries, with the "attitude of skepticism" now even applying to one of the main sources of critical reflection in the post-Enlightenment period – the scientific worldview itself. The accumulation of scientific knowledge and the social and technological "advances" made possible by science have stimulated a growing critical awareness of the expanding global risks and dangers directly traceable to these scientific and technological developments.[6]

The erosion of confidence in science and technology is a marker of what some see as a much more powerful source of growing uncertainty in the world today, a process that they claim has brought us to a new phase in human history. The increasing risk of humanly produced disasters in the "global risk society" is rooted in a more fundamental historical development that Ulrich Beck and his collaborators term as "reflexive modernization."[7] The emergence of reflexivity in the contemporary global system makes it possible to distinguish a "late" or "second" modernity that follows the "early" or "first" modern phase of nation states, industrialism, and scientific legitimacy. In the second modernity, indeterminacy in human experience does not derive only from critical reflection on the intellectual foundations of truth and moral consciousness, but is rooted more fundamentally in the erosion of first modern institutions – nuclear family, ethnic group, class, nation state – and individual self-distancing from roles that interface with these structures.[8] Thus, if Nietzsche's phrase the "death of God" captures the annihilation of absolutes, the "death of the social" designates the demise of the ontological foundations of a social "reality sui generis" that serves as the empirical ground for social scientific analysis

Connecting Nietzsche's "death of God" and Jean Baudrillard's "death of the social"[9] to reflect on the putative historical transition from first to second modernity is more than a rhetorical exercise. Although risk-society theorists do not typically employ either of these phrases, both are relevant to key contrasts drawn by these theorists in conceptualizing the two distinct phases of modernity. For instance, Scott Lash indirectly references Nietzsche's critique of the foundational discourses of the first modernity by exploring the contrast between reflection and reflexivity:

> [T]he individual of the first modernity is reflective while that of the second modernity is reflexive. The idea of reflective belongs to the philosophy of consciousness of the first modernity.... To reflect is to somehow subsume the object under the subject of knowledge. Reflection presumes apodictic knowledge and certainty. It presumes a dualism, a scientific attitude in which the subject is in one realm, the object of knowledge in another.[10]

By contrast, dualism between subject and object has no place in the reflexive consciousness of the second modernity: "Reflexive ... has more to do with reflex than reflection. Reflexes are indeterminate. They are immediate. They do not in any sense subsume."[11] Lash's description of reflexive consciousness echoes Nietzsche's "perspective" approach to consciousness, which "recognize[s] that each person's body, biography, and location are unique optics,"[12] and accepts that "we have access only to our own perspectives on things, with the result that we can never exit from our perspectives to know reality as it is in itself."[13] This position is consistent with Beck's phenomenologically based approach to consciousness which emphasizes the partiality of our knowledge of the object and the interest-oriented perspective of the knower. Beck asserts that "the objectivity of simple-modernity knowledge is replaced by the *intentionality* of knowledge in the second modernity," which is related to one of the key dynamics of reflexive modernization – the fact that "what is intended leads to the most extraordinary unintendedness, to side-effects, to unintended consequences."[14]

As late modern individuals gravitate toward various cultural expressions of perspectivism and increasingly reject the foundationalism of early modernity, one of the ontological pillars supporting an objective reality of "the social" begins to crumble. With the clear absence of a Durkheimian "collective conscience" serving as an interpretive reference for cooperative endeavors and self-reflection, the ontology of structurally formed agents reproducing institutional arrangements and constructing cohesive narrative biographies is progressively eroded. As Lash notes, this does not mean that the subject and knowledge disappear: "The subject is still with us and so is knowledge. Only knowledge itself is *of* uncertainty.... It is itself precarious as distinct from certain, and what that knowledge is about is also uncertain – probabilistic, at best; more likely 'possibilistic'."[15] Thus, the "death of the social" is partly a consequence of the shift from the dualism of reflection to the monism of reflexivity, but even this change points to the deeper transformation that is at the heart of reflexive modernization. To understand this deeper movement, we need to appreciate the immanent character of reflexivity – an immanence that erases the distinction between structure and agency entirely.

If first modern social life is characterized by the dominance of structures and systems that have a determinant impact on agency, the second modernity is distinguished by the immanent termination of structural determinacy. In this expression of second modern reflexivity, social structures and systems acquire characteristics that diminish their determinant impact on agency. In the early work of some risk society theorists, this aspect of reflexivity was discussed in terms of the increasing separation of agency and structure.[16] More recently, however, Lash has proposed the idea of *non-linear* reflexivity as a way to avoid the implicit dualism involved in the earlier conceptualization.[17] While linear systems move toward a state of equilibrium that can only be disturbed by external forces, non-linear systems are characterized by change and dis-equilibrium produced by forces internal to the system. "It is the 'chaos' or noise of the unintended consequences that leads to system dis-equilibrium."[18] Thus, agency within non-linear systems does not exist independently from structure, but rather emerges as a reflex response to structure:

> Reflexivity ... is characterized by choice, where previous generations had no such choices.... [T]his choice must be *fast*, we must – as in a reflex – make quick decisions.... We must live, are forced to live, in an atmosphere of risk in which knowledge and life-chances are precarious.[19]

The type of structure/agency blend that Beck and Lash envision here accords with Manuel Castells'[20] notion of a social universe governed by the logic of flows:

> Beck's notions of unintended consequences, of ever-incomplete knowledge, of not irrationalism but a rationality that is forever indeterminate is comfortable in the logic of flows. Beck's chronic indeterminacy of risk and risk-taking, of living with risk is much more of a piece with, not the determinacy of structure but the partial, the elusive determinacy of flow.[21]

Applying Castells' metaphor of flow to structure/agency relation, we have an additional way to distinguish between first and second modernity: while the first modernity is rooted in the logic of structures, the second modernity is governed by the logic of flows.

Thus, at a point in the historical process when the logic of structures gives way to the logic of flows, when the dualism of reflection collapses into the monism of reflex, where cosmopolitanism supplants nationalism, and the family is fragmented by divorce, long-distance marriage, and the distancing effects of new communication technology on parents and children, it is possible to say that the domain of the social, as it was understood and experienced in early modernity, has largely disintegrated. In the new post-social universe of late modernity, functions are no longer tied to roles but are managed in ad hoc fashion by subjects detached from first modern institutions. There is a general move to greater complexity and chaos, but the chaos is regularized at a higher level. This involves, in part, what Lash refers to as "a normalization that institutionalizes abnormality,"[22] a process of institutionalizing the exceptional rather than the normal. These are the general changes that constitute what we want to term the "death of the social" in the era of late modernity.

Promise and peril in the risk society

> I am stupid, and all I do is need and want things. My tiny life. My tiny little shit job. My Swedish furniture. I never, no, never told anyone this, but before I met Tyler [and joined fight club], I was planning to buy a dog and name it "Entourage." This is how bad your life can get.
> (Chuck Palahniuk, *Fight Club*)

What would an existentialist appraisal of the social configurations of the risk society indicate about our collective human prospects in era of the second modernity? One theme in existentialist thought that is clearly missing from Beck and Giddens' assessment is attention to the moral and emotional implications of people's confrontation with the consequences of reflexive modernization. While both theorists emphasize the contradictory mix of threat and liberation that conditions life in the risk society, neither is particularly attuned to the terror that both of these experiences produce in most people. In contemplating the broad range of global dangers that confront us in the twenty-first century, from the threat of environmental catastrophe, pandemic disease, nuclear annihilation, financial panics, terrorist attacks, and the like, most of us understandably harbor deep fears about what global tragedy we may witness or experience on any given day. At the same time, however, the loosening of structural ties between individuals and first modern institutions, and the subsequent confrontation with seemingly infinite choices in how we manage our lives, is also a potential source of terror. In a context in which daily living requires that we come to terms with the logic of flows in order to insure our survival, Marx's famous phrase "all that is solid melts into air"[23] aptly describes a kind of horrifying weightlessness that characterizes the lived experience of growing numbers of people. What existentialists would ask about this experience of "normal chaos"[24] and "ontological insecurity"[25] is "How do people respond to these conditions and how do these responses contribute either to the destruction or emancipation of the human spirit?"

First, it is clear that individuals exposed to the unpredictable flows of the risk society are likely to respond in many different ways. One response that has acquired great geopolitical importance in recent years is the move to re-legitimize tradition in the wake of its steady erosion under the conditions of reflexive modernization. Giddens describes this response as a two-pronged movement in which defenders of tradition either justify it by acknowledging the plurality of worldviews and arguing that traditions have value within that plurality or by embracing reactionary moves to fundamentalist orientations that reject any form of critical scrutiny and assert "formulaic truth without regard to consequences."[26] From an existentialist standpoint, the conservative/fundamentalist response is particularly destructive of human freedom, representing little more than a cowardly retreat into what Nietzsche called the "slave morality." According to Nietzsche, individuals subscribing to such moralities become so thoroughly domesticated that they lose all capacity for creative expression and uniqueness, and ultimately succumb to the "herd instinct of obedience."[27] Their moral judgments are guided by the ethical/emotional sense of *ressentiment*, in which one's suffering is given meaning by blaming others who then become the focus of imaginary revenge. What may be most destructive about the desire to reclaim tradition, however, is its link to a deep-seated hatred for the world that actually exists. For Nietzsche, this hatred is "a product of nay-saying and negativity, a symptom of the resentment of individuals who cannot live fully in the actual world."[28]

If neo-conservatism and fundamentalism define one general reaction to the normal chaos of the risk society, we also see a pronounced movement in the opposite direction, toward a positive acceptance of the principle that "anything goes." With its focus on nihilism as a response to the radical doubt engendered by modernism, existentialism calls attention to a moral and emotional issue that is curiously absent from the risk society perspective. While theorists of reflexive modernization emphasize the decline of structural determinacy and the expanding choices available to individuals freed of institutional constraints, they rarely acknowledge the feelings of "lack" or "absence" that these conditions generate. In the midst of the "pandemonium of free spirits," it is not surprising that many people experience a profound loss of meaning and develop a cynical stance toward all systems of value and truth. This state of mindless drifting and general indifference supports the sense that everything is permitted but nothing is particularly inspiring. For Nietzsche, these conditions are emblematic of the cultural exhaustion that is taking place in Western societies after an extended history of rationalization. His anticipation of the contemporary shift to reflexive agency is strikingly revealed in the following passage:

The entire West has lost those instincts out of which institutions grow, out of which the *future* grows.... One lives for today, one lives very fast – one lives very irresponsibly: it is precisely this which one calls "freedom." That which *makes* institutions institutions is despised, hated, rejected: whenever the word "authority" is so much as heard one believes oneself in danger of a new slavery.[29]

With the decline of normative controls and legitimate authority, behavior increasingly "follows the grooves of habit, organizational routine, and mass culture or is simply disoriented."[30]

As an observer of late-nineteenth-century social life, Nietzsche could not have imagined what the nihilist response would look like at the beginning of the twenty-first century. Had he been able to observe this late modern strategy for living, he would have likely regarded it as another slave system no less destructive than the slave morality of conservatism and fundamentalism. Contemporary nihilists not only follow the grooves of habit and organizational routine in their work life, they commit levels of time and energy to these routines that are unmatched by workers in past decades.[31] Long hours at work and forsaken vacations do not reflect necessarily any special meaning and value assigned to one's occupational or professional status. Rather, commitment to work is justified by a basic desire to maximize one's economic resources for participating in the mediated world of consumer culture. Today's nihilists work hard in order to consume more, not because the commodities they acquire have intrinsic value for them but because they are a source of fleeting stimulation or part of a continuous flow of status signifiers. Indeed, the value of all things, including objects, ideas, relationships, experiences, or any other tangible resource, are ultimately reduced to commodity exchange value, since everything is for sale in the late modern marketplace. The nihilist orientation even extends beyond that which is commodified to the actual *advertising* of commodities as consumers become sophisticated interpreters of print ads and television commercials and cease to be moved by standard advertising appeals. This fuels a spiral of new advertising approaches, which at each turn seek to incorporate the cynical interpretations of previous approaches into the new format. In the most recent turn in this process, print and electronic advertising abandon all pretense of making a logical case for the superiority of a product and lapse into complete incoherence as a way to attract the consumer's attention.

In what sense is this shift to consumer-driven nihilism a destructive force rather than a liberating one? To be free of institutional constraints and normative controls would seem to create new opportunities for self-development, interpersonal exploration, and structural innovation, and yet the lives of late modern nihilists appear to be distinguished most by increasing uni-dimensionality. The enslaving nature of the "work to consume" lifestyle leaves little room for the development of one's individual and interpersonal powers: people work more only to be able to spend more. And as traditional normative constraints on spending habits are relaxed and spending actually exceeds many workers' earning capacity, they become even more tightly bound to their jobs by the weight of their mounting debt. Although reflexive modernization creates greater *potential* for multidimensional self-development, this potential remains unrealized for most people in the consumer culture of late capitalism.

Whether one seeks to escape late modern anxiety by finding refuge in early modern traditions or by embracing the one-dimensional lifestyles of the consumer nihilists, there is little possibility for individual freedom in either of these responses to the immense uncertainties of the risk society. Although existentialists confronting the institutional dislocations of other periods have argued for immersion in intense emotional experience as a way to achieve deep insight into one's moral predicament, even this avenue of self-exploration has been cut off in a market system that has extended the commodification process into the affective dimension. In late capitalism, powerful emotional experiences can be purchased just as easily as a pair of shoes or a box of cereal, particularly with the rapid development of media technology in recent decades. Consequently, the reflexive value of intense affective experience has been cheapened by the same market processes that have devalued most other sources of meaning in consumer culture.

In short, an existentialist interpretation of the changes in structure and agency that characterize the risk society seems to cast doubt on a key premise of the reflexive modernization thesis: whatever liberating potential may be found in the greater range of choices available to people in the risk society, this freedom of choice is overridden by the delimiting consequences of the dominant lifestyle responses to the uncertainties of the present age. In this analysis, the increasing importance of risk as a system-level imperative is not only reflected in the growing likelihood of human-made global disasters, it has also inspired individual-level responses to the new uncertainties in the direction of increasingly unidimensional lifestyles, comparable in many ways to Herbert Marcuse's "one-dimensional man" complex.[32] However, the picture may not be as bleak as it first appears. By contextualizing risk in ways not previously considered by risk society theorists and incorporating the concept of "edgework" into the framework, we will demonstrate how the type of emancipatory experience envisioned by existentialists does in fact emerge within the risk society.

Corporal transaction, life-world, and system in the risk society

We expand the analysis at this point by linking it to an ongoing theoretical project that offers a way to explore in greater depth the relevance of existentialist themes to the conditions of social life in the second modernity. This theoretical project consists of an effort to reformulate Jurgen Habermas' Theory of Communicative Action (TCA)[33] by deepening the theory's connection to ideas associated with the American pragmatism tradition and by incorporating the human body into the framework. The reformulation has yielded an approach that Lyng and Franks designate as the Theory of Corporeal Transaction.[34]

Space limitations preclude a detailed description of the Theory of Corporeal Transaction (TCT) here, so we will discuss only those elements of the framework directly relevant to the present focus on the existentialist dilemmas posed by the risk society. The crucial concepts for dealing with this problem are captured by Habermas's distinction between the "life-world" and "system." Although Habermas employs these concepts as key conceptual devices for synthesizing a broad range of social theories, including phenomenology, pragmatism, semiotics, and various versions of systems theory, the impressive synthesis accomplished by TCA is deeply rooted in a rationalist ontology that some pragmatists find troubling. For example, Shalin, Halton, and a number of other pragmatist critics of Habermas criticize the privileging consciousness and discursive practices in TCA.[35] This approach is problematic because it employs a conception of reason that "has no obvious relation to the human body and non-cognitive processes (emotions, feelings, sentiments)."[36]

In an effort to address this problem, Lyng and Franks strengthen TCA's connection to the pragmatist ontology by substituting the notion of "corporeal transaction" for Habermas' "communicative action" in the action–theoretical framework.[37] With this alteration of the theory, analysis of the life-world can now be expanded beyond the exclusive focus on symbolic interaction to consider other bodily transactions involved in a wide range of social practices in the realms of production, consumption, and social interaction. The transactional approach puts *embodied* actors at the center of the life-world, which allows us to see transacting bodies as the ontological foundation of the conflicting forms that constitute this domain.

With this conceptual modification, it is possible now to discern the key problem of the life-world as involving the need to discover ways to *terminate* the inherent *indeterminacy* of the body. This problem is implicated in the specific meaning that pragmatists give to the concept of "transaction." According to Dewey,[38] transaction can be understood as the actualization of intentions to alter a world that responds indifferently to these acts. The body's capacity for the manipulation of objects to achieve specific ends is the foundation of the double-edged process by which environmental objects are constituted and sensitivities and capacities of the organism are developed. Thus, the over-riding experience of the body is found in the dialectic between its subjective and objective aspects – the sense of both *being* a body and *having* a body simultaneously. Indeed, these two dimensions cannot be separated in actual experience because it is in the action of the body as subjective agent that we discover its ego-alien unpredictability. The latter experience – the sense of the body's objective contingency or indeterminate reality – forms the key problem for the embodied actor, a problem that can be addressed only through corporeal transactions in a world of objective resistance. Thus, corporeal transaction is the principal means by which human actors 'terminate indeterminacy' by bringing out some of the potentialities of the body and "render[ing] obscure its other possible determinations."[39]

In Habermas' TCA framework, increasing rationalization of social life in the evolution of modern societies eventually leads to the decoupling of the system and life-world, with the rationalization process taking different forms in each dimension.[40] However, with the conceptual shift to corporeal transaction in TCT, system rationalization of production, consumption, and interaction practices can now be seen as a process of *disembodying* these practices. That is, corporeal transactions directed by the rationalization imperative terminate the body's indeterminacy only in ways that reflect system needs and, in doing so, narrowly inscribe bodies in accordance with the structural logics of prevailing work regimens, consumption patterns, and discourse systems. Since corporeal transactions shaped by the system are no longer specifically focused on the life-world problem of bodily contingency, the full range of potential terminations that can be explored in *embodied* production, consumption, and interaction are "rendered obscure." Thus, system colonization of the life-world, manifested concretely as the promotion of rational efficiency, conspicuous consumption, and ideological domination, gives rise to distinct styles of body usage that reflect the different ways in which the system inscribes bodies. Following Arthur Frank, these body styles can be designated as the *disciplined body*, the *mirroring body*, and the *dominating body*, which accord with the production, consumption, and interaction practices, respectively.[41]

Framing our analysis of reflexive modernization and risk society in terms of TCT offers a way to further develop this analysis in some useful directions. First, it is possible now to orient the risk society perspective to an embodied form of agency. Although it should be self-evident that human action involves most fundamentally the action of human bodies, the longstanding cognitive bias in social science has tended to obscure this fact. Moreover, as Scott Lash notes, the cognitive bias can also be found in Beck and Giddens' conceptualization of the key idea of "reflexivity."[42] What makes reflexivity possible for both Beck and Giddens are the flows of conceptual symbols that pass through the information structures of the risk society, whether these symbols arise in the sub-political critiques of the institutions of science (Beck) or they are mediated by "expert systems" such as psychology, psychoanalysis, and sociology (Giddens).

However, by employing the ideas of "corporal transaction" and "system colonization of the life-world" as developed in TCT, it is possible to understand the crucial role of the body in how people respond to the uncertainties of the risk society. In addition to Beck and Giddens' cognitive reflexivity, in which information structures yield the cognitive categories that enable reflection on first modern institutions and roles, members of the risk society engage in embodied expressions of the nihilistic and fundamentalist responses to late modern uncertainties. On the one hand, the late modern nihilistic response of "working more to consume more" inscribes the disciplined body in routines of work and the mirroring body in consumption practices, even as worker–consumers adopt a cynical stance toward all existing systems of truth and value. On the other hand, the fundamentalist response of "asserting formulaic truth without regard for consequences" takes the form of the dominating body, which seeks to eliminate contingency in the other by drawing on its own contingent nature to transform or destroy the other. Thus, each of these body styles refers to corporeal transactions emerging within the life-world, although each arises through system colonization of this domain.

The second advantage of linking our analysis to TCT is that we now have a way to explore in more systematic terms how emancipatory experience can arise in the risk society. To deal with this issue, we must return to Habermas' distinction between system and life-world and consider how these concepts figure into his emancipatory agenda. For Habermas, the force of reason in the modern era is a double-edged sword insofar as the rationalization process has differential effects on the system and life-world. While he is deeply committed to the modernist project and its promise of liberation through reason and rational discourse, Habermas is also attentive to the subversion of reason by "systematically distorted" communications of the "money-bound," media-steered" system.[43] In this respect, he is indebted to Max Weber, whose analysis of reason gave prominent attention to the triumph of formal rationality over substantive rationality. Reason may have its roots in the historical development of a system becoming increasingly dominated by formal rationality, but this historical process also transforms the life-world by creating universal discursive standards for the collective discussion of social issues. Such discussions take place within "ideal speech situations," where "only reason should have force" in mediating issues of truth, justice, and authenticity.[44] Thus, the ideal speech situation is an environment in which appeals to established custom eventually give way to procedural rules for achieving communicative rationality. In this sense, Habermas sees rationalized communicative action within the life-world as an emancipating force that counters the influence of the instrumental-rationality of the system.

Although TCT's reformulation of Habermas' framework is based on an alternative conceptualization of the life-world, it is also possible to envision a further reformulation based on a different conceptualization of the system. As we have seen, Habermas' indebtedness to the classical canon leads him to identify formal rationality as the central imperative of the system. But what if Beck and Giddens are correct in asserting that we have entered into a second modern era increasingly dominated by the logic of risk? In this conceptualization of the system, risk calculation emerges out of instrumental rationality, since "risks arise precisely from the triumph of the instrumentally rational order."[45] Thus, the new system imperative involves a form of risk consciousness that treats unpredictability as "cognizable through probabilistic calculation."[46] As Lash points out, "[t]he risk society is ... not so much about the distribution of 'bads' or dangers as about a mode of conduct centered on risk."[47] This way of conceptualizing the central structural logic of the system therefore shifts the focus away from the "systematically distorted communications" at issue in Habermas' treatment of the system to Beck's concern with the "unanticipated consequences" of risk calculation and action involved in the implementation of scientific and technological programs.

Our principal concern here, however, is gauging the impact of the emergence of risk consciousness and agency on corporeal transaction and the life-world. To be sure, Beck and Giddens and their collaborators have devoted significant attention to how life-world institutions have been either created or transformed by the unanticipated consequences of the risk society, even though they do not make use of the conceptual distinction between system/life-world specifically. What remains to be addressed, however, is how risk consciousness has affected corporeal transactions involved in dealing with uncertainty, i.e. people's embodied orientation toward, and encounter with, uncertainty. As the system compels social actors take on new risks and responsibilities by becoming "probabilistic calculating subjects," they develop a certain familiarity with the experience of uncertainty and an expanding faith in their abilities as individuals to effectively managed it. Thus, in the transition from first to second modernity, we witness a basic transformation in the general stance toward uncertainty – it becomes something to be embraced rather than avoided.

What we find in the evolution of the life-world from the first to second modernity, then, is the growing influence of risk consciousness and agency on corporeal transaction, a process that is comparable to Habermas' conception of the rationalization of communicative action. Of course, the *system* is also affected by the expanding impact of risk consciousness and agency with this process transforming purposive-rationality at the system level and unleashing the *disembodying* forces that deform the corporeal transactions of the life-world. Thus, the colonization of the life-world by these system forces serves to severely restrict the possibilities for terminating the indeterminacies of the body. This can be seen in the styles of body usage that emerge within the life-world under the influence of the colonization process – the disciplined, mirroring, and dominating bodies mentioned above – each of which terminates corporeal contingency in a narrow way consistent with system demands in the spheres of production, consumption, and interaction.

Standing in opposition to these unidimensional, narrowly defined body styles, however, is an embodied practice that expands the range of possible terminations of corporeal contingency, a practice that emerges as a direct consequence of the new willingness to embrace risk. Voluntary risk-taking assumes special significance in the late modern context as increasing numbers of people develop a sense of their capacities to manage risky situations and are increasingly drawn to the risk-taking experience. What they discover in this experience is a new way to achieve self-empowerment and transcendence. We assert that the voluntary risk-taking experience – or what can be termed as the "edgework" experience – is the key to understanding the distinctly late modern form of emancipation. Once again, the structure of our argument parallels Habermas' approach in TCA: in the same way that he sees the rationalization of communicative action creating the possibility for free and open communication within the ideal speech situation, we posit that the shaping of corporeal transaction by risk consciousness/action generates the possibility for free agency within the edgework experience. Thus, while Habermas' approach to emancipation focuses on "speech acts," ours is concerned with "embodied experience"; and while his analytical reference point and political objective is "free communication," ours accords with the existentialist emphasis on "free agency." As we will see next, examining the nature of edgework activities as an expression of risk consciousness/action within the life-world will reveal how free agency is achieved through a form of self- and hermeneutic reflexivity that can only be experienced at the edge.

Edgework and the will to power

The concept of edgework applies to voluntary risk-taking behavior in various domains of social life, including extreme sports,[48] dangerous occupations,[49] high-risk finance,[50] and even certain forms of street crime.[51] By highlighting the significance of a consequential edge or boundary condition in extreme risk taking, the edgework concept can account for the distinctive experiential characteristics of many high-risk endeavors. Researchers have paid particular attention to the sensual pleasures and aesthetic arousal experienced by edgework participants. In all such activities, one confronts an "other-world" experience consisting of time and space implosions, where time passes either much faster or slower than normal, and spatial boundaries collapse as the edge is approached. This gives a "hyper-real" quality to edgework activities, which are experienced as more "authentic" than everyday reality. The feelings of authenticity are accompanied by a sense that the experience is ineffable – words cannot adequately describe what it's like to negotiate the edge.

Edgework typically produces a sense of self-determination or self-actualization. The heightened sense of self represents another dimension of the "authentic" character of edgework experiences: in addition to confronting an exaggerated, transcendent reality, edgeworkers also experience a sense of self that they regard as their authentic or "true" self. They emphasize the innate capacity of their bodies to respond creatively, appropriately, immediately, and automatically in life-and-death conditions. Thus, edgework skills are regarded as non-cognitive and fully embodied in nature.[52]

The analytical power of the edgework idea derives from its usefulness for understanding the ontological foundations of the unusual experiential patterns described here. The concept calls attention to the importance of consequential "edges" or "boundaries" in the emergence of these powerful sensations and perceptions. As revealed in the work of well-known social theorists like Victor Turner, Michel Foucault, and Gilles Deleuze,[53] approaching, managing, and crossing edges or "limits," in the context of either collective ritual or private exploration, often generate powerful experiences that may include instances of personal transcendence and transformation. Also, as indicated by Lyng, edgework sensations and perceptions become more intense as they move closer to the critical line between order and disorder. Consequently, participants in high-risk endeavors often try to get as close to the edge as possible without actually crossing it.[54]

In a recent effort to orient edgework to the risk-society model, Lyng suggests that the edgework experience may represent a special form of reflexivity.[55] Lash points out that Beck and Giddens conceptualize reflexivity in terms of what can be called "structural" and "self" reflexivity.[56] Structural reflexivity is best understood as "agency, set free from the constraints of social structure, [which] then reflects on the 'rules' and 'resources' of such structure." By contrast, self-reflexivity designates a reflexive subject who makes an object of itself – "agency reflect[ing] on itself" in the form of self-monitoring and self-construction. While both forms of reflexivity distinguish Giddens' "new social universe of action and experience" dominated by uncertainty and risk, reflexivity in edgework is achieved at a much deeper level than the reflexive processes described by Beck and Giddens. The distinctive edgework perceptions and sensations described above are consequences of a type of "hermeneutic reflexivity"[57] attained by those who venture close to the edge in high-risk activities. Hermeneutic reflexivity refers to deep perception that extends well beyond structural "rules and resources" and focuses on the nature of reality itself – the socially constructed categories of time and space normally taken for granted in people's everyday experience.

An identical claim can be made for self-reflexivity as a dimension of anarchistic experience at the edge. Lash's summary of Beck and Giddens' work on self-reflexivity focuses on the historical shift from "heteronomous monitoring of agents" engaged in role performance to the self-monitoring or "autonomous monitoring of life narratives and love relationships."[58] However, when we turn to the experience of self in edgework activities, we confront a form of self-reflexivity that involves much more than the autonomous monitoring of life narratives. The feelings of "self-determination" and "self-actualization" reported by edgeworkers point to a sense of self that cannot be consigned to a narrative structure. Actors experience agency in edgework as fully embodied and ineffable; and the self is empowered through externalization of previously undiscovered human capacities. Self-reflexivity in edgework is perhaps best captured by Michel Foucault's description of the "limit experience," which closely resembles edgework in most respects.[59] As Foucault describes it, this experience represents a form of self-creation, an "act of liberation" involving "work carried out on ourselves by ourselves as free beings."[60]

By integrating the concept of edgework with ideas borrowed from pragmatism and the risk society perspective as part of the TCT reformulation of Habermasian critical theory, it is now possible to envision the nature of emancipation in the late modern context. As risk consciousness and agency transform the system and life-world in the transition from first to second modernity, edgework emerges as a special zone of corporeal transaction where one experiences free agency in the form of self- and hermeneutic reflexivity. In the process of negotiating consequential edges, one's spontaneous embodied (trans)actions are separated not only from existing institutional structures, but also from existing self-definitions and the cultural "consentient set" employed in the social construction of reality. All of the distinctive sensations and perceptions of the edgework experience arise in this "space outside of culture" that individuals enter as they approach the edge. Alterations in the perception of time and space, the sense of mental control over environmental objects, and the ineffable nature of the experience are all due to the annihilation of the social mind and immediate projection of a contingent body into the flow of action. As edgeworkers "body forth" in responding to the threat at hand, they experience the indeterminacy of the natural world in completely novel ways – "terminating indeterminacy" in ways that breach the cultural consentient set with which they normally construct reality. They discover "authentic" selves rooted in the objective uncertainty of their bodies and an alternative reality in which culturally defined time and space distinctions are dissolved and reconstructed.

What is revealed in the experience of self- and hermeneutic reflexivity at the edge is a form of liberation particularly attuned to the existentialist themes discussed above. While not all edgeworkers are proto-existentialists in search of meaningful experience, it is entirely plausible that the power of the edgework reality inspires a deep appreciation of "freedom" in the existentialist sense. To be set free from the social and cultural constraints involved in everyday problem solving and achieve direct personal author-ship of one's actions in edgework involves the singular experience of moving beyond the "facticity" of normal social existence. Thus, the sense of self-determination and authentic reality reported by edgeworkers arises through the kind of transcendent experience that existentialists see as the antidote to complacent absorption in society. As a profoundly emotional experience that involves embodied reflex rather than cognitive reflection, edgework offers deep insight into the conditions of our personal and collective existence.

But, to fully understand the edgework experience, we must also take account of the overriding sense of empowerment involved in negotiating the edge. Thus, by "going beyond" what they presently are, edgeworkers exhibit the quality that Nietzsche termed the "will to power." They are drawn to the edge because it is the place where they can explore what Hunter S. Thompson has referred to as the "place of definitions."[61] In this sense, edgeworkers are akin to Nietzsche's "free spirits" or "overmen" who seek that which is "to be overcome." They are commit-ted to the pursuit of spontaneous and creative action "in which the only goals are self-expansion, the multiplication of perspectives, and the ceaseless drive to overcome everything that has come to seem 'self-evident' and beyond dispute."[62]

Ultimate Fighting as edgework

Having presented a rather complex conceptual framework for understand-ing the nature of risk, reflexivity, and freedom in the contemporary social order, we now demonstrate the empirical relevance of our abstract analysis by discussing data from an ongoing field study of a distinctive form of vol-untary risk taking – the sport of Ultimate Fighting.[63] Our decision to focus on this newly evolving high-risk sport as an illustration of the theoretical idea presented in this chapter reflects two basic concerns. First, we believe that this illustrative material will offer important insights about the role of violence, domination, risk taking, and existential transcendence in the violent encounters that characterize certain forms of street crime. To be sure, Ultimate Fighting is not a criminal enterprise, but we believe that this activity incorporates many of the same experiential dynamics found in violent street crime, elements of the phenomenological "foreground"[64] accessible only through an embodied emersion in the experience. For obvious ethical reasons, participant observation is problematic as a method for studying violent street criminals. Consequently, our ethnogra-phy of Ultimate Fighting seeks to uncover some of the embodied social forces operating in violent criminal acts without actually crossing the line into criminality.

A second consideration in choosing to focus on Ultimate Fighting relates to the existentialist themes of this chapter. Among the important implications of the conceptual framework developed here, one will likely strike many readers as particularly troubling – the idea that some violent criminal events may be experienced by perpetrators as acts of liberation in the existentialist sense. This issue is discussed in more detail below, but we want to emphasize at this point the importance of separating the moral dimensions of liberating experiences from the structural and sensual dynamics that give rise to such experiences. Although Ultimate Fighting is not a morally neutral enterprise, it is less suffused with moral considerations (relating to issues of consent, legality, etc.) than violent street crime is. Thus, we can better ensure that the moral dimensions of violent encounters do not cloud the analysis of the existential consequences of these encounters by using Ultimate Fighting to illustrate our theoretical ideas.

What can be seen in our interview and participant observational data on Ultimate Fighting is an edgework project that can best be described as the quintessential late modern sport. Expressed in terms of the conceptual categories of our analytical framework, Ultimate Fighting involves corporeal transactions within the life-world that have been organized around the subcultural appropriation of colonized body styles and the active embrace of risk consciousness and agency. Although we will restrict the discussion here to the dominating and disciplined bodies, all three of the colonized body styles discussed above have been creatively combined within the subculture of Ultimate Fighters for the purpose of doing edgework. And, as with other forms of edgework, fighters discover opportunities for self and experiential transcendence at the edge that continues to draw them to this zone of hermeneutic reflexivity.

Contingency and indeterminacy in No Holds Barred (NHB) fighting

Because of the indeterminate nature of the sport itself and the multiple ways in which participants have broken with the traditions of old paradigms of fighting, NHB fighting can be described as "liquid" in the sense of Bauman's concept of "liquid modernity."[65] As Bauman observes,

> [W]hat is happening at present is … a redistribution and reallocation of modernity's "melting powers."… Configurations, constellations, patterns of dependency and interaction were all thrown into the melting pot to be subsequently recast and refashioned; this [is] the "breaking the mould" phase in the history of the inherently transgressive, boundary breaking, all eroding modernity.[66]

The refashioning of fighting arts, some of which have been around for hundreds (if not thousands) of years has created a sport that is largely open-ended. It is a sport where an infinite number of solutions may be applied to an infinite number of problem sets. For example, there are currently hundreds of books explaining the various permutations of submission holds, counters, and counters to counters.[67] To the uninitiated viewer, NHB matches have been described as "free for alls," or brawls without rules. To dismiss such contests as battles between unskilled athletes, however, would be a serious misrepresentation of events. NHB fighters are trained specifically in multiple forms of martial arts, taking the most effective techniques and blending them together in unique ways. NHB fights are paradoxical in nature – they are chaotic and wild events in which emergent creativity on the part of participants creates order *and* chaos.

For fighters and fans alike, the chaotic and often unpredictable nature of NHB fighting provides much of the allure. Many fighters cultivate what Katz has termed "the ways of the badass" by creating a world of violence and projecting an aura of uncertainty, akin to an animal that is not quite tamed.[68] This characteristic is typified in the self-reflection of one fighter in our study who described himself as "fighting like a cat in a bag." Because of the relative lack of rules and boundaries within the sport, there are simply too many ways in which someone can win or lose a fight. Fighters, then, must be able to both deal effectively with a potentially very chaotic environment and to simultaneously create one when the opportunity arises.

NHB fighters are like other edgeworkers in that they do not seek an experience where they are entirely out of control. The calculated production of uncertainty and the calculated engagement of risk nurture a sense of possible and future selves (e.g. the path to self-awareness, discovery, etc.). Thus, NHB edgeworkers seek to find limits without transgressing them and to avoid crossing into the abyss of chaos where they are no longer in control. They see Ultimate Fighting as a kind of chess game. Chess is a highly complex game involving more calculations of possible moves than any one human can imagine. Illustrating this, an NHB fighter in an interview with *Sports Illustrated* suggested that NHB fighting is "a kinetic chess kind of thing."[69] This analogy to chess is a common theme among the fighters in our study.

As participants in edgework, NHB fighters are preoccupied with their competency in fighting from a variety of positions (i.e. standing, on the ground, in the clinch), maintaining their stamina in a fight, and their ability to end a fight. Since published research on NHB fighting is presently non-existent, we draw upon the research on boxers as a point of comparison. Like boxers, NHB fighters must also have the skill to control a situation that verges on chaos – one that a "normal" person would find impossible to endure. Unlike boxers, however, NHB fighters must contend with a much larger set of threats to their own safety (e.g. kicks to the head, body and legs, submission attempts, take-downs, etc.). NHB fighters believe that the only way to control such uncertainty is to develop an embodied capacity to deal with many different fighting styles and situations. Lyng originally termed this as the "survival skill," wherein participants must master not only

> activity-specific skills but also a general ability to maintain control of a situation that verges on total chaos. It is this ability that edgeworkers believe most determines success or failure in negotiating the edge, and the chance to exercise this "survival skill" seems to be what they value most.[70]

Inherent in such edgework experiences are the sensations of "self-realization," "self-actualization," or "self-determination."[71] These sensations are evident in NHB fighters' descriptions of their activities. In their view, the experiences they have fighting are "pure" – success or failure depend on their ability to keep another person from beating them into submission or unconsciousness, or from breaking joints (while simultaneously attempting to do the same things to them). One such fighter expressed this idea well in a recent interview with *Sports Illustrated* when he said:

> [I]t seems like there are fewer and fewer opportunities to find out who you really are. With this combination of violence and discipline – brains and brawn, you have a hell of a way to find out. Same thing from the fan's perspective. There's no B.S. Two guys are stripped down. One wins, one loses. Where do you find that anymore?[72]

At the same time, NHB fighters, like other edgeworkers, "dislike placing themselves in threatening situations involving circumstances they cannot control."[73] Chief among these situations are sparring sessions in the days before a fight. Fighters must hone their skills while also avoiding injury. Fighters believe that among those things that may cause injury prior to a fight is sparring with a much less experienced opponent. Inexperienced sparring partners prove to be unacceptably risky in two ways. First, the more experienced fighter begins "over-thinking," not wanting to hurt the less-experienced sparring partner by going "full out." A second source of uncertainty is their sparring partner's lack of experience in throwing kicks, punches, and executing submission holds. In this way, uninitiated partners prove too risky in that they are likely to behave in erratic and unpredictable ways. This parallels Wacquant's observation that it is difficult for uninitiated boxers to spar with those who are more experienced. He writes of his first full-contact sparring session:

I hit the bull's eye, a straight right dead center in Butch's mullin. Instinctively, I almost say "sorry!" out loud to Butch – but it's impossible with my mouthpiece in. Jeez, I definitely don't have a boxer's mentality! *I feel vaguely guilty about having bopped him right in the schnoz, since I don't have any intention of hurting him. But mainly I fear his retaliation* [emphasis added].[74]

Indeed, it is common for the experienced fighter to react to such an offense by an inexperienced sparring partner by "lighting him up" (i.e. punishing him with kicks and punches) to re-establish his dominance. Occasionally, however, such attempts are mistakenly received as an invitation to increase the intensity of the sparring session, rather than decrease it. As Hoffman notes with boxers, there are normative structures that effective sparring partners must understand – chief among them not to seriously hurt one another.[75] If the partner is not conversant in the norms of sparring, then he may try to "win" the sparring session by increasing the level of intensity, which is exactly the wrong thing to do.

Unlike boxers, however, NHB fighters must contend with takedowns and submission attempts, both of which can cause injury if done incorrectly. Submission attempts that involve leverages to joints are particularly dangerous, as the margin between getting an opponent to "tapout"[76] and breaking bones or damaging ligaments is razor thin. More-experienced fighters understand how much pressure to apply to an elbow joint to get their partner to submit, while an inexperienced fighter does not. This fact makes sparring with inexperienced fighters a potentially risky proposition, and some of the advanced fighters refuse to spar with anyone who they believe to be so inexperienced as to be dangerous.

At the most basic level, however, the defining experience (and perhaps much of the allure) in NHB fighting is the encounter with a "resistant other" once they step into the ring. While training is used to manage the contingent nature of the resistant other, no amount of training will ever fully prepare a fighter for all of the possible things that may happen during a fight. Indeed, a fight, while constrained by rules, is also an emergent interaction between two participants, each of whom possesses both a reflexive consciousness and determinate body. Several of the inexperienced fighters in the gym we studied viewed their training as adequate preparation for a fight – having a distorted sense of not only themselves as prepared fighters, but also of the risks involved. Nevertheless, the only "test" of whether a fighter is ready is to actually fight, and so it was not uncommon for lower-level fighters to enter their first fight within a few months of serious training.

Fighters often experience humiliation and self-doubt after losing a fight in front of several thousand people, many of them who have come to watch them fight (one fighter in particular had sold over 50 tickets to his family and friends, only to be knocked out in the first round). Many inexperienced fighters never return to the ring (or gym) after suffering such defeat, suggesting that perhaps for some, the most serious risks may be to their egos. Such explorations between the ego and risk taking may prove to be fruitful in the future. However, given the relative inattention to the embodied nature of risk taking, we believe that exploring this dimension may help to advance our understanding of how the body is mobilized for an edgework project like Ultimate Fighting. This is the problem to which we now turn.

Appropriating the dominating and disciplined bodies

> When we invented fight club, Tyler and I, neither of us had ever been in a fight before. If you've never been in a fight, you wonder. About getting hurt, about what you're capable of doing against another man. I was the first guy Tyler ever felt safe enough to ask, and we were both drunk in a bar where no one would care so Tyler said, "I want you to do me a favor. I want you to hit me as hard as you can."
>
> (Chuck Palahniuk, *Fight Club*)

We have discussed how NHB fighting has emerged as an edgework practice in late modernity, incorporating the system's risk taking imperative and offering its participants a life-world experience of emancipation rooted in self- and hermeneutic reflexivity. When Ultimate Fighters report experiencing their "authentic selves" in NHB encounters, as they explore the limits of their physical, psychological, and spiritual abilities to cope with chaos in the cage, they reveal their engagement with a Nietzschean "will to power" actualized in their reflexive self-development. Intertwined with this sense of self-authenticity is the perception of an "authentic reality" found in the hermeneutic reflexivity that fighters experience at the edge. Thus, fighters are drawn into the NHB enterprise by the seductive nature of the edgework experience of reflexively reconstructing self and reality. However, while the voluntary embrace of risk and uncertainty is at the center of the NHB project, it is important to recognize that this project is undertaken within a life-world that has been colonized by the system, which is reflected in corporeal transactions of the mirroring, dominating, and disciplined bodies (only the latter two forms will be discussed here). Consequently, to adequately describe the NHB phenomenon, it is necessary to demonstrate how fighters have creatively appropriated the dominating and disciplined bodies in order to conduct this form of edgework.

The dominating body

To see domination as a key element of NHB fighting would seem to acknowledge the obvious since the primary goal of the sport is to "submit" one's opponent – that is, to force the opponent into state of helpless submission. However, a careful examination of the corporeal transactions associated with the dominating body reveals the more complex character of domination in Ultimate Fighting, particularly as it relates to the edgework problem of managing chaos. If overcoming corporeal contingency is the primary problem that social actors must address in the life-world, then the dominating body deals with this problem by "seek[ing] out contingency in others and constitut[ing] itself by overcoming other-contingency."[77] The dominating body uses corporeal contingency as a source of resistance to being dominated by the other. At the same time, this contingency can be a force used by one body to dominate another. Arthur Frank draws on the work of the German social theorist Klaus Theweleit in *Male Fantasies* to develop this idea.[78] Theweleit's analysis focused on the ways in which *Friekorps* soldiers projected their internal contingency onto others, "the need to dominate the other is a need to control the projection of the internal contingency which threatens them."[79]

Katz has explored similar processes at work among violent criminals, in what he describes as the previously mentioned "ways of the badass."[80] The badass projects an image of toughness and indifference to others, as well as the capacity for violence. The badass must present himself as willing and capable of instantaneously creating a "world of chaos" for the other. This contingent self is then thrust upon the other to dominate him. Lyng and Franks note the paradoxical nature of the dominating body, writing that,

> in dealing with his own corporeal contingency, the dominating body seeks and destroys other bodies that threaten contingency. However, in order to prevail in this project, the dominating body must draw on its own capacity for chaotic action to meet the unpredictable responses of its victims.[81]

In other words, the badass controls contingency – both his own and that of the other – by intentionally creating chaos. Given the contingent nature of NHB fighting, such a strategy of creating chaos may give one fighter an advantage over the other. Fighters often refer to this in terms of being "pulled from their comfort zone," or "being in someone else's world." Some fighters do this by "getting off first," which entails a very aggressive assault on the other, right from the beginning of the fight with a barrage of punches and kicks. In other instances we have seen fighters rush across the ring to "swarm" their opponent, grabbing them and slamming them on the mat before they can react. Such strategies draw on the very things they fear the most – uncertainty, unpredictability, and chaos.

The dominating body can also control contingency by literally dominating the opponent's body and ending the fight through a submission (tapout) or rending them unconscious (which may be done through choking or punching). Examples of such strategies include gaining what are known as dominant positions (i.e. a position that places the opponent in such a vulnerable state that he cannot respond, like placing their body weight on the opponent's chest, "mounting" them). Indeed, much of what fighters talk about strategically is controlling their opponent in order to finish the fight. An often-heard quote among fighters experienced in controlling the bodies of their opponents is "position before submission," which means that one should strive to achieve a dominant position with their opponent before either applying a submission hold (i.e. joint lock) or punches (e.g. "ground and pound").

However, some opponents are able to resist submissions, either through enduring a tremendous amount of pain (often suffering serious bone or ligament injury in the process), or escaping the hold. Indeed, we have witnessed fighters who have suffered dislocated joints – both in training and during fights. Some fighters refuse to "tap," which is generally viewed as an unwise decision since the risk of long-term, permanent injury is always prevalent. One fighter, addressing the issue of opponents who refuse to tapout, noted that he prefers to choke his opponents into submission. In his words, "some guys just won't tap, and I'm not gonna take a chance on some guy getting out of an armbar. If I choke him, either he taps or he goes to sleep [is rendered unconscious due to lack of blood flow to the brain]. Either way the fight is over."

In terms of our general theoretical framework, the key point to make about the role of the dominating body in NHB fighting is that it functions less as a motivational force in bringing individuals into the sport (although it can serve this function) and more of a resource for pursuing a special kind of edgework project that gives fighters access to a liberating experience. NHB fighters rarely take up the sport to fulfill a need to dominate others. Rather, the emphasis on domination is more often a challenge that must be met: are they capable of doing what is necessary to force another person to submit to their will? Can they deliver a punch and take a punch? Do they have the capacity to "go to the limit" in a violent encounter with a person whose limits are uncertain? Answering these kinds of questions is a critical part of the reflexive process of self-creation, of the act of liberation at the center of Foucault's "limit experience."[82]

The disciplined body

While the dominating body represents one colonized domain of corporeal transaction expropriated by Ultimate Fighters for doing edgework, another colonized body style appropriated for this purpose is the disciplined body. For NHB fighters, as with all edgeworkers, the body is a critical problem – bodies are capable of defying the wishes of the most forceful mind, creating increased risk for injury. Lyng and Franks define the disciplined body as

> the relationship between self-conscious intentions and a body that responds either predictably or unpredictably to these intentions. Thus, the primary issue of the disciplined self is coming to terms with the contingency of the body – overcoming the body's resistance (which derives from its contingency) to one's intentions.[83]

Wacquant (2004) has explored elements of this disciplined body in boxers, when he writes about the notion – often repeated by professional fighters – that if you are "thinking" you can't fight.[84] He has suggested that the schemata of the mind and body actually change through vigorous training. The body must also be trained to do those things that are counterintuitive.[85]

For example, when watching a fighter spar for the first time, it is common to see him run away from a barrage of punches, to forget to cover himself from the punches, turn his back to his opponent inviting a choke, or all three – despite all of his previous training. Inexperienced fighters also do this in the ring during real fights. It takes a tremendous amount of discipline to not do what is intuitive. In a live situation, there is no time to think about techniques – one must simply employ them. "Steve," an experienced fighter, describes the transformation that is necessary:

> there's a lot of things that go against your natural instincts, how to turn, where to turn, you know, what to do, so there's – that's something that you have to learn, to go against your natural instincts, you know there's a punch and you pull away, but you should roll into it, but yeah, there are some things you have to learn and that takes practice, to make it an instinct rather than a thought.

Another fighter suggested that what separates fighters is the ability of one fighter to persist in their efforts to control the opponent, "despite being smashed in the face" while doing it.

Fighters believe that the best way for movements to become instinctual is to train them through constant repetition, so much so that they no longer think at all – things become a matter of reaction. This parallels Wacquant's observations of boxers when he notes that the distinction between thought and action must be erased by the fighter:

> theoretical mastery is of little help so long as the move is not inscribed within one's bodily schema; and it is only after it has been assimilated by the body in and through endless physical drills, repeated ad nauseum that it becomes in turn fully intelligible to the intellect.[86]

The disciplined body, then, must become comfortable with "naturally and instinctively" doing things that seem counterintuitive at first blush. The subtle shift in weight, from one foot to another, moving toward an opponent to avoid getting hit, rather than away from him, and being comfortable fighting from one's back are all examples of this transformation that NHB fighters experience.

It is common to hear fighters tell one another that they are "thinking too much" and that they need to "let their hands fly" (which loosely translates into punch more often without thinking about specific combinations – to simply see the opening and react). Therefore, while NHB fighters are developing the disciplined body as a vehicle to control others and manage risk, they are also engaged in a project of self-control. The contingency of the corporeal body – both theirs and their opponent's – must be managed.

The question of why someone would engage in such a project may be answered – at least in part – by going back to the idea of self-discovery through edgework, and the desire of edgeworkers to find their own "truth." The corporeal body is yet another arena where such truth projects, self discovery, and self-actualization are undertaken. Sheridan observes that fighters

> train hard to win fights, so that no one will be able to dominate them, to damage them where they have been damaged – but in the end, they train hard to make themselves better. The test is necessary. It completes the training, and it changes you. Fighting is not just a manhood test; that is the surface. The depths are about knowledge and self-knowledge, a method of examining one's own life and motives. *For most people who take it seriously, fighting is much more about the self than the other* [emphasis added].[87]

In this sense, the disciplined body becomes the vehicle through which the fighter's journey of self-discovery travels. The disciplined body must be focused, well trained and controlled. "John," one of the fighters in our study, termed this process "conscious living," noting:

> you've got to keep a certain amount of discipline, you have to keep a certain amount of, I would almost say integrity because you don't want to go out there and just "oh I'm a fighter I'm tough" and start bar room brawling with everyone.

At the same time, the relationship between the body and mind is dialectical. The mind is capable of interfering with what the body needs to do, and the body can defy the desires of the mind. "Swimming in deep water" is a phrase that is used by many NHB fighters to describe the state at which the body becomes so physically exhausted that even the most simple movements become nearly impossible. Some fighters believe that the mind is capable of making the body do what it doesn't want to, even under such extreme conditions. The body, no matter how well conditioned, though, will eventually succumb to the laws of physiology at some point – lactic acid will increase to an intolerable level, preventing muscle movement, and oxygen deprivation will cause temporary paralysis – oxygen deprivation to the brain from a carotid artery choke will render the fighter unconscious. Herein lies the essential problem to be overcome: at the point at which the contingency of the corporeal body is expressed as paralysis and there is nobody there to help, NHB fighting is viewed by its participants as an ultimate test of the self.

Conclusions

Our goal in this chapter has been to introduce and illustrate a framework for linking together several strands of theoretical and philosophical thought that, we believe, assume special relevance in the present historical context of twenty-first century post-industrial society. By weaving together ideas borrowed from the risk society and edgework perspectives with elements of existentialist thought and rooting these ideas in the micro–macro theory of embodied transaction, we have attempted to demonstrate how the increasing prevalence of risk and uncertainty in the contemporary global system has become the source of both new threats to human well-being and new possibilities for human freedom. If our emphasis on risk consciousness and agency in late modernity is appropriate, then one could expect to find this curious mixture of danger and emancipation even in social domains where it is generally believed that these two possibilities cannot co-exist in any meaningful way. Our use of the framework presented here to theoretically interpret the new violent sport of NHB fighting was designed to provide some empirical support for this proposition. In concluding the chapter, we want to suggest a possible extension of this proposition by considering the implications of our interpretation of Ultimate Fighting for another unlikely pathway to liberating experience – the pursuit of violent street crime.

Although we lack the space here to systematically explore these implications, it is possible to identify the general outline of the argument to be constructed. As indicated in the discussion of our field data on Ultimate Fighting, there are strong empirical connections between our data and Jack Katz's phenomenologically based study of violent street crime.[88] Thus, it would make sense to extend the scope of our framework by using Katz's study as a starting point for an exploration of the major themes discussed in this chapter. One important theme is the problem of contextualizing the "foreground" elements of violent criminal events in terms of the structural dimensions of the risk society. Doing this would allow us to see risk and uncertainty as more prominent features of the experiential patterns Katz describes, at the level of both structure and agency. Moreover, by linking structure and agency in this way, the foreground elements emphasized by Katz can be theoretically organized in terms of the edgework concept and related to a broader range of risk taking activities, a connection that other scholars have made in previous research.[89] Most importantly, applying the edgework/risk society framework to Katz's phenomenology of violent crime yields a parsimonious micro–macro explanation of this type of crime, an explanation that gives attention to the powerful influence of the risk imperative in the late modern context.

Connecting Katz's work on street crime to the risk imperative of late modernity also makes it possible to orient his phenomenological framework more strongly to the existentialist themes of our analysis. To be sure, the influence of certain strands of existentialist thought – in particular, the work of Nietzsche – can be readily seen in Katz's analysis of crime, as reflected in his discussions of the "transcendence of chaos"[90] and related ideas. However, by examining the careers of violent street criminals against the background of the growing uncertainties produced by reflexive modernization, it is possible to see the "seductions of crime" arising out of the experiences of objective embodiment, self-creation, and authentic reality that contrast so dramatically with the "liquid" character of institutional flows within the social system. Paradoxically, these seductive qualities are the experiential consequences of an active embrace of risk calculation, which is the same calculus that has contributed to the increasing uncertainties of the system and the "death of the social." It is this paradox, brought into stark relief through our analysis of risk at the levels of both system and life-world, which opens up a critical theory agenda that is left implicit in Katz's work – for understandable reasons. However, we believe that critical criminologists and other social scientists must come to terms with the disturbing implications of a theoretical approach to crime that finds it impossible to clearly separate liberating experience and the violent victimization of others.

Finally, it is clear that Katz's phenomenology of violent crime also accords with the emphasis on embodiment and corporeal transaction in our theoretical framework. Katz's discussions of "the criminal hardman" and "ways of the badass" provide rich empirical support for our analysis of the role of the disciplined and dominating bodies in edgework projects devoted to violent exchanges. What our framework adds to Katz's analysis is the understanding that capacities for discipline and domination derive from body styles that violent edgeworkers expropriate, body styles that ultimately arise through system colonization of the life-world. This formulation is more in line with Katz's performative approach to issues of gender, ethnic, and criminal identity – the focus on "doing" these identities as opposed to "being" them. Moreover, we can see the expropriation of the disciplined and dominating bodies as another expression of an existentialist project devoted to the reformulation and refashioning of existing social forms for the purpose of self-expansion and transcendence.

The development of the branch of "existential criminology" we propose here will no doubt present us with many dilemmas and unanswered questions. However, it is time to begin the difficult task of addressing these concerns.

Notes

1 C. Palahniuk, *Fight Club*, New York: W.W. Norton & Company, 1996.
2 D. Fincher, *Fight Club*, 20th Century Fox, 1999.
3 U. Beck, A. Giddens, and S. Lash, *Reflexive Modernization: Politics, Tradition and Aesthetics in the Modern Social Order*, Stanford: Stanford University Press, 1994.
4 S. Lyng, "Edgework, risk, and uncertainty," in J. Zinn (ed.) *Social Theories of Risk and Uncertainty*, London: Blackwell Publishing, 2008, pp. 106–137.
5 C. Guignon and D. Pereboom, *Existentialism: Basic Writings*, Indianapolis: Hacket, 1995, p. 93.
6 U. Beck, *Risk Society: Towards a New Modernity*, Newbury Park: Sage Publications, 1992.
7 U. Beck, W. Bonss, and C. Lau, "The theory of reflexive modernization: problematic, hypotheses and research program," *Theory, Culture, and Society*, 2003, 20, 1–33.
8 S. Lash, "Reflexivity as non-linearity," *Theory, Culture, and Society*, 2003, 20, 49–57.
9 Although we employ Baudrillard's term "death of the social" in this analysis, our development of this idea departs in some important ways from Baudrillard's formulation, as revealed below.
10 Lash, op. cit., p. 51.
11 Ibid.
12 R. Antonio, "Nietzsche's antisociology: subjectified culture and the end of history," *American Journal of Sociology*, 1995, 101, 1–43.
13 Guignon and Pereboom, op. cit., p. 101.
14 Lash, op. cit., p. 51.
15 Lash, op. cit., p. 52.
16 See A. Giddens, "Living in a post-traditional society," in U. Beck, A. Giddens, and S. Lash (eds) *Reflexive Modernization: Politics, Tradition, and Aesthetics in the Modern Social Order*, Stanford: Stanford University Press, 1994, pp. 56–109; S. Lash, "Reflexivity and its doubles: structure, aesthetics, community," in U. Beck, A. Giddens, and S. Lash (eds) *Reflexive Modernization: Politics, Tradition, and Aesthetics in the Modern Social Order*, Stanford: Stanford University Press, 1994, pp. 110–173.
17 Lash, "Reflexivity as non-linearity," *Theory, Culture, and Society*, 20, 2003.
18 Lash, op. cit., p. 50.
19 Lash, op. cit., pp. 50–51.
20 M. Castells, *The Informational City*, Oxford: Blackwell, 1989.
21 Lash, op. cit., p. 49.
22 Lash, op. cit., p. 52.
23 K. Marx, *The Communist Manifesto*, New York: Monthly Review Press, 1964.

24 U. Beck and E. Beck-Gernsheim, *The Normal Chaos of Love*, Cambridge: Polity, 1995.
25 Giddens, op. cit.
26 Giddens, op. cit., p. 100.
27 Antonio, op. cit., p. 7.
28 Guignon and Pereboom, op. cit., p. 108.
29 Nietzsche, 1968a, 93–94, as quoted in Anotonio, op. cit., p. 9.
30 Antonio, op. cit., p. 9.
31 For empirical documentation of increasing demands on US workers, see L. Mishel, J. Bernstein, and J. Schmitt, *The State of Working America*, Ithaca, NY: Cornell University Press, 2005.
32 H. Marcuse, *One Dimensional Man: Studies in the Ideology of Advanced Industrial Society*, Boston: Beacon Press, 1964.
33 J. Habermas, *The Theory of Communicative Action. Volume 1, Reason and the Realization of Society*, Boston: Beacon, 1984; J. Habermas, *The Theory of Communicative Action. Volume 2, Life World and System: A Critique of Functionalist Reason*, Boston: Beacon, 1987.
34 S. Lyng and D. Franks, *Sociology and the Real World*, Lanham: Rowman & Littlefield, 2002; see also S. Lyng, "Crime, edgework, and corporeal transaction," *Theoretical Criminology*, 2004, 8, 359–375.
35 D. Shalin, "Critical theory and the pragmatist challenge," *American Journal of Sociology*, 1992, 98, 237–279; E. Halton, *Bereft of Reason*, Chicago: University of Chicago Press, 1995; R.J. Antonio and D. Kellner, "Communication, modernity, and democracy in Habermas and Dewey," *Symbolic Interaction*, 1992, 15, 154–163; H. Joas, "An underestimated alternative: America and the limits of 'critical theory'," *Symbolic Interaction*, 1992, 15, 261–275; and D. Sciulli, "Habermas, critical theory, and the relativistic predicament," *Symbolic Interaction*, 1992, 15, 299–313.
36 Shalin, op. cit., p. 254.
37 Lyng and Franks, op. cit., 2002.
38 J. Dewey, *Knowing and the Known*, Boston, MA: Beacon, 1949; see also M. Emirbayer, "Manifesto for a relational sociology," *American Journal of Sociology*, 1997, 103, 281–317; M. Emirbayer and A. Mische, "What is agency?," *American Journal of Sociology*, 1998, 103, 962–1023.
39 Shalin, op. cit., p. 258.
40 Habermas, op. cit., 1987, pp. 153–155.
41 A. Frank, "For a sociology of the body: an analytical review," in Mike Featherstone, Mike Hepworth, and Bryan S. Turner (eds) *The Body: Social Process and Cultural Theory*, London: Sage Publications, 1995, pp. 36–102.
42 S. Lash, "Reflexivity and its doubles: structure, aesthetics, community," in U. Beck, A. Giddens, and S. Lash (eds) *Reflexive Modernization: Politics, Tradition, and Aesthetics in the Modern Social Order*, Stanford: Stanford University Press, 1994, p. 111.
43 Habermas, op. cit., 1987, pp. 256–282.
44 J. Habermas, *Toward a Rational Society: Student Protest, Science, and Politics*, Boston: Beacon, 1970, p. 7.
45 U. Beck, "The reinvention of politics: towards a theory of reflexive modernization," in U. Beck, A. Giddens, and Scott Lash (eds) *Reflexive Modernization: Politics, Tradition, and Aesthetics in the Modern Social Order*, Stanford: Stanford University Press, 1994, p. 9.
46 Lash, op. cit., 1994, p. 140.

47 Lash, op. cit., 1994, p. 141.
48 J. Ferrell, D. Milovanovic, and S. Lyng, "Edgework, media practices, and the elongation of meaning," *Theoretical Criminology*, 2001, 5, 177–202.
49 J. Lois, "Gender and emotion management in the stages of edgework," in S. Lyng (ed.) *Edgework: The Sociology of Risk Taking*, New York: Routledge, 2005, pp. 177–152.
50 D. Zwick, "Where the action is: Internet stock trading as edgework," *Journal of Computer-Mediated Communication*, 2005, 11 (electronic file).
51 J. Katz, *Seductions of Crime*, New York: Basic Books, 1988; P. O'Malley and S. Mugford, "Crime, excitement, and modernity," in G. Barak (ed.) *Varieties of Criminology*, Westport: Praeger, 1994, pp. 189–211; W.J. Miller, "Adolescents on the edge: the sensual side of delinquency," in S. Lyng (ed.) *Edgework: The Sociology of Risk Taking*, New York: Routledge, 2005, pp. 153–171.
52 L. Wacquant, "The pugilistic point of view: how boxers think and feel about their trade," *Theory and Society*, 1995, 24, 489–535; Lyng, 2004, op. cit.
53 V. Turner, *The Ritual Process: Structure and Anti-Structure*, Chicago: Aldine Publishing Co., 1969; M. Foucault, *Discipline and Punish: The Birth of the Prison*, Middlesex: Penguin, 1977; see also J. Miller, *The Passion of Michel Foucault*, New York: Simon and Schuster, 1993; G. Deleuze, *Negotiations*, New York: Columbia University Press, 1995.
54 Lyng, S., "Edgework: a social psychological analysis of volunteer risk taking," *American Journal of Sociology*, 1990, 95, 851–886.
55 S. Lyng, "Risk-taking in sport: edgework and reflexive community," in K. Young and M. Atkinson (eds) *Tribal Play: Subcultural Journeys Through Sport*, New York: Elsevier Ltd, 2008, pp. 83–109.
56 Lash, op. cit., 1994, p. 115.
57 Lash, op. cit., 1994, pp. 165–168.
58 Lash, op. cit., 1994, p. 116.
59 See M. Foucault, "How an 'experience-book' is born," in R. Goldstein and J. Cascaito (trans.) *Remarks on Marx: Conversations with Duccio Trombadori*, New York, 1991. There are strong similarities between limit experience and edgework but also important differences. In limit experiences, the goal is movement *across* boundaries while in edgework the goal is to move *close to* boundaries without actually crossing them. Thus, limit experience is devoted to *transgression*, while edgework involves *transcendence*; see also S. Lyng, "Sociology at the edge: social theory and voluntary risk taking," in S. Lyng (ed.) *Edgework: The Sociology of Risk Taking*, New York: Routledge, 2005, pp. 17–49.
60 M. Foucault, *The Foucault Reader*, New York: Pantheon, 1984, p. 47.
61 H. Thompson, *Hell's Angels: A Strange and Terrible Saga*, New York: Ballantine, 1966.
62 Guignon and Pereboom, op. cit., p. 106.
63 Data for this chapter are part of an ongoing field study that began two years ago. The study has relied on participant observation as well as a series of semi-structured interviews with more than a dozen professional mixed martial arts fighters. Rather than a systematic analysis of our data, this section is designed to identify themes that are relevant to, and provide preliminary support for, the theoretical framework developed throughout the chapter.
64 J. Katz, op. cit., 1988.
65 Z. Bauman, *Liquid Modernity*, Malden: Blackwell, 2000.
66 Bauman, op. cit., p. 6.
67 One such example is the "arm lock" encyclopedia, which has step-by-step

demonstrations of 85 ways to employ an arm lock (which is a hyperextension of the elbow joint).

68 Katz, op. cit., 1988.
69 L. Wertheim, "The new main event," *Sports Illustrated*, May 28, 2007, p. 56.
70 Lyng, op. cit., 1990, p. 871.
71 Lyng, op. cit., 1990, p. 860.
72 Wertheim, op. cit., p. 60.
73 Lyng, op. cit., 1990, p. 862.
74 Wacquant, op. cit., 2004, p. 76.
75 S. Hoffman, "How to punch someone and stay friends: an inductive theory of simulation," *Sociological Theory*, 2006, 24, 170–193.
76 The term "tapout" is used among NHB fighters and other grapplers to signify submission. For example, if one fighter is choking the other, and the person being choked wants to submit, they do so by "tapping" their hand on their opponent. Many fighters will wait for the referee to intervene at this time, rather than simply letting their opponent go, so that there is no question whether he tapped out. If the submission hold is particularly tight, or the opponent doesn't tap soon enough, the margin for error is greatly reduced, and injuries often occur in such situations.
77 Lyng and Franks, op. cit., p. 129.
78 Frank, op. cit., 1995.
79 Theweleit, as cited in Lyng and Franks, op. cit., p. 130.
80 Katz, op. cit., 1988.
81 Lyng and Franks, op. cit., p. 131.
82 Foucault, op. cit., 1991.
83 Lyng and Franks, op. cit., p. 117.
84 Wacquant, op. cit., 2004.
85 Ibid.
86 Wacquant, op. cit., p. 69.
87 S. Sheridan, *A Fighter's Heart*, New York: Atlantic Monthly Press, 2007, p. 297.
88 Katz, op. cit., 1988.
89 O'Malley and Mugford, op. cit., 1994; Miller, op. cit., 2005; K. Hayward, *City Limits: Crime, Consumer Culture and the Urban Experience*, London: Cavendish Press, 2005.
90 Katz, op. cit., pp. 231–236.

Chapter 5

Scrounging
Time, space, and being*

Jeff Ferrell

Introduction

A few years ago I resigned a tenured professorship at a large state university and set out to see if I could survive on my own, sans salary, book contract, or research grant. Given my long-standing interest in recycling and second-hand living, I decided to become an urban street scrounger – a 'dumpster diver', in common American parlance. Adopting a way of life that was equal parts field research and free-form survival, I spent each day walking or riding my old bicycle around the city, digging through trash piles and trash bins, and then heading home to sort my take. As the days rolled by, I discovered that I could indeed live from what I scrounged; and while ultimately I did return to academia, I still continue to scrounge whenever I can, so seductive did I find the experience.

Among the seductions was urban scrounging's uncanny ability to undermine the existing order of things. As consumers set out yesterday's goods on the curb or discard them in the trash bin, and as scroungers explore these marginal accumulations, sorting and saving and reusing what they find there, consumers and scroungers alike cooperate to subvert all manner of neatly dualistic categories: commodity versus trash, public versus private, possession versus dispossession. Part of this subversion is transgressive; the daily, informal exchange of second-hand goods keeps the city's boundaries open, its situations porous and permeable, and in so doing erodes revanchist strategies for partitioning the city by social class and privilege. Other aspects of this subversive dynamic are economic. Operating as a far-flung underground economy, the 'empire of scrounge', as I came to call it, connects homeless scroungers, independent scrap haulers, scrap yards denizens, junk artists, and yard sale aficionados – and, more remarkably, exists as an underground economy that offers for many of them a lived alternative to the very consumer economy on whose discards it operates. As a practice of boundary transgression and economic independence, urban scrounging also subverts conventional legal categories; despite the stern efforts of legal and political authorities to criminalize it, scrounging continues to float somewhere between property theft and ecological salvation, social problem and celebrated self-reliance. And in each of these cases, I found, the subversive power of urban scrounging builds from its inherent humanity; as an ambiguous and largely autonomous human process, its ever-shifting meanings and slippery contexts erode the certainty of law, property, and commerce.

But for all that, my life as an urban scrounger, and my ongoing participation in urban scrounging since, have suggested to me some deeper subversions as well. I would call these subversions *existential*, since they seem to expose and undermine fundamental, everyday notions of existence, meaning, identity, and purpose. Similarly, these subversions might be distinguished from scrounging's economic and legal dynamics to the extent that they shape and reshape moments of *personal* experience – though, as we will see, this is not to say that they aren't soundly political and economic as well. In fact, it may well be that these existential subversions offer avenues into social issues, and insights into issues of crime and justice, as important as those routes more conventionally taken. Whatever their broader implications, though, these subversive understandings did in fact emerge for me as an accumulation of lived moments. Walking and bicycling mile after mile, scavenging curbside trash piles and diving dumpsters day after day, I came to realize that I was scrounging more than material artifacts. It seemed I was scrounging time and space. Or maybe I was scrounging myself.

Time

In the day-to-day process of scrounging by foot or bicycle, a distinct sort of pace emerges – and one that is distinctly different from the usual pace set by workday automotive commutes, office hours, and suburban mall shopping. The physiology of walking and the physics of a simple second-hand bicycle begin to set this pace; when utilized for scrounging, both move the body and the mind through urban space at a dawdler's velocity. Yet this slow, uncertain movement occurs by intention as well as by physical limitation; spotting a hidden dumpster and easing over to it, rolling up on a curbside trash pile, walking the street's gutters while looking for coins or aluminum cans or auto parts, the scrounger is well served by a pace geared to the slow process of noticing and investigating. Certainly the low-cost, do-it-yourself economy of walking or bicycling fits the cash-poor economy of urban scrounging – but in fact so does the attentive pace that these modes of transportation offer. Wandering a mile or so of street in an hour, rather than driving down that street at 60 miles an hour, offers the scrounger advantages of both time and money.

In my experience, another practical advantage accrues: the scrounger arriving by foot or bicycle presents less sense of threat or intrusion than does the scrounger arriving by pickup or car, and so elicits less concern and reaction on the part of home- or store-owners. On the other hand, in comparison to car travel, foot or bicycle scrounging certainly elicits more numerous informal interactions from other dawdlers, pedestrians, bicyclists, and hangers-out – and when these interactions occur, the pace of such scrounging slows further still. Engaged with the particulars of the urban environment, and all but certain to become engaged with the city's varied on-the-street citizenry, the scrounger moving about by foot or bike sets a slow rhythm punctuated by pause and interruption.

As the days of scrounging accumulate into weeks and months, the ongoing process of surviving off a world of found objects replicates this uncertain rhythm. The daily zigzag through streets and alleys slowly builds into a complex personal map of the city, an accretion of little understandings about situations, tendencies, and opportunities. Favorite trash bins emerge from repeated discoveries of useful items inside them; dangerous alleyways, aggressive homeowners, and fouled trash bins are remembered on the next ride, and avoided; routes known to yield particular types of scrap metal are replicated, if imperfectly, when needed. And even this slowly developing grid of street knowledge holds within it still other bits of lag time, other requisites of patience and pace. Big roll-away trash receptacles at a construction site contain clues as to the stage of the construction process, and so suggest a time for returning when the electricians and plumbers later arrive, with their discards of copper and brass. Thrown away in the street, beer cans still wet with warm beer and spittle are noted but not picked up, to be revisited instead when sufficiently compacted by car traffic and dried by the sun; the length of this lag time is in turn uncertain, contingent as it is on weather conditions and volume of street traffic. An office dumpster discovered at 2 p.m. suggests a safer return visit after the 5 p.m. departure of the office workers; in the meantime, curbside trash piles in a nearby neighborhood can be visited while homeowners are away at some identical office building elsewhere.

The dumpsters and trash bins themselves, and the items they contain, offer further moments that linger and loop back on themselves. Last Christmas' hot-selling, must-have toy is found baking in this year's overheated summer dumpster; a little lost Cupid figurine shows up in a trash pile on the ninth of April, two months after his holiday. Some juxtapositions of then and now are more immediate. One of the most commonly discovered is the old appliance – often a microwave oven or television – tossed in the trash bin along with the box and packaging from its newly purchased replacement. Other juxtapositions are of greater duration, and tragedy. As I discovered time and again, decades-old baby photos and college annuals, century-old diplomas and first-edition books are simply thrown away, and so left to intermingle in trash bags and trash bins with soiled diapers, greasy pizza boxes, and remodeling debris; in moments of family dissolution, the long cycle of birth and death catches up to the ever-shorter cycles of contemporary consumption and waste. As a scrounger, one's own life and the lives of others are indeed lived in lag time. Momentary or millennial, the delays emerge amidst the residues of past wants and aspirations, and always after the fact.

Yet my sense of living my scrounger's life in lag time took shape most sharply – though as always, slowly – as I developed a practical rhythm for utilizing my accumulations of scrounged items. The empire of scrounge, I found, offered most everything I needed for surviving outside a cash-based consumer economy – but it almost never offered it quickly or predictably. As the weeks and months rolled by, needed items were found, little problems solved, to-do lists crossed off, if only I had the patience to let the solutions emerge. The ability of the empire to provide, in time, the particulars of my daily life I found remarkable. A locking latch for the back window of the house, fencing for the back yard, an 11 mm wrench, some additional bins for scrap storage, a carrying bag for my bicycle's rear deck, another pair of sturdy shoes, a couch for the living room, a lamp to go with it – it was all there, not efficiently, but eventually. Whether attributable to the power of selective perception or the kindness of the universe, a needed item was more than once found as soon as I began to look for it; in other cases I would find, months later, the precise part that I had all but forgotten I needed. In the end, I never wanted – unless what I wanted was immediate resolution.

Supplementing this slow-paced process were the gradual dynamics of recuperation and conversion, as I learned through experimentation and hard-earned wisdom to put found objects and their constituent parts to a range of uses never intended nor imagined. A handcrafting process running in reverse, the ongoing use of a hacksaw, hammer, table vice, and pair of wire cutters to break down found items into usable components led also to emergent understandings of sorting and categorization, and so to a growing collection of bins for holding parts with similar uses. Like the thrift store and the flea market, I found, the dumpster and the trash bin teach – enforce, actually – patience and an openness to possibility for those who would employ them successfully.[1] Ultimately, it seems they teach a larger, leisurely lesson about life and the dynamics through which we live it: perhaps learning to wait, and to want what you eventually find, are as important as going out to find what you already want.

Of course, I could afford to learn this lesson, to follow this pace, precisely to the extent that scrounging allowed me to acquire necessary items without benefit of money. Not needing to convert my time into money by way of employment, and only occasionally looking to sell some of my scrounged goods, I was free to reverse the usual clichéd equation: if time is money, then little need for money means little need to rush. Recalling inquiries as to how he and his dumpster-diving, shoplifting friends could continue to survive without access to cash, the young author of the book *Evasion* explains something more of this reversal:

> 'Money?' they ask, the implication being that without money our system was flawed, incomplete. When in fact our lifestyle had stripped money of its value, reduced it to an inefficient and indirect means of acquiring what we just stole or pulled from the trash.[2]

And while we're deconstructing clichés, there's one more that came into focus during my time outside the consumer economy, during all those days of imagining new uses for found objects and the parts they yielded. It's true, I realized, necessity *is* the mother of invention; it's a hard-worked wellspring of personal creativity and innovation. But if so, wouldn't the opposite hold true of existence *within* contemporary consumer culture – that when nothing of yourself is needed, when everything is bought new and delivered complete, convenience becomes the mother of existential complacency?

As suggested by this question, and by these reversals of cultural truisms about time, money, and motivation, I found the temporal rhythms of urban scrounging to challenge understandings at the core of contemporary economy and existence. In fact, I would argue, scrounging's slow-paced dynamics – the dawdling movement through urban space, the lag time in encountering and utilizing the products of consumer culture, the inevitable procrastination in problem-solving, the looping non-linearity of then and now – collide head-on with contemporary cultural structures of efficiency, productivity, and personal satisfaction. After all, the mass consumer culture of late capitalism operates on twin schedules – an overdriven pace of a panicked daily life, and accelerating cycles of consumption and waste – that intertwine in the presumed "right" of the consumer to the immediate and efficient addressing of needs and desires. Drive-through lattes, high-speed Internet access, on-line bill paying, grocery express lanes, speeding tickets, sales that Must End Saturday – all coalesce into a consumer culture of perpetual panic intermingled with momentary, gulping gratification. From this view, scroungers and scavengers slowly making their way through the city and its trash piles aren't just bums because of their predilection for back alley trash or their inattention to fashion trends; they're *time bums*, unwilling or unable to keep pace with contemporary status and respectability.[3]

Except, of course, that this pace of contemporary status-acquisition is all a self-perpetuating fraud. An addiction to immediate gratification guarantees no lasting gratification at all, only an itch for the next quicker fix, an insatiable desire for the faster and the more efficient. Sold like so much crack cocaine, the corporate promise of greater convenience persuades the consumer to perceive today as an unbearable inconvenience, and to pay for tomorrow's imagined resolutions. As the pace of this cycle accelerates, and feeds off existing patterns of hyper-consumption, a sort of binge-and-purge panic emerges, a consumptive bulimia; consumers purchase products mostly for the immediate pleasure of doing so, then return them for a refund and repeat the cycle – or, as I regularly discovered while scrounging their dumpsters, choose a more convenient and efficient solution, tossing them into the trash, unopened and unneeded.[4] In the process of offering a temporal alternative to consumer culture, it turns out, scrounging serves also to excavate consumerism's fast-accumulating temporal ruins.

And it is here, in the realms of individual experience and social relations alike, that we can begin to understand urban scrounging as temporal subversion – to understand that the alternative way of life that urban scrounging offers, the critique of consumer society that it provides, are as much temporal as they are practical and economic. If the plethora of purchased items scrounged from contemporary trash piles reveals something of consumer society's wasting of human and planetary potential, so does the pace with which they have arrived there. Likewise, if scrounging can be differentiated from corporate employment by degrees of autonomy and self-sufficiency, it can also be distinguished by orientations toward time and temporal efficiency. As I discovered, to become an urban scrounger is to feel, over time, the tight-wound panic of late modernity begin to unravel. To dawdle from dumpster to dumpster as cars and commuters whiz by, to forego a fast trip to the store for the slow solutions offered by chance and accumulation, is to undermine in some small way the temporal foundations of the social order. Chris Carlsson characterizes bicycling, or more specifically the choice to bicycle rather than to purchase and operate an automobile, as 'an act of desertion from an entire web of exploitative and demeaning activities, behaviors that impoverish the human experience and degrade planetary ecology itself.'[5] If so, then slow-paced bicycle scrounging would seem a sort of double desertion, a withdrawal from both time and money.

Significantly, it seems to me, temporal desertions, transgressions, and subversions of this sort are hardly confined to the world of scrounging. During my years in the hip-hop graffiti underground I discovered a sense of time as aggressively unconventional as the sense of art; the graffiti artists resolutely and proudly refused to be bound by the straight world's norms of temporal propriety.[6] Residing in an inner-city neighborhood in Denver, I watched working-class Latino street cruisers and low riders commit the legal offense of driving too slowly, not too fast. Living for a while in Arizona, I listened time and again to Anglos honking and complaining while stuck behind slow-moving Navajo and Hopi drivers – and watched those Navajo and Hopi drivers maintain that same slow, steady pace in response. Beyond this, food activists have organized a 'slow foods' movement in response to the corporate peddling of 'fast food' – and anthropologists have documented the tyranny of the industrialized world's chronometric 'clock time' in contrast to longer and more leisurely temporal rhythms elsewhere in the world.[7] Time, it seems, is both cultural and political. A welter of laws and regulations is aimed at those who don't keep to the pace of the dominant culture, prodding them to move more quickly or efficiently – and a tissue of temporal resistance likewise connects them, defines them, as they go about living at the margins of the political order.

But if time is cultural and political, it is also personal, even existential; as we organize time, so it organizes and defines the frameworks within which we live. The accelerated pace of contemporary consumption incorporates not only the consumer's illusory right to immediate gratification, but also a sense of personal status derived from the control of time and the on-demand domination of goods and services.[8] In this sense, while the ideology of consumerism certainly defines identity in terms of successful goods acquisition, it also defines identity in terms of *control*: control of time, of pleasure, of the world and our existence in it. An existential embracing of materialism, contemporary consumerism is equally an existential affirmation of domination and control. In contrast, a practice like urban scrounging, in abandoning the accelerated pace of consumerism, at the same time forfeits temporal control over the world of material goods, instead encountering and utilizing them as they come and go. To scrounge, then, is to in some way desert time, money, control – and one's own identity, to the extent that one's identity has developed as an internalized machinery of the dominant consumer culture. Dare I say, it is to embrace a sort of Zen, a Zen of scrounging, an existential sense of not wanting what one doesn't have, a humility and patience in waiting for possibilities to emerge outside one's own control.[9] It is to develop an existential orientation that gently subverts the temporal foundations of consumer culture. After all, riding the slow, rhythmic currents of their own lives, scroungers find, amidst all that consumer trash, an existential calm that others can't.

Space

As already seen, scrounging's leisurely pace allows for a slow accretion of everyday understandings as to the dangers and opportunities offered by the city's trash. While these understandings may over time develop into dislocated insights about people and their disposal habits, in the day-to-day process of scrounging they remain situated firmly in the particulars of urban space. To be an urban scrounger, I found, is not to mine the city as an undifferentiated stockpile of discarded consumer goods, but rather to encounter the city as a series of spaces and situations, each requiring on-the-spot evaluation and negotiation. Successful scrounging of course involves a daily search for discarded items; as much so, though, it necessitates a daily search for spatial arrangements, an ability to discover situations and make sense of potential linkages between them. In this way much of the daily process of scrounging becomes a process of *mapping*, a fluid task of interpreting and coordinating the spatial possibilities offered by the city and its trash.

The scrounger maps the city as a series of subdivisions, telescoping in from broad spatial understandings to small details of street and alley. As a daily scrounger I came to understand particular sorts of neighborhood boundaries – those defined by trash pick-up and dumpster-emptying schedules, for example, and by the limits of bicycle or pedestrian accessibility. In turn I created a set of roughly defined bicycle routes within and across these neighborhoods, often coordinating these routes with city trash-collection schedules, at other times varying them with particular needs or integrating them with other errands to be run by bicycle. But riding these routes day after day was never as simple as following a predetermined time and path – nor was it meant to be. Routes were designed in part to take me by as many intersecting cross-streets as possible, so that in looking down these cross-streets as I rolled along, I could spot and evaluate the maximum number of curbside trash piles, dumpsters, and trash bins. Depending on what was spotted, of course, the street and the route necessarily changed.

No matter what the street, though, smaller mappings also emerged. I learned to look for little triangular islands of street debris, created by the patterned movement of automobile tires through intersections; such islands often held lead weights, small auto parts, and coins. (Dawdling along so as to catch a red light affords time to examine such islands.) I came to pay special attention to the pavement as I passed large potholes or speed bumps; their concussive possibilities sometimes jar loose a lead wheel weight or dislodge a tool from the back of a service truck. In fact, such a tool found in the street merits continuation down that same street for awhile, even if not initially intended; more than once a first discovery led to others, sequentially, apparently the result of tools bouncing out of an unsecured tool box block after block.[10] On the other hand, tire store lots offer not sequentiality but concentration, a mother lode for all those lead tire weights, with thousands used each day to balance car wheels as they are fitted with new tires. If, upon cycling up after closing time, the dealer's lot remains dirty from the day's work, lost and discarded weights will be found scattered around the lot and in front of tire changing bays; if clean, they're likely to have been swept into a pile near a dumpster or washed together into a gutter.

In parallel parking spots along streets, or in parking lot parking spaces, I likewise learned to look for coins (valuable in their own right) and keys (valuable because made of brass) – especially on the driver's door side of the parking space, or near park-and-pay kiosks. My larger mapping of lost coins, keys, and other valuables integrated time, space, and direction. Reinventing a trick I learned over the years in searching for glass marbles and glass insulators along railroad tracks, I paid special attention to the pavement while biking east into the morning sun or, more often, west into the afternoon sun. Equipped with a good pair of scrounged sunglasses – a large supply of which I always had on hand – I could use the sun's reflection to show me coins, jewelry, and other bits of shiny value. So effective was this technique, in fact, that I often changed course, at least temporarily, so as to traverse a parking lot or ride a street directly into the sun. And while we're on the pavement, I should mention one further spatial contingency: pausing to pick up a lead weight or a sunlit coin I found to be far more appealing when bicycling a flat street or parking lot than when flying down a big hill or grinding my way up it. On a bicycle, momentum is a terrible thing to waste.

Stopping to investigate a curbside trash pile or an alley dumpster, a new sort of mapping would begin – a careful calibration of space measured not in feet or yards, but in the potential for unpleasantness and interruption. In fact, as a scrounger I developed a keen sensibility for nearness and juxtaposition – or perhaps more accurately, resurrected the same sort of sensibility that I earlier acquired as an alley-wandering graffiti writer.[11] I learned to avoid curbside trash piles or alley dumpsters situated too close to parked cars – especially expensive parked cars – lest the owner misread my presence as a precursor to stereo removal or auto theft. Likewise I learned to check the proximity of a business's back door to its dumpster, and to look for windows from which someone might disapprovingly discover me in the trash pile. Forgetting this precaution in one case, too eager to investigate a full dumpster situated between a small business and an apartment building, I was startled by a voice from above, by what at first seemed the voice of some redneck deity: 'Leave that alone! I'm fixin' to bring that up here.' Thankfully, as it turned out, the guy in the second floor apartment just wanted the dumpstered piece of furniture whose knobs and handles I was at that moment removing. As a researcher, I valued the insights offered by human interaction; as a scrounger, living off what I found, I learned how to be left alone when needed.

Moving in this way from the broad boundaries of neighborhood access to the minutiae of pot holes and alleyway arrangements, scrounging created for me an idiosyncratic map of urban possibility. In a real sense this map became my method. Some 40 years ago, in fact, certain sociologists began to talk about this sort of phenomenon in terms of 'ethnomethodology' – that is, the practical, situated method by which people and groups construct the reality of their daily existence. Exploring what Harold Garfinkel called the 'constitutive phenomenology of the world of everyday life,' ethnomethodologists attempted to document the small, often unnoticed practices through which people make sense of, or 'accomplish,' their lives.[12] Though this documentary work could at times led ethnomethodologists to efflorescences of excruciating detail, it did offer one profoundly humanistic insight: all of us – dirt farmers, drug users, school kids, sex workers, janitors, musicians, scroungers – develop and utilize intricate, elaborately nuanced methods for negotiating the contingencies of our everyday lives. And another important thing about this perspective, by the way: conventional hierarchies of the learned and the ignorant, the accomplished and the incompetent, can't hold. As Hugh Mehan and Houston Wood put it, all sorts of folks develop "elegant knowledge" of their own lives and situations, knowledge saturated with "intricacies and sophistication."[13]

Urban scroungers do indeed develop sophisticated methods out of their practical, experiential engagement with the urban environment. Close and quick determinations of on-the-spot street value, subtle interpersonal negotiations of possession and dispossession, innovative applications and material reinventions make up these methods – and so do the intricate reconstructions of time and space by which scroungers learn to salvage from the city all they can. Recalibrating consumer time, remapping the city's spaces, urban scroungers invent a way of life that is extraordinary in its accomplished everyday practicality.

And yet, for all their practicality, these methods are surely subversive as well. It's not just that scroungers' everyday methods lead them into confrontations with legality, into moments of trespass or accusations of theft, as they work their way through the city on their own terms. It's that their methods subvert and reinvent the city itself. For just as scrounging's dawdling pace serves to undermine consumer culture's temporal foundations, its peripatetic remapping of the city begins to unravel official forms of spatial organization.

The practice of subversively remapping urban space is of course hardly the province of scroungers alone; others have also noted, and participated in, its transformative power. The long-standing tradition of the urban *flâneur*, for example – the unfettered individual walking the city's streets – has referenced for many not only a sort of endless urban wandering, but a special, perhaps subversive, sort of spatial knowledge. As Michael Keith puts it, the self-knowledge gained from the flâneur's negotiation of the city's streets becomes also a form of valuable social information, confronting 'the will to power implicit in the aerial view of the urban plan,' giving lie to 'the metanarrative certainties of the plan, the scheme, the totalizing view....'[14] Lost to the flow of the city's streets, the flâneur is in reality not lost at all, manufacturing instead an emergent, microscopic map of city life – a map that, in its slow-paced human engagement, subverts the gridded certitude and hurried efficiency of city planners, law enforcers, and corporate developers. And in this way the flâneur's map – like the scrounger's map always changing, always open to amendment – reconfigures the city itself, defining the city less by street numbers and property boundaries than by emergent human possibility.

Urban theorist Michel de Certeau saw in informal city life the possibility of this same subversive dynamic. For de Certeau, the city of the 'city planner or cartographer' was an aggressive abstraction, a totalizing arrangement of street grids, privately protected spaces, and legal regulations designed for efficiency, profit, and control. And yet, de Certeau argued, an irony emerges. The ongoing and inevitable flux of urban life within this bureaucratic city 'increasingly permits the re-emergence of the element that the urbanistic project excluded'; by occupying the city, by walking its streets and sidewalks, by moving around and with one another, the city's inhabitants unravel the certainty of the planned city. Those walking the city's crowded streets write a new story of the city, a new urban text, out of their interactions; they 'compose a manifold story that has neither author nor spectator, shaped out of fragments of trajectories and alterations of spaces.' In this way, urban dwellers don't simply occupy the spaces set up for them by city planners and legal authorities; they reconstruct them as they move through them on their own terms. Likewise, urban scroungers don't simply obey or disobey the law, trespass on private property or not; they reinvent the experiential meaning of such legal abstractions, they remap the city itself, as they go about their work. Walkers, scroungers, bicyclists, loiterers – all engage a sort of collective ethnomethod that subverts the mythology of the city as a place of planned and efficient control. Together, as de Certeau says, 'their intertwined paths give their shape to spaces.' They 'weave places together' in a way that the authorities, with their cost-per-square-foot coefficients and spatial controls, cannot.[15]

The peripatetic remappings undertaken by scroungers, walkers, and flâneurs suggest transformations that are at the same time existential and collective in nature, suggest everyday practices that merge peculiarities of individual method with accretions of urban transformation. And for still another group of urban inhabitants, this double transformation of self and city was not only a suggestion, but precisely the point – and the point was a 'revolution of everyday life.' The Situationists – a disreputable collection of left intellectuals, artists, and cultural dissidents – sought to overthrow the everyday banality of consumer society; their ideas became the spark for the 1968 student and worker revolts in France and the insurgent British punk culture of the 1970s, and continue to animate various urban and environmental movements today.[16] Revolutionists of everyday situations, saboteurs of taken-for-granted meanings and emotions, the Situationists were radicals who didn't bother with guns or bombs. Instead, they employed two weapons designed to shoot down assumptions and blow up common sense: *détournement* and the *dérive*. *Détournement* denoted a radical reversal of meaning, a subversive theft of understanding, such that the stultifying stability of everyday life might be disrupted. A corporate billboard transformed by graffiti into a call for revolt against corporations, a banal cartoon strip illicitly reprinted as a commentary on banality, a work of art made ugly, a religious situation made sacrilege – all might offer, the Situationists hoped, a healthy shock of social and existential uncertainty, perhaps even an unraveling of the social order.

In the particular context of urban scrounging and spatial subversion, though, it's the second Situationist strategy that is perhaps more instructive. The Situationists designed the *dérive* as a disorienting, drifting walk through the city, a bit of existential magic by which the vast, accumulated boredom of everyday street signs, office towers, and traffic grids might reappear as excitement and surprise. An abandonment of fixed coordinates, a discarding of the maps made by work and consumption and habit, the *dérive* offered at its best a shock of its own: a startled awakening from the somnambulant shuffle of everyday existence. In this way the *dérive* was meant to transform its participants and the city alike; as with the wanderings of the flâneur, it could invent new existential orientation out of personal disorientation, and sketch a new map of the city by annihilating the old.

Formulating in 1953 a Situationist 'new urbanism,' for example, Ivan Chtcheglov imagined a city that replaced 'frigid architecture' with 'changeable decors,' a city in which 'the main activity of the inhabitants will be *continuous drifting*. The changing of the landscapes from one hour to the next will result in total disorientation.'[17] Elaborating on the *dérive's* 'psychogeographical effects,' emphasizing the *dérive's* 'primarily urban character ... in the great industrially transformed cities – those centers of possibility and meaning,' Guy Debord a few years later offered a clarification uncanny in its similarity to the everyday practices of urban flâneurs and urban scroungers. The *dérive*, Debord argued, is not merely a matter of 'chance'; instead it is a 'letting-go' mixed with its opposite, the 'knowledge and calculation' of the city's otherwise unnoticed terrain.[18] The *dérive* is the cartography of possibility and surprise.

Now a half-century old, this notion of spatial subversion and reinvention continues to surface in a variety of venues. Groups like Critical Mass, a loose confederation of urban bicyclists, 'dis-organize' collective bike rides featuring emergent routes and destinations, alter the pace of urban traffic and urban life (often illegally) while slowly riding the city's streets, and in this way work to invent a new city, to 'live the way we wish it could be.'[19] Tracing their lineage to the Situationists and the tradition of the flâneur, contemporary psychogeographers use one city's map to navigate another, set off on 'algorithmic' walks defined by 'directions but no map,' and engage in 'reverse shoplifting' by surreptitiously placing objects on store shelves – all while promising that 'when you remake your environment, or find wonderful things in it, it breaks you out of the machine.'[20] Writing about her own experiences as a field researcher, anthropologist Stephanie Kane notes that 'powerful insight can arise out of walking down a street by mistake. Serendipity can realign data...' She goes on to argue that 'we may even be able to engineer incidents of mistaken identity' in order to develop new insights into 'social control and resistance.'[21] Wandering the country, living out of dumpsters, the author of *Evasion* offers a similar insight. 'I always secretly looked forward to nothing going as planned,' he says. 'That way, I wasn't limited by my imagination. That way anything can, and always did, happen.'[22]

Wandering the streets of Fort Worth, this is what I looked forward to as well, and what I found. Engaged in intensely practical activity – mapping the city on my own terms so as to scrounge enough goods to get by – I reinvented the city as a place of subversion and surprise. The conventional map of the city was reversed, read backwards, *détourned*, as I went about my work. I followed provisional routes made up of back alleys more than major thoroughfares. I looked not for the best of situations but waited to find the worst, aiming not for tourist attractions and symbols of civic pride but for demolition sites, accumulations of trash, and the residues of broken relationships. I came to appreciate stores and strip malls not by their bright signage and display windows but by the depth and quality of their back-lot dumpsters. I judged the desirability of neighborhoods not by housing prices and school standards but by the quantity and value of curbside trash. Adopting a back alley slouch, timing my travels to arrive not at events but at their aftermath, I found myself rearranging the city as I moved through it.

Out of this *détourning* of the city's meanings, out of this scrounger's *dérive* through its forgotten spaces, there emerged a vast landscape of possibility. Working the spatial margins of consumer society, reading the city in reverse, I found that anything was possible, so long as I didn't expect it. Culture, history, meaning collided in a series of absurd juxtapositions, by turns tragic and funny, and always surprising. Antique door knobs on top of cheap microwave ovens, lag bolts left lying next to discarded lipstick, copper wire piled on a pretty overstuffed sofa – every dumpster, every trash pile offered an implosion of oddball surprises. Once, scaling a huge roll-away, then climbing down deep inside it, working my way underneath a ton of remodeling debris in search of copper and brass, I found a little antique green and white bowl, unbroken, unchipped even, resting in a small pocket accidentally formed by the tossed-in cross-layering of lumber and sheetrock panels. Other times it was a shiny camera found at the bottom of a dirty trash bin, foreign currency discovered inside a purse inside a garbage bag underneath a trash pile, 1950s baby doll shoes buried beneath a pile of furniture, still fresh in their little pink and white boxes – and of course the everyday chance encounters with homeowners, homeless folks, and others.

In an urban environment increasingly subject to close surveillance and legal control, I found myself salvaging surprise and adventure as surely as consumer discards. The tyranny of the ordinary, the tight circuitry of the city's legal and spatial control, fell away as the process of scrounging reversed everyday meanings and transformed ordinary situations into extraordinary events. As with the Situationists, this little revolution of everyday life didn't require bombs or guns – only spatial subversion. Its excitement didn't flow from a fast motorcycle or new sports car, but from the slow pedaling of an old bicycle; its endless surprises didn't come from consuming the latest product innovations, but from sorting through yesterday's consumer discards. Drifting from situation to situation, mapping the spaces between one moment and the next, I found I could escape the banality of the consumer city not by running away from it, but by losing myself in it, and so overturning it.

In fact, this realization paralleled a practical one, and together the two drew me deeper and deeper into scrounging: in the same way that urban scrounging offered all the tools and clothes I needed to remain functionally self-sufficient, it offered all the excitement and surprise I needed to remain existentially alive. By conventional terms of bureaucratic planning or commercial success, each day of scrounging was an accident, an impossibility – and a dirty one at that. And yet, for me, scrounging came to constitute a seductive sort of existential and urban magic, like the *dérive* a trick of meaning and experience that could transform the same old city into the 'breathtakingly beautiful wasteland' that Raoul Vaneigem and the Situationists imagined.[23]

Come to think of it, maybe this magic trick – this transmogrification of urban banality into situations of uncertainty and surprise – explains something of crime's broader existential seductions as well.[24] Burglars, street racers, skate punks, graffiti writers, gang members – all read the everyday functionality and legality of the city in reverse, remaking the urban grid in their own image and animating it with their own illicit desires. In their worlds the most common of urban spaces – freeway on-ramps, stairwells, alleys and alley walls, front stoops and back doors – are reimagined as illegal staging areas, entry points, escape routes. As with urban scrounging, these remappings are of course practical matters essential to the success of criminal enterprise or illicit activity. But these remappings are also epistemic, and emotional; their alteration of the city can be measured not just in broken locks and spray-painted walls, but in the illicit illumination of urban life for those involved. Moving through the city, casing houses or grinding handrails, the city's outsiders rewrite its everyday geography into a map of alternative meaning, a shifting grid of illicit danger and existential excitement.

The geographer Edward Soja has called for 'a more flexible and balanced critical theory that re-entwines the making of history with the social production of space, with the construction and configuration of human geographies.'[25] Conventional criminology could likewise benefit from a critical theory of transgression that better integrates the making of crime, the experiential and emotional production of urban space, and the policing of time, space, and being. After all, aren't city spaces and their meanings constructed out of the perceptions and desires of those who use them as much as by the stern efforts of legal authorities and economic planners? Don't urban dwellers of all sorts invest the city with meaning as they map and remap it, deciding safety and risk, creating preferred routes and little isolated pleasures, denoting favorite buildings or dangerous pathways? If so, then conventional criminological notions of 'broken windows' and their allegedly predictable effects – and likewise, reductionist notions of 'rational choice' as the key to crime and crime prevention – would seem to reflect not the intricacies of urban transgression, but criminologists' own intellectual arrogance and experiential vacancy.[26]

Being

But, in any case, this much I do know: in writing an illicit map of the city, scrounging made a new map out of me. In the same way that it confirmed for me the existential pleasures of slowing down, it affirmed the possibilities available in an everyday life on the spatial margins, a life reconstructed by back alleys and abandoned urban spaces. Much of this personal transformation merged with, and emerged from, what I might call *existential ethnography*. With no research grant, no book contract – hell, with no job, academic or otherwise – I was able to at least approach the point of 'becoming the phenomenon,' of scrounging the city not as a research project or field experiment, but as existence. In this way scrounging resituated me in time, in space – and in the web of social relations that constitutes urban life. Catching the scornful stares of respectable folks while digging through their trash, hearing other times offers of kindness from them or from other scroungers, finding frustration in a dumpster locked against those of us who would add to or subtract from it – all were moments of real insight, it seems to me, precisely because they were moments of existential reorientation as well. They taught me about scrounging, and about the world of urban scroungers, by teaching me something about myself and my emotional existence as a scrounger.[27] Humility and humiliation, gratitude, independence, pride, pleasure – as they became part of who I was, as they animated the scrounging situations in which I found myself, I became better able to understand those who shared those situations with me. And so, it seems, we arrive again at the urban *dérive*, or maybe at some sort of existential understanding of scrounging and of life ... where wandering away is the only place to be.

Notes

* This contribution is a revised version of a chapter in *Empire of Scrounge: Inside the Urban Underground of Dumpster Diving, Trash Picking, and Street Scavenging* (2006). New York University Press are thanked for their permission to reprint materials here.

1 See J. Ferrell, 'Degradation and Rehabilitation in Popular Culture,' *Journal of Popular Culture*, 1990, 3, 89–100.

2 Anonymous, *Evasion*. Atlanta: CrimethInc., 2003, p. 80.

3 See *Evasion*, p. 78, emphasis in original:

But we were prepared, in true transient form, to *wait* by the dumpster, for hours or forever, until they threw away a batch. I've always respected and enjoyed the company of the grumpy, old, scruffy homeless guys that hung out by the supermarket dumpsters just drinking hairspray and spitting on people all day.

And as Raoul Veneigem writes in *The Revolution of Everyday Life* (London: Rebel Press, 2001 [1967], p. 226), 'Economic imperatives turn people into walking chronometers, with the mark of what they are around their wrists. This is the temporality of work, progress, productivity, production deadlines, consumption and planning.'

4 For a different metaphorical take on social bulimia, see J. Young, 'Cannibalism and Bulimia: Patterns of Social Control in Late Modernity,' *Theoretical Criminology*, 1999, 4, 387–407. And thus Vaneigem:

The world of reification is a world without a centre, like the new prefabricated cities that are its décor. The present fades away before the promise of an eternal future that is nothing but a mechanical extension of the past.
(R. Vaneigem, 'Totality for Kids,' reprinted in D. Star (ed.) *Beneath the Paving Stones: Situationists and the Beach, May 1968*. Edinburgh: AK Press Europe, 2001 [1962–1963], pp. 38–61 [quotation p. 59])

5 C. Carlsson, 'Cycling Under the Radar: Assertive Desertion,' in C. Carlsson (ed.) *Critical Mass: Bicycling's Defiant Celebration*. Oakland: AK Press, 2002, pp. 75–82 (quotation p. 82).

6 See J. Ferrell, *Crimes of Style: Urban Graffiti and the Politics of Criminality*. Boston: Northeastern University Press, 1996. And as itinerant artist and activist Bob Waldmire writes on his hand-drawn postcards and posters: 'Small is beautiful, old is beautiful, slow is beautiful, safe is beautiful.'

7 See R. Levine, *A Geography of Time*. New York: Basic Books, 1997; C. Honore, *In Praise of Slowness*. San Francisco: HarperCollins, 2004; J. Ferrell, 'Speed Kills,' *Critical Criminology*, 2003, 3, 185–198.

8 And in contrast to the consumer class' 'need to worry and betray time with urgencies false and otherwise, purely anxious and whiney,' we might consider the beat-down temporal wanderings of Kerouac and Cassady, 'the point being that we know what *it* is and we know *time* and we know that everything is really *fine*.' J. Kerouac, *On the Road*. New York: New American Library, 1955, p. 172, emphasis in original.

9 As Gary Snyder says,

In the Buddhist view, what obstructs the effortless manifestation of this natural state is ignorance, fed by fear and craving.... Modern America has become economically dependent on a fantastic system of stimulation of greed which cannot be fulfilled, sexual desire which cannot be satiated, and hatred which has no outlet except against oneself or the person one is supposed to love.

> (G. Snyder, 'Buddhist Anarchism,' in M. Blechman (ed.) *Drunken Boat (#2)*. Brooklyn: Autonomedia/Left Bank Books, 1994, pp. 168–170 [quotation p. 169])

My thanks also to Trey Williams for his comments on scrounging, time, and social theory.

10 Once, while bicycling down a bumpy dirt road in the forest outside Flagstaff, Arizona, I found scattered over the course of three or four miles an almost complete set of wrench sockets, each a few hundred yards farther along from the last.

11 See Ferrell, *Crimes of Style*.

12 H. Garfinkel, *Studies in Ethnomethodology*. Englewood Cliffs: Prentice-Hall, 1967, p. 37.

13 H. Mehan and H. Wood, *The Reality of Ethnomethodology*. New York: John Wiley and Sons, 1975, p. 117; as they point out, the phrase 'elegant knowledge' originates with David Sudnow. And as Garfinkel says in introducing his *Studies in Ethnomethodology*:

> The following studies seek to treat practical activities, practical circumstances, and practical sociological reasoning as topics of empirical study, and by paying to the most commonplace activities of everyday life the attention usually accorded extraordinary events, seek to learn about them as phenomena in their own right.
>
> (p. 1)

14 M. Keith, 'Street Sensibility? Negotiating the Political by Articulating the Spatial,' in A. Merrifield and E. Swyngedouw (eds) *The Urbanization of Injustice*. New York: NYU Press, 1997, pp. 137–160 (quotation pp. 143–4).

15 M. de Certeau, *The Practice of Everyday Life*. Berkeley: University of California Press, 1984, pp. 93, 95, and 97. As de Certeau says, 'In short, *space is a practiced place*. Thus the street geometrically defined by urban planning is transformed into a place by walkers" (p. 117, emphasis in original). And as Stephanie Kane notes in relation to ethnographic research:

> The linkage of map and text makes culture accessible as culture *area*, holistically rendered.... I wonder, though, if we are reifying such boundaries, as a matter of convenience, without establishing whether or not people render them significant in the course of what we catch ourselves describing as their everyday lives.
>
> (S. Kane, 'The Unconventional Methods of Cultural Criminology', *Theoretical Criminology*, 2004, 3, 303–321; quotation p. 307)

See K. Hayward, *City Limits: Crime, Consumer Culture, and the Urban Experience*. London: Glasshouse, 2004.

16 See, for example, R. Vaneigem, *The Revolution of Everyday Life*; G. Debord, *Society of the Spectacle*. Detroit: Black and Red, 1983; G. Marcus, *Lipstick Traces: A Secret History of the Twentieth Century*. Cambridge: Harvard University Press, 1989; J. Ferrell, *Tearing Down the Streets: Adventures in Urban Anarchy*. New York: Palgrave/Macmillan, 2002.

17 I. Chtcheglov, 'Formulary for a New Urbanism,' 1953. Reproduced at www.bopsecrets.org, emphasis in original.

18 G. Debord, 'Theory of the Derive,' 1958. Reproduced at www.bopsecrets.org. Interestingly, Debord also references the work of the Chicago School of sociology/criminology on concentric urban zones.

19 Quoted in Ferrell, *Tearing Down the Streets*, p. 114; see also Carlsson, *Critical Mass*.
20 Quotations from http://socialfiction.org/psychogeography; and J. Hart, 'A New Way of Walking,' *Utne Reader*, July–August 2004, pp. 40–43 (quotation p. 41). See also S. Plant, *The Most Radical Gesture*. London: Routledge, 1992; http://glowlab.blogs.com; *Year Zero One Forum Issue #12 – Summer 2003: Psychogeography – Space, Place, Perception* (www.year01.com/issue12.htm).
21 S. Kane, 'Unconventional Methods,' p. 317; S. Kane, 'Reversing the Ethnographic Gaze: Experiments in Cultural Criminology,' in J. Ferrell and M. Hamm (eds) *Ethnography at the Edge*. Boston: Northeastern University Press, 1998, pp. 132–145 (quotation p. 143).
22 Anonymous, *Evasion*, page 12.
23 Vaneigem, *The Revolution of Everyday Life*, p. 264:

> One evening, just as night fell, my friends and I wandered into the Palais de Justice in Brussels. The building is a monstrosity, crushing the poor quarters beneath it and standing guard over the fashionable Avenue Louis – out of which, some day, we will make a breathtakingly beautiful wasteland.

See Anonymous, *Evasion*, p. 120, for a similar experience. See also J. Ferrell, 'Boredom, Crime, and Criminology,' *Theoretical Criminology*, 2004, 3, 287–302.
24 See J. Katz, *Seductions of Crime*. New York: Basic Books, 1988.
25 E. Soja, *Postmodern Geographies*. London: Verso, 1989, p. 11; see Ferrell, *Tearing Down the Streets*, on transformations in spatial meaning and experience spawned by skateboarding and other illicit urban activities. See also Hayward, *City Limits*.
26 See, for example, J. Wilson and G. Kelling, 'Broken Windows: The Police and Neighborhood Safety,' reprinted in E. McLaughlin *et al.* (eds) *Criminological Perspectives*. London: Sage, 2003, pp. 400–411; D. Cornish and R. Clarke, 'The Rational Choice Perspective,' in S. Henry and M. Lanier (eds) *The Essential Criminology Reader*. Boulder: Westview, 2006, pp. 18–29.
27 See J. Ferrell, 'Criminological Verstehen: Inside the Immediacy of Crime,' *Justice Quarterly*, 1997, 1, 3–23.

Chapter 6

White-collar offenders after the fall from grace

Stigma, blocked paths and resettlement

Ben Hunter

Introduction

Existing work on resettlement in the community after a prison sentence emphasises the importance for ex-prisoners of a change in identity and in the sense of who they are.[1] For resettlement to be 'successful' (i.e. accompanied by desistance from crime), such changes should be supported in the post-release world. Ex-prisoners need to be able to construct a sense of who they are in terms of their future as a means of working to achieve that future self. While existing work on resettlement and desistance from crime is extensive, one group of offenders whose experiences of resettlement have, by and large, not been considered are white-collar offenders.

The intention here is to highlight the resettlement experiences of white-collar offenders, framing them with an understanding of existential sociology, itself derived from broader existentialist tenets.

The chapter starts by considering the salient features of existentialism and existential sociology for the consideration of white-collar offenders' resettlement. Following this, a brief review of the literature that has considered resettlement will highlight what has been identified as being of importance for successful resettlement and how this relates to an understanding of white-collar offenders' experiences following release from prison. The data used in this chapter are drawn from published autobiographical accounts written by white-collar offenders. Therefore, in recognising the somewhat unusual nature (at least, for criminology) of the chosen method, there is a brief outline of what utilising autobiographical accounts can add to an understanding of particular social experiences before moving to the way in which resettlement was faced by white-collar offenders. Although not used extensively in criminology, drawing upon autobiographical accounts allows direct access to what was of relevance in the resettlement experience as it was encountered by white-collar offenders. In doing this, autobiographies provide an understanding of an area of criminology that is often theorised but has yet to be explored.

The focus of the resettlement experiences of white-collar offenders is upon how they used various 'cues' to come to terms with who they were in the world following their release from prison. These cues took the form of the negative reactions they received from others and also a realisation that future opportunities they may have taken for granted were to be denied them. Such experiences affected the sense of self they had upon their release. Beyond this, the challenge these white-collar offenders faced in resettling was in part constituted in a return to the 'legitimate' world, which was something of which they had previously been a part. It is suggested that for them, attempting to take up 'legitimate' practices in the wake of release from prison was more difficult than for ex-prisoners more generally, because a return to the familiar denied them the opportunity to demonstrate their change to being ex-offenders through their actions.

Resettlement following a prison sentence

Issues and concepts

Resettlement (also called re-entry[2]) is identified as the implementation of strategies designed to reintegrate the ex-offender into the community.[3] Reintegration in this context is taken to mean anything and everything that is intended to reduce the chance of re-offending once a prisoner has left prison.[4] Recently, work on ex-prisoner resettlement and reintegration has highlighted the importance for those who wish to desist from crime of being able to fashion a new pro-social identity to aid their attempts. Forming such an identity may be achieved in part through commitment to family or work roles,[5] long identified by the desistance from crime literature as having a 'positive' function in terms of reducing the likelihood of re-offending.[6] In addition to these, a key part of achieving and maintaining a pro-social identity is engagement in roles that the individual identifies as holding a civic function, such as roles that enable something to be 'given back' to the wider community.[7] This has some resonance with the study of citizenship and the feeling that one can be a participant in wider society, a feeling that may pervade all aspects of the individual's life. In short, 'ex-felons must become a productive citizen at work, a responsible citizen at home and an active citizen in the community'.[8] Farrall and Calverley[9] also draw explicit links between citizenship and desistance. They note that those members of their sample identified as desisters were more likely to subscribe to liberal values espousing the importance of honesty and being involved in one's community. Related to this, it is through interactions with others and reflecting on what these interactions 'mean' that the individual comes to feel their own attempts at change are successful.[10] Such thinking echoes the literature on desistance from crime more generally. The general thrust of such work is that a new identity aids attempts to desist from crime by helping the offender to realise that they can have a life free of offending. They can 'be' someone else[11] and through fashioning a new identity they come to place a different meaning upon their lives relative to that which they had done before.[12] Maruna[13] suggests that desistance is only possible when offenders 'develop a coherent pro-social identity for themselves', while Giordano et al.[14] observe that being able to envision a different future self to 'replace' who one is now is important if attempts to stop offending are to be successful. This highlights the importance of the concept of understanding who one is and who one can be for an understanding of desistance. This observation suggests that a key part of forming a new identity is being able to be future oriented and being able to identify who one wants to 'be' as a prelude to making attempts to get 'there'. In short, desistance is about making a new way to live that is incompatible with a continued commitment to deviant activity.

In sum then, for the ex-prisoner, post-release circumstances should ideally represent a means of helping them live lives consistent with who they feel they are by providing structures that encourage them to feel their attempts can be successful and resources to make their aspirations a reality.

The resettlement experiences of white-collar offenders

The resettlement of white-collar offenders has been left largely unconsidered by the criminological literature. White-collar crime here will be defined, following Edelhertz, as: 'An illegal act or series of illegal acts committed by non physical means and by concealment or guile, to obtain money or property, to avoid the loss of money or property, or to obtain business or personal advantage.'[15] For the purposes here, a white-collar offender will be anyone convicted of a white-collar crime defined in the above terms.

Shover and Hochstetler[16] suggest that white-collar offenders may be able to draw on support networks that do not encourage criminal behaviour that they had developed prior to their incarceration to ease their resettlement, while other offenders are likely to lack such extensive resources.[17] However, the presence of these networks does pose a different problem that white-collar offenders may face and that other offenders may find less of an issue. Specifically, the problem of the loss of social status and reputation following a criminal conviction which, it is suggested, is particularly acute amongst white-collar offenders.[18] Weisburd et al.[19] suggest that there is no relationship between the informal sanctions associated with arrest and imprisonment and the likelihood of re-offending. However, the notion that arrest and imprisonment creates a stigma that it is hard to rid oneself of, and does so particularly for white-collar offenders, is an oft-cited feature of research.[20] The impact of such a stigma (if it does indeed exist) on subsequent behaviour is unclear, however (Weisburd et al.'s[21] observations notwithstanding), as the presence of such stigma tends to be something that is theorised rather than firmly identified.

What is clear from the above literature on resettlement is the importance of understanding the lived world of offenders who are attempting to resettle and how the experiences they have are of relevance to them. This is of particular relevance with regard to attempts to fashion and present a non-offender identity. One means of doing this is by drawing upon existentialist tenets to highlight what was of particular salience for white-collar offenders following their release from prison.

Existentialism and existential sociology

Existentialism

Existentialist thought generally emphasises that to exist is to be in encounter with the world. MacQuarrie[22] identifies three key 'characteristics' of existence. First, there is the dynamic and future-oriented nature of the individual's existence as they strive constantly to achieve an ideal self. In doing this, however, there will always be a certain tension, as one's ideal self is always, to a greater or lesser extent, separate from the self as it stands in any particular moment. Second, to exist is to exercise choice. Third, to exist is to be unique within the world (and to assert that uniqueness through one's own existence), to have feelings, experiences and encounters that are relevant to oneself only. In total then, to exist is to be capable of thinking, feeling and initiating action, as these processes comprise the whole spectrum of existence.[23]

It is through thinking and, as a result of this thinking, exercising choice that the individual becomes uniquely oneself.[24] Freedom of choice and the exercise of that freedom is the individual's means of deciding upon a future and making a commitment to pursuing one particular possibility (and therefore one particular self) over all others.[25] Such a choice cannot be completely 'free', however, first because one's past choices will have a bearing on the way in which choices are constructed and attended to.[26] That is, in choosing our future we must have regard for the 'fact' of our past, although we may choose to change the meaning of it.[27] Second, the need to create an authentic self will drive the individual to maintain a unitary self-identity that is only possible if the values and ideals that are reflected in one's choices are kept constant.[28]

Existentialist writers emphasise the importance of emotions generally, as it is through emotions that we interact with (i.e. exist within) the world. To feel anger or joy (for example) is to understand something about how we interpret the world. A brief consideration of guilt as an emotion may better highlight this. To feel guilt is to know that one has failed in attempting to achieve the self that one wishes to view oneself as.[29] However, feeling guilt may ultimately be seen as a positive experience, in this instance because it can provide the individual with the will to change, to strive to realise their future potential self.[30] To feel guilt and shame can then represent a commitment to the future and one's future ideal self. It is through emotions then that we interact with (i.e. exist within) the world. To feel anger or joy (for example) is to understand something about how we interpret our experiences and what they mean to us in terms of who we are. To express an emotion is to express our sense of self.

While thinking and feeling are both important elements in contributing to one's own existence, it is through action that that existence becomes realised.[31] 'Action' is not merely the observable act, but is rather the fusion of thinking and feeling and the meaning this fusion has for the individual. Action therefore represents the 'total person'. As an individual acts, they are in the process of projecting themselves forward, of making themselves, of existing.[32] To act is therefore to constitute oneself.[33]

Part of existence involves managing the tension between one's past, present and future self and also recognising that who one is now and who one may yet become is grounded in who one was. Because we become our past, in this way we already are our future.[34] Although we may not be able to change our past, we can, however, change the meaning of it[35] and it is in this way that we actively construct a future.

Existential sociology

Some writers have sought to utilise the ideas suggested in existentialist thought for a more thorough consideration of human behaviour (see, for example, edited collections by Douglas and Johnson,[36] Kotarba and Fontana[37] and Kotarba and Johnson[38]). Such 'existential sociology' provides a means of considering the internal processes that underlie behaviour change, and the influence of the existentialist thought may be seen in the core concerns of existential sociology: the importance of the sense of self, the role of feelings and emotions and the importance of individuals' values and beliefs.

The importance of self

The sense of self that all individuals hold, but cannot necessarily rationalise,[39] is developed as a result of the need to negotiate the various situations that the individual will encounter over the course of their life. It is through the sense of self that the individual comes to understand their place in the world and the options this offers to them. It situates them with reference to others and also with reference to their own past, present and future.[40] Douglas describes the role of the self in considering human interaction: 'Just as the sense of inner self is the cornerstone of any healthy life, so is it the cornerstone of any basic model of human nature in the social world and, thus, of any theory of social life.'[41] The self is constantly becoming.[42] That is, it develops in response to the lived reality of its being in the world.[43] Fundamental to the conceptualisation of the self, then, is an understanding of how it reacts to the possibility of its own change. If an experience that suggests the possibility of change is perceived as something that can be easily coped with, possibly by accommodating it within the current conception of the self, then the individual is unlikely to feel a sense of ontological insecurity; the sense that one's very being is threatened.[44] However, if the change is viewed as a threat, because the individual feels they lack the resources to cope, then they are likely to experience the dread that is concomitant with their inner self – their very being – being put at risk.[45] A situation that threatens change is likely to be an unsettling time as the individual's place in the world is suddenly less certain, the meaning they place on their existence in jeopardy. The experience of stigmatisation is one such situation. To be stigmatised is to suffer the threat of self-degradation as one's general worth is called into question. The source of potential change in this instance coming through introspection may lead to the transformation of the self as a result of the guilt or shame suffered.[46]

Several writers have highlighted the importance of the self evolving through social encounters and the notion that who one 'is' is constructed through interaction with others.[47] Who we are is in part constituted in social encounters and will necessarily be reconstructed as one moves between social encounters and social institutions.[48] An important related issue to the notion that others help to define who we are is that answering questions regarding our place in the world can be done through an understanding of others' beliefs about us. Answering such questions is important to derive some meaning from existence: 'Where do I come from? Where am I? Where am I going? must be answered, at least in some implicit way to *give physical direction to our life-processes*.'[49]

Through an understanding of our 'place' in the world can such questions be answered. To be within the world is to have who we are in part defined by others,[50] and an awareness of who others are and their relationship to us informs an understanding of our place in the world. Identity is that which others perceive our self to be, and the tension between our sense of self and others' perception of that self (i.e. our identity) characterises the tension of being within the world.[51]

Individual values and beliefs

Existential sociology also highlights the importance of values and beliefs for an understanding of the self. Living in accordance with such values is likely to produce feelings of pride, while, conversely, acting in a manner contradictory to one's values may bring about shame as the individual is forced to confront (via their actions) the possibility that they are less capable or have less integrity than is consistent with their sense of self.[52] Douglas describes the problems that would be faced by a self without values:

> Socially we would be continuously *lost*. An individual who violates his own basic rules or those of the groups in which he is emotionally grounded feels that he has betrayed his self, and he experiences the pain of severe guilt or shame; this pain in turn reinforces the rules, making it more likely that he will not betray his self next time.[53]

Values and beliefs anchor us to the world and to particular spheres over others. In this way, then, our values help us to orient ourselves in relation to the world and the values that individuals hold themselves to become self-reinforcing. They protect the sense of self from shame by prompting the individual to behave in a manner more in accordance with the prevailing conception of self.

Feelings and emotions

In keeping with the existentialist literature more generally, the role of emotions in human life are also emphasised by existential sociologists, particularly with regard to providing the impetus for human action. Clark[54] argues that rather than rejecting the part that emotions contribute to the human experience, we should consider them alongside a perspective that views humans as rational actors who behave according to a carefully considered cost–benefit analysis. Emotions are social products, arising out of our interactions with the world[55] and consequently are also of importance because they are a means of confirming (or altering) the relationships we hold with others, based upon an understanding of our relationship with them. Such expressions of emotion help to reaffirm to the individual a meaningful self-identity.

> Emotions play a crucial part in the process of exchange, connection, and division because emotions concern the self, others, and the self in relation to others. ... Further, emotions such as disdain, gratitude, liking, annoyance, obligation, fear, love, distrust, and sympathy provide data or 'intelligence' that social actors need to orient them toward others.[56]

Essentially, individuals act upon their feelings.[57] Reason, although still employed by individuals, is viewed as being 'weak' and prone to high levels of variability depending upon the situation the individual has encountered. In this position, feelings are all-pervading, underlying and driving forward all aspects of the human experience.

With its focus upon being within the world and the relevance of defining oneself by reference to others, in addition to the emphasis placed upon the future-oriented becoming of the self, existential sociology provides a deeper means of understanding the processes inherent in successful resettlement. The task here is to provide a more concrete illustration of this by applying the concerns of existential sociology to a consideration of resettlement after prison for white-collar offenders. This will be done using information from autobiographical accounts written by individuals convicted of a white-collar crime.

Autobiographical accounts

Autobiography is, essentially, the telling of a story about oneself and may take spoken or written form. For Lejeune, autobiography is 'A retrospective prose narrative produced by a real person concerning his own existence, focusing on his individual life, in particular on the development of his personality.'[58] Added to this, Roberts[59] suggests that other ephemera such as memoirs, diaries and journals all provide sources of autobiographical data. Being a story of the life, or part of the life, an autobiography is focused upon the past, or, perhaps more appropriately, *a* past, that being the past that is recalled by the teller. Autobiography represents one of the myriad forms of 'human documents'[60] through which individuals express themselves. In autobiography, past events are interpreted and recounted for the meaning they have to the autobiographer. Such meaning is not a stationary construct, with the meaning of particular events possibly subject to reconstruction. Recounting the life is therefore an active process, with meaning constructed as the past is recalled.[61] Although, as the above definition suggests, autobiography may be written or spoken, the focus here is upon written autobiographies or what Smith and Watson[62] refer to as 'life narratives'. As a text, a life narrative is

> a historically situated practice of self-representation. In such texts, narrators selectively engage their lived experience through personal storytelling. Located in specific times and places, they are at the same time in dialogue with the personal processes and archives of memory.[63]

Smith and Watson[64] note that only through a life narrative (such as that represented by autobiographical text) may we encounter the writer's self, as only the author can comment on their own subjectively viewed experiences. Indeed for some, the search for a self is what characterises autobiography.[65] Autobiographies give an indicator as to the writer's subjectively experienced past. As a result they include what was important to them, which of their life experiences were of relevance, which encounters shaped them and in which ways.[66] They are a means of understanding how the self experiences itself.[67] For the current discussion, this is of most interest when considering accounts of change. Autobiography permits a demonstration that one has changed, but also allows, through presenting the context for that change, the opportunity to say how.

McAdams[68] asserts that it is through the telling of stories that individuals come to attain a sense of meaning and self-identity so as to reaffirm their sense of unity and purpose. This gives individuals' accounts a unique place in contributing to an understanding of their experiences, with the relevance of historical facts relegated to a secondary role behind establishing the 'truth' of events for the individual. Attending to narratives in such a manner means to relinquish notions of 'fact' and recognise that just as one experiences events subjectively, they will also come to recall and recount these events in a similarly personal manner,[69] indeed 'autobiographical truth is a [different matter to autobiographical claims, e.g. date of birth], it is an intersubjective exchange between narrator and reader aimed at producing a shared understanding of the meaning of a life'.[70]

Far from being a disadvantage for those wishing to understand human experience, assessment of autobiographical accounts may represent a 'truer' reading of one's experience because such accounts add to that which has been lived.[71] The autobiographer reflects on their life, their significant experiences and what these mean in terms of the life as a whole. Any use of autobiography as a research tool must reflect this. Plummer, who views life history as analogous to autobiography, being the full-length account of a person's life in his or her own words, makes this point explicit:

> It is however clear what [life documents, e.g. autobiography] are not: they refuse to be social scientists' second-order accounts that claim to be external and objective truth ... They all attempt to enter the subjective world of informants, taking them seriously on their own terms and thereby providing first hand, intimately involved accounts of life ... What matters, therefore, in life history research is the facilitation of as full a subjective view as possible, not the naïve delusion that one has trapped the bedrock of truth.[72]

Autobiographies are a means of creating a 'posthumous propaganda'[73] for the teller of their own life story, a means of self-justification for some.[74] In addition to this, Sheridan[75] highlights the possibility that the construction of an autobiography acts as a means of confirming one's existence to oneself. We might go beyond this to consider that the construction of an autobiography helps one to understand who 'they' are, and for McAdams[76] this is an important part of writing one's autobiography, even if it is never to be read by another. Generating a coherent life story allows the teller of it to gain a sense of meaning, situating their life in relation to broader historical and social contexts.[77] Constructing a narrative is an important part of understanding who one is.

Methodological issues in studying autobiographies

Drawing upon published autobiographical accounts is not without problems, however. Most significant perhaps are issues surrounding the lack of 'tailoring' of data to the specific focus of the research and the extent to which authors have 'ownership' of what is written. First, there is the issue that the researcher who wishes to use published autobiographical data for the investigation of a particular phenomenon has no means of controlling what is written, nor how adequately it pertains to the topic of study. However, while this may be problematic for some studies, where the issue of investigation is individual experience (as is the case here) data that has not been 'sullied' by the researcher's opinions and preconceptions might be said to be a boon. As Maruna[78] observes, the written autobiography reflects what the author wants the reader to know and does so better than any interview. Second, we might add that it is important to understand the extent to which the author has 'ownership' over what is written. The use of a ghost writer and the impact of editorial influence may both have a bearing on what is said and the way in which information is presented. Both Maruna[79] and Katz[80] identify the concern that the drive to publish a marketable book may have a significant bearing on what is written, hiding the author's intentions beneath a wave of prose designed to sensationalise. Ultimately, however, it might be expected that at some level what is produced is the author's own story or at the very least is approved by them. In addition to this, Maruna[81] suggests that such issues are likely to be no more relevant than with the oral histories collected by sociologists.

Study of autobiographies in criminology

The use of published autobiographical accounts in this manner is not unprecedented within criminology. Maruna's[82] study of desistance from crime illustrates the advantage of employing published autobiographical accounts for a consideration of offender behaviour by considering the common themes in plot structure that were expressed by 20 offenders through their autobiographies that aided them in the creation of a 'prototypical reform narrative'.[83] More recently, Shover and Hochstetler[84] drew upon the published autobiographies of white-collar offenders who had spent time in prison to illustrate the angst that the prison situation prompted in them, while Farrall has used such sources to consider the experience of release from prison for those wrongfully convicted.[85] Morgan,[86] in his reading of prisoner autobiographies, highlights that it is through the study of such texts that we might gain an understanding of processes that are otherwise difficult to access: '[Prison autobiographies] represent some of the most extended narratives and analyses of a particular social experience normally hidden from public view.'[87] Similarly, Oleson,[88] in considering the autobiographies of several 'genius' (i.e. having a high IQ) offenders, notes that: 'Their writings are insightful and often eloquent, and serve as a window into a social world about which virtually nothing is known.'[89]

In a similar vein to the above studies, which have considered published autobiographical accounts, the intention here is to investigate a particular phenomenon that has remained largely unexplored. The distinctive advantages that autobiographical data provides will be used to investigate the resettlement process as it is experienced by white-collar offenders. The reading of such autobiographies will be done so as to take account of encounters most relevant to them after their release from prison. Existential sociologists, while not privileging a particular methodological stance over any other, have tended towards naturalistic methods in investigating human experience. Individuals are encouraged to tell their 'own story' as a means of conveying the uniqueness of their experience.[90] Furthermore, the focus is on understanding how the context of the life as a whole influences the emphasis placed upon particular experiences.[91] In short, the very concerns that it is suggested above may be served by an analysis of textual autobiographical data.

The sample

The data used were drawn from the published autobiographical accounts of nine individuals convicted of a white-collar offence. All nine were successfully considered to have resettled. That is, none had been convicted of a further offence after their release from prison as far as could be ascertained by searches of media archives. Ten books were used in total.[92] Three of the individuals (Leeson, Bond and Timilty) wrote their books in conjunction with a named co-author. In all cases this co-author was a literary 'professional', i.e. they were employed to write books. All of those whose books were considered spent time in prison and dedicated a portion of their book to writing about their experiences after release. Books were analysed to consider common themes in authors' experiences of their arrest and punishment and their life in the aftermath of this.

Stigma and blocked paths: the reality of resettlement

The immediate aftermath of release from prison was a confusing and insecure time for these men. Nevertheless, when these white-collar offenders left prison they all had a sense of who they were. The prison experience had been harrowing for some, but they all thought of themselves as non-offenders, either because they denied any original guilt or because they had come to view their actions as 'wrong'. However, their post-release circumstances would challenge this view and the hope they had that they would have unfettered opportunity to live as they wished. In particular, the accounts of the experience of release from prison highlighted that these white-collar offenders experienced stigmatisation from others and also came to realise that certain of their life paths were 'blocked'.

Ultimately, there was no uniform experience for these white-collar offenders. All encountered stigma and blocked paths in ways unique to their past and all viewed the future in terms similarly informed by that past. The intention here is to outline a broadly shared experience of resettlement, simultaneously recognising that reaction to such experiences is highly individual.

Stigma

The uncertainty and questions that for some characterised the anticipation of their release from prison and its immediate aftermath continued for some time after release as these white-collar offenders attempted to negotiate who they were in their post-release world. Challenges were faced as interactions with others that they anticipated while in prison finally became a reality. During such interactions, these offenders came to understand how others viewed them in light of their offence and what this might mean for their future. What is prevalent in these accounts is the experience of negative reactions from others as the ex-prisoner made their way in the world. This in turn had an impact upon how the individuals saw themselves. Robert Berger, who served 38 months in prison for corporate income tax evasion and bribery while CEO of Royce Aerospace Materials, discovered that the reactions of others were too much for him to deal with and that he needed to 'restart' his life: 'The stigma of my incarceration weighed heavily on the outside, like a big dark cloud. I found myself cast adrift from old, pre-incarceration friends and associations.'[93] Further example of stigma suffered is given by Barry Minkow, who was convicted on 54 counts of securities fraud, embezzlement, mail fraud, tax evasion and bank fraud related in part to defrauding investors in his company 'ZZZZ Best', and spent seven years in prison. After leaving prison Minkow attempted to demonstrate his change (i.e. that he was no longer a 'con man') through working to uncover fraud. For him, this showed his reformed character. However, despite this work, Minkow was shocked to find some people still did not trust him. A friend informed him that a speaking engagement at an international conference had been cancelled because the American Fraud Association had refused to participate if he was the main speaker. Shortly after, he was informed that a magazine editor had stated he will never publish something positive about him:

> I sank deeper into my chair as the shocking reality of his words filtered through to my brain. After I hung up the phone, I tried to shake off the shackles of my past ... The devastating reports ... exploded like shrapnel in my mind, leaving a torrent of pain.[94]

Interactions with others were not solely negative. When John Dean, convicted of obstruction of justice following his role in Watergate, was first released from prison he received many calls from those wishing to welcome him home, in addition to receiving letters and telegrams from people sending him fond wishes, as well as many requests for interviews. This attention boosted his self-esteem, which was fragile following the fall out from Watergate that had affected him and his time spent in prison:

> I began to feel strangely like a hero being welcomed home, instead of a released prisoner. While I tried to shrug it off, I liked the attention, particularly the flattery of the repeated job offers – and each day brought another one. These bolstered my self-confidence tremendously, and it needed the bolstering.[95]

There was, therefore, sensitivity on the part of these men as to how the world would treat them. However, just as positive encounters with others provide hope for the future, so negative encounters are taken as a barometer for general feeling about the individual. Dean's confidence was fragile, as evidenced by his reaction to being asked to market pornographic films: 'This call bothered me because it made me think about how others saw me. I knew the estimation must be low or I would not have received such a call.'[96] Dean was bothered by what association with such films suggested about him as a person. The – as he saw it – sordid nature of pornography and the 'sleazy' reputation it had were being directly associated with him. In some people's view he was the 'sort of person' who would market pornography. In addition, Dean was painfully aware of how he might be judged by others and what that meant in terms of his own sense of self. On holiday on a remote island three weeks after his release, he reflects on his interactions with others in a journal entry:

> I don't want to see people because I'm embarrassed – even, at times, ashamed – to be who I am, or to be who they think I am. I really don't know how to deal with these feelings. I understand now that we judge ourselves to a greater extent than I've ever before admitted, through the eyes of others. I know it is difficult for any person to consider himself evil, or greedy, or stupid, since he must live with himself. Yet

the mirror of my identity is partly in the eyes of others, and I find I keep checking to see how I look. For a while I thought I looked pretty good. Although I've always known I would have to wear the 'scarlet letter of Watergate,' as I once described the stigma I felt to a newsman, I didn't think it would be for very long.[97]

By an awareness of oneself in the eyes of others, one's place in the world may be better understood,[98] one's sense of self being forced to reflect on what the reactions of others mean.[99] These men suffered the stigma that white-collar offenders more generally are asserted to experience following a criminal conviction.[100] The difficulty of experiencing stigma was for them rooted in the contrast between their own self-conception as non-offenders and the image of themselves that society presented them with. The experience of being stigmatised acted to signal to these ex-prisoners who they 'were' in the world and was thus an important source of information in understanding themselves as beings.[101] The stigma they suffered indicated to them that who they were in the world had changed and was at odds with how they identified themselves. The pain of suffering stigmatisation came from being forced to reflect on who they really were in the world.[102]

Blocked paths

In addition to the stigma encountered, these white-collar offenders discovered that opportunities were denied them because of their deviant past. Such 'blocked paths' are different from the experience of stigma because they represent structural impediments to living one's life rather than specific negative reactions from others. William Laite spent five months in prison for perjury and making false statements to avoid paying employee wages while he was owner of a building company. Laite's concern upon leaving prison was to become again who he felt he had been before his sentence: 'I had to re-establish myself as a man – as a family man, and as a man involved in the business and social life of the community.'[103] His search for employment proves problematic, however, preventing him from achieving his goal:

> I was angry and frustrated. Here I was with a formal education, trying to get a job – I would have taken any kind of job, I wasn't particular. I'd paid any debt I might have owed to society – paid it in the Tarrant County jail and in Eglin AFB [Air Force Base] Prison. Still no luck. I could easily see how other ex-cons with less education might soon give up, turn again to crime, and return again to prison.[104]

Jonathan Aitken, convicted of perjury, also faced problems establishing himself. His status as a convicted offender proved a hindrance to gaining a place at university. It also impeded his attempts to become a professional writer when he was left unable to travel to America by a refusal of the US Embassy to issue him with a visa:

> This development plunged me into a black mood of despair. No visa meant no book contract and no prospects of travel to a country I loved ... It felt as though I was being punished twice over, with imprisonment in Britain being followed by exile from America. The visa refusal worsened my money problems. If I could not write books for my US publishers, could I earn a living as an author? The answer was far from clear. To add to my gloom, my plan to study theology at Wycliffe Hall, Oxford, looked as though it might be crumbling.[105]

Much of one's resettlement involves looking to the future and what one will do, who one will become. Invariably, however, it will be discovered that not all options are open to the ex-prisoner. Some will be denied the opportunity to return to old careers. At the same time, many may 'self-block', feeling for whatever reason that they will not or cannot go back. More generally, some will find that as convicted offenders they cannot engage in activities previously available to them. Therefore, as part of ongoing attempts to forge a meaningful future for themselves and to determine who they 'are', some individuals must face the reality that they may not be able to achieve what they wish.

To know that much is denied them may be difficult, even if denied options were not things that may have been previously coveted. John Dean describes his feelings three weeks after his release from prison:

> The distance from prison still felt very short, and, while my body had escaped, my head was still struggling to break free ... I wondered if [my wife] thought of me as an 'ex-con,' a felon no less. Of course not, I decided, because she knew me and what I really was. But I knew too, that to the rest of the world I was someone who had 'done time.' I began to think about what it might mean.[106]

He goes on to realise that in many of America's states he will have greatly reduced civil rights and that as a result the confidence he had upon leaving prison that his life was going to continue as it had before Watergate may have been misplaced:

> I sat in the dark, on the edge of my bed, numbed by the vision of these horrible consequences ... I knew I had been deluding myself in feeling that I had come through Watergate unscathed, smelling like a rose.[107]

Part of asking about one's future involves considering one's past.[108] This, accompanied by the opportunity for time to reflect that is offered by one's time away from prison, allows for a reappraisal of what life means now. Dean's realisation was of who he 'was' in this world and of what that meant to others. Such a realisation affected his sense of self. Dean recognised that he was no longer the man he had been upon his arrest. The 'horrible consequences' cited by Dean reflect a concern with his ability to be able to participate in civic activities. For Dean, who was formerly actively involved in politics, such an inability to participate was particularly troubling.

As part of ongoing attempts to forge a meaningful future for themselves, some individuals must face the reality that they may not be able to return to their old life. Because of their offence and the fall out from it, some options may be denied them. The realisation is that one is an ex-offender and that being such brings with it a certain number of responsibilities and expectations as well as removing some opportunities. As has been touched upon, for some these opportunities relate to an inability to return to specific work which engaged them before and dealing with this realisation is likely to be difficult. Jonathan Aitken came to realise this while still in prison shortly before his release during a conversation with his former political colleague Michael Howard:

> As Michael described his talks in Washington (my home from home for many years), I felt a rare pang of wistfulness for the life of politics. He was involved with exactly the same interests, issues and influential people that I would have liked to be associated with on the international stage if my life had not gone pear-shaped and prison-shaped. These were not envious thoughts. I was simply being realistic ... our conversation brought home to me he was talking about a way of life which had slipped away from me forever.[109]

Once again, there is the realisation that one may yet be changed as they are forced to reject what previously was an important part of their identity. More generally as well, the notion of such paths being blocked is quite problematic because once again, it clashes with a strong sense of who one is. All these individuals had an idea of how they would like their lives to develop if given unfettered opportunity. The concerns expressed regarding leaving prison and finding one's way in the world express a desire to return to old spheres, and concerns with such issues as one's role as a responsible citizen. Knowing one's options are limited has an impact upon that. Change as 'inflicted' upon the self upsets a previously taken-for-granted world and prompts a certain amount of 'soul searching', a struggle to determine who one now is.

Similar to the way in which stigma suggests to the individual who one is, where paths are blocked because of an individual's convicted offender status, such information also helps to frame an understanding of the place one has in the world. In addition, however, while stigma is an indication of who one is 'now', the information provided by a knowledge of which paths are blocked is knowledge of who one can be. It has, therefore, a future-oriented element that may be lacking in other information 'cues'. The despondency expressed is a result of the realisation that the feelings of freedom and choice that characterised the euphoric period of release from prison have been shown to be false. Stigma and blocked paths force a restructuring of the self and a reappraisal of who one is. Further, they deny the opportunity to achieve a specifically viewed future self, necessitating that a new self is envisioned.[110] A realisation that paths are blocked means to feel that one is not free to choose oneself.

Returning to the familiar

The negative reaction to having one's plans frustrated is hardly surprising. The frustration and gloom that is reported comes from one's reformed character not being recognised as credible by others. In addition to this, if such plans are identified as the means through which one might re-establish oneself, then their failure represents a risk that once again one's life has been irreparably changed by prison. The above highlights how fundamental for one's well-being are one's hopes that the future will hold something positive. The importance of hope that the future may be meaningful is underlined here.[111]

It is clear from the above accounts that there is a need to reconcile the post-release and resettlement experience with one's own sense of self and one's awareness of who one is in the world. Ultimately, stigma and blocked paths are messages to ex-prisoners about themselves. These make individuals aware of the changes that have taken place within their world, what this means in terms of their future and how a change of their status in it has been forced upon them. It is in this way that change is experienced, as thrust upon offenders and it is this that makes it so troubling. Resettlement represents a threat to these offenders' ontological security. The identity the world presents them with prompts a reconsideration of their 'place' in the world relative to others.[112]

These offenders have to negotiate their identity, reconciling the firm notion of themselves as a non-offender with the identity society presents them with and the place in the world that this consigns them to. It is the strong conception of who they are that in part causes the angst they feel at suffering stigma. They share the values and beliefs of the world they are attempting to re-enter. They recognise the wrong inherent in their actions but no longer see these actions as a part of who 'they' are. The way that change has been conceived of in the desistance literature more generally is with the notion of quite extensive changes in identity being necessary for desistance to occur.[113] The individual who is attempting to resettle is expected to develop a new coherent pro-social role to replace their previous deviant identity.[114] Almost a prerequisite for this is identifying a blueprint for a future self that one will 'become',[115] a new self. The notion of a blueprint is still useful as a means of understanding how individuals measure their own success in resettling, but in the case of those here it was realised in different ways. For example, some (Laite, Berger, Timilty) attempted to realise the self they perceived they had prior to their offence. They attempted to return to the world as the men they 'were'. In contrast, others (Aitken, Minkow, Lawson) identified new selves that wished to 'be', for them based upon their own personal conversions to Christianity that they had undergone. As much as they wished to return to their previous 'world', they did so with new selves.

For those who identified a blueprint for the future based upon their past rather than a blueprint being one of a new future self, it represented the person they once were with a focus upon getting back the trappings of the former life. These trappings were identified in terms of both material and less concrete measures of success such as ideas around citizenship, for example. Those who identified new selves they wished to be did so within a context of returning to a familiar world as this new self.

As has been shown, however, stigma and blocked paths had an impact upon the ability to envision a desirable future, whether this future was based upon a 'new' or 'old' self. In identifying a future that is predicated upon a legitimate past, there is a tension inherent in doing so from a present in which one is an ex-offender. The past as it was can never be regained because in that 'world' one was not an ex-offender. Using the past as a blueprint for the future meant recognising the 'imperfect' nature of this future. When living a legitimate life after a conviction, resources can be re-accrued, status can be regained, but the past will always constitute one as an ex-offender.

Part of what made the resettlement experience different for these white-collar offenders is that they were encountering a familiar world from an unfamiliar perspective. Because they were attempting to re-enter the 'legitimate' world they already knew what was required. They had goals to attain. At the same time, they knew the 'rules' of the legitimate world.

The majority of other ex-offenders who are attempting to desist from crime must make their way into the world of (for example) legitimate work and encounter it as a challenge because it is something new. For those considered here, however, the familiarity of it was precisely what made the challenges difficult. These individuals, in attempting to show the world they were in fact ex-offenders, were on the threshold of the legitimate world and were attempting to re-enter it. In the same way that to be an ex is different from never having been,[116] to attempt to enter a world that one was previously in but was then ousted from is difficult and different from attempting to enter it for the first time. The problem this created for these white-collar offenders was that it was difficult for them to demonstrate their change to the oft-cynical world they found themselves presented with. To take on the meaningful employment and family responsibilities associated with the formation of a pro-social identity was to return to the world they existed in before their offence. However, for offenders more generally, what such responsibilities do is act to demonstrate one's change of character, a means of living who one is now. The difficulty for these white-collar offenders was that living such lives did not demonstrate their change to the world.

It was difficult for them to live and demonstrate their change through the lives they wished to have, because they could not 'be' their change[117] if they returned to old spheres. One can demonstrate to the world one's change in who one is through locales frequented, attire and activities undertaken.[118] Ex-prisoners who are attempting to desist from crime and resettle can show their change through gaining employment and being part of the community in ways that they were not before[119] and having their attempts recognised by others.[120] They can live who they wish to be and also signal their change in who they are to the world.

The white-collar offenders presented here lacked this means of demonstrating their change. The irony of their situation was that they were once part of the world they were attempting to resettle in and this made it difficult for them to live the life they wished. For them, their attempts were truly about *re*settling, but to gain employment, to be active participants in their communities meant to be what they were before their offence, which simultaneously made it difficult to signal to the world that change had taken place. They all had hope that their lives would continue unproblematically after prison but the stigma they suffered and the realisation that their paths were blocked forced them to reconsider this position. It is noteworthy that several of these men, after initial setbacks, made what might be termed 'grand gestures' in how they lived their lives. Some made public their conversion to religion or attempted to make reparation to their victims beyond that prescribed by the courts, for example. Finally, and most obviously, all of them wrote books about their conviction, their life now and why they were not offenders. These gestures were a means of being who they felt they were, but also of demonstrating this to the world.

Conclusions

Little is understood about the experiences that white-collar offenders have following their release from prison. What is 'known' is based largely on statistical portraits of offenders' movements. While useful, such portraits do not provide an understanding of what it feels like to resettle as a white-collar offender. The experiences recounted above suggest that not all white-collar offenders ease back into society in as straightforward a manner as might sometimes be thought.[121] Anxiety over one's place in the world is exacerbated by the reactions offenders experienced from others and the realisation that the future would not necessarily be lived out as they wished. Their criminal pasts constituted a particular future for them.[122] The place these offenders had in the world had changed and they were forced to come to terms with that in the period following their release from prison. Stigma and blocked paths made them realise that they would forever be ex-offenders and that any future they had would be predicated upon this. In short, their future would forever be informed by their past.[123] The problems they had were exacerbated by their desire to return to old spheres of life, such spheres denying them the opportunity to demonstrate the manner in which they had changed. It was difficult for them to be who they felt they were. Existential sociology allows for an understanding of the peculiar problems that face white-collar offenders in terms of these issues.

Future research should aim to consider how meaning is made of the resettlement experience, with particular reference to how the meaning of these events is structured. Also of interest would be a consideration of white-collar offenders who attend to stigma and blocked paths in a manner very different from those considered here. All of these white-collar offenders attempted to return to a familiar world. The experience of resettlement would likely be very different for those who reject the notion of a future self predicated on a familiar world.

Notes

1 C.A. Visher and J.T. Travis, 'Transitions from prison to community: understanding individual pathways', *Annual Review of Sociology*, 2003, vol. 29, 89–113; S. Maruna, *Making Good: How Ex-Offenders Reform and Reclaim Their Lives*, Washington, DC: American Psychological Association Books, 2001; S. Maruna and S. Farrall, 'Desistance from crime: a theoretical reformulation', *Kölner Zeitschrift für Soziologie & Sozialpsychologie*, 2004, vol. 43, 171–194; S. Farrall, 'On the existential aspects of desistance from crime', *Symbolic Interaction*, 2005, vol. 28, 3, 367–386.
2 S. Maruna, R. Immarigeon and T.P. LeBel, 'Ex-offender reintegration: theory and practice', in S. Maruna and R. Immarigeon (eds), *After Crime and Punishment: Pathways to Offender Reintegration*, Portland: Willan, 2004, pp. 3–26.
3 P. Raynor and G. Robinson, *Rehabilitation, Crime and Justice*, New York: Macmillan, 2005.
4 Maruna *et al.*, op. cit.
5 Visher and Travis, op. cit.
6 J.H. Laub and R.J. Sampson, 'Understanding desistance from crime', in M. Tonry (ed.), *Crime and Justice: A Review of Research (vol. 28)*, London: University of Chicago Press, 2001, pp. 1–69.
7 Maruna, op. cit.; C. Uggen, J. Manza and A. Behrens, 'Less than the average

citizen: stigma, role transition and the civic reintegration of convicted felons', in S. Maruna and R. Immarigeon (eds), *After Crime and Punishment: Pathways to Offender Reintegration*, Portland: Willan, 2004, pp. 261–293.

8 Uggen *et al.*, op. cit., p. 266.

9 S. Farrall and A. Calverley, *Understanding Desistance from Crime: Theoretical Directions in Resettlement and Rehabilitation*, Maidenhead: Open University Press, 2006.

10 T. Meisenhelder, 'Becoming normal: certification as a stage in exiting from crime', *Deviant Behaviour*, 1982, vol. 3, 137–153; M. Maguire and P. Raynor, 'How the resettlement of prisoners promotes desistance from crime; Or does it?', *Criminology and Criminal Justice*, 2006, vol. 6, 1, 19–38.

11 Maruna, op. cit.

12 Farrall and Calverley, op. cit.

13 Maruna, op. cit., p. 7.

14 P.C. Giordano, S.A. Cernkovich and J.L. Rudolph, 'Gender, crime and desistance: toward a theory of cognitive transformation', *American Journal of Sociology*, 2002, vol. 107, 990–1064.

15 H. Edelhertz, *The Nature, Impact and Prosecution of White-Collar Crime*, Washington, DC: USGPO, 1970, p. 8.

16 N. Shover and A. Hochstetler, *Choosing White-Collar Crime*, London: Cambridge University Press, 2006.

17 M.L. Benson and K.R. Kerley, 'Life course theory and white-collar crime', in J.L. Smith, D. Shichor and H.N. Pontell (eds), *Contemporary Issues in Crime and Criminal Justice: Essays in Honor of Gilbert Geis*, Upper Saddle River, NJ: Prentice-Hall, 2001, pp. 121–136.

18 Shover and Hochstetler, op. cit.

19 D. Weisburd, E.J. Waring and E.F. Chayet, *White-Collar Crime and Criminal Careers*, Cambridge: Cambridge University Press, 2001.

20 M.L. Benson, 'Denying the guilty mind: accounting for involvement in white-collar crime', *Criminology*, 1985, vol. 23, 4, 583–607; Weisburd *et al.*, op. cit.; Benson and Kerley, op. cit.; Shover and Hochstetler, op. cit.

21 Weisburd *et al.*, op. cit.

22 J. MacQuarrie, *Existentialism*, London: Penguin Books, 1972.

23 MacQuarrie, op. cit.

24 J.P. Sartre, *Being and Nothingness: an Essay on Phenomenological Ontology*, original English translation by H.E. Barnes, New York: Philosophical Library, 1958.

25

> [T]he freedom which escapes toward the future can not give itself any past it likes according its fancy ... It has to be its own past, and this past is irremediable ... If the past does not determine our actions, at least it is such that we can not take a new decision except in terms of it.
>
> Sartre, op. cit., p. 517

27 Sartre, op. cit.

28 MacQuarrie, op. cit.

29 MacQuarrie, op. cit.

30 MacQuarrie, op. cit.

31 Sartre, op. cit.

32 MacQuarrie, op. cit.

33 G.M. Kenyon, 'Philosophical foundations of existential meaning', in G.T. Reker and K. Chamberlain (eds), *Exploring Existential Meaning: Optimizing Human Development Across the Life Span*, Thousand Oaks, CA: Sage, 2000, pp. 7–22; Farrall, op. cit.

34 Sartre, op. cit.; 'I am as having been', M. Heidegger, *Being and Time*, translated by J. MacQuarrie, New York: Harper and Row, 1962, p. 373.
35 Sartre, op. cit.
36 J.D. Douglas and J.M. Johnson (eds), *Existential Sociology*, London: Cambridge University Press, 1977.
37 J.A. Kotarba and A. Fontana (eds), *The Existential Self in Society*, Chicago: Chicago University Press, 1984.
38 J.A. Kotarba and J.M. Johnson (eds), *Postmodern Existential Sociology*, Oxford: Rowman and Littlefield, 2002.
39 J.D. Douglas, 'The emergence, security and growth of the sense of self', in J.A. Kotarba and A. Fontana (eds), *The Existential Self in Society*, Chicago: Chicago University Press, 1984, pp. 69–99.
40 J.M. Johnson and J.A. Kotarba, 'Postmodern existentialism', in J.A. Kotarba and J.M. Johnson (eds), *Postmodern Existential Sociology*, Oxford: Rowman and Littlefield, 2002, pp. 3–14.
41 Douglas, op. cit., p. 69.
42 Sartre, op. cit.
43 A. Fontana, 'Introduction: existential sociology and the self', in J.A. Kotarba and A. Fontana (eds), *The Existential Self in Society*, Chicago: Chicago University Press, 1984, pp. 3–17.
44 I. Yalom, *Existential Psychotherapy*, New York: Basic Books, 1980; A. Fontana, 'Short stories from the salt', in J.A. Kotarba and J.M. Johnson (eds), *Postmodern Existential Sociology*, Oxford: Rowman and Littlefield, 2002, pp. 201–218.
45 Douglas, op. cit.
46 Douglas, op. cit.
47 E. Goffman, *Stigma*, Harmondsworth: Penguin Books, 1963; E. Goffman, *The Presentation of Self in Everyday Life*, Harmondsworth: Penguin, 1969; J.D. Douglas, 'Existential sociology', in J.D. Douglas and J.M. Johnson (eds), *Existential Sociology*, London: Cambridge University Press, 1977, pp. 3–73.
48 H.R.F. Ebaugh, 'Leaving the convent: the experience of role exit and self-transformation', in J. Kotarba and A. Fontana (eds), *The Existential Self in Society*, Chicago: Chicago University Press, 1984, pp. 156–176.
49 Douglas, 1977, op. cit., p. 12 (emphasis in original).
50 Kenyon, op. cit.
51 Fontana, 1984, op. cit.
52 T. Scheff, 'Shame and the social bond: a sociological theory', *Sociological Theory*, vol. 18, 1, 2000, pp. 84–99.
53 Douglas, 1984, op. cit., p. 83 (emphasis in original).
54 C. Clark, 'Taming the "brute being": sociology reckons with emotionality', in J.A. Kotarba and J.M. Johnson (eds), *Postmodern Existential Sociology*, Oxford: Rowman and Littlefield, 2002, pp. 155–182.
55 Clark, op. cit.
56 Clark, op. cit., p. 172.
57 Douglas, 1984, op. cit.
58 P. Lejeune, 'The autobiographical contract', in T. Todorov (ed.), *French Literary Theory Today: a Reader*, translated by R. Carter, Cambridge: Cambridge University Press, 1982, pp. 192–222.
59 B. Roberts, *Biographical Research*, Buckingham: Open University Press, 2002.
60 K. Plummer, *Documents of Life 2: An Invitation to a Critical Humanism*, London: Sage, 2001, p. 18.

61 S. Smith and J. Watson, *Reading Autobiography: A Guide for Interpreting Life Narratives*, Minneapolis: University of Minnesota Press, 2002.
62 Smith and Watson, op. cit.
63 Smith and Watson, op. cit.
64 Smith and Watson, op. cit.
65 Plummer, op. cit.
66 Smith and Watson, op. cit.
67 Smith and Watson, op. cit.
68 D.P. McAdams, *The Stories We Live by: Personal Myths and the Making of the Self*, New York: Guilford, 1993.
69 Smith and Watson, op. cit.
70 Smith and Watson, op. cit., p. 13.
71 G. Gusdorf, 'Conditions and limits of autobiography', in J. Olney (ed.), *Autobiography: Essays Theoretical and Critical*, Princeton, NJ: Princeton University Press, 1980, pp. 28–48.
72 K. Plummer, *Documents of Life: An Introduction to the Problems and Literature of a Humanistic Method*, London: George Allen and Unwin, 1983, p. 14.
73 Gusdorf, op. cit., p. 36,
74 Gusdorf, op. cit.
75 D. Sheridan, 'Writing to the archive: mass-observation as auto/biography', *Sociology*, 1993, vol. 27, 1, 27–40.
76 McAdams, op. cit.
77 McAdams, op. cit.
78 S. Maruna, 'Going straight: desistance from crime and life narratives of reform', in A. Lieblich and R. Josselson (eds), *The Narrative Study of Lives (vol. 5)*, London: Sage, 1997, pp. 59–93.
79 Maruna, 1997, op. cit.
80 J. Katz, *Seductions of Crime: The Moral and Sensual Attractions of Doing Evil*, New York: Basic Books, 1988.
81 Maruna, 1997, op. cit.
82 Maruna, 1997, op. cit.
83 Maruna, 1997, op. cit., p. 71.
84 Shover and Hochstetler, op. cit.
85 Farrall, Chapter 7, this volume.
86 S. Morgan, 'Prison lives: critical issues in reading prisoner autobiography', *The Howard Journal of Criminal Justice*, 1999, vol. 38, 3, 328–340.
87 Morgan, op. cit., p. 337.
88 J.C. Oleson, 'The celebrity of infamy: a review essay of five autobiographies by three criminal geniuses', *Crime, Law and Social Change*, 2003, vol. 40, 391–408.
89 Oleson, op. cit., p. 403.
90 Kotarba and Johnson, op. cit.
91 Farrall, 2005, op. cit.
92 J. Aitken, *Porridge and Passion*, London: Continuum, 2005; R.L. Berger, *From the Inside*, New York: iUniverse, 2003; A. Bond, *Bond*, London: HarperCollins, 2003; J. Dean, *Lost Honor*, Los Angeles: Stratford Press, 1982; W. Laite, *The United States vs. William Laite*, Washington: Acropolis Books, 1972; S. Lawson, *Daddy, Why Are you Going to Jail?*, Illinois: Harold Shaw, 1992; N. Leeson, *Rogue Trader*, London: Little, Brown and Company, 1996; N. Leeson, *Back from the Brink: Coping with Stress*, London: Virgin Books, 2005; B. Minkow, *Cleaning Up: One Man's Redemptive Journey*

Through the Seductive World of Corporate Crime, Nashville, TN: Nelson Current, 2005; J. Timilty, *Prison Journal*, Boston, MA: Northeastern University Press, 1997.

93 Berger, op. cit., p. 195.
94 Minkow, op. cit., p. 312.
95 Dean, op. cit., p. 13.
96 Dean, op. cit., p. 15.
97 Dean, op. cit., p. 19.
98 J.P. Sartre, *Saint Genet: Actor and Martyr*, translated by Bernard Fretchman, New York: Pantheon, 1963.
99 Fontana, 1984, op. cit.
100 Weisburd *et al.*, op. cit.; Benson and Kerley, op. cit.; Shover and Hochstetler, op. cit.
101 Sartre, 1963, op. cit.
102 Douglas, 1984, op. cit.
103 Laite, op. cit., p. 227.
104 Laite, op. cit., p. 231.
105 Aitken, op. cit., p. 186.
106 Dean, op. cit., p. 24.
107 Dean, op. cit., p. 24.
108 Douglas, 1984, op. cit.
109 Aitken, op. cit., p. 127.
110 Girodano *et al.*, op. cit.
111 See also Farrall and Calverley, op. cit.; C. Simpson, 'When hope makes us vulnerable: a discussion of patient–healthcare provider interactions in the context of hope', *Bioethics*, 2004, vol. 18, 5, 428–447.
112 Fontana, 1984, op. cit.
113 Maruna, 2001, op. cit.; Girodano *et al.*, op. cit.; Farrall and Calverley, op. cit.
114 Visher and Travis, op. cit.
115 Maruna, 2001, op. cit.; Girodano *et al.*, op. cit.
116 H.R.F. Ebaugh, *Becoming an Ex: The Process of Role Exit*, Chicago: Chicago University Press, 1988.
117 Kenyon, op. cit.
118 Ebaugh, 1984, op. cit.
119 Visher and Travis, op. cit.
120 Meisenhelder, op. cit.
121 Benson and Kerley, op. cit.
122 Sartre, 2003, op. cit.
123 Heidegger, op. cit.

Chapter 7

'We just live day-to-day'

A case study of life after release following wrongful conviction[1]

Stephen Farrall

Introduction

Research on the resettlement of offenders after they have served periods of imprisonment is (again) in vogue. Partly this is due to the periodic re-emergence of core criminological topics, and partly it is due to the growing numbers of women and men sentenced to custody in many jurisdictions in the US and the UK. This chapter, however, turns its attention away from this body of work to consider the resettlement (if such a word dare be used in this context) of the wrongfully convicted. In a number of essays, Adrian Grounds and Ruth Jamieson[2] have explored in depth the experiences of some of those men and women who have been wrongfully convicted and sentenced to imprisonment in the UK and North America. Their work is at the forefront of efforts to understand the impacts of wrongful imprisonment. Towards the end of one of their essays they refer in passing to the concept of the loss of the assumptive world – that is, the loss of all of those things that help to orient people, make them feel secure and that provide them with meaning. This chapter is an attempt to develop the notion of the loss of the assumptive world within wider existentialist concerns as a way of understanding the experiences of those who have been wrongfully convicted.

In the remainder of this introduction I discuss definitions of wrongful conviction, review what is known about its incidence, and summarise the experiences of the wrongfully convicted. Following this, I outline existential sociology and its main preoccupations, then, in a third section, introducing the notion of the assumptive world and its loss. The section following applies these insights to one case study, that of Angela Cannings. I then close with a discussion of the wider contexts of her case and some of the lessons this analysis implies for the wider study of life after punishment.

Defining wrongful conviction

There is no one clear definition of a wrongfully convicted person. However, each of the studies cited herein usually takes some element of the following as a key part of its definition: People who have been arrested and charged with a criminal offence, and who have pleaded guilty to the charges or been found guilty of the charges in a court of law, but who are in fact innocent of that charge[3] either because they did not commit the crime, or because no crime actually took place.[4] Some researchers include those who are released without a retrial or whose conviction is overturned in court or, in some cases, pardoned,[5] whilst others hold that all successful appeals, including those in lower courts, ought to count as 'justice in error'.[6]

How common are wrongful convictions?

It is, as one might imagine, very hard to produce statistics with any sort of reliability on the number or rate of cases whose convictions may be considered 'unsafe', either in the UK or further afield. Despite this, a number of reasonable estimates based on experiences in North America or reviews of the work of the English and Welsh Criminal Cases Review Commission (CCRC) have been made. For example, Radelet[7] reports that between 1972 and 2002 in the US, over 100 inmates have been released from 'death row' because of doubts about their guilt or proof of their innocence. Similarly, Radelet et al.[8] argue that some 23 innocent persons have been executed in the US alone. More recent research[9] reports that 25 per cent of initial suspects in sexual assault cases were ruled out in the light of DNA evidence. Huff,[10] using data from a survey of legal professionals in the US, suggests that around 7,500 people are wrongly convicted for index crimes (i.e. the most serious offences in the US) each year. This survey (reported on in full in Huff et al.[11]) suggested that around 0.5 per cent of index convictions were wrongful. In Australia, an enquiry into corruption among New South Wales police officers found 35 claims of wrongful conviction (cited in Martin[12]).

Martin[13] reports that in England and Wales, 37 cases involving 49 individuals were reported to the Home Secretary between 1980 and 1987. During the same period, the Home Secretary paid compensation to 60 individuals. In the UK the CCRC has received over 4,000 applications between 1999 and 2004.[14] An analysis of cases from the CCRC for the period 1999–2002[15] suggested that the annual case load for the service was running at about 70 cases per annum. The Scottish Criminal Cases Review Commission (SCCRC) reports that it received 807 applications between April 1999 and May 2006. The CCRC's annual report for 2005–2006 stated that the convictions of 31 out of the 44 cases referred back to the courts were quashed (representing some 70 per cent[16]). The same report notes that the CCRC has received some 8,540 applications since its inauguration in 1997, and that 'the long-term trend suggests that there will be continue to be a high level of applications'.[17] Similarly in Scotland, the SCCRC reported in its 2006 annual report that it had again seen a rise in applications, up around 40 per cent of the previous year's number. In short, it appears that there are a considerable number of cases each year over which some uncertainty hangs.

What is the wrongful convictee's experience?

There have been very few accounts of the experience of being wrongfully convicted.[18] Most of those studies that have been conducted either report on small numbers of cases (Campbell and Denov[19] rely on interviews with five cases, while Grounds[20] uses data derived from around 30 cases, several of them 'Irish cases', others drawn from work in Canada). Despite this, a number of experiences have been highlighted. Weisman[21] suggests that the wrongfully convicted prisoner is inhibited from expressing remorse or sadness for the victims of the crime for which they have been found guilty. Because the wrongfully convicted often maintain their innocence for several years or for their entire prison sentence, they are unlikely to be seen by the criminal justice system as having taken their first steps along the road to rehabilitation: namely admission of wrongdoing and remorse[22] (see Campbell and Denov[23]). As such, these individuals come to be treated as if they presented a *greater* risk of harm to others, and are, in terms of institutional cultures, unlikely to be able to create the identity of someone who is ready to be returned to the community. Such treatment also creates troubling emotions for the wrongfully convicted as their guilt is assumed.[24] Campbell and Denov[25] suggest that the uncertainty over their release date (and the general lack of preparedness for it) causes the wrongfully convicted great stress. The unwillingness to admit to the offence often made such prisoners ineligible for early release or parole schemes. This perhaps goes some way towards accounting for the psychiatric problems identified among this group of prisoners[26]; depression, self-harm and attempts to kill themselves are all common.[27] Grounds' studies of a number of long-term wrongfully convicted prisoners have suggested that they experience enduring personality changes and other psychiatric problems.[28] These problems include always feeling 'on edge' or 'panicky', vividly re-experiencing the events surrounding their trial or experiences in prison, substance use, insomnia and emotional problems. As with ordinary prisoners,[29] many of the wrongfully convicted report the emotional troubles associated with visits from their family members[30] and the recognition that in some respects *not* having such visits was easier. Like many of those who have been imprisoned for long periods of time, Grounds also found that many of the wrongfully convicted had lost practical or social skills by the time they were released. Many also experienced difficulties with their relationships with family members (who had often learned to live without the wrongfully convicted individual present, either physically or emotionally). In short, their life-courses were altered dramatically and in a way that was hard to undo. Grounds concluded that the wrongfully convicted bore more resemblance to soldiers returning from combat than they did to 'ordinary' ex-prisoners.

Existential sociology[31]

In a number of edited volumes,[32] a loosely affiliated research group has charted what it has referred to as 'existential sociology'. This existential sociology they have variously defined (or just described) as being concerned with the following issues:

> Existential sociology is defined descriptively as the study of human experience-in-the-world (or existence) in all its forms.... The goal is to construct both practical and theoretical truths about that experience, to understand how we live, how we feel, think, act.[33]

As one would expect, these definitions draw heavily upon philosophical existentialism, which Manning defines in the following manner: 'Existentialism is ... a philosophy arguing that through his life, man makes decisions and builds up meanings in line with them (if possible), and is in fact forced to act, to accept freedom'.[34] More specifically, existential sociology attempts to understand the above via a detailed concern with the following.

The search for a meaningful identity

As well as importing the existential preoccupation with the 'futility of existence',[35] existential philosophers and sociologists have highlighted the individual's search for a meaningful identity (e.g. Sartre,[36] Manning[37]), and the feelings and angst this entails. Numerous of the existentialists whose work is reviewed herein are engaged in exploring how individuals – often following a period of change – seek, adapt and maintain a meaningful identity.[38] Of course, and as hinted at above, these processes of change are neither simply linear nor without their moments of self-doubt, as recorded by Ebaugh:

> The application [to leave the convent] came, I [Ebaugh] put it away in my desk drawer, and for three weeks was unable to look at it. It was not so much a process of intellectually weighing the pros and cons but of becoming comfortable with the idea of no longer being a nun.[39]

As this quotation suggests, the search for a meaningful identity – be it a 'new' identity or the ongoing project of 'self' – presents certain threats to an individual at an existential level. The extent to which such threats create intense feelings of ontological insecurity is a core focus of existential philosophy and hence also of existential sociology (see, for example, Douglas[40]). Applied to the study of reforming alcoholics, Denzin writes that an individual 'comes to define herself in terms of who she no longer wants to be',[41] adding that over time 'the self that is moving forward judges the momentum of this movement in terms of where it used to be'. Thus, 'being for itself' becomes an ongoing project, continually striving to understand and improve itself in some way. In this respect, as others have observed,[42] the self is continually being projected forward into the future (Heidegger, on being and time[43]), as this becomes the temporal space in which the 'for itself' (Sartre[44]) is realised.

'Self' and 'Other'

It ought to be clear from the foregoing discussion that another of the core foci of existential interest surrounds changes in the self and definitions of 'oneself'.[45] As MacQuarrie writes, 'To exist is to project oneself in to the future. But there is always a lack or disproportion between the self as projected and the self where it actually stands'.[46] In this respect one of the chief concerns of existential sociology has revolved around the 'slowly evolving sense of inner self'[47] and transformations in self-identity that occur as individuals move from one social setting or institution to another,[48] or adapt to new social roles.[49] Of course, as individuals' sense of who they are develops, or as they leave one social institution and/or join another, so their relationships with other individuals may also change.[50] This is another central preoccupation of existential sociology and refers not just to specific individuals, but also to social groups or types of relationships. For example, Ebaugh's study describes how ex-nuns found themselves forging new relationships not just with specific others, but with certain social groups and types of 'role occupants' (e.g. landlords, classmates, work colleagues and male friends). These then were not just changes in specific relationships, but changes in terms of who one *could* and *needed* to associate with.

Feelings and emotions

Almost all the existential sociologists writing at the core of the school emphasise understanding the role of feelings and emotions in the human experience.[51] Of particular importance is the experience of conflicting emotions and how these are resolved (or not) and the impact this has on the subject's self identity.[52] In this respect, as Ebaugh's research on ex-nuns suggests, existential sociology charts the peculiar mix of rational and non-rational elements that imbue many human experiences, and especially those periods characterised by processes of change and transition. Thus existential sociology provides a welcome break from the 'rational'/'non-rational' dichotomy that haunts much criminological thinking.

This fusing together of thoughts and feelings brings us to one of the other core foci of existential sociology, namely a focus on an individual's values. Beliefs about what is 'right' or 'wrong' and how (and when) these beliefs are translated into feelings is another preoccupation of existential sociologists. As Douglas writes, 'basic values, supported by strong feelings of pride when we live by them and shame and guilt when we do not, orient us towards our social world.[53] Beliefs and the feelings associated with them are key to helping the individual make sense of the wider world and particular activities within it. The extent to which and the ways in which the sense of oneself and of one's behaviour are uniquely linked are summarised by Douglas in the following passage:

> It is our sense of self that gives us the feeling that 'that is not like me', 'but I'm not like that', 'but I'm not the sort of person who would do such a thing', 'but I could never', 'but I feel violated', 'I would not feel right', 'I just sense that it's wrong for me', and so on, all the time. We cannot generally say exactly why 'it is not like me'. We do not know in words, but we know immediately.[54]

This insight brings us to a consideration of two recurring themes in existentialism and the sociology that it has inspired: guilt and shame.[55] These powerful emotions help individuals to understand 'who' they are and 'what' they believe to be 'right' and 'wrong'. Of course, there is almost certainly a feedback loop between such feelings and the ongoing production of a sense of self: feeling shame at one's past actions or deeds helps to engender a sense of 'who' one is. This sense in turn may influence which things one thinks to be right or wrong, which in turn may find expression in new actions that reinforce the emerging self-identity and so on. In many respects, it is these sorts of issues that get to the heart of one of the other central concerns of existentialism: problems of freedom and choice.[56] This concern with freedom and choice is most obviously articulated in the writings of Sartre,[57] and is a key organising principle in Ebaugh's study of ex-nuns.[58] The ex-nuns finally initiated leaving the convent when they realised that they had the freedom to decide whether or not to remain a nun. As Ebaugh reports, this moment was often associated with a strong feeling of elation.[59]

The existential methodological stance

Although, as Fontana[60] notes, existential sociologists have not devoted much of their energies to outlining a uniquely existential methodology, a number of principles do suggest research strategies. The first principle is a focus on 'natural settings'.[61] This commitment to study humans in their 'natural' habitat comes from a desire to gain an understanding of the individual's everyday life world.[62] This orientation has most commonly encouraged existential sociologists to engage in in-depth interviews, ethnographies, participant observation and introspection. For example, Ebaugh relied upon interviews with ex-nuns, ex-doctors, ex-teachers and a range of other 'exes' for her study of changing identities.[63] Similarly, Fontana[64] relied upon his own experiences to discuss how he was able to adopt a new role of racing enthusiast, while Warren and Ponse[65] relied upon participant observation and interviews for their study of gay communities.

In this chapter I rely on a published autobiography (that by Angela Cannings[66]) and media interviews for my data. Criminology has a long tradition of using autobiographies, and in particular there has been a resurgence of interest in this methodology.[67] The life-history approach – within which I place the use of autobiographies – has been described by some as the best way of investigating the 'inner world' of respondents, sharing a great deal with ethnographic writings.[68] Various challenges present themselves, including the impossibility of anonymising the data and issues surrounding the accuracy of the accounts presented. My approach to autobiographies is to focus on their ability to present 'internal' truths rather than strict 'factual' truths (for example, the recounting of precise events). As such, the use of autobiographies means focusing on *subjective truths* and relinquishing notions of factual truth. In this way, autobiographies need to be read alongside other accounts of similar events. In this manner, as well as reading Angela Cannings' autobiography, I read a number of other autobiographies of the wrongfully convicted at the same time.[69] Through this triangulation of resources I was able to develop an appreciation of the experiences related by Angela Cannings herself. Autobiographies also represented an ethical solution to the subject matter at hand. Researching the lives of those men and women who have undergone miscarriages of justice presents considerable ethical problems since many of these people simply wish to be left alone to rebuild their lives. Further interviews with these cases may have hindered their recovery. In this respect, the use of autobiographies represents a non-invasive research tool.

The second principle embodied within existential sociology is a concern with capturing the 'total person'.[70] Whereas quite exactly what is meant by the focus on the 'total person' is never fully spelt out, it is not unreasonable to assume that this idea refers to a desire to capture in detail all of the nuances of individual lives. The fusion of the rational and the irrational, the heady mix of emotional states (sometimes intense, sometimes mundane), the specific locating of individuals in particular times and spaces, the uniqueness of their experiences and the desire to combine both 'the human' and 'the social' in one account best represent what is meant by the attempt to capture the 'total person'.

Existentialist thought within criminology

There have been very few studies that have either drawn directly from existentialist thinking, or that have employed closely related concepts.[71] Among these is the study of drug dealers/smugglers by Adler[72] whose ethnography reveals how these individuals, feeling disenchanted with their lives, retreated into 'heavy-end' drug smuggling in order to avoid pain, achieve pleasure and satisfy their brute inner drives.[73] Their chosen lifestyle allowed them to feel excitement, glamour, spontaneity and to attend to their inner drives for impulsive self-expression. As Adler writes, 'they ceased to think of their selves as something to be "attained, created and achieved", and focused instead on discovering and satisfying their deep, unsocialized inner impulses'.[74]

As Morrison notes,[75] the work of Jack Katz,[76] while not directly referring to existentialist thought in any depth, resonates with many of the concerns of existential sociologists. Relying on a number of sharply focused studies of specific types of crime or criminal (for example, the thrill of breaking and entering a neighbour's house), Katz draws our attention to the experiential aspects of offending. Morrison's work demonstrates how, by emphasising the sensuality of crime, one is given a new perspective on both crime and criminals – a perspective that encourages one to reconsider not just why people offend, but what may be done to discourage such behaviour.[77] Other criminologists[78] have discussed existential concerns in the study of crime, but few have explicitly tied existentialist concerns directly to the issues confronting contemporary criminological enquiry.

Just as the study of deviancy can help illuminate the basic contours of social order and the ways in which fundamental desires clash head-on with social conventions, thereby creating possibilities for social change,[79] an existentially inspired understanding of crime, criminals, victims and innocents can help illuminate current criminological preoccupations. In particular, the existential perspective is especially insightful when applied to the concept of changes in the criminal career.[80] When people try to stop offending, try to make amends for past behaviour and succeed in so doing, they are not merely 'no longer offending', but in some cases have gone through lengthy periods of rebuilding, remodelling or remaking their own social identities. By understanding these processes of change (sometimes self-initiated, sometimes supported by criminal justice agencies, and almost always 'propped up' by partners, parents and offspring) we are able to understand how people 'remake' themselves.

It must be said that some of the best work on change in identity with criminology has started to echo some of the core interests of existentialism. For example, in their study of female desistance, Giordano et al.[81] rely on the concept of a 'blueprint' for a replacement self. Their four-part 'theory of cognitive transformation' involves the following stages: 'general cognitive openness to change'; exposure and reaction to 'hooks for change' (turning points); the envisioning of 'an appealing and conventional "replacement self"'; and transforming the way the actor views deviant behaviour. Additionally, they focus on the emotional aspects of the desistance process.[82] Other studies of ex-offenders resonate with existentialism: for example Cusson and Pinsonneault's research[83] on 'shocks' that force the individual to embark upon a period of renegotiation of 'who' they are and 'what' they do; Shover's study[84] on changes in goals, 'tiredness' and the impact these processes have on self-identity; Bull's work[85] on feelings of despair and the motivation to change; or Meisenhelder's investigation[86] of an individual's use of social locales to reinforce the projection of a new personal identity. Maruna[87] shows that while catalysts for change were external to the individual, desistance was reported as an internal process that enabled the 'real me' to emerge. Without explicitly referring to it, many of these commentators have been following a research agenda that mirrors many of the concerns associated with existential sociology.

The loss of the assumptive world

The notion of there being an 'assumptive world' grew out of work on grief, mourning and thanatology.[88] The assumptive world refers to those beliefs that ground, secure, stabilise or orient people and that accordingly give them a sense of purpose and meaning to their lives as well as providing feelings of belonging and connection to others.[89] Parkes writes that the assumptive world 'is the only world we know and it includes everything we know or think we know. It includes our interpretation of the past and our expectations of the future, our plans and our prejudices'.[90] Beder suggests that

> the assumptive world is an organised schema reflecting all that a person assumes to be true about the world and the self on the basis of previous experiences; it refers to the assumptions, or beliefs that ground, secure, and orient people, that give a sense of reality, meaning and purpose to life.[91]

Most accounts of the assumptive world stress the importance of the notions of safety, control and justice in the assumptive world. The assumptive world is terribly mundane; such assumptions lead individuals to the belief that their life has a structure which is 'knowable' to themselves and (largely) rewarding and satisfying. The world is understandable, predictable, manageable and largely benign.[92] Alongside these assumptions come the assumptions that oneself is a worthy individual that others care for, and that others are trustworthy.[93] In short, our assumptions about our social worlds make us think that the world is understandable, worth caring about and investing in, and unthreatening to ourselves.

In some respects, the assumptions about the world as held by individuals are illusory internal constructs, rather than real objective externalities. The assumptive world is shaped by past experiences, relationships and investments, but is usually approached as being future oriented.[94] Kauffman[95] argues that 'assumptive world convictions maintain belief in the future, maintain an open horizon to the future. No safe future imaginable means that no future is imaginable' (as such there are parallels with the writings by key existentialists, most notably a concern with developing a sense of a future self (becoming) that is coherent and a meaningful identity (authenticity), the problematic nature of life (nihilism) and the anxiety associated with the search for meaning).

However, such assumptions are not readily admitted to, nor do many individuals consciously acknowledge their assumptions until such assumptions are radically called into question.[96] Only at this point are social actors forced to recognise just how much of their world they had come to take for granted, become accustomed to or assumed was stable and predictable. No two sets of assumptions will be alike, and each will be, of course, structured by age, gender, ethnicity, social class and life experience. Similarly, historical, cultural and social contexts will influence the nature of any one individual's assumptive world. Assumptive worlds are not static either; as individuals age and develop socially, so their assumptions about the ways in which the remainder of their lives will be spent will change. A young mother aged 25 will have a different set of assumptions from those she is likely to have when she is 50 and her children have left home. Our assumptions change as we grow and our lives unfold, and in so doing they become modified and renegotiated.[97]

When such assumptions are shattered, ruptured or altogether lost – either through the death of a loved one, divorce or some other form of traumatic loss – the individual concerned can experience a rampant devaluation of much that was important to them. Such experiences can lead to a crisis of meaning,[98] existential uncertainty[99] and to periods of confusion and disorientation[100] as the self and one's narrative about oneself becomes discontinuous.[101] Taken as a whole, such phenomena can lead to a loss of self-identity, with many who experience such losses feeling as if they have been betrayed,[102] leading to an existential search for a meaningful identity. Neimeyer and colleagues note how many people who suffer traumatic loss attempt to re-impose their 'old self' as a way of maintaining their sense of narrative:

> Our first impulse when faced with invalidation of our scripts of identity often focuses on becoming our 'old self' again. Unfortunately, such a 'narrative rewind' is impossible by definition, as we cannot turn back time and must instead struggle with ways of bridging what once was and what now is.[103]

They go on to note how attempts to create new narratives draw upon a range of resources, both practical and symbolic, which are derived from relationships with family members, the wider community and culture. However, these narratives may be very restrictive or limiting, and the individual concerned may wish to resist accepting these conceptions of themselves. To this one could also add religious beliefs. Attig[104] suggests that such 'relearning' of the world requires the person who has suffered the loss to learn new ways of being and of acting in the world. The establishment of a new assumptive world may be a long and painful process.[105] In short, the work surrounding the assumptive world and its loss resonates with core concerns of existential sociology in that both are interested in how people make sense of their self in relation to others and wider social institutions and organisations during or following periods of uncertainty.

Angela Cannings

Angela Cannings was found guilty of the murder of two of her children in February 2002, and was released on appeal in December 2003 after almost two years in prison. I focus exclusively on Angela's case for a number of reasons. First, hers is an extremely well-known case, at least in the UK, which resulted in the Attorney General, Lord Goldsmith, ordering a review of 297 convictions of parents accused of killing a child aged less than two years during the decade prior to her case. The entry of the phrase 'post-Cannings' into the legal lexicon and the choice of the BBC to make a documentary about her case are testimony to the importance, legally and culturally, of this case. Second, and for the above reason, hers is an extremely well-documented case. As well as Angela's autobiography, there exist a number of interviews with her and members of her family in the media. For someone interested in her life *after* she had been released, her autobiography makes ideal material, devoting the best part of 100 pages of text to her and her family's experience after her release with an extraordinary level of openness and candour. As such, Angela Cannings' story is both an extremely moving one, and one that is fitting to use as a 'way into' the problems facing those who are released from prison following successful appeal against their conviction.

Angela's story

Angela Cannings saw herself as an 'ordinary mother'[106] of two children living with her husband in a provincial English town (Salisbury). This was, she described, 'a normal family life'[107] in which she cared for her two children, worked part-time at a local supermarket and ran a home. Angela had lived with her husband, Terry, for the previous 15 years or so. With the exception of the tragic deaths of their first two children due to cot death (or Sudden Infant Death Syndrome, SIDS), their lives had been pretty uneventful. Following the deaths of their first two children, Gemma and Jason, Angela and Terry went on to have two further children, Jade and Matthew. When he was a little over four months old, Matthew too died (again of SIDS, it transpired), sparking a train of events that led to Angela spending almost two years in prison for his and Jason's murders.

Almost as soon as Matthew had died, Angela was in the grip of a criminal investigation that would see her forced to live apart from her family (in case she harmed her three-and-a-half-year-old daughter). She endured this torment for two-and-a-quarter years before her trial commenced – at which she was found guilty of the murders of her two sons, Jason and Matthew.[108] Most of the extracts below come from her autobiography.

Upon reception at Eastwood Park, Angela quickly became accustomed to the routine of the prison, and within a couple of days knew where and when meals would be served, how to order food, where to go for medicines and such like. However, she reports feeling like 'a pencil drawing half rubbed out, the lines all blurry'[109] as she struggled to grow accustomed to her new life and what this meant for her. During the period, she refers to herself as 'grieving for her lost life'[110] and as feeling 'tormented by the life that should have been mine'.[111] Family visits, perhaps unsurprisingly, caused some of the greatest heartache, partly as these brought home what had been lost: 'You never know what you've got until it's gone and just to be able to move around freely with [Jade], to touch [Jade], to have a few hours in which to watch [Jade] properly, filled me with happiness'.[112] However, visits were no place in which to be a 'real mummy',[113] and Angela started to withdraw emotionally from her daughter.

Such emotional closure was mirrored by her husband, Terry, too. In part, this process had started before the trial, as Terry started to prepare for life without Angela. Terry later told Angela that he had cut himself off emotionally from her as he thought that she would be gone for years.[114] Angela's presence at home in the run up to her trial also caused problems – her mere presence started to remind Terry of what they were about to lose. While in prison, as is the case with many relationships, Angela and Terry's started to struggle. Letters back to Terry were too hard for Angela to write, and so she chose not to write at all, wishing not to worry him further. When Angela did write, often her letters to Jade went unopened and Terry hid from Angela Jade's loss of interest in her mother during this period. In short, that is to say while she was in prison, imprisonment damaged the relationship between Angela and her family more than one could possibly imagine.

I want to focus, however, on Angela's experiences after she left prison, following her successful appeal against her conviction (on 10 December 2003), since my primary concern is with documenting Angela's life after her formal punishment had ended. Like many former prisoners (wrong-fully *or* legitimately convicted), Angela struggled with a number of features of everyday life to which she had become unaccustomed. These included money,[115] the noise of traffic[116] and the 'bewildering choice' associated with modern life.[117] All of these things made Angela feel 'like an alien'.[118] These findings are consistent with other studies of the release of the innocent.[119]

Angela also found it hard to re-establish her place in the family. While she had been in prison, Terry and Jade had had four holidays together. They had become used to making their own holiday arrangements and doing their own packing, leaving Angela with little to do.[120] The strength of the relationship between Terry and Jade – who had lived without close contact with Angela for the best part of four years – created further distance from Angela. In part this was due to Jade no longer being the little girl Angela had left behind:

> I was still taking in all the changes in her. She was so different to the little girl I remembered. I think part of me had expected to get back the three-and-a-half-year-old I'd been separated from on the day of Matthew's death. But Jade was now nearly eight.[121]

Part of the trauma for Angela was that her role in the family – that of main carer – had been destroyed. When Jade wanted affection or reassurance it was Terry, not Angela, she turned to. Angela added in an interview in the *Yorkshire Post* that she felt 'permanently scarred'[122] by her experiences and said six months later that she

> felt that my body was broken in two and I'm still trying to mend it now. Whilst I was in prison Terry was Jade's mummy and daddy, but suddenly Mummy has come home. I'm concentrating on us being a family again but we all have traumas to get over.[123]

In her autobiography, Angela describes the 'emptiness' caused by, ironically, her release: 'There had been something to fight for so long – first an arrest, then a trial, then the appeal – and it almost felt strange to face each other again without having to look over our shoulders.'[124] This emptiness was partly due to the role-vacuum caused by her imprisonment (whereby she was no longer the main care-provider for her child) and the vacuity of a life without a job, a day-to-day role or a clear sense of what the future would hold or how it may be shaped. This sense of emptiness forced Angela and Terry to confront the future in a way that they might not have had to before: 'Real life lay before us like a blank canvas and we were slowly edging towards living it.'[125] A year after her release from prison, Terry said in one interview that

Some days when I wake up, all I can think about is going back to bed. I don't want to go out; I can't meet people. My only security is my bedroom and my living room. I'm not the bloke I was.[126]

A matter of months after being released, Angela became convinced that all three of them needed to leave their home town, Salisbury:

I still felt uncertain among people, as if I would never know who was friend or foe and there were constant echoes of the past – the magistrates court in the middle of the city centre, the sign for the A&E department of the hospital where I went for a check-up on my Bell's Palsy, the police station at the end of the Road where Claire lived – buildings once part of the safe life we'd had before losing Matthew were now almost threatening.[127]

Relationships with immediate family and friends were another reason for wanting to leave Salisbury. Initially after Angela's arrest, there had been many well-wishers, but soon that ceased and people had started to avoid Terry, leaving him feeling hurt and abandoned. Although Angela's family would travel to see her while she was in prison, they did not visit to see Terry or Jade, who were living in the same town. Asking her family to give them time to readjust after release backfired: after not seeing her father for a month or so, Angela's father wrote to her stating that he wished to cut off all contact with her as she had not been in contact enough. Angela and Terry decided, in the light of all of this, to leave Salisbury to seek a new life. In any case, neither of them was working since Terry had given up his job to look after Jade full-time – a decision that saw him having to move into local authority accommodation.

Deciding to start a new life in Cornwall (since they had recalled happy memories of holidays there), however, did not solve many of their problems and Angela started to realise how difficult the next phase of their lives would be:

Gradually I had realised how naive I'd been about what would greet me when I came out. Terry was no longer the confident, smiling, generous, hard working people-pleaser I'd known.[128]

I was also increasingly aware, though, of problems we had not left behind in Salisbury. What I had seen in the first six months of freedom had frightened me[129] and it was only now beginning to dawn on me just how much work was needed to repair my relationship with my husband and daughter.[130]

After they had left Salisbury, Terry and Angela found their lives got harder, not easier: Jade refused to go to school (fearing that her parents would not be there when she returned), refused to take part in any Christmas activities, was not eating properly and was having trouble sleeping. Similarly, Terry's drinking had become worse, Angela started to argue with both Jade and Terry and found it harder to comfort both of them. All three of them started counselling. This general situation persisted for over a year, and Angela admits that she found Jade increasingly tiring to build a relationship with.[131] Angela later said that she had expected to be back at work by this stage, but that she was still not ready.[132] The efforts required to build relationships with Terry and Jade had meant that all of her energies had been put into them, and relationships with others suffered, and they spent less and less time in Salisbury. For Angela it felt as if neither Terry nor Jade wanted her at home.[133] In counselling, Terry admitted that he had struggled with Angela's return to the family home:

> Since Angela has come home I've had to try and get used to the fact that we're all back together. When she was away from me and given a life sentence, which we understood was going to be for years, I got it into my head that she wouldn't be coming out until I was well into my sixties. I had to learn how to live with it and forced myself to. Now I can't get past that. What I have done is emotionally detach myself from her. That is how I feel today.[134]

At this time Angela reported that she did not know how to look forward anymore and felt as if she was 'a failure'.[135] Terry described the change in their relationship as 'it's a crappy relationship now. We're very distant'.[136] He adds, in the same interview, this comment:

> I suffered because of what all this did to me as a man. On the 12th November, 1999, I was five stone thinner than this. I was a guy who worked 60 hours a week. I'd never been in trouble with the police. I ran the top money-making Tesco bakery in Great Britain and I was a dad and a husband. But from the moment Ange was arrested, they stripped that all away from me.

Terry elsewhere has described himself and Angela as more like brother and sister since her release,[137] adding that it felt like they had lost their futures. Looking to the future, to the extent that it can be discerned, provides only a further source of worry for Angela:

> The judges gave me my freedom back and what I desperately want is to embrace life now and I hope that somewhere in the future we can pick some of the pieces up. But my fear is that the way things are at the moment, it may never come to that.[138]

Towards the end of her autobiography, Angela reflects on what the future holds for her and her family:

> where I have some sense of optimism about my future with Jade, there is only uncertainty with Terry. I wish I could give you a happy ending but I cannot. We both made mistakes when I came out, he needed softness and I could not give that to him, he shut off from me and would not build bridges. We had both changed and struggled to adjust to the people we found waiting for us. He believes he will see Gemma, Jason and Matthew in another life, but the comfort I found in religion while in prison has not extended to life on the outside.[139]

It is clear from Angela Cannings' autobiography that she felt not just a profound loss at the death of her children, but also at the shattering of her assumptions about the way the world 'was', the person she was and who others saw her as, and the loss of her assumptions about the future course of her life, as the following quotations attest:

> For a split second when I woke on the morning after Matthew's death, I thought my world was still complete. In those first waking moments of 13th November 1999, as I hovered between a fitful sleep and wakefulness, *I was in the life I should have been living.*[140]

> I'd thought constantly about Matthew since coming home. Every so often, as I did the housework or walked to pick up Jade from school, I'd think back to our home in Waterloo Road and wonder *what life would have been like* if we were still there, the four of us.[141]

> To be deprived of your freedom for something you did not do goes to the *very core of beliefs you have about society and your place in it, your sense of safety and trust.* I don't talk to anyone, even Terry, about it all and, while I have tried as much as possible in this book, there are some things I cannot explore with myself or another. I want to move on. I don't want to be heartbroken forever.[142]

Echoing the loss of the world she had assumed she would lead, Angela writes, in connection with the death of her first child, Gemma, that 'losing a baby isn't just about losing that tiny person – it's about losing your dreams, your hopes for the future'.[143] It is also clear that Terry suffered a similar process[144] and that they both suffered a devaluation in what had previously been important to them.

For Angela, the conviction and her imprisonment, regardless to some extent of her release (since the word 'innocent' was never used by any court official to describe her), has left her in an unusual position. Her identity has been spoiled in a very direct and readily observable way, however, the ease with which she can rebuild her identity and re-assume the identity of a respectable person is fraught with challenges too. As Angela says: 'I've been given a label – and I will carry that to my grave. But I cling on to the hope that happiness is there in the future.'[145] However, it is unclear to Angela how she ought to set about altering that label. Unlike ex-criminals who can embark on rehabilitation via 'good works' (such as Tookie Williams[146]), Angela had done nothing wrong in the first place for which she can 'make amends'. She cannot embark upon a series of pronouncements about her 'true self' having emerged from the wreckage of her former life,[147] since, if anything, the *reverse* is closer to the truth: her true self has been obliterated by her conviction. Angela has no obvious way of 'unspoiling' her identity. Initially she assumed that she could return to her old life and become her 'old self' (an assumption made by many whose worlds have been shattered[148]). However, this strategy, she quickly realised, was not open to her. Instead she creates a 'phantom normalcy'[149] in which she lives with her husband and Jade as they try to assess what the future holds for them. In so doing, Angela is required to develop a new set of assumptions that are less certain and more fluid than her previous (i.e. pre-conviction) assumptions. Gone is the assumption that she will spend the rest of her life with Terry, or that they will enjoy a happy and successful marriage. Gone are her assumptions that she will return to work as her children age. At best, Angela will not gain a new identity for some time, but rather will gain the identity of someone who has overcome extreme hardship.[150] This 'mortification of the self'[151] is particularly painful since there was (a) nothing wrong with Angela's self, behaviour or identity prior to the death of Matthew, and (b) the arrest, conviction, imprisonment, etc. was unwarranted.

Goffman argues[152] that those dealing with stigma often elect to tell a small number of people everything about their stigma while keeping most others unaware of their past and their spoiled identity. Those brought into the fold in this way are 'employed' to assist the individual dealing with the stigma cope with ordinary, everyday obstacles. Angela Cannings, however, has employed almost the reverse of this strategy: she has been extremely candid about her feelings and her and her family's struggles since Matthew died. This strategy is best suited to her position as someone with nothing whatsoever to hide (and having committed no wrongdoing at all she had no need for a 'confessional moment' in which to recruit assistance). In any case, concealing her identity would leave her open to the danger of arousing others' suspicions if her identity were uncovered. The uncovering of her true identity would lead to accusations of dishonesty (or deceitfulness), in turn raise suspicions about other aspects of her life and could lead to further social ostracism since honesty is seen as the bedrock of friendship relationships.

Another approach, in this case taken by Sally Clark,[153] another of the women wrongfully found guilty of murdering their children on the basis of the faulty evidence provided by Professor Roy Meadows,[154] is to withdraw socially for some period of time until the collective memory of her and her case has subsided. In April 2003 Sally elected not to attend the Court of Appeal to hear their judgment in her case. She posted the following on her web page by way of explanation for her decision not to attend court that day:

> something important happened to me last week which made me take the difficult decision to stay away from court today. Something that many of you will, I hope, empathise with and understand. I took my little boy to the park and struck up a conversation with the other mums there. Not one of them knew who I was. How I have longed for that day – to be a normal mum, doing normal things, which had been denied to me, without fear of being recognised, without any self-consciousness.[155]

This, then, represents the dilemma facing many of the wrongfully convicted: the strategies for social reintegration – for want of a better phrase – are extremely painful. Either they require an openness about family relationships that may lead to more pain and hurt, or they require self-imposed social ostracism which may last for years. Either way it is clear that the loss of the assumptive world brought on by wrongful convictions leaves the wrongfully imprisoned in an existential limbo, feeling for some considerable time that they no longer fit in to the social world[156] or are caught between two worlds.[157] The strategies for repair open to the released wrongfully convicted person are not numerous, nor are they likely to be successful in the short or even medium term. What is clear is that the life courses of the individuals concerned are changed forever more, as hinted at in this quotation from Angela Cannings:

> We just live day to day. I love [Terry] but somewhere along the way it's been damaged because he's a different man now. I've seen him kicked in the teeth and don't seem to be able to help him through that. It's not that I don't love him because I do.[158]

A further set of problems faced by the wrongfully accused is to be found with their relationship with the state. The sense of betrayal felt by most wrongfully convicted persons comes from not having been believed all the time they were telling the truth, and from having been harmed by the state. The state is the body that has done most to harm the wrongfully convicted person's life. They are arrested, prosecuted, sentenced and imprisoned in the name of the state. The state, therefore, which in Western democracies has positioned itself (at least until the 1980s) as the ultimate care-giver, has damaged almost irreparably the relationship between itself, the wrongfully convicted person and their family. The initial sense of betrayal by the state makes it hard, therefore, for individual statutory agencies, even if they had an obligation to do so, to assist in resettlement, since such bodies will be tainted in the eyes of the wrongfully convicted. This, however, goes further still, as the painful memories associated with the trial and imprisonment are brought back to the fore during resettlement attempts.

The wider contexts of the Cannings case

The case surrounding Angela Cannings, along with women accused of similar crimes such as Sally Clark,[159] Tripti Patel,[160] Margaret Smith,[161] Julie Ferris[162] and Donna Anthony,[163] is embedded in a wider social and political context, of course.[164] Part of this is the demonisation of mothers who work (during her trial Sally Clark was described as being 'career obsessed'[165]). But part of this also is the rise of medical expertise and the importance placed upon such forms of knowledge in the widely heralded 'knowledge economy'.[166] In times and situations of uncertainty, experts are called upon to make judgements about decisions about which it would otherwise be near-impossible to come to any firm conclusion. This development took place alongside others, some documented, others not. There has, as Sparks and Loader point out,[167] been a rise in our awareness of other forms of crime and other sorts of criminals. The ordinary and mundane have become among those who it is reasonable to express suspicion about. In this light, as well as 'new' forms of crime coming to our attention (child sexual abuse, abuse by parents, children and partners, abuse of positions of privilege or power, such as those used by Dr Harold Shipman or Nick Leeson), so too 'ordinary' mothers came to be suspected as potential murderers. This new awareness led to an understandable backlash against such offenders (witness the protests against paedophiles in many of the UK's cities) and a moral panic about such crimes. This backlash Angela Cannings and Sally Clark experienced firsthand for themselves on arrival at prison, where they were subjected to threats of harm, some of which were made good. Like any theory, Meadows' theory of Munchausen Syndrome by Proxy (MSbP) needed evidence to support it – and Angela Cannings was part of such evidence. As others have argued,[168] such arguments started to become circular, as the professional knowledge supported the legal prosecution process, success in which was cited as further evidence of the validity of the professional knowledge. When the scientific basis for the diagnoses collapsed (and other causes for sudden, repeated cases of childhood death in the same family emerged), so the legal basis of the convictions being safe evaporated. Behind all of this, arguably, are changes in the nature of childhood and attitudes towards children. In times in which many couples attempt to conceive children for several years and in which assisted conceptions are costly and less than fully effective, so those who harm or endanger the lives of children are seen as especially worthy of hatred.

Lessons for research on rehabilitation and resettlement

At this juncture I wish to return to one of the main points of focus of my own research and to attempt to distil some lessons from the consideration of the experiences of the wrongfully convicted for it. In short, what does an examination of the resettlement experiences of the wrongfully convicted tell us about what we need to examine in wider resettlement research? It is clear from Angela Cannings' case that she was not the only person affected by her imprisonment: her husband and daughter's lives were changed forever more too. So too were her relationships with her family of origin.[169] In this sense her conviction and eventual release started a 'domino-effect' cascade of harm and hurt which ran through several family units and across three generations. This is not one of those features one routinely encounters in resettlement research. True, we know that very many family relationships will be damaged by imprisonment, but what is not widely recognised is the harm, not so much done *by* release, but realised *through* release and the need to confront the immediate past and the uncertainties of the future. This is not, of course, to argue that no one ought to be released, but rather that if fewer people were imprisoned, fewer would need to be released. Research on rehabilitation and resettlement has made some inroads into recognising the assistance provided by family members in helping to build futures for those men and women processed by the criminal justice system, but more work needs to be done on the life trajectories of family members of the imprisoned. In this respect such research ought to recognise the damage inflicted via the processes of punishment on proximal others.

Another lesson to be learned from the above concerns the discontinuous nature of many biographies. It is well documented[170] that many people who have had their assumptive worlds shattered feel that their sense of self becomes discontinuous. A similar process was cited by Maruna[171] to account for why some desisters appeared able to put their pasts behind them and to move on to pastures new. However, here we see something of the reverse: instead of a 'bad' former self being abandoned we observe amongst the wrongfully convicted a 'good' former self being not so much abandoned but remaining unobtainable. A similar process is in operation, although with differing causal elements and with quite opposite outcomes. 'Re-biographing' has only taken place once with the wrongfully convicted: they have had their old ('good') selves obliterated and a new ('bad') self imposed upon them through the courts and the internalisation of external messaging. In some respects they are unable to 'move on' since what they desire most is that past (unlike, for example, those ex-offenders who wish to 'go straight' and who are only too willing to leave behind their pasts). Thus the past is desired but unobtainable, while what is desired can only be located in the past, which leaves the released wrongfully convicted person in a limbo whereby they have no meaningful social identity. What is required post-release is a further re-biographing to occur. Maruna (referring to the rightfully convicted) refers to this as a redemption ritual. Such a terminology is, of course, inappropriate for those who have committed no offence (and who therefore are not in need of redemption), but nevertheless such a ritual is needed, for, as both Sally Clark and Angela Cannings say: 'Because of the way the legal system works, appeal judges do not say "we proclaim Sally Clark innocent of all crimes". They just say "Her convictions are unsafe" ';[172] 'I was guilty until my conviction was declared unsafe, but no one used the word "innocent". It is not a concept the law recognises when dealing with appeals.'[173] Angela Cannings had experienced something approaching a 'decertification ceremony'[174] when the Court of Appeal gave its reasons for quashing her conviction:

> This was no dry legal document but one written in a language I could understand and mentioning each of my children, Gemma, Jason, Jade and Matthew, by name. They were no longer exhibits, objects to be prodded as the ultimate prove of my guilt. As page after page was read out, I felt as if some of the horror of my trial was washed away as my children became individuals again and, within the formal confines of their judgement, the judges seemed to reach out to Terry and me and acknowledge our family tragedy. I felt touched by their humanity.[175]

However, the absence of the word 'innocent' from the judges' description of her (merely that her conviction was 'unsafe') robs her and others in her position of feeling that they have been fully vindicated. Until the Court of Appeal declares the wrongfully convicted to be de facto innocent, such people will remain uncertain as to whether or not others see them as innocent.[176] This can only further impede the processes of recovery for them.

Summary

Those wrongfully convicted face numerous problems on release from prison. Initially, their joy at release is overwhelming. However, slowly they start to realise both how damaged they are and how hard they will have to work in order to recover any sense of a meaningful identity. This search, which may often last years, entails coming to terms with the past life they have lost and investing in a new life that lies ahead of them. The loss of

their assumptive worlds often means that there is no or only limited investments in future selves, since the traumas of the past are still so painful and
raw. Unlike 'ordinary' ex-prisoners, for whom 'drawing a line' underneath
the past may be a relatively straightforward and beneficial endeavour
which provides them with a renewed sense of life and narrative,[177] the
wrongfully convicted have no immediate desire to cast aside their pre-
convictions selves – which were in many cases both fully formed and non-
deviant. The wrongfully convicted's experiences of loss and readjustment
leave them experiencing the effects of imprisonment for far longer than is
ordinarily recognised by those studying the effects of imprisonment. Only
through marrying existential work with analyses of the loss of assumptive
world and psychiatric assessments[178] can the full horrors of the world they
face become recognised.

Notes

1 I would like to express my thanks to the editors for comments on this chapter.
   I would also like to extend my thanks to Ruth Jamieson for comments on an
   earlier draft, and to Adrian Grounds for discussions in this general arena.
   Errors and omissions remain the sole responsibility of the author. I additionally wish to thank University of California Press for their permission to
   reprint sections from an earlier article: S. Farrall, 'On the existential aspects of
   desistance from crime', *Symbolic Interaction*, 2005, 28(3), 367–386.
2 A. Grounds, 'Psychological consequences of wrongful conviction and imprisonment', *Canadian Journal of Criminology and Criminal Justice*, 2004, 46(2),
   166–182; A. Grounds, 'Understanding the effects of wrongful imprisonment',
   in M. Tonry (ed.), *Crime and Justice: A Review of Research*, Chicago: University of Chicago Press, 2005, vol. 32, pp. 1–58; R. Jamieson and A. Grounds,
   'Release and adjustment: perspectives from studies of wrongfully convicted
   and politically motivated prisoners', in S. Maruna and A. Liebling (eds), *The
   Effects of Imprisonment*, Cullompton: Willan Publishing, 2005, pp. 33–65.
3 C. Huff, A. Rattner and E. Sagarin, *Convicted but Innocent: Wrongful Conviction and Public Policy*, London: Sage, 1996.
4 D.L. Martin, 'The police role in wrongful convictions: an international com-
   parative study', in S.D. Westervelt and J.A. Humphrey (eds), *Wrongly Convicted: Perspectives on Failed Justice*, New Brunswick: Rutgers University
   Press, 2005, pp. 77–95.
5 C.R. Huff, 'Wrongful convictions and public policy: The American Society of
   Criminology 2001 Presidential Address', *Criminology*, 2002, 40(1), 1–18.
6 M. Naughton, 'Redefining miscarriages of justice', *British Journal of Criminology*, 2004, 45(2), 165–182.
7 M. Radelet, 'Wrongful convictions of the innocent', *Judicature*, 2002, 86(2),
   67–68, September–October.
8 M. Radelet, H.A. Bedau and C. Putnam, *In Spite of Innocence*, Boston, MA:
   Northeastern University Press, 1992.
9 B. Scheck and P. Neufeld, 'DNA and innocence scholarship', in S.D. Westervelt and J.A. Humphrey (eds), op. cit, pp. 241–252.
10 C.R. Huff, 'Wrongful convictions: the American experience', *Canadian
   Journal of Criminology and Criminal Justice*, 2004, 46(2), 107–120.

11 C.R. Huff *et al.*, op. cit.
12 D.L. Martin, 'The police role in wrongful convictions', op. cit.
13 Ibid.
14 A. Grounds, 'Psychological consequences of wrongful conviction and imprisonment', op. cit.
15 P. Shore, *Assistance to Prisoners Released on Successful Appeal against Conviction*, 2001, independent report to the Home Office Working Group on Assistance to Prisoners Released on Successful Appeal against Conviction, London.
16 Criminal Cases Review Commission, *Annual Report and Accounts 2005–06*, London: HMSO, 2006, Table 1, pp. 38–39.
17 Ibid., p. 20.
18 K. Campbell and M. Denov, 'The burden of innocence: coping with a wrongful imprisonment', *Canadian Journal of Criminology and Criminal Justice*, 2004, 46(2), 139–163, at p. 140.
19 Ibid.
20 A. Grounds, 'Psychological consequences of wrongful conviction and imprisonment', op. cit.
21 R. Weisman, 'Showing remorse: reflections on the gap between expression and attribution in cases of wrongful conviction', *Canadian Journal of Criminology and Criminal Justice*, 2004, 46(2), 121–138.
22 Ibid., p. 127.
23 K. Campbell and M. Denov, op. cit., p. 152.
24 A. Grounds, 'Psychological consequences of wrongful conviction and imprisonment', op. cit., p. 170.
25 K. Campbell and M. Denov, op. cit., p. 140.
26 A. Grounds, 'Psychological consequences of wrongful conviction and imprisonment', op. cit.
27 K. Campbell and M. Denov, op. cit., p. 148.
28 A. Grounds, 'Psychological consequences of wrongful conviction and imprisonment', op. cit., pp. 168–170.
29 T. Meisenhelder, 'An essay on time and the phenomenology of imprisonment', *Deviant Behaviour*, 1985, 6, 39–56; C. Jose-Kampfner, 'Coming to terms with existential death: an analysis of women's adaptation to life in prison', *Social Justice*, 1995, 17(2), 110–125.
30 A. Grounds, 'Psychological consequences of wrongful conviction and imprisonment', op. cit., p. 170.
31 This section draws on S. Farrall, 'On the existential aspects of desistance from crime', *Symbolic Interaction*, 2005, 28(3), 367–386.
32 J. Douglas and J. Johnson, 'Introduction', in J. Douglas and J. Johnson (eds), *Existential Sociology*, Cambridge: Cambridge University Press, 1977, pp. vii–xviii; J. Kotarba and A. Fontana (eds), *The Existential Self in Society*, Chicago, IL: Chicago University Press, 1984; J. Kotarba and J. Johnson (eds), *Postmodern Existential Sociology*, Walnut Creek: Altamira Press, 2002.
33 J. Douglas and J. Johnson, op. cit., p. vii.
34 P. Manning, 'Existential sociology', *Sociological Quarterly*, 1973, 14, 200–225, at p. 209.
35 A. Fontana, 'Introduction: existential sociology and the self', in J. Kotarba and A. Fontana, op. cit., pp. 3–17.
36 J.P. Sartre, *Being and Nothingness*, London: Routledge, 1958 [1943].
37 P. Manning, op. cit.
38 J. Douglas, 'The emergence, security, and growth of the sense of self', in

J. Kotarba and A. Fontana, op. cit., pp. 69–99; H. Ebaugh, 'Leaving the convent', in J. Kotarba and A. Fontana, op. cit., pp. 156–176, at p. 167; J. Johnson and K. Ferraro, 'The victimized self: the case of battered women', in J. Kotarba and A. Fontana, op. cit., pp. 119–130; A. Fontana, 'Short stories from the salt', in J. Kotarba and J. Johnson, op. cit., pp. 201–218; J.P. Sartre, op. cit.

39 H. Ebaugh, op. cit.
40 J. Douglas, op. cit., pp. 76–83.
41 N. Denzin, *The Recovering Alcoholic*, London: Sage, 1987, pp. 158–159.
42 T. Meisenhelder, op. cit.
43 M. Heidegger, *Being and Time*, Oxford: Blackwell, 1996 [1926].
44 J.P. Sartre, op. cit.
45 J. Douglas, op. cit., p. 69; H. Ebaugh, op. cit., p. 156; A. Fontana, op. cit., p. 11.
46 J. MacQuarrie, *Existentialism*, Harmondsworth: Penguin Books, 1972, pp. 202–203.
47 Ibid., p. 69.
48 H. Ebaugh, op. cit.
49 A. Fontana, 'Short stories from the salt', op. cit.
50 J. Douglas and J. Johnson, *Existential Sociology*, op. cit.
51 E.g. C. Clark, 'Taming the "Brute Being"', in J. Kotarba and J. Johnson, op. cit., pp. 155–182, at p. 157; J. Douglas, op. cit., p. 10; J. Douglas and J. Johnson, 'Introduction', op. cit., p. xii; H. Ebaugh, op. cit., p. 159; A. Fontana, 'Introduction: existential sociology and the self', op. cit.; J. Johnson and J. Kotarba, 'Postmodern existentialism', in J. Kotarba and J. Johnson, op. cit., p. 3; M. Lester, 'Self: sociological portraits', in J. Kotarba and A. Fontana, op. cit., pp. 18–68, at pp. 53–57; P. Manning, op. cit., p. 209.
52 M. Lester, op. cit., p. 58.
53 J. Douglas, 'The emergence, security, and growth of the sense of self', op. cit., p. 83.
54 Ibid., p. 97.
55 J. Douglas and J. Johnson, *Existential Sociology*, op. cit., p. 45; J. MacQuarrie, op. cit.
56 J. Johnson and J. Kotarba, 'Postmodern existentialism', op. cit., pp. 3–15, at p. 3.
57 A. Fontana, 'Introduction: existential sociology and the self', op. cit., p. 5.
58 H. Ebaugh, op. cit., pp. 165–166.
59 Ibid., p. 166.
60 A. Fontana, 'Toward a complex universe: existential sociology', in J. Douglas, P.A. Adler, P. Adler, A. Fontana, C.R. Freeman and J.A. Kotarba (eds) *Introduction to the Sociologies of Everyday Life*, Boston, MA: Allyn and Bacon, 1980, pp. 155–181, at p. 156.
61 B. Arrigo, 'Shattered lives and shelter lies?', in J. Ferrell and M.S. Hamm (eds), *Ethnography at the Edge*, Boston, MA: Northeastern University Press, 1998, pp. 65–86, at pp. 74–75; J. Douglas and J. Johnson, *Existential Sociology*, op. cit., p. 22; J. Douglas and J. Johnson 'Introduction', op. cit., p. ix; R. Quinney, *Bearing Witness to Crime and Social Justice*, New York: SUNY Press, 2002.
62 M. Lester, op. cit., pp. 56–57.
63 H. Ebaugh, op. cit.
64 A. Fontana, 'Short stories from the salt', op. cit.
65 C. Warren and B. Ponse, 'The existential self in the gay world', in J. Douglas and J. Johnson, op. cit., pp. 273–290.

66 A. Cannings, *Against All Odds: The Angela Cannings Story*, London: Time Warner Books, 2006.

67 For example, J. Katz, *The Seductions of Crime*, New York: Basic Books Inc., 1988; S. Maruna, 'Going straight: desistance from crime and life narratives of reform', *The Narrative Study of Lives*, 1997, 5, 59–93; N. Shover and A. Hochstetler, *Choosing White Collar Crime*, Cambridge: Cambridge University Press, 2005.

68 B. Harrison and E.S. Lyon, 'A note on ethical issues in the use of autobiography in sociological-research', *Sociology*, 1993, 27(1), 101–109.

69 K. Callan, *Kevin Callan's Story*, London: Time Warner Paperbacks, 1998; A. Maguire, *Miscarriage of Justice*, Boulder: Court Wayne Press, 1994; R. Wyner, *From the Inside*, London: Aurum Press, 2003; G. Conlon, *Proved Innocent*, London: Penguin, 1993; P.J. Hill, *Forever Lost, Forever Gone*, London: Bloomsbury, 1995; N. Fellowes, *Killing Time, Lifeshaping Ministries*, Wotton-under-Edge, 1996; and J. Ward, *Ambushed: My Story*, London: Vermilion, 1995.

70 A. Fontana, 'Introduction: existential sociology and the self', op. cit., p. 5.

71 W. Morrison, *Theoretical Criminology*, London: Cavendish Publishing, 1995, p. 351.

72 P. Adler, *Wheeling and Dealing*, New York: Columbia University Press, 1985.

73 Ibid., pp. 151–152.

74 Ibid., p. 154.

75 W. Morrison, op. cit., p. 358.

76 J. Katz, op. cit.

77 W. Morrison, op. cit., p. 37.

78 J. Ferrell, 'Criminological Verstehen', in J. Ferrell and M.S. Hamm (eds), op. cit., pp. 20–42; R. Quinney, op. cit.

79 J. Kotarba, 'Existential sociology', in S.G. McNall (ed.), *Theoretical Perspectives in Sociology*, New York: St. Martin's Press, 1979, pp. 348–368, at pp. 359–360.

80 See, for example, S. Farrall, op. cit.; B. Hunter, Chapter 6, this volume.

81 P. Giordano, S. Cernkovich and J.L. Rudolph, 'Gender, crime and desistance', *American Journal of Sociology*, 2002, 107, 990–1064.

82 Ibid., p. 1042.

83 M. Cusson and P. Pinsonneault, 'The decision to give up crime', in D. Cornish and R. Clarke (eds), *The Reasoning Criminal*, New York: Springer, 1986, pp. 72–82.

84 N. Shover, 'The later stages of ordinary property offender careers', *Social Problems*, 1983, 31(2), 208–218.

85 J. Bull, *Coming Alive: The Dynamics of Personal Recovery*, unpublished PhD thesis, 1972, University of California, Santa Barbara, cited in N. Shover, ibid.

86 T. Meisenhelder, 'An exploratory study of exiting from criminal careers', *Criminology*, 1977, 15, 319–334; also 'Becoming normal: certification as a stage in exiting from crime', *Deviant Behaviour*, 1982, 3, 137–153; and 'An essay on time and the phenomenology of imprisonment', op. cit.

87 S. Maruna, *Making Good: How Ex-Convicts Reform and Rebuild Their Lives*, Washington, DC: American Psychological Association Books, 2001.

88 J. Kauffman, 'Introduction', in J. Kauffman (ed.), *Loss of the Assumptive World: A Theory of Traumatic Loss*, New York: Brunner-Routledge, 2002, pp. 1–9.

89 J. Beder, 'Loss of the assumptive world – how we deal with death and loss', *OMEGA: Journal of Death and Dying*, 2004, 50(4), 255–265; J. Kauffman,

op. cit.; J. Kauffman, 'Safety and the assumptive world', in J. Kauffman (ed.), op. cit, pp. 205–211.

90 C.M. Parkes, 'Psycho-social transition: a field of study', *Social Science and Medicine*, 1971, 5, 101–115, at p. 102.

91 J. Beder, op. cit., p. 258.

92 See I.S. Landsman, 'Crises of meaning in trauma and loss', in J. Kauffman (ed.), op. cit., pp. 13–30.

93 See A.P. DePrince and J.J. Freyd, 'The harm of trauma', in J. Kauffman (ed.), op. cit., pp. 71–82.

94 T. Attig, 'Questionable assumptions about assumptive worlds', in J. Kauffman (ed.), op. cit., pp. 55–68.

95 J. Kauffman, 'Safety and the assumptive world', op. cit., p. 207.

96 Ibid., p. 62.

97 C.M. Parkes, 'Postscript', in J. Kauffman (ed.), op. cit, pp. 237–242.

98 J. Kauffman, 'Introduction', op. cit., p. 5.

99 I.S. Landsman, op. cit.; J. Beder, op. cit.

100 T. Attig, op. cit.

101 J. Kauffman, 'Safety and the assumptive world', op. cit.

102 J. Kauffman, 'Introduction', op. cit., p. 6.

103 R.A. Neimeyer, L. Botella, O. Herrero, M. Pacheco, S. Figueras and L.A. Werner-Wildner, 'The meaning of your absence', in J. Kauffman (ed.), op. cit., pp. 31–47.

104 T. Attig, op. cit., p. 64.

105 J. Beder, op. cit., p. 260.

106 A. Cannings, op. cit., p. xiii.

107 Ibid., p. xiv.

108 The death of Gemma was not prosecuted as insufficient medical evidence could be provided by the Crown Prosecution Service.

109 A. Cannings, op. cit., p. 165.

110 Ibid., p. 171.

111 Ibid., p. 185.

112 Ibid., p. 203.

113 Ibid., p. 216.

114 Ibid., p. 316.

115 Ibid., p. 244.

116 Ibid., p. 246.

117 Ibid., p. 248.

118 Ibid., p. 249.

119 See R. Jamieson and A. Grounds, op. cit.; A. Grounds, 'Psychological consequences of wrongful conviction and imprisonment', op. cit.; A. Grounds, 'Understanding the effects of wrongful imprisonment', op. cit.

120 A. Cannings, op. cit., p. 254.

121 Ibid., p. 255.

122 *Yorkshire Post*, 23 January 2004.

123 *The Sunday Times*, 6 June 2004.

124 A. Cannings, op. cit., p. 259.

125 Ibid., p. 259.

126 *Daily Telegraph*, 20 December 2004.

127 A. Cannings, op. cit., p. 270.

128 Ibid., p. 273.

129 Terry had started drinking heavily and was physically and emotionally distant from Angela, and Jade appeared to resent Angela's presence in the home.

130 A. Cannings, op. cit., p. 277.
131 Ibid., p. 298.
132 *Daily Telegraph*, 20 December 2004.
133 A. Cannings, op. cit., p. 303.
134 Ibid., p. 313.
135 Ibid., p. 312.
136 *Independent on Sunday*, 21 May 2006.
137 *Observer*, 20 February 2005, p. 20.
138 *Lincolnshire Echo*, 10 June 2006.
139 A. Cannings, op. cit., p. 328.
140 Ibid., p. 40, emphasis added.
141 Ibid., p. 270, emphasis added.
142 Ibid., p. 325, emphasis added.
143 Ibid., p. 27.
144 Ibid., pp. 288–289.
145 *Lincolnshire Echo*, 10 June 2006.
146 S.T. Williams, *Blue Rage, Black Redemption: A Memoir*, Pleasant Hill: Damamli Publishing Company, 2004.
147 S. Maruna, *Making Good*, op. cit.
148 R.A. Neimeyer *et al.*, op. cit., p. 23.
149 E. Goffman, *Stigma*, London: Penguin Books, 1963, p. 148.
150 Ibid., pp. 19–20.
151 E. Goffman, *Asylums*, New York: Doubleday Anchor, 1961; R. Weisman, op. cit.
152 E. Goffman, *Stigma*, op. cit., p. 117.
153 Sally Clark was originally found guilty of murdering two of her children. She was released after her second appeal, having served just over three years in prison. Sally Clarke died accidentally aged 42 in mid-March 2007 from acute alcohol intoxication (S. Gaines and D. Pallister, 'Sally Clark's death accidental, coroner rules', *Guardian*, 7 November 2007).
154 One of the expert witnesses who gave evidence against Angela Cannings.
155 Sally Clark's Letter to Supporters, 11 April 2003: www.sallyclark.org.uk/Sally0403.html.
156 J. Kauffman, 'Safety and the assumptive world', op. cit.
157 H. Ebaugh, op. cit.
158 *Lincolnshire Echo*, 10 June 2006.
159 See note 153 above.
160 Tripti Patel was charged with murdering three of her children, but was acquitted at her trial as questions surrounding Prof. Roy Meadow's evidence started to emerge. During the trial it emerged that Mrs Patel's maternal grandmother had lost five of her own children in early infancy, suggesting that a genetic disorder accounted for the deaths.
161 Margaret Smith was accused of smothering her child but acquitted at a retrial.
162 Julie Ferris was originally found guilty of killing her two children, but was released on bail pending a retrial after being held under the Mental Health Act for four years. The Crown Prosecution Service decided to drop all charges against her after Prof. Roy Meadow's evidence had been discredited. During her time in custody she was encouraged to allow herself to be sterilised so that she could have no further children.
163 Donna Anthony was originally found guilty of murdering her two children. She was released on appeal, having served six years in prison.
164 These cases are just those that are widely known about because the proceedings

against them took place in the criminal courts. In the Family Courts, where the standard of proof is lesser ('balance of probability' rather than 'beyond all reasonable doubt'), proceedings are held in secret. Some (e.g. J. Le Fanu, see note 166 below) have estimated there to be 'several hundred cases per year' heard in such courts.

165 J. Batt, *Stolen Innocence*, London: Ebury Press, 2004, p. 459.
166 J. Le Fanu, 'Wrongful diagnosis of child abuse – a master theory', *Journal of the Royal Society of Medicine*, 2005, 98(6), 249–254.
167 J.R. Sparks and I. Loader, 'States of insecurity: contemporary landscapes of crime, order and control', in M. Maguire, R. Morgan and R. Reiner (eds), *The Oxford Handbook of Criminology, 3rd edition*, Oxford: Oxford University Press, 2002, p. 85.
168 J. Le Fanu, op. cit.
169 M. Naughton, op. cit.
170 J. Kauffman, 'Safety and the assumptive world', op. cit., p. 209.
171 S. Maruna, *Making Good*, op. cit.
172 Sally Clark, quoted in J. Batt, op. cit., p. 456.
173 A. Cannings, op. cit., p. 324.
174 T. Meisenhelder, 'Becoming normal', op. cit.
175 A. Cannings, op. cit., p. 265.
176 J. Batt, op. cit., p. 256; A. Cannings, op. cit., pp. 323–324.
177 S. Maruna, *Making Good*, op. cit.
178 A. Grounds, 'Understanding the effects of wrongful imprisonment', op. cit.

Chapter 8

The seductions of conformity

The criminological importance of a phenomenology of exchange

Simon Mackenzie

Introduction

In 1776 Adam Smith published *Wealth of Nations*, a book that would entrench certain structures of thought that would come to dominate economic, social, political, academic and common-sense public thinking for the next 230 years. Among these are the conventional wisdom (a) that humans are by their nature self-interested and (b) that in allowing the free pursuit of individual self-interest beneficent aggregate social results would ensue. Despite it being widely known and remarked that Smith was not the thoroughgoing advocate of a natural human propensity to undiluted self-interest he is often made out to have been, his attempts to explore our relational orientations – in particular 'sympathy' as he and his friend Hume had it – have been rather ignored, most notably by economic theory, which has worked until very recently with a model of a rational actor who is assumed to be self-interested. Claims of parsimony in explanation have supported this assumption, alongside pragmatic suggestions that to assume the worst of people is a sensible precaution for architects of governance; this latter approach having informed the grand political structures of Hobbes and Hume among others: 'in contriving any system of government ... every man ought to be supposed to be a knave and to have no other end, in all his actions, than his private interest.'[1] Of course there has always remained suspicion, not least in sociological and anthropological quarters, that despite the parsimony and precaution of the self-interest assumption, its premise remained to some extent false, but it is surprising that it has taken so long for economics to begin to undermine its assumption from within.

The proposal at (b) above was demonstrated to be wrong by Mancur Olson in 1965. He showed that in certain collective action settings – those we call 'public-goods' problems – each individual who might contribute to the public good is best advised in his own self-interest not to do so. In its most basic terms, this is because if enough others are contributing to sustain the general provision of the public good (e.g. a free communal bus service), then self-interest dictates that I should enjoy the service without contributing myself, whereas if not enough others are contributing to sustain the service then my contribution will be a cost incurred for no benefit. Given this 'equilibrium' position of non-contribution for all self-interested individuals, none in fact would be predicted to contribute and a potentially useful public good will not materialise.[2]

The assumption at (a) above that people are a priori self-interested has persisted, however, but has recently been challenged by data gathered by a group of experimental economists.[3] It emerges that in collective action situations such as the public-goods problem, people do not generally adopt the dominant strategy for self-interested individuals, and 'free ride'. Rather, the population seems to be composed of a substantial number of reciprocators as well as those who are essentially self-interested. Current estimates place around two-thirds of the population as 'strong reciprocators', with the remaining one-third tending to self-interest. A reciprocal strategy repays like with like. In an individual relationship of exchange this would manifest as returning kind actions with kind actions (positive reciprocity), and unkind with unkind (negative reciprocity).[4] In a public-goods model, reciprocity manifests as contributing so long as a sufficient number of others also contribute. Kahan explains:

> In collective action settings, individuals adopt not a materially calculating posture, but rather a richer, more emotionally nuanced *reciprocal* one. When they perceive that others are behaving cooperatively, individuals are moved by honor, altruism and like dispositions to contribute to public goods even without the inducement of material incentives. When, in contrast, they perceive that others are shirking or otherwise taking advantage of them, individuals are moved by resentment and pride to withhold their own cooperation and even to engage in personally costly forms of retaliation.[5]

So it seems that not only have Smith's interpreters been wrong to suppose that free markets in self-interest would benefit all, but they have also been mistaken in their assumption that the majority of people would behave in terms of optimal strategies of self-interest even if given the chance. And *contra* Olson, a high number of contributors in a public-goods model does not increase the temptation on any given individual to free ride, but increases the normative pressure on the individual to reciprocate by contributing.

An action scale of civility and the norm of reciprocity

In my conclusion to this chapter I will suggest that the criminological implications of a phenomenology of exchange are wide-ranging and worth sustained research attention. In order to support this conclusion, I will make an argument in this chapter for the potential importance of such theorising which is rather severely restricted in its orientation and subject matter. This restriction, made in an effort to make the best use of limited space, will involve, on the theoretical front, focusing the issue of exchange around the concept of reciprocity, and on the substantive front, focusing my criminological gaze on the currently vogue discourse of 'community activation', which is linked to a particular construction of the problems of crime and anti-social behaviour facing 'communities' that tends to highlight the issue of 'incivility'.[6] My approach to this substantive issue involves working with a particular model of 'civility'.

Civility can be conceived of as a collective-action problem, concerned with the many relationships between mutually observing individuals and a central pool of 'public good'. Tim Hope has used the idea of club goods to analyse individual contributions to group security by way of measures such as neighbourhood watch;[7] I suggest here that civility is amenable to interpretation as a larger-scale study of this sort of contribution. The exchange basis of such collective-action cooperation problems is clear: civility as a public good is something to which one contributes, but also a benefit on which one draws. We can go further and say that contributions to the public good of civility exist on an 'action scale' which runs from the minimal to the maximal. At the minimal end of the scale the contribution required from the individual is only in terms of norm obedience: politeness, tolerance, civil inattention, not engaging in crime or anti-social behaviour, etc. – all of the constituent parts of the norm of civility, in other words. At the maximal end of the scale, contributions can be made to norm enforcement: bystander intervention, chastisement of deviators from the norm, and other forms of informal social control.

There are, we should note, at least two norms at play in a situation where civility is reciprocally reproduced as a public good. One is the norm of civility and the routines and actions it involves, as indicated in shorthand above. The other is the norm of reciprocity itself. Perhaps the best way intellectually to separate these two norms is to think of a situation where the primary norm (civility in our case) is not something a particular individual values. Nonetheless, they may still feel compelled to contribute to the supposed public good because of their observations of the contributions of others, and their internalisation of the norm of reciprocity. There is therefore a complementarity, and at times tension, between the two norms. For example, depending on my individual preference structures as regards the two norms, I may in the event contribute to the civil norm no matter who else reciprocates this contribution (the committed contributor), I may not do so even if others do (the committed non-contributor), or I may decide not to contribute because even though I value the civil norm highly, I attune my contributions primarily to the reciprocal norm and (if few others are contributing) this determines the outcome for me. Much more could be said about the relationship between the two norms, but the central point is that they are both relevant to the production of civility.

Gouldner has claimed reciprocity as a moral norm, hypothesising it as one of the universal 'principal components' of moral codes.[8] Elster has distinguished moral norms from other behavioural influences that might look confusingly similar: social norms (like moral norms but without the moral import; use of appropriate cutlery for example); legal norms (norms with the force of law behind them); convention equilibria (breach involving social opprobrium like norms, but unlike social norms guided by outcomes in a substantive sense, and unlike moral norms, without moral import; driving on the left for example); private norms (self-imposed rules that attract no public sanction if broken), habits and compulsive neuroses (relatively unconscious as compared to norms); tradition (again, comparatively mindless); and 'other cognitive phenomena' (decisions that are purely rational, for example).[9]

By way of extending Gouldner's seminal analysis, it seems that as well as being a moral norm, reciprocity can be found in all of Elster's other behavioural influences. It can be a social norm, such as where acquaintances exchange Christmas cards. It can be a legal norm, such as where I abide by my part in a contract so long as you abide by yours. It can be a convention equilibrium – indeed it is essential to the maintenance of such equilibria – such as where I drive on the left so long as everyone else does too. It can be a private norm, such as where I resolve to make regular donations to charity in response to the opportunities afforded me by society which I have exploited to secure my comfortable position. It can be a habit, such as where boxers train themselves to trade blows instinctively without resort to conscious deliberation.[10] It can be a tradition, as is the case with the welfare state – a social programme that embodies reciprocity in various forms. And finally it can present as 'other cognitive phenomena' as where in Gouldner's example I make a rational choice to help others as I perceive this to increase the likelihood that others will help me in return.[11]

Further, it is likely that the emotional phenomenology of the acting out of reciprocity is different across each of these categories, ranging from a minimal sense of security and satisfaction in the acting out and observing of convention equilibria, to the pride and collective effervescence experienced by those acting out and sustaining traditions or rituals, which have a considerably greater cohesional effect in terms of the emotions they foster.[12] This is of particular importance for the discourse of community activation in crime control: when we express a desire for more 'active' communities this is often done against a background of erstwhile community ritual which if revitalised might, it is thought, achieve anti-criminogenic effects. Current barriers to this sort of activation are thought to be (amongst others) trends in fear of crime, social atomisation and consumptive attitudes to matters such as safety and security. The subject-ive emotional dynamics of participating in group activities which generate collective effervescence through reciprocal contribution seem to provide a shaft of light towards which we can orient ourselves in searching for a *reason* for individual members of a community to 'activate' towards maximal contributions to the civility norm, which is of sufficient subjective value or merit as to be taken as more than simply an invitation to 'do the police's job for them'.

Civility, in the reciprocal public-goods model outlined here, emerges from a phenomenological investigation of social-exchange mechanisms as something considerably more vibrant than it may seem from conventional operations of the concept. These conventional operations portray civility often in terms of absence (it involves a liberal non-intervention in the lives of others) or otherwise in rather emotionally inert terms, where manners are characterised by a polite self-restraint or, at most, unobtrusive exten-sion of an offer of aid where a fellow citizen appears troubled. The idea that civility is a reciprocal ritual, or a community tradition, and may there-fore form part of a community's collective identity, is largely overlooked. To recall Elster's typology, we might say that civility is generally con-sidered to be a convention equilibrium. In my argument, the emotional dynamics which are part of the exchange mechanism that supports civil behaviour, and which will be explored in what follows, render it quite amenable to (re)interpretation, and indeed promotion, as a ritual or social tradition, and therefore as a rather unexpected source of collective effer-vescence. As we shall see, however, although I have suggested above that tradition can be 'comparatively mindless', the reciprocal determinants of civil behaviour bring with them all of the category-identifiers laid out by Elster. Therefore, while amenable to suggestions of tradition, the social co-production of civility rests on moral, social and legal normativity, and in some degree on bounded rationality, which render it in many instances a particularly mindful tradition.

Reciprocity and existentialism

The emerging transition in economic theory from the model of the human actor as self-interested to a more rounded view of strong reciprocators in fact finds its mirror in certain trends in the development of existentialism in the mid twentieth century. This is particularly apparent in Simone de Beauvoir's attempts to theorise 'the bonds of freedom'. In places, this theo-retical move has been noted, perhaps in a rather overblown way, as a rejection of a Sartrian position. The Sartrian position in question is that taken in *Being and Nothingness*,[13] that saw one's freedom as being forged in conflict with the freedom of others. Sartre's position on the question of social cooperation as we have phrased it here varies in his output, as might be expected in a programme of developing a philosophy sensitive to the constant tension inherent in a 'hopeful and pessimistic vision of the *groupe-en-fusion*'.[14] Some works, such as the 1943 *L'Etre et le Néant*,[15] and 1960's *Critique de la Raison Dialectique*,[16] tend to emphasise his rejection of structuralism and determination, attending to his conception of freedom with the above-mentioned 'hope and pessimism' for collectivity. In the 1946 *L'Existentialisme est un Humanisme*,[17] however, we find less emphasis on the competitive implications of the existential life, and considerable attention paid to developing a cooperative view of moral freedom, which necessitates a dependence on and collaboration with others.

By contrast with this reductionist portrayal of the Sartrian view at the edges of this timeline, but quite complementary to the humanism in the middle, de Beauvoir can be seen to create a theory of moral freedom which, in her interpreter Kristana Arp's terms, finally discovers in *The Ethics of Ambiguity*[18] the proposition that working with others gives human life meaning. Arp traces the process of the development of this line of thought in de Beauvoir's work and shows *The Ethics* to be the culmination of a process of incremental movement away from the strong antagonism between individuals in Sartre's interpretation of the Hegelian Master–Slave dialectic, which informs de Beauvoir's prior work *She Came to Stay*,[19] as disclosed most overtly by the book's epigraph, drawn from Hegel: 'Each consciousness seeks the death of the other.'[20] This is a rather unfair caricature of Sartre's view: as mentioned, a more sympathetic reading of his work[21] accepts his observations of the constant potential for conflict but takes him as seeing the Heideggerian authentic life as involving exercises of freedom that tend towards the establishment of a community of mutual respect in the making of choices. Rather than the overwriting of Sartre that Arp sees in de Beauvoir's *Ethics*, I would suggest that in the late 1940s we find both writers having rather similar thoughts; a suggestion lent support by the socio-historical post-war context of hope and reconstruction in which these works were forged.

At any rate, we certainly find in *The Ethics* a new tilt: an acceptance of the need for reciprocity in acting out the self–other relation based upon an analysis of the joint production of social meaning; what existentialism terms the disclosure of the world, but social scientists might be more comfortable talking of, *mutatis mutandis*, as social construction. The processes of the social construction of reality being based in mutuality of observation and the attendant negotiation and accommodation of definitional claims by individuals, we can perhaps see that processes of reciprocal social exchange are an important part of subjective internalisations of normative viewpoints, and tie the 'disclosure' of Sartrian individual ontological freedom into social structures of reality negotiations which are premised on self–other differentiation (at least to the extent that I am aware that others may think differently from me, and that I am well advised to consider their ideas in some measure when making my choices; safety in numbers, as it were), but which nonetheless bind selves and others together in the disclosure mechanism.

Mutuality in the processes of production of social meaning is an integral part of the systems of cooperation that reciprocity theory identifies. The theory would predict that if I am a 'strong reciprocator' then in considering whether to intervene in an emerging criminal situation to attempt to prevent it happening, I would ask some questions about how many others would be likely to do similar, what precisely they would be prepared to do, and suchlike. There are, however, also a series of meaning-related questions which operate at the level of social construction, such as what definition others would place on the situation unfolding before me, how my first impression might fit with their definition, what standards I might use to resolve any ambiguity, etc., and the same raft of questions can be applied not only to the practical definition of the act unfolding but to its moral or normative import.

Cooperation, collaboration, reciprocity, being *together* in the world: these are not therefore concepts alien to the existentialist tradition. What an existentialist frame of analysis of collective action encourages us to do, however, is to maintain a penetrating focus on the subjective in our investigations. Thus, in locating subjective perceptions in the context of social reference as part of the background of decision-making about undertaking norm-abiding or norm-enforcement activities, we might further ask what the texture of those subjective perceptions are. The existential view of the acting subject draws our attention to freedom of choice on all levels, such that individuals are thought to remain free to choose, among other things, to define a situation as having this or that 'meaning'. If this is so, it becomes very interesting to explore why, in the face of such a tyranny of possible choices, the exercise of existential freedom so often manifests in the choice to conform. In particular, are there sensual attractions to rule-observance and norm-enforcement similar or comparable to those held to be attendant upon criminal activity?

If there has been sufficient output in criminology to warrant an identification of an existential approach as an established field of theory and research in relation to crime and deviance, the strongest themes of this field have been the phenomenology of the seductions both of the activities involved in the crimes in question[22] and the transformative or freedom-asserting attractions of rule breaking in itself.[23] In my suggestion, these approaches, which we might for the sake of shorthand term the 'existential attractions of transgression', present only one side of a full existential science of crime and deviance. The invaluable insights these expositions of the attractions of transgression provide require to be matched by an equally nuanced existential exposition of the attractions of conformity.

Clearly that exposition, an existential mirror of the question at the heart of control theory ('why doesn't everyone commit crime?'), is too large an endeavour for a brief chapter such as this. But in dissecting the matter of conformity so as to ignore many of its component parts, we can focus purely on the norm of reciprocity as an exchange-based mechanism for the production of cooperation in society. In asking what the emotional phenomenology of that mechanism is for the individuals involved in this exchange process, I want to at least sketch an existential argument that allows us to expose the emotional dynamics operating at the micro-level of individual exercises of freedom of choice, which produce aggregate social patterns that manifest at the macro-level as conformity.

To match the literature on the existential attractions of transgression, which has provided a substantial foil to long-held assumptions of instrumentalism towards material gain as the model of criminal action, we should perform the same task on norm- and rule-obedience in order similarly to disrupt assumptions of cooperation as motivated by material instrumentalism, and expose the 'existential attractions of reciprocity' as part of a longer-term endeavour to match Katz's contribution with a full exposition of 'the seductions of conformity'. Such a project seems important to criminology in at least the following ways: as a contribution to the literature on effective interventions to assist desistance from crime; as an aid to understanding mechanisms of community activation, with particular regard to encouraging bystander intervention and other forms of informal social control; and as an indication of how engaging those under the lure of the seductions of crime in particular types of social-exchange networks might provide alternative seductions with a 'replacement value' sufficient to supplant the attractions of transgression. We can examine some of the apparent sensualities of cooperation here.

Exchange and emotions

I have used the term 'phenomenology' several times already in this chapter. In its broad meaning, this term invokes the study of 'phenomena',[24] in other words how things appear to us in our consciousness. This is therefore a method, or philosophy, that calls attention to subjectivity, or the lived experience of the 'lifeworld' in first-person terms. Most generally, we might ask of an actor after an 'experience': 'how did that seem/feel/appear to you?'. There are several considerably more precise uses of the term phenomenology, reflecting its interpretation and adaptation by philosophers such as Merleau-Ponty, Heidegger, Sartre and others. The various points I raise in this chapter are, I think, amenable to useful interpretation using simply the outline definition presented above, although the particular phenomenology I have in mind when I make these points is that of Edmund Husserl.[25] Husserl's view of the 'intentionality' in our experience of objects in the world is very well suited to the discussions of exchange, and objects of exchange processes, that will follow; in which we discover that people's experiences of satisfying exchange processes tend to take the form of 'feelings' about 'objects', such as exchange partners or social entities. Wishing to make an argument for the importance of subjective experiences of exchange processes, rather than an argument for a Husserlian interpretation of phenomenology, I have submerged the particularities of this framework, as much as possible, in the text.

As Kahan's excerpt above implies, relationships of social exchange are suffused with emotion ('honor, altruism, and like dispositions ... resentment and pride'). Social-exchange theory, therefore, once typified by 'assum[ing] self-interested actors who transact with other self-interested actors to accomplish individual goals that they cannot achieve alone',[26] now must not only work to accommodate the idea that not all actors are self-interested, but also to accommodate that exchange is premised on, and generates, feelings:

> A close examination of many common exchange relations suggests that emotions both enter and pervade social exchange processes. Friendship relations are often propelled by strong affection or feelings of joy; corporate mergers may result from fear or anger; economic partnerships may thrive because they produce positive feelings such as confidence or pleasure ... The processes of exchange may cause individuals to feel good, satisfied, relieved, excited, and so forth.[27] The outcome of social exchange may generate pride or shame directed at one's self[28] or anger or gratitude directed toward the other.[29]

The importance of a phenomenology of exchange is in its focus on the deeply subjective experience of exchange relations, including the emotional aspects of these subjective experiences. Such an existential enquiry operates at a level that has largely been overlooked in the experimental economic research that has informed our understanding of the importance of reciprocity as a decision-making tool. One exception to the absence of experiential data in the development of reciprocity theory comes in several related theories of the role of emotions in exchange developed by Edward J. Lawler.

The bonding capacity of reciprocal exchange is represented in Lawler's 'theory of relational cohesion', which contends that 'repeated exchange with the same others generate[s] positive emotions that, in turn, promote[s] perceived cohesion and commitment behaviour'.[30] The idea that social-exchange processes can generate 'interpersonal attraction' has been around for some time,[31] but Lawler and colleagues have refined this observation to produce a theory that predicts both the precise emotional content of the attraction so formed, and its place in reinforcing the behaviour that produced it. In producing this theory, Lawler has built on a range of approaches to the emotions, of which one of the most important for the civility-as-collective-action dilemma which is the subject of this chapter is Frank's theory of moral sentiments.[32]

In Frank's theory, emotions are strategic, in the sense that they provide a solution to collective-action problems. Frank calls the free-rider problem in public-goods situations 'the problem of commitment'; a problem that includes not only the provision of public goods but that affects any situation in which two or more (assumed) self-interested individuals come together in a collaborative relationship that would dissolve without mutual commitment. The temptation to defect from a steady course of cooperation – for businessmen to cheat on their partners, perhaps, or for husbands and wives to cheat on theirs – is resisted by the operation of emotions that tie people together. In Frank's theory these include such feelings as love, sympathy and sorrow. Importantly, Frank acknowledges that for these emotions to achieve a lasting bonding effect they must be reciprocated; in this way emotional reciprocators overcome the destructive effects of self-interest on collective-action problems by establishing processes of emotional exchange with like-minded others.

Lawler's theory of relational cohesion builds on these insights to posit three stages of emotional exchange. In the first stage, an exchange relationship delivers beneficial results to an individual. In the second stage, this manifests 'global', 'primitive'[33] emotions of pleasure/satisfaction and interest/excitement, the source of which actors are motivated to discern and understand. In the third stage, attempts to cognitively address the source of the positive emotions leads the actor to view the exchange relation or group as a cohesive object, 'and they then are willing to take risks or make sacrifices on its behalf'.[34] Lawler has produced several studies[35] that 'demonstrate that the endogenous process – from exchange frequency, to positive emotions, to perceived cohesion – produces commitment to exchange relations. Through this process, the exchange relation becomes an expressive object of attachment for actors'.[36] The relational cohesion theory can be summarised as an 'endogenous process – *exchange to emotion to cohesion* – that links social structure to commitment behaviour'.[37]

Lawler has also produced an 'affect theory of exchange', which is intended to extend and complement the theory of relational cohesion. One component of the affect theory is of particular relevance to our existentially oriented discussion of the importance of emotions in exchange. This is the idea that what Lawler, in the language of social psychology, calls 'self-efficacy', is related to individual perceptions of collective efficacy through the medium of the structural form of joint tasks which in exchange processes create collective effects (such as public goods). Self-efficacy, for existentialists, might be said to be an evaluative aspect of the effects of ontologically free choices. For the layman, it might be said to be a perception of how good one is at getting certain things done. One of the 'affects' of collective enterprises is a sense of shared responsibility allowing 'pride in self and gratitude toward the other to occur in tandem'. Exchange processes such as public-goods problems that are successfully navigated by way of high levels of individual contribution can therefore be thought to reinforce in the individual a sense that 'self-efficacy is "socially mediated" – that is, contingent on collective efficacy'.[38]

In the next section of this chapter we will explore some of the more direct criminological implications of both reciprocity theory and an emotional theory of exchange. However, it is worth noting here some points of importance raised by Lawler's theories for the notion of community crime control. Much policy discourse at present – and not just in criminal justice – seeks the holy grail of 'community activation' which, it is generally felt, will involve raising levels of social capital in communities (seen as a latent resource which lies in wait of 'activation'), allowing communities to sort out their own problems with decreasing formal policing support. This is thought to involve increasing instances of informal social control, including bystander intervention, and the routinisation and internalisation of pro-social norms. The precise role of the police as external agent in kick-starting and supporting this activation remains rather unclear,[39] not least to many senior police in charge of the endeavour (personal communications). Lawler's theory suggests that the important precursor of generalised routine exchange of various benefits between individuals in a community may depend on their identifying the 'community' as an 'expressive object of attachment' and therefore as something that an individual can engage in an exchange relation with. The identification of the community as such an object will depend on its being seen by individuals as the group or entity that was the cause of positive emotions in relatively frequent prior exchanges.[40]

This may begin to seem rather circular: people are likely to engage in exchange relations with the 'community', which makes them feel good, if they have previously been actively and frequently engaged in exchange relations with the community, which made them feel good. It does suggest, however, that the police role in 'activating' communities is a delicate one. Where the police provide responsive services to individuals, *they* are likely to be seen as the object of the positive emotions that are created by the exchange, rather than the community. The most productive approach to the apparent paradox that community activation is most likely to occur in communities that are already active is to promote police intervention in communities in a role in which their identity as external organ of state control is lost, or at least seriously diluted, such that what services they provide take on the appearance of having been provided by 'the community'. Models of the police and community working in partnership to address problems of crime and incivility tend towards this state of presentation, particularly when they involve 'selective privatization' of policing functions,[41] and the police organise community meetings at which the identity of the local 'community' can be confirmed and reconfirmed by its members. The widely praised Chicago Alternative Policing Strategy is notable for its inclusion of many of these sorts of features.[42] Perhaps the most important thing we can do in order to give community the best chance of becoming an object perceived by individuals to be deserving of their (pro-social) contributions is not acquiesce to proponents of the view that there is no such thing as community, or worse still, society.

Taking an existential lens to the exchange framework of analysis promoted here points us to a third of Lawler's emotional-exchange theories that he has called a 'choice process theory of person-to-group commitments'.[43] This 'proposes that people become more strongly committed to social units (relations, groups, organisations) that give them a sense of control'.[44] In a recent paper, he and colleagues use experimental data to confirm the hypothesis – based on both the theory of relational cohesion and the choice process theory – that people commit more to exchange relations where they choose their exchange partners than they do to exchange relations where their partners are predetermined. The sense of control in the former is seen as an important factor inducing commitment: that is, the freedom of choice involved in negotiated 'enabling' voluntaristic exchange relations generates commitment to continued exchange through the generation of positive emotions which appear to be, in part at least, contingent upon the experience of exercising the choice itself. To make the existential connection here clear, we can refer to Williams' suggestion that 'freedom itself can be and often is a commitment, value, preference and motivation guiding human behavior'.[45]

Note that although the term 'commitment' is shared with Hirschi's control theory, it carries a more general meaning here, while still retaining its general advertence to social bonding. For Hirschi, commitment defined the rational considerations of those with a stake in conformity.[46] For Lawler and colleagues, commitment is a more general concept that is displayed as a preference to stay with a particular exchange partner, even in spite of 'good alternatives',[47] and is also characterised by various forms of altruistic and forgiving behaviour. While not ignoring rational considerations, it therefore focuses attention on what in Hirschi's theory of social bonds was called 'attachment' – in other words an 'affection for and sensitivity to others'.[48] There is a rather obvious connection with sociological 'community' criminology in this discovery that acts of free choice to enter exchange relations with specific others promote this sort of commitment to those relations as externalised object, through the mediator of positively valued emotions. That connection is to the conceptual categories of 'communities of choice' and 'communities of fate'; the former being 'associative communities where our common endeavours are at least partially chosen', and the latter being 'constitutive communities which reflect our associations with others that we were born into'.[49] Our reading of emotions in exchange so far would predict that commitment to social-exchange relations in communities of choice would be stronger than in communities of fate. This is notable for being, on the face of it, precisely the opposite to what celebrated philosopher and one-time existentialist André Gorz has said about bonds in these different kinds of communities: he has argued that the bonds in communities of fate are the stronger, as the bonds in communities of choice are amenable to dilution in terms of the choices we make as to how much commitment to award them.[50] There may be ways to resolve this discrepancy, but one would need to do so with reference to the empirical evidence that while it is of course possible to subsist in a community of choice in a state of relative detachment, in fact people tend to commit more to exchange groups they have chosen than to those they have been lumbered with, and further tend to commit more of their personal resources, including time and energy, to such communal projects if others appear to be making their share of such contributions too.

The criminological implications of a phenomenology of reciprocal exchange

Thus far, we have suggested that: civility can be viewed as a collective-action problem; contributions and withdrawals in respect of this public good depend in some measure upon reciprocity; civility can therefore be represented as a structure of exchange; processes of exchange can engender emotional commitment to the object of the exchange, and a perception of joint enterprise in efficacy between self and exchange partners; this emotional commitment is stronger when the exchange relation is characterised by a voluntarism in attachment; and conformity to exchange norms therefore has considerable phenomenological seductions.

The implications of this position are so numerous, and individually in some cases of such great importance, that I can only advert to some of them here, and even then only in sufficient detail to – I hope – offer some food for further research thought. In this section I will raise some of the more direct criminal justice policy implications of the theories behind these suggestions. I will do this with particular reference to current attempts to regulate incivility in the UK, which have given rise to the 'Respect Agenda',[51] and a trend towards a form of pseudo-reciprocal mechanism of 'control' that has become known as 'contractual governance'.[52] Although my comments are thus targeted, it will be apparent that similar considerations affect many of the more 'traditional' mechanisms of criminal justice.

The first point to be raised is whether it is wise to have such a public agenda at all, in relation to the apparent decline of a social commodity such as 'respect'. Kahan's review of strategies of governance of tax evasion[53] suggests that publicity campaigns in relation to tax evasion, drawing attention to an apparently high number of evaders, result in more rather than less evasion. In a population of reciprocators, 'evidence' that high numbers of others are not contributing to a public good is reason to cease one's own contributions. This theory would suggest that public bemoaning of a general dearth of respect by government can lead to even greater attrition in respectful contributions to the public good of civility.

More productive than the publicisation of deviance is likely to be the informal social control exercised by individuals who intervene in order to control or chastise others who contravene the norm of civility. Evidence from laboratory simulations suggests that when the rules of the 'game' under study allow reciprocators to punish free riders, cooperative equilibria can be enforced and maintained even when there are strong material incentives to free ride. The 'reciprocal types' in a population are prepared to 'vigorously punish free riders even when the punishment is costly for the punisher',[54] and the knowledge of this among the would-be recipients of punishment helps diminish instances of free riding. Absent such informal social controls, the opposite can occur: rather than reciprocal types in a population persuading the selfish to conform, the presence of uncontrolled free riding by selfish individuals can induce reciprocators to withhold their contributions; and a situation that may originally have been characterised by reciprocal contribution unwinds.[55] Given the observed relationship between trust, social capital and coordinated action or voluntaristic intervention,[56] disorganised high-crime communities are likely to tend towards the second model rather than the first, their reciprocal types withholding contributions to public goods of collective interest, such as safety and civility, based on a lack of supporting displays of contribution by others, or assurances of similar action which would require a degree of cohesion that is not present. The contributions withheld in these situations may range from maximal to minimal on our 'action scale' of civility, for failure to intervene in preventing crime when one is in the role of bystander can be in the nature of a 'withheld contribution' just as can the performance of a disrespectful act. The role of official 'capable guardians', such as the police and others, in supporting unofficial sanctioning of non-contribution to the civil norm is, as has been mentioned, a key point of contention here. Communities with low contributory equilibria would seem in clear need of external agency support in helping them to 'activate'.

More formal controls, however, may not have the same effects as the informal social controls of 'game' participants, or community members in the real world. Where the sort of publicisation of deviance discussed above is accompanied by penalties for non-compliance, there is some evidence that these penalties can have the opposite to their intended effect, 'crowding out' pro-social tendencies.[57] This can be thought to occur in several ways: first, as the presence of incentives magnifies the publicisation of deviance mentioned above, and perhaps draws attention to the state's failure to deliver safety, or civility, in practice, further dissipating trust among mutually observing reciprocators, in each other and in 'the system';[58] second, as actors attend to the letter of the law rather than the spirit of its underlying message,[59] hitherto assumed and very possibly extended; third, as reciprocal types react against the implied assumption that they are free riders and need incentives to keep them in line; and fourth, as incentives may make pro-social voluntary contributions appear forced even where they are not, reducing their influence in encouraging similar voluntary contributions by observing reciprocators.[60]

While I have been pressing a public-goods analysis of (in)civility and crime here, it is of course also the case that, as I suggested in the introduction, reciprocal social relations do not only exist within such a model. Rather, there also pertain one-on-one social-exchange relations where individuals meet one another unmediated by a central pool of public good, and these relationships may also be characterised by reciprocity. The state's relationship with actual and potential offenders can be thought to be one such exchange structure,[61] and here in the context of the UK we find, among other things, an explosion of contractual and quasi-contractual mechanisms that involve at-risk populations in exchange relations with a range of public and private bodies. These include Anti-social Behaviour Orders, Acceptable Behaviour Contracts and Introductory Tenancies.[62] While some of these, such as ASBOs, are rather in the nature of straightforward imperatives rather than invitations to any real sort of contractual dialogue, others, introductory tenancies for example, are more obviously reciprocal in being premised on the state or local authority's grant of a benefit to the individual; in this case social housing. Conditionality in the provision of such social services is achieved by linking their grant to acceptable behaviour by the recipient.[63]

Might such 'productive' direct-exchange relations between the individual and the state, or one of its agents, give rise to emotional commitment to the exchange relation that supports the behavioural norm sought? Aside from the obvious fact that the exchange partner here is the very definition of one not 'chosen' by the individual, a further difficulty occurs in the fact that the benefits given by the state as its part of the bargain are not new, but are social provisions that were previously entitlements. Making welfare entitlements conditional upon the non-infringement of behavioural norms does not therefore fit a model of positive reciprocity, where reward begets reward, gift begets gift. Rather it appears more like negative reciprocity where what was once given without such strings will be taken away in the case of incivility by the benefit claimant; cessation of welfare entitlement appears as a punishment, rather than its grant as a gift.

This difficulty in achieving genuine positive reciprocity in the relationship between the state and the individual is not easily overcome, for as

readers of the tabloid press well know, benefit given to offenders in reciprocation of a satisfactory response to the state's demand for civility can
appear an insult to those who contribute to this public good without
express incentive. What then of more general incentives, to which all
theoretically have access? It is possible to find in the myriad forms that
populate the field of contractual governance some initiatives that incorporate this sort of positive reciprocity in their activities. In a discussion of
anti-social behaviour and housing, Flint and Nixon note 'the growing use
of reward schemes by social landlords' such as where 'in addition to a
small financial payment, tenants who have demonstrated appropriate
conduct (paying rent promptly and not engaging in anti-social behaviour)
may also access improved repairs services which are not available to
tenants not eligible for rewards'.[64] Where these are new benefits rather
than the re-working of services and payments previously universally
granted, we have an example of positive reciprocity. Flint and Nixon criticise the creation of such a two-tier service for the civil and the uncivil. The
question a phenomenology of reciprocal exchange would ask is to what
extent the subjective impression of non-receipt of a benefit given to others
is experienced by individuals in the lower tier as a punishment; in which
case retaliatory cycles of negative reciprocity (i.e. mutual punishment)
may result.

There are other aspects of the subjective experience of the contractual
governance of crime and incivility that may militate towards the entrenchment of cycles of negative reciprocity: notably that in the branding of dispositions such as ASBOs as behaviour-control tools given by the state to
communities, it is the proximate 'community' or sometimes even specific
members of the community involved in reporting the offences in question,
rather than the distant state, that can come to be seen by the offender in
receipt of such an Order as the exchange partner responsible for delivering
this negative result. The negative emotional response, which promotes a
negative reciprocal response by the offender, may therefore be aimed at
local neighbours rather than a more distant exchange partner. There is
something of a delicate balance between punishment, whether perceived to
be the work of the state or the community, being received as an incentive
to cooperate by the individual, and it being received as inviting a retaliatory negative reciprocity by the individual (see, for example, the revelatory
research into the importance of the emotional mannerisms of criminal
justice officials in predicting re-offending).[65] In Axelrod's famous computer
models, the mutual benefit of cooperation to be gleaned in iterated interactions with the 'tit for tat' strategy in a prisoner's dilemma depended on the
capacity of the other player to 'get the message' from the negative reciprocity that followed defection, and turn to cooperation instead.[66] Persistent
defection would indeed lead to a cycle of mutual negative reciprocity with
'tit for tat'.

The emerging 'emotions and justice' literature[67] shows that criminology is quite aware of the need to endeavour to ensure that the punishment exchange relation between citizen and state encourages in the former a more socially useful emotional response than that which characterises negative reciprocity (rejection, withdrawal, anger, vengefulness).[68] Restorative Justice attempts to attend to precisely this emotional response to the particular exchange relation in question, tending to identify 'shame' as the ideal outcome of a justice intervention. The increasing sensitivity of criminal justice to the emotional results of its exchanges does not seem to have become a concern central to its activities outside this discourse of restorative practices, however. Contractual governance remains an increasingly popular tool for state-based attempts to regulate behaviour in the UK, but displays none of this concern with the emotional effects of social-exchange processes for offenders. Given the ill feeling measures like ASBOs can create in individuals subject to them, and given further the fact that these individuals are generally thought not to be among those sectors of society most approximating pure rational maximisation, cycles of negative reciprocity rather than positive reciprocity or rational maximising behaviour seem likely. If, as Kahan says, 'citizens reciprocate respectful treatment with cooperation and obedience and disrespectful treatment with resistance',[69] the question of the contractual governance of anti-social behaviour becomes one of the phenomenology of the legitimacy of legal intervention as experienced by those subject to state controls.[70]

Conclusion: for social inclusion by contribution rather than consumption

If the above are a selection of the practical implications of our outline phenomenology of exchange, let me now move towards a conclusion with more ambition in paradigmatic movement.

Community exists in the context of economic market relations rather than outside them.[71] Economic and quasi-economic calculations are widespread everyday features of social life, and lead to such oft-observed tendencies as that of individuals to measure their status and 'success' against others. Calculations such as these are an important component in extended versions of exchange theory, as for instance in Adams' theory of 'inequity in social exchange' where employees consider themselves to be treated fairly when the ratio of their inputs to outcomes is equivalent to the ratio of inputs to outcomes of comparable others around them.[72] Contemporary concerns with the 'super-rich' in society can be explained in part by the capacity of such wealth to warp the balance of social observation contained in theories that relate happiness to the monitoring of others. If reciprocators would make the effort to act with respect for others so long as they perceived most others doing the same, acts of self-interest in accumulative practices which are sometimes labelled 'gross' or 'disproportionate' can provide models of disrespect for the common pool of public good which may reduce contributions more generally. The sharp issue here is that reciprocation ties individual pro-social practices to symbolic representations of levels of contribution or self-interest among others, and when particularly visible groups symbolically cast the obligations of collective life aside, this symbolism resonates in the unwinding of a willingness to make reciprocal pro-social contributions among observers of these signs.

There are, of course, many hypotheses suggesting links between social dislocation and breakdown on the one hand, and advanced-capitalist individualism on the other. Against these, 'community' is often set up as occupying one half of a conceptual dichotomy between the public and the private, or 'communal life' and 'business enterprise'. Using this paradigm, the idea that community might be influenced by the personal economic choices of a relatively few high-net-worth individuals is often portrayed as rather too much of an empirical stretch. The idea of civility as a collective-action problem provides a different paradigm, however. This is one possible theoretical conceptualisation of the bonds each of us enjoys with a central pool of behavioural public good, and it seems quite plausible that our subjective emotional relationships with the public good do not discern in a clear-cut manner between various types of contribution, withdrawal, or disavowal in terms of these bonds. This framework allows us to bring ostentation, greed and a range of other 'top-end' manifestations of self-interest within the ambit of a discourse of 'incivilities', affecting the emotional lives and conformist commitments of us all, through their abuse of conceptions of the public good of civility.

In exchange relations, agents seem constrained and enabled by structures of exchange possibility which they encounter on a subjective level often as already formed,[73] and it is within – or sometimes in rejection of[74] – these constraints and opportunities that agency as the exercise of choice occurs. Mauss's anthropology of the Gift[75] very well embodies the recursivity of the structuring effects of individual agentic choices and the structured constraints within which those choices are made; the production and reproduction of ritual. It has been observed that Mauss, in his attempt to explore 'alternative moralities', has left us a framework within which to critique the Western trend towards societies characterised by accumulation or consumption.[76] This view pays particular heed to Mauss's outline of an alternative conception of social and economic exchange, through which status became fused with giving. Here, therefore, we can see the emergence of an attempt to produce an anthropologically grounded philosophy of social contribution through interpersonal and group exchanges.[77] Criticism of the alleged Maussian project to link identity-work (status, self-image) to a philanthropic rather than an enterprise-based spirit has involved observation of a not inconsiderable tendency to rational strategising in the manipulation of the gift mechanism by its users, across a range of societies. This, it might be said, dilutes what attractions we may find in the social-bonding technologies of 'the gift', for power and exploitation will find a way to use any social system.

To the contrary, and not without caution, I think the recent emergence of evidence as to the positive emotional effects of productive exchange, and the role of these effects in sustaining contributions to that exchange process, coupled with the parallel discovery of the presence of strong reciprocal tendencies in the dispositions of agents previously theorised as purely self-interested, brings the constitutive message of the Gift back onto the agenda as a centrepiece for contemporary social analysis. Let us consider a passage from Simon Jarvis in order to make the point more clear:

> In Mauss's idea of a gift-society, more is happening in an exchange or in a gift than can really be adequately thought with the help of the term 'economy'. In an 'economy', properly so-called, some kinds of exchange have become indifferent with respect to the legal status of the exchange partners. I go into the supermarket; I remain a subject of the state with the legal and political status pertaining to such a subject whether or not I buy anything. There is a lived theory that my economic and legal status are indifferent with respect to each other. In Mauss's gift-societies this is not necessarily the case. So-called 'economic' exchange is often the very medium in which so-called 'political' status is determined.[78]

My suggestion, supported by a considerable body of critical work in the social sciences, is that the 'lived theory' that my rights as citizen adhere irrespective of any particular economic activity I choose to undertake, is rather obviously in the nature of a contemporary ideology. Economic activities – production and, increasingly especially, consumption – have in serious ways become entry requirements to the enjoyment of certain rights of 'citizenship', which term comes to be a synonym for club goods rather than universal recognition. This argument has been made by many writers, included among them Nikolas Rose,[79] who has suggested a view of contemporary society bifurcated into circuits of inclusion and circuits of exclusion (see also Bauman's suggestion that consumerism is a dominant new paradigm for social integration).[80] The acceleration of late capitalism is premised on the 'invisible hand' argument of Adam Smith, which is based on the notion that consumptive choices are an effective way for the population to exercise democratic will, in relation to the direction of the cut-and-thrust of the economy at least. In this way, every organic turnip bought is a vote against GM food, and every can of cheap beans is a vote in favour. And if you are not buying anything, or are constrained in such consumptive choices by your financial means, you are not voting, or are doing so only under duress. Erving Goffman noted as long ago as 1963 that the 'lived theory' above was an empirical nonsense, when he remarked that being present on public footpaths demanded certain displays of productive intent, such as rushing to be somewhere apparently important or, if loitering, to ensure one had a legitimate subordinate involvement in the situation, such as admiring displays in shop windows.[81] As Goffman knew, and as has now become much more widely recognised with the explosion of literature on private security and 'semi-public' places, loiterers in shopping malls or supermarkets will be ejected if identified, and if it is judged that they are not in fact capable of or likely to make any productive economic choices.

My argument here of course is that far from late modern individuals in advanced capitalist nations enjoying economic rights separate from their legal or constitutional rights, the two sets of rights are fused. Granted, they are fused in a manner which seems to approximate the antithesis of the utopianism in Mauss's exchange model, but given the presence of the fusion we might be given licence at least to retain attention to the progressive possibilities of an economy–exchange–rights–identity nexus. That is, if identity practices can be linked to exchange through the medium of emotions, then the possibility arises of engaging models of reciprocal exchange as policy tools across a wide spectrum of social initiatives, incorporating some of the insights of a Maussian exchange structure as the basis of a broader philosophy of social contribution. This is a radically different model to current neo-liberal approaches to governance. Where neo-liberal governance sees individuals 'rowing' in their self-interest, primarily socially defined by their consumptive preferences, and amenable in some measure to being 'steered' by incentive structures established by government (which structures are often contradicted by market forces), a more progressive model might see communities, defined in their membership boundaries by contribution, and with self-organising capacities (i.e. both steering and rowing) based on the emotional seductions of common virtue and mutual support. In developing such a model, we might find we have created social and economic structures that 'gift' reward back to those who themselves are the best 'givers', rather than allowing reward to settle with the most accomplished 'takers'.

All of these considerations suggest the need for a sustained programme of research into the crime-preventive capacities of reciprocal exchange as implemented in the field as opposed to the laboratory, from where most of the current data has come. The review performed here suggests that in further exploring the existential aspects of pro-social, anti-social and criminal action, we would do well to attend to a more fully developed phenomenology of exchange in criminology.

Notes

1 D. Hume, 'Of the independency of parliament', in *Essays Moral, Political and Literary*, Oxford: Oxford University Press, 1963 [1741], p. 40.
2 M. Olson, *The Logic of Collective Action*, Cambridge, MA: Harvard University Press, 1965.
3 H. Gintis, S. Bowles, R.T. Boyd and E. Fehr (eds), *Moral Sentiments and Material Interests: the Foundations of Cooperation in Economic Life*, Cambridge, MA: MIT Press, 2005.
4 E. Fehr and S. Gächter, 'Fairness and retaliation: the economics of reciprocity', *The Journal of Economic Perspectives* 14(3), 2000, 159–181; A. Falk and U. Fischbacher, '"Crime" in the lab: detecting social interaction', *European Economic Review* 46, 2002, 859–869, at p. 861.
5 D.M. Kahan, 'The logic of reciprocity: trust, collective action, and law', *Michigan Law Review* 102, 2003, 71–103, at p. 71, his emphasis.
6 A. von Hirsch and A.P. Simester (eds), *Incivilities: Regulating Offensive Behaviour*, Oxford: Hart, 2006; J. Bannister and N. Fyfe, 'Review issue: (in)civility and the city', *Urban Studies* 43(5/6), 2006, 853–1023.
7 T. Hope, 'Privatopia on trial? Property guardianship in the suburbs', in K. Painter and N. Tilley (eds) *Surveillance of Public Space: CCTV, Street Lighting and Crime Prevention*, New York: Criminal Justice Press, 1999; T. Hope, 'Inequality and the clubbing of private security', in T. Hope and R. Sparks (eds) *Crime, Risk and Insecurity*, London: Routledge, 2000; T. Hope and A. Trickett, 'Angst Essen Seele Auf ... But it keeps away the burglars! Private security, neighbourhood watch and the social reaction to crime', *Kölner Zeitschrift für Soziologie und Sozialpsychologie* 43, 2004, 441–468.
8 A.W. Gouldner, 'The norm of reciprocity: a preliminary statement', *American Sociological Review* 25(2), 1960, 161–178.
9 J. Elster, *The Cement of Society: a Study of Social Order*, Cambridge: Cambridge University Press, 1989, pp. 97–106.
10 See L. Wacquant, *Body and Soul: Notebooks of an Apprentice Boxer*, Oxford: Oxford University Press, 2003.
11 Gouldner, op. cit., p. 173.
12 R. Collins, 'On the microfoundations of macrosociology', *American Journal of Sociology* 86(5), 1981, 984–1014; R. Collins, 'Toward a neo-median sociology of mind', *Symbolic Interaction* 12(1), 1989, 1–32; E. Durkheim, *The Elementary Forms of the Religious Life*, New York: Free Press, 1965.
13 J.-P. Sartre, *Being and Nothingness*, New York: Philosophical Library, 1956 [1943].
14 A.C. Danto, *Sartre*, 2nd edn, London: Fontana Press, 1991, p. 141.
15 Sartre, op. cit., 1956 [1943].
16 J.-P. Sartre, *Critique of Dialectical Reason*, London: Verso, 2004 [1960].
17 J.-P. Sartre, *Existentialism and Humanism*, London: Methuen, 1948 [1946].
18 S. de Beauvoir, *The Ethics of Ambiguity*, Secaucus, NJ: Citadel Press, 1948.
19 S. de Beauvoir, *She Came to Stay*, New York: Norton, 1990 [1943].
20 K. Arp, *The Bonds of Freedom: Simone de Beauvoir's Existentialist Ethics*, Chicago and La Salle, IL: Open Court, 2001, p. 21.
21 And taking into account particularly Sartre, op. cit., 1948 [1946].
22 J. Katz, *Seductions of Crime: Moral and Sensual Attractions in Doing Evil*, New York: Basic Books, 1988.
23 C.R. Williams, 'Engaging freedom: toward and ethics of crime and deviance', in B.A. Arrigo and C.R. Williams (eds) *Philosophy, Crime, and Criminology*, Urbana and Chicago, IL: University of Illinois Press, 2006, 167–196.

24 See Crewe, Chapter 1, this volume, note 32.
25 E. Husserl, *Logical Investigations*, London: Routledge, 2001 [1900–1901]; E. Husserl, *Ideas Pertaining to a Pure Phenomenology and to a Phenomenological Philosophy*, Dordrecht: Kluwer Academic Publishers, 1983 [1913].
26 E.J. Lawler and S. Thye, 'Bringing emotions into social exchange theory', *Annual Review of Sociology* 25, 1999, 217–244, at p. 217.
27 E.J. Lawler and J. Yoon, 'Commitment in exchange relations: test of a theory of relational cohesion', *American Sociological Review* 61, 1996, 89–108.
28 T.J. Scheff, 'Socialization of emotions: pride and shame as causal agents', in T.D. Kemper (ed.) *Research Agendas in the Sociology of Emotions*, New York: SUNY Press, 1990, 281–304.
29 B. Weiner, *An Attributional Theory of Motivation and Emotion*, New York: Springer-Verlag, 1986; Lawler and Thye, op. cit., p. 218.
30 E.J. Lawler, 'An affect theory of social exchange', *American Journal of Sociology* 107(2), 2001, 321–352, at p. 322 and E.J. Lawler and J. Yoon, 'Power and the emergence of commitment behavior in negotiated exchange', *American Sociological Review* 58, 1993, 465–481; Lawler and Yoon, op. cit., 1996, 89–108; E.J. Lawler and J. Yoon, 'Network structure and emotion in exchange relations', *American Sociological Review* 63, 1998, 871–894; E.J. Lawler, S. Thye and J. Yoon, 'Emotion and group cohesion in productive exchange', *American Journal of Sociology* 106, 2000, 616–657.
31 D. Byrne and R. Rhamey, 'Magnitude of reinforcement as a determinant of attraction', *Journal of Personality and Social Psychology* 2, 1965, 889–899; A.J. Lott and B.E. Lott, 'Liked and disliked persons as reinforcing stimuli', *Journal of Personality and Social Psychology* 11(2), 1969, 129–137; R.M. Emerson, 'Social exchange theory', *Annual Review of Sociology* 2, 1976, 335–362.
32 R.H. Frank, *Passions with Reason: the Strategic Role of Emotions*, New York: Norton, 1988; R.H. Frank, 'The strategic role of emotions: reconciling over- and undersocialized accounts of behavior', *Rationality and Society* 5(2), 1993, 160–184.
33 Weiner, op. cit.
34 Lawler and Thye, op. cit., p. 237.
35 E.J. Lawler and J. Yoon, 'Structural power and emotional processes in negotiations: a sociological exchange approach', in R. Kramer and D. Messick (eds) *Negotiation as a Social Process*, Newbury Park, CA: Sage, 1995; Lawler and Yoon, op. cit., 1993, 1996, 1998.
36 Lawler and Thye, op. cit., p. 237.
37 E.J. Lawler, 'Micro social orders', *Social Psychology Quarterly* 65(1), 2002, 4–17, at p. 6, original emphasis.
38 Ibid., p. 11.
39 S. Herbert, *Citizens, Cops, and Power: Recognizing the Limits of Community*, Chicago, IL: University of Chicago Press, 2006.
40 See also P.L. Berger and T. Luckmann, *The Social Construction of Reality: A Treatise in the Sociology of Knowledge*, Harmondsworth: Penguin, 1971 on the group as object in social constructionism – a 'third force' besides self and other.
41 D.M. Kahan, 'Reciprocity, collective action, and community policing', *California Law Review* 90, 2002, 1513–1539.
42 W.G. Skogan, *Police and Community in Chicago: a Tale of Three Cities*, New York: Oxford University Press, 2006.
43 E.J. Lawler, 'Choice processes and affective attachments to nested groups: a

theoretical analysis', *American Sociological Review* 57, 327–339, 1992; E.J. Lawler, 'Affective attachments to nested groups: the role of rational choice processes', in J. Skvoretz, J. Szmatka and J. Berger (eds) *Status, Networks, and Structures: Theory Development in Group Processes*, Stanford, CA: Stanford University Press, 1997; C.W. Mueller and E.J. Lawler, 'Commitment to nested organizational units: some basic principles and preliminary findings', *Social Psychology Quarterly* 62, 1999, 325–346.

44 E.J. Lawler, S.R. Thye and J. Yoon, 'Commitment to structurally enabled and induced exchange relations', *Social Psychology Quarterly* 69(2), 2006, 183–200, at p. 184.

45 Williams, op. cit., p. 193. See also G.C. Homans, *The Human Group*, New York: Harcourt Brace and Jovanovich, 1950 for similar assertions made from the very different perspective of a rational choice theory of exchange.

46 T. Hirschi, *Causes of Delinquency*, Berkeley, CA: University of California Press, 1969.

47 Lawler *et al.*, op. cit., 2006, p. 188.

48 G.B. Vold, T.J. Bernard and J.B. Snipes, *Theoretical Criminology*, 5th edn, New York: Oxford University Press, 2002, p. 184.

49 A. Little, *The Politics of Community: Theory and Practice*, Edinburgh: Edinburgh University Press, 2002, p. 158.

50 A. Gorz, *Reclaiming Work: Beyond the Wage-based Society*, Cambridge: Polity Press, 1999.

51 Respect Task Force, 'Respect action plan', London: Home Office, 2006.

52 A. Crawford, ' "Contractual governance" of deviant behaviour', *Journal of Law and Society* 30(4), 2003, 479–505; S. Mackenzie, 'Second-chance punitivism and the contractual governance of crime and incivility: new labour, old Hobbes', *Journal of Law and Society*, 35(2), 2008, 214–239.

53 Kahan, op. cit., 2003.

54 Fehr and Gächter, op. cit., p. 160.

55 J.O. Ledyard, 'Public goods: a survey of experimental research', in J.H. Kagel and A.E. Roth (eds) *The Handbook of Experimental Economics*, Princeton, NJ: Princeton University Press, 1995; T.C. Schelling, *Micromotives and Macrobehaviour*, New York: W.W. Norton & Co., 1978; E. Fehr and K. Schmidt, 'A theory of fairness, competition and cooperation', *Quarterly Journal of Economics* 114, 1999, 817–868, proposition 4.

56 J.S. Coleman, *Foundations of Social Theory*, Cambridge, MA: Harvard University Press, 1990; T. Hope and S. Karstedt, 'Towards a new social crime prevention', in H. Kury and J. Obergfell-Fuchs (eds) *Crime Prevention: New Approaches*, Mainz: Weisse Ring Verlag-GnbH, 2003; R.J. Sampson, 'Neighbourhood and community: collective efficacy and community safety', *New Economy* 11, 2004, 106–113.

57 E. Fehr and S. Gächter, 'Do incentive contracts crowd-out voluntary cooperation?', *Working Paper No. 34*, University of Zurich: Institute for Empirical Research in Economics, 2000.

58 Cf. Hope and Karstedt, op. cit.; D.J. Smith, 'Changing situations and changing people', in A. von Hirsch, D. Garland and A. Wakefield (eds) *Situational Crime Prevention: Ethics and Social Context*, Oxford: Hart Publishing, 2000.

59 D. McBarnet, 'After Enron will 'whiter than white collar crime' still wash?', *British Journal of Criminology* 46(6), 2006, 1091–1109.

60 B.S. Frey, *Not Just for the Money: an Economic Theory of Personal Motivation*, Aldershot and Lyme, NH: Edward Elgar, 1997; Kahan, op. cit., 2002.

61 S. Mackenzie, 'Tit for tat: criminal justice policy and the evolution of co-operation', *The Scottish Journal of Criminal Justice Studies* 13, 2007, 58–71.
62 Crawford, op. cit.; Mackenzie, op. cit., 2008.
63 A. Deacon, 'Justifying conditionality: the case of anti-social tenants', *Housing Studies* 19(6), 2004, 911–926; C. Hunter, 'The changing legal framework: from landlords to agents of social control', in J. Flint (ed.) *Housing and Anti-social Behaviour: Perspectives, Policy and Practice*, Bristol: Policy Press, 2006.
64 J. Flint and J. Nixon, 'Governing neighbours: anti-social behaviour orders and new forms of regulating conduct in the UK', *Urban Studies* 43(5/6), 2006, 939–955.
65 T.R. Tyler, *Why People Obey the Law*, New Haven, CT: Yale University Press, 1990; T.R. Tyler and Y.J. Huo, *Trust in the Law: Encouraging Public Co-operation with the Police and Courts*, New York: Russell Sage Foundation, 2002.
66 R. Axelrod, *The Evolution of Co-operation*, London: Penguin, 1990 [1984].
67 E.g. W. de Haan and I. Loader (eds), 'Crime, punishment and the emotions', *Theoretical Criminology* 6(3), 2002; S. Karstedt, 'Emotions, crime and justice: exploring durkheimian themes', in M. Deflem (ed.) *Sociological Theory and Criminological Research: Views from Europe and the United States*, Sociology of Crime, Law and Deviance series, Amsterdam: Elsevier, vol. 7, 223–248; L.W. Sherman, 'Reason for emotion: reinventing justice with theories, innovations and research', *Criminology* 41, 2003, 1–38; S. Karstedt, I. Loader and H. Strang (eds), *Emotions, Crime and Justice*, Oxford: Hart, forthcoming.
68 See also the pertinent and comparable points made by 'peacemaking' criminologists in respect of (among other things) empathy, honesty, conversation, and the counter-productive value placed on displays of remorse by Western criminal justice systems. The discomfort Pepinsky feels when he sees the plea-bargaining incentive structure cajoling defendants into humiliating public declarations of remorse seems rather a good example of the failure of the system to prioritise the emotional effects of the exchange relation: H.E. Pepinsky, 'A criminologist's quest for peace: Chapter 4, empathy works, obedience doesn't', *Critical Justice* 1(1), 2005.
69 Kahan, op. cit., 2002, p. 1525.
70 Cf., again, Tyler, op. cit.; T.R. Tyler, 'Trust and law abidingness: a proactive model of social regulation', *Boston University Law Review* 81, 2001, 361–406; Tyler and Huo, op. cit.
71 J. Boswell, *Community and the Economy: the Theory of Public Co-operation*, London: Routledge, 1990.
72 J.S. Adams, 'Inequity in social exchange', in L. Berkowitz (ed.) *Advances in Experimental Social Psychology*, New York: Academic Press, vol. 2 1965, 267–299.
73 A. Giddens, *The Constitution of Society*, Cambridge: Polity Press, 1984.
74 Williams, op. cit.
75 M. Mauss, *The Gift: the Form and Reason for Exchange in Archaic Societies*, London: Routledge, 2002 [1950].
76 D. Graeber, *Fragments of an Anarchist Anthropology*, Chicago, IL: Prickly Paradigm Press, 2004, p. 21.
77 D. Graeber, *Toward an Anthropological Theory of Value: the False Coin of Our Own Dreams*, New York: Palgrave, 2001.
78 S. Jarvis, 'Problems in the phenomenology of the gift', *Angelaki, Journal of the Theoretical Humanities* 6(2), 2001, 67–77, at p. 72.

79 N. Rose, 'Government and control', in D. Garland and R. Sparks (eds) *Criminology and Social Theory*, Oxford: Oxford University Press, 2000.
80 Z. Bauman, *Intimations of Postmodernity*, London: Routledge, 1992, p. 51.
81 E. Goffman, *Behavior in Public Places: Notes on the Social Organization of Gatherings*, New York: The Free Press, 1963.

Chapter 9

Existentialism and the criminology of the shadow

Bruce Arrigo and Christopher Williams

Introduction

Criminologists are increasingly looking to philosophical sources to unravel critical tensions in contemporary discourse on crime, law, and justice (e.g., what is crime? Who is a criminal?).[1] That these challenges are firmly – if not thoroughly – rooted in philosophical questions means that they are equally ripe for philosophical speculation and interrogation.[2] Ontological, epistemological, ethical, and esthetical assumptions underlie our definitions and explanations of crime, as well as policy initiatives designed to prevent and/or control it. Moreover, philosophical traditions such as existentialism, postmodernism and post-structuralism, as well as the humanist critique, offer a rich assortment of themes and insights the consideration of which present innovative tools and new directions for criminological theorizing.

In this chapter, we suggestively examine several such themes and insights, relating them to what Arrigo and Milovanovic describe as the 'criminology of the shadow.'[3] Several lines of critique within postmodernist and post-structuralist thought are explored. However implicitly at times, prominent themes within the works of Foucault (the bio-physics of power),[4] Baudrillard (hyper-reality),[5] Lacan (the subject as 'lack'),[6] and Fromm (negative freedom and escape)[7] are linked with broader existentialist themes such as identity, alienation, choice, and authenticity. Specifically, the ways in which possibilities for choice, commitment, and authentic existence are artificially limited by forces social and cultural are characterized as harms of reduction (limits on being) and harms of repression (denials of becoming). Throughout, we concentrate on the (often obscured) means by which these harms are cultivated, nurtured, and sustained.[8] For illustrative purposes, several pressing issues within criminology and criminal justice (i.e., evidence-based research, actuarial penology, and the policing of risk) are highlighted as exemplars of the criminology of the shadow and the dynamics of harm.

Conceptualizing the criminology of the shadow

The phrase, *the criminology of the shadow*, is a relatively recent expression used to account for punitive public attitudes[9] and, to a lesser extent, the underlying psychoanalytic dimensions of Garland's[10] thesis on the culture of control and penal policy.[11] In this chapter, we employ the phrase as an instrument of existentialist critique which aims to deconstruct those covert forces that discipline the body, implode the reality–appearance dichotomy, and impose limitations on human agency, choice, and ultimately freedom.[12] These limitations, we suggest following constitutive criminology, can be described as *harms* of reduction (i.e., limits on one's possible being) and repression (i.e., denials of one's possible becoming).[13] Produced and reproduced through structure and culture, harms are 'energized by ... offenders ... victims, criminal justice practitioners, academics, commentators, media reporters and producers of film and TV crime shows.'[14] What all harms share, whether they emanate from conventionally defined crime or other stifling elements of power relations, is their role in 'denying or preventing us from becoming fully social beings.' As Henry and Milovanovic write, 'Being human is to make a difference to the world; to act on it ... If this process is prevented or limited we become less than human; we are harmed.'[15]

As employed hereinafter, 'harm' thus assumes a Sartrean character, describing processes of objectification, alienation, and displacement.[16] It is not merely something that individuals do to one another, but results as well from relations of power and domination that repress or reduce prospects for being and becoming. Indeed, as Sartre suggested in *Being and Nothingness*, what ultimately makes us human is what we *become*.[17] Authentic existence – meaningful existence – stems from freedom, choice, commitment, and engagement with self-defined projects. To the extent that others dictate or limit our capacity to act upon the world in meaningful ways, possibilities for authentic existence are replaced by an alienated relationship with the world.[18] Crime itself, Henry and Milovanovic suggest, '*is the expression of some agency's energy to make a difference on others and it is the exclusion of those others who in the instance are rendered powerless to maintain or express their humanity*' (emphasis in the original).[19]

The criminology of the shadow thus calls for a reflexive interrogation of criminology, criminal justice, and their associated values, policies, and practices. In the remainder of this section, we explore the works of several crucial figures in contemporary philosophy – Michel Foucault, Jean Baudrillard, Jacques Lacan, and Erich Fromm. Although preliminary and suggestive, our analysis borrows liberally from each in an effort to shed greater light on the dynamics of reduction and repression and their subsequent effects on the struggle to be human.

Foucault: the bio-physics of power and panopticism

The development and refinement of Foucault's disputation on power was revisited by him, time and again, throughout his intellectual life.[20] At the core of this exploration was the conviction that 'power [expressed through words] produces; it produces reality, it produces domains of objects and rituals of truth.'[21] This is the context in which his sophisticated critique of power – particularly as a discursive mechanism for social control, surveillance, and disciplining (i.e., punishment as harm) – is most germane to understanding the criminological shadow.[22] Foucault systematically explained that the manifestation of punishment in society represents 'a system of power and regulation which is imposed upon a population.'[23] This system of governmental or state-sponsored domination is built around regulatory institutions (e.g., the legal, the psychiatric, and the penal), that promote particularized regimes of knowledge/truth whose effect is the panoptic inspection, and normalization of the subject.[24] For Foucault, this condition of discursive power, as embedded in dominant discourses and as a form of knowledge/truth, was both pervasive and insidious.[25]

To illustrate, the legal, the medical, and penal apparatuses operate to advance totalizing representations of power as knowledge/truth. This is 'not because [power] embraces everything but because it comes from everywhere.'[26] Thus, medicine represents an all-encompassing expression of knowledge/truth enacted through the instrumentality of scientific discoveries (e.g., functional magnetic resonance imaging as brain-scanning technology) and medical breakthroughs (i.e., their application in the case of interrogating criminal suspects/offenders or in determining juvenile waiver for trial fitness purposes). The law (especially the criminal justice apparatus) represents an all-encompassing expression of knowledge/truth when it functions to police or socially control these discoveries and breakthroughs through the activities of codification, reification, and legitimation.[27] These are particularized or circumscribed renditions of reality construction undertaken in the juridic sphere.

Indeed, Foucault's treatment of power, mobilized and activated through speech codes or even entire systems of communication, indicates that the symbiosis of language as power is itself a form of ideology.[28] Ideology or the regimes of knowledge/truth to which Foucault referred included 'doctrinal texts' as well as 'discursive practices' that reconstituted privileged standpoints into 'lived experience.'[29] These lived experiences, as 'strategies of power'[30] or as expressions of ideology, seep unconsciously into the bodily core of the individual and signify a type of 'bio-power' or a 'micro-physics of power.'[31] It is at this point that the mechanisms of power (e.g., the grand narrative of science as the arbiter of truth, reason, and justice) exert their material will and force on the subject's 'soul.'[32] Foucault's notion of the soul refers to the internalization of disciplinary knowledge/truths, absent the need for external mechanisms of restraint or coercion (e.g., torture, banishment, ostracism). This is the point at which the individual is thoroughly disciplined and rendered a *docile body*. Indeed, as Foucault, observed,

> in thinking of the mechanisms of power, I am thinking rather of its capillary forms of existence, the point where power reaches into the very grain of individuals, touches their bodies, and inserts itself into their actions and attitudes, their discourse, learning processes, and everyday lives.[33]

For Foucault, whether exploring the genealogy of madness,[34] medicine/science,[35] sexuality,[36] or penology,[37] this emphasis on the techniques or strategies of institutional power not only defined the subject but the structural relations and human actions of which subjects were a part.[38] These apparatuses – as increasingly inventive, productive, and technical – were themselves emblematic of a culture of 'domination and subordination.'[39] Further, commenting on the Foucauldian construct of power, Garland observed that such omnipotence 'shapes the actions of individuals and harnesses their bodily powers to its ends. In this sense, power operates "through" individuals rather than "against" them and helps constitute the individual who is at the same time its vehicle.'[40] This very mobilization represents a sort of internal political essentializing in which the organization of power and its concrete forms subject the individual's soul to the unfettered and normalizing gaze of panoptic governmental authority.[41]

Consider, for instance, contemporary penology, especially in societies such as the United States. Here, the emphasis on the discourse of 'corrections' (e.g., 'secure housing units,' 'electronic monitoring and/or surveillance,' 'intensive probation supervision,' and 'solitary confinement') draws attention to the apparatuses of power – to the doctrinal texts and discursive practices – that render the subject's soul docile. Through such instrumentality, the 'perfection of power' is borne, making its actual exercise (i.e., the infliction of physical harm) 'unnecessary.'[42] Thus, Foucault's account of power as knowledge/truth, of the body as territorialized by the state, and of the instruments and techniques of control they entail, represented 'a prolonged assault' on what he took to be 'the myths of the Enlightenment' and the development of Western civilization.[43] In such instances as these, the icons of modernist reasoning (e.g., positivist science, categorical truth, absolute progress) were all understood through the totalizing and oppressive exercise of power. Under conditions such as these, *the shadow is omnipotent*!

Baudrillard: technologized and hyper-real culture

Foucault's thesis on power, knowledge, and the body was critically embraced and radically explicated in the work of Jean Baudrillard.[44] Indeed, as Agger noted, 'Baudrillard goes farther than Foucault in that he argues that postmodernity moves into a mode of simulation and information, displacing the roots of power from sources of material production (cf. Marx) to information and entertainment.'[45] Consistent with this perspective, Gane asserted that 'Baudrillard elaborates the genealogy of the orders of simulation over the period of European history since the Renaissance.... [I]t rivals that of Foucault ... in its vast ambitions to elaborate not theoretical modes of production but modes of simulation.'[46] Commenting still further, Gane noted:

> And yet despite similarities to his predecessors, Baudrillard takes us into a whole new era of social development: beyond Marx, beyond neo-Marxism, beyond the Situationists, beyond modernity, and beyond theory itself. We leave behind the society of the commodity and its stable supports; we transcend the society of the spectacle and its dissembling masks; and we bid farewell to modernity and enter the postmodern society of simulacrum, an abstract non-society devoid of cohesive relations, shared meaning, political struggle, or significant change.[47]

How, then, does the transition from Foucault to Baudrillard further our understanding of the criminology of the shadow, its associated harms, and their implications for freedom, choice, and authenticity? Much like Foucault, Baudrillard maintained that 'social texts' (e.g., the discourses of religion, politics, science, law, engineering, and fashion) were the locus of disciplinary control;[48] however, according to Baudrillard, the ontological statuses of these texts were themselves the subject of considerable examination.[49] For Baudrillard, social texts referred to the mass-mediated messages of our times: smartly crafted consumable images that signify 'the passage out of the metallurgic [tactile] into the semiurgic [intangible spoken] society.'[50] These media-manufactured messages operate at the level of simulation. They are efficacious discourses or stylized word and sight re-presentations of the 'real world' 'dispersed in everyday life' that are taken to be more authentic, more factual, and, thus, more legitimate than the reality on which they are based.[51] This is because simulations as social texts possess sign-exchange value.[52] Sign-exchange value refers to 'the process of symbolic exchange in a consumer-oriented society.'[53] This is a world in which counterfeit realities or imitations of the authentic – replicated, reproduced, and circulated – are consumed and devoured for their representational, although temporary and conditional, meanings.[54] To illustrate, consider the example of the fast-food eatery, McDonald's. The commodity that is consumed is not merely the food items that the company sells but a sense of family, community, and fun. Thus, the representational meaning for the McDonald's advertisement campaign – commodified through its chain-store distribution efforts – is one in which the public devours an *evolving* McDonald's world and the messages its architects assign to it.[55]

As consumable symbolic meanings abound, these image objects and their corresponding sign-exchange values become hyper-real social texts.[56] Following Baudrillard's thesis, the 'hyper-real is the end of a new result of a historical simulation process in which the natural world and all its referents have been gradually replaced with technology and self-referential signs.'[57] But as these imitations of the real infiltrate 'people's sentient environments,'[58] the divide separating the reality and appearance dichotomy vanishes.[59] This is the realm of 'simulation proper.'[60] During the stage of simulation proper, imitation models of the real 'come to constitute the world, and overtake and finally "devour" representation.'[61] Moreover, these 'simulation models generate simulacra, [linguistic] representations of the real, that are so omnipresent that it is henceforth impossible to distinguish the real from simulacra.'[62] Correspondingly, the grounding of the artificial, the counter-factual, and the replica are undone because these are 'mere representations of an intangible, unreal existence.'[63] In other words, as this virtual non-reality has no foundation which it can claim as its own, 'the subject-object distance is erased' and altogether obliterated;[64] in short, reality is imploded.[65]

Under these postmodern conditions, the end of the social seems both immanent and undeniable.[66] This is a world in which 'language no longer coheres in stable meanings ..., [where] originals are endlessly reproduced in copies, and ... [where] signs no longer refer beyond themselves to an existing, knowable word.'[67] Computerized technology, digitized images, and cybernetic codes – all facets of the instantly accessible mass-mediated information superhighway – both exaggerate and accentuate the undoing of social life.[68] As Baudrillard explained,

> Now the 'structural law of value' reigns, and models take precedence over things, while 'serial' production yields to generation by means of models.... Digitality is its metaphysical principle ... and DNA its prophet. [The conditions of] a capitalist-productivist society [give way] to a neo-capitalist cybernetic order that aims at total control.[69]

Accordingly, 'the real is produced from miniaturized units, from matrices, memory banks and command models – and with these it can be reproduced an infinite number of times.'[70] In the end, what is taken to be real 'is not only what can be reproduced, but that which is always already reproduced.'[71] When everything can be technically reproduced 'reality is dissipated and depleted; it loses its power and force through its cultural processing, through mechanical reproduction and the proliferation of illusions and pseudo-forms.'[72] These forms as stylized and manufactured imitations of the real are replicated, marketed, and circulated by profit-minded and business-savvy corporate executives, sensitive to the consumable needs of an insatiable public.[73] Thus, what the subject is left with are artificial choices whose subtext is control and 'programmed differences.'[74] Self-definition and the establishment of identity (products of choice, decision, commitment) meet with adversative forces. As Heidegger and Sartre remind us, our identities and subsequent projects and behaviors become meaningful – authentic – only to the extent that they are *ours*. This is Kellner's point when he soberly warns,

> The society of simulations thus comes to control an individual's range of responses and options for choice and behavior ... Baudrillard ... offers a new model of social control in which codes and programming become the principal of social organization, and individuals are forced to respond to pre-coded messages and models in the realm of economics, politics, culture, and everyday life. Although one is allowed a range of choices – indeed such choice is constantly demanded – the options are predetermined and pre-coded.[75]

Consequently, the disciplinary society of which Michel Foucault wrote is radically transformed by Jean Baudrillard. The latter posits a simulated hyper-reality where the ubiquitous message as transmutating sign-exchange value 'becomes a secret text.'[76] This text conveys multiple and evolving meanings yet represents nothing 'real,' or 'true,' or 'permanent.' Moreover, this narrative as illusory non-reality defines, shapes, and regulates *ad infinitum* the subject's corporeal soul. Thus, in Baudrillard's hyper-reality of simulation and simulacra, the individual no longer is a subject, an object, or a fixed image; rather, the social reality (i.e., the ontology) of the individual is dramatically re-conceptualized where the absence of anchored meaning or stable identity (i.e., the void) gives way to illusion that is taken to be authentic even though it is not.[77] This is how exclusion as harm is sustained at the everyday level of experience. The *shadow is omnipresent*! However, what remains to be seen is how such harm is appropriated and reified at the intra-psychic level. To address this matter, the seminal contributions of Jacques Lacan are reviewed.

Lacan: the subject as 'lack' in discourse

Foucault's critique indicates how panoptic bio-power renders human subjects 'docile bodies, bodies of abject utility and mere functionaries of the state.'[78] Baudrillard's investigation of hyper-reality and technologized culture explains how simulated meanings – 'miniaturized models of reality, imitation units of authenticity'[79] – are ubiquitously produced and rapaciously consumed. However, both psycho-philosophic approaches are insufficient for purposes of interpreting the degree to which the criminological shadow operates deep within one's psyche. In short, what is absent from the discussion thus far is how felt exclusion stemming from Foucault's bio-physics of power and Baudrillard's media-manufactured reality is embodied in *unconscious desire*. This assessment of a shadow criminology, of circumscribed desire that renders the subject *pas tout(e)* or as 'lack,' draws critical attention to the protean relationship between discourse and subjectivity and the contexts in which human agency is conceived, spoken, and knowable.

Lacan was a Freudian revisionist and he reconsidered the latter's developmental theory as profoundly addressing the relationship between language and symbolic representation.[80] In re-conceptualizing Freud's formulations on the unconscious,[81] Lacan recognized that the subject (the self) was intimately bound to discourse (to language).[82] Indeed, the spoken (or written) word represented a 'stand-in,' a substitute, for the identity of the individual; that is, it spoke for or on behalf of the self.[83] Further, Lacan argued that the unconscious was structured much like a language.[84] Not surprisingly, then, he examined 'the inner workings of that discourse located within the ... unconscious ... This [domain was] the repository of knowledge, power, agency, and desire.'[85] As such, he was particularly interested in deciphering the organizing parameters of meaning that 'defined the language in use.'[86]

Lacan's (1981) attention to the unconscious and to the desire embodied in language that spoke the person, led him to identify two planes of subjectivity or two levels of the self.[87] These included the *subject of speech* and *the speaking subject*. The first of these represents the content or narrative of what the 'I' (the person) says or writes. It is the text itself. However, when a person speaks, 'another plane is hidden which is the locus of the actual producer of the narrative or text.'[88] This is the concealed, postponed, or deferred self, absent in the spoken or written narrative. The second plane of subjectivity is the *speaking subject*. It signifies the 'scripted' meaning that is uttered. Psychoanalytically, it is the language of the 'Other' (of the unconscious) that often passes through and functions as a substitute for the identity, individuality, and humanity of the one who speaks or writes. This 'Other' is not directly or immediately accessible. Despite this, the question Lacan explored throughout the course of his considerable career was one of identifying the voice (language) and way of knowing (desire) that spoke for and on behalf of the subject (the self).[89]

Lacan's position that language speaks us (that it often represents a stand-in for the 'real' subject whose identity, regrettably, remains dormant, silenced, and repressed), significantly recasts the established view of human agency.[90] In effect, contrary to the modernist conception of the resolute, rational subject developed through the insights of Enlightenment philosophy and Cartesian epistemology,[91] the subject is not so much in control of his or her thoughts whose effects include purposeful and utilitarian action; rather, the subject is much more de-centered, divided, and unstable. The question, then, is whose desiring voice (way of knowing) speaks and embodies the criminological shadow? In other words, whose desire insists in the omnipotent (Foucault) and omnipresent (Baudrillard) message that engulfs the divided self?

Lacan's critique of human agency descriptively specifies the depth to which unconscious (and circumscribed) desire is lodged within the language the subject employs, whether engaged in speech or writing. As the Lacanian *discourse of the master* indicates, system-maintaining forms of meaning and sense-making prevail. Further, as the *discourse of the hysteric* makes evident, efforts to convey subjectivity (desire) outside such restricted parameters of communication are thwarted.[92] Under conditions such as these, *the criminological shadow is omniscient*! However, what has yet to be delineated is the character of such system-endorsing speech. In other words, mindful of our thesis on the criminological shadow, what *does* the omnipotent, omnipresent, and omniscient message privilege? This question implicates the perceptive work of Erich Fromm.

Fromm: negative freedom, displaced spontaneity, and mechanisms of escape

The insights of Foucault, Baudrillard, and Lacan represent a compelling critique of power, a gripping assessment of culture, and a provocative reworking of human agency respectively. However, it is Fromm's analysis that squarely addresses the quality of personal freedom and social responsibility amid a climate of expanding forms of state-sanctioned capitalism;[93] constructions that presumably liberate, democratize, and humanize.[94] Interestingly for Fromm, the effects of monopoly/late capitalism represented a 'crisis of contemporary society' stemming from the 'great promise of unlimited progress – the promise of domination of nature, of material abundance, of the greatest happiness for the greatest number, and of unimpeded personal freedom.'[95] Among other forces, Fromm traced this crisis to advances brought about by the industrial age, including 'the substitution of the computer for the human mind [which led to the belief that] we were on our way to unlimited production and, hence, unlimited consumption; that technique made us omnipresent; that science made us omniscient.' However, according to Fromm, the 'illusion' of such advances was linked to an understanding of two fundamental modes of human existence: having versus being.[96]

Why is Fromm's critique of the political economy and the social-psychological exclusion rendered through this apparatus relevant for purposes of deconstructing the criminological shadow? In short, issues of autonomy and individuality are significant because they direct attention to the quality of our existences in which the presence of power – fuelled by materialist culture and unconscious desire – nurtures, sustains, and endorses a new form of existence. For Fromm, this existence was marked by *escape* and was expressed through psychic unrest and social discord (e.g., mechanistic conformity, human destructiveness, domination, and criminality).[97] It is this escape that directs us to the existential dilemma the subject confronts given the omnipotent, omnipresent, and omniscient shadow.

The essence of Fromm's argument was targeted toward the capitalistic mode of production, the industrial and technological means by which it functioned, and the new psychological states and social relations it therefore produced.[98] On the one hand, capitalism established a heightened personal independence expressed through 'individualistic activity.'[99] Indeed, 'capitalism not only freed [us] from traditional [feudal] bonds, but it also contributed tremendously to the increasing of positive freedom, to the growth of an active, critical, responsible self.'[100] This sense of autonomy and freedom 'put the individual entirely on his [or her] own feet,' advancing the growth 'process of individualization.'[101] In the extreme, as Fromm noted,

> [t]he achievement of wealth and comfort for all was supposed to result in unrestricted happiness for all. The trinity of unlimited production, absolute freedom, and unrestricted happiness formed the nucleus of a new religion, Progress.... It is not at all astonishing [therefore] that this new religion provided its believers with energy, vitality, and hope.[102]

On the other hand, the effect of capitalism fostered isolation, fear, and loneliness for the ostensibly self-made citizen, imbuing the person 'with a feeling of insignificance and powerlessness.'[103] For Fromm, these more negative dimensions of freedom, linked as they were to accumulation for its own sake, subordinated the identity of the individual and rendered the person nothing more than an instrument of the capitalistic apparatus.[104] As he cautioned,

> It becomes [the individual's] fate to contribute to the growth of the economic system, to amass capital, not for purposes of [one's] own happiness or salvation, but as an end in itself. [The individual therefore becomes] a cog in the vast economic machine – an important one if he [or she] has capital, an insignificant one if he [or she] has none – but always a cog to serve a purpose outside of the [self].[105]

Elsewhere, Fromm draws a similar conclusion. As he observed,

> the dream of being independent masters of our lives ended when we
> began awakening to the fact that we ha[d] all become cogs in the
> bureaucratic machine, with our thoughts, feelings, and tastes manipu-
> lated by government and industry and the mass communication that
> they control.[106]

Fromm's disputation on capitalism and its debilitating consequences for
various facets of our everyday lives, led him to question whether individuality[107] and identity[108] were even possible. He argued that notwithstanding
the accomplishments of capitalism, 'negative freedom' prevailed. As
Fromm explained,

> By making the individual free politically and economically, by teach-
> ing [the person] to think for [self] and freeing [the person] from ...
> authoritarian pressure[s], one hoped to enable [the person] to feel 'I' in
> the sense that he [or she] was the center and active subject of his [or
> her] powers and experienced himself [or herself] as such. [However]
> for the majority, individualism was not much more than a façade
> behind which was hidden the failure to acquire an individual sense
> of identity.[109]

This concern for the pretence of identity and the illusion of individuality
led Fromm to question whether positive freedom was even realizable.
As he noted, the possibility of positive freedom was associated with
one's capacity for spontaneous conduct.[110] In other words, *'positive
freedom consists in the spontaneous activity of the total, integrated
personality'* (emphasis in the original).[111] His more humanistic regard
for the retrievability of this notion occupied considerable attention in
his subsequent writings.[112] In partial response to his query on the
veritable existence of positive freedom, Fromm examined the techniques
people employed in order to cope with the economic fall-out of
their oppressive and repressive realities.[113] Fromm described these
strategies as 'mechanisms of escape.'[114] Linked to these strategies was
his concern for whether expressions of independent thought and
affect were possible, absent intrusion from or regulation by the state. As
he explained,

> *The right to express our thoughts, however, means something only if
> we are able to have thoughts of our own;* freedom from external
> authority is a lasting gain only if the inner psychological conditions
> are such that we are able to establish our own individuality.[115]
> (Emphasis in the original.)

Again, one is reminded of Heidegger's position that authenticity requires thoughts, feelings, projects, etc. to be *one's own*.[116] Like actions, thoughts are authentic only if they are chosen or 'authored' by oneself (to use a Nietzschean tone).[117]

Fromm's mechanisms of escape consisted of two principal forms.[118] Authoritarianism is the tendency on the part of the subject to rely on sadistic and/or masochistic activities that are rationalized. In this respect, then, 'authority is not a quality one person "has," in the sense that [one] has property or physical qualities. Authority refers to an interpersonal relation in which one person looks upon another as somebody superior to him [or her].'[119] Outwardly, the rationalizations of authority are expressions of wanting to dominate others (sadist) and wanting to be dominated by others (masochist). However, the more covert explanation for these inclinations is that the person is 'terrified' by the freedom that he or she lacks in which (unhealthy) dependency is at the core.[120] In other words, 'both the masochistic and sadistic strivings tend to help the individual to escape his [or her] unbearable feeling of aloneness and powerlessness.... [The person is] filled with a terror of aloneness and insignificance.'[121] In this context, then, sadistic and/or masochistic strivings reflect the subject's 'inability to bear the isolation and weakness of one's own self.'[122] Indeed, these authoritarian propensities symbolize the desire '*to get rid of the burden of [negative] freedom*.'[123]

Automaton conformity is the second mechanism of escape and, for Fromm, it represented the 'solution' most people appropriated given the lack of true individuality and authentic identity they experienced.[124] As Fromm aptly summarized it,

> [T]he individual ceases to be [a self and] adopts entirely the kind of personality offered to him [or her] by the cultural patterns; and [the person] therefore becomes exactly as all others are and as they expect [the person] to be. The discrepancy between 'I' and the world disappears and with it the conscious fear of aloneness and powerlessness.... The person who gives up his [or her] individual self becomes an automaton, identical with millions of other automatons ..., need not feel alone and anxious any more. But the price [the person] pays, however, is high; it is the loss of the self.[125]

Under conditions such as these, whether exclusion assumes the form of authoritarianism or automaton conformity, *the shadow* is *all-encompassing*!

The criminological shadow as exclusion: applications in crime and justice

Recently, three forms of exclusion have appeared on the criminological horizon, emblematic of the phenomenology of the shadow as specified throughout this chapter. These include: (1) evidence-based criminal justice research; (2) actuarial penology; and (3) the policing of risk. Although certainly interrelated, each of these phenomena is summarily described below. This commentary is followed by a preliminary analysis of how these notions collectively further what we might call 'existential harm' – exclusion, alienation, and corresponding limitations on choice-making and positive freedom more generally. Implicated are those harms of reduction (limits on one's being) and repression (denials of one's becoming) that are nurtured, sustained, and reified in crime and justice studies – not to mention associated policies and practices. In order to address these concerns, the contributions of each luminary as discussed throughout this chapter (i.e., Foucault, Baudrillard, Lacan, and Fromm) are suggestively linked to the three forms of harm identified above.

Evidence-based research, actuarial penology, and the policing of risk

Current efforts to advance a rigorous 'science' of criminology focus on what works.[126] In this approach, reliance on the tools of the scientific method (e.g., theory-testing, quantification and measurement, objectivism and positivism) are all prominently featured. At issue is the discovery of reliable, valid, and replicable outcomes that can be harnessed to advance worthwhile crime policies whose principal goal is to abate violence and reduce victimization.[127] This same logic finds its way into the 'new' penology movement.[128] Understood to be a form of actuarial justice, an expanding number of classification schemas (e.g., 'high-risk offenders,' 'serial sadistic killers,' 'death row felons,' 'sexually violent predators,') are employed to combat or contain crime.[129] The expressed purpose of such categorization is to forecast risk and to promote management.[130] Moreover, the aim is to develop effective programming and treatment strategies whose objective is crime reduction.[131]

Both evidence-based criminal justice and actuarial penology are particular manifestations of the risk society.[132] Policing the risk society implicates late modernity and the global economy.[133] Specifically, efforts to maximize personal safety and social welfare are of central concern, and the proliferating advances in industry, medicine, government and the like are thought to be essential pathways to guaranteeing such security.[134] However, the growth of this 'progress,' steeped in technological innovations or breakthroughs, also fosters hazards.[135] In particular, although focused on the elimination of social inequalities and class divisions, the preoccupation with avoiding threat or reducing risk makes obsolete the free-thinking role of the individual in society. Indeed, excessive investments in technology displace the creative contributions of the individual.[136] Within the 'science' of criminology, the mechanistic regulation of citizens occurs through offender-monitoring techniques (e.g., intensive probation supervision, boot camps, mandatory-minimum sentences, three-strikes legislation, transfer of juveniles to the adult system) that seek to ensure compliance and/or minimize transgression.[137] More problematic, however, is the extent to which evidence-based criminal justice, actuarial penology, and the policing of risk promote exclusion consistent with the criminology of the shadow.

Foucault, the criminological shadow, and the risk society

For Foucault, power is linked to discourse such that this binary and unalterable relationship produces expressions ('texts') of knowledge/truth. In contemporary culture, the locus of these forms of knowledge/truth, as governing systems of power, resides in regulatory institutions whose purpose is to police, inspect, and discipline the individual. One such regulatory institution is the academy itself whose gate-keeping activities include, among other things, monitoring the academic publication process. In short, the mechanism of peer review, as an extension of the academy, vets what does or does not 'count' as meritorious knowledge. The significance of this disciplinary regulation is most acute (and is most problematic) when publication choices are made by 'high-impact' periodicals or other prestige outlets whose distribution reaches a large readership or whose content is acknowledged *sui generis* as a significant contribution to the literature. This is the realm where power and control is transformed into knowledge and authority.[138]

The 'text' of criminology – increasingly proliferated through scholarship that advances evidence-based research, actuarial penology, and the policing of risk – is an expression of knowledge/truth and it falls squarely within the regulatory ambit of the (criminal justice) academy. As such, and consistent with Foucault, this communicative system of power represents an 'ideological' view[139] in which a range of (existential) concerns (e.g., deconstructing the risk society) and the lived experiences pertaining to them (symptoms of the phenomenology of the shadow) can be and, according to the modern episteme of materialist culture,[140] should be interpreted.

The hyper-vigilant and near-obsessive preoccupation with which the criminological community now embraces, endorses, and extols scientism (e.g., evidence-based research, actuarial penology) is an overly reductionistic and deterministic perspective on the human condition. This notwithstanding, as a discursive practice and operating at the level of Foucauldian bio-power, this grand narrative or doctrinal text conveys de facto the message that the burden and privilege of discovering truth, advancing knowledge, and promoting progress rests upon the mantle of science, despite the considerable limits of such an approach.[141] Moreover, functioning within the sphere of Foucault's microphysics of power, the investigator is required to appropriate the tools of the scientific method as a basis to undertake a legitimate scholarly inquiry; the peer referee is charged with maintaining rigorous standards of research acumen as a way of discerning the relative worth of a manuscript; and the Editor of a (high-impact) journal is obliged to inspect both, ensuring that the investigator's analysis is meritorious and the reviewer's critique equally commendable, always already consistent with the logic and language of science. Once published and disseminated to the periodical's audience (other criminologists), recipients are encouraged to accept the superiority of such 'findings,' especially when appropriated for strategic use beyond the (criminal justice) academy (e.g., to advance crime policy). Thus, the exercise of state-sanctioned authority vis-à-vis the educational apparatus is transformed productively, power is ingrained corporeally, and dissent/disagreement gives way to docility. The omnipotent criminological shadow endures.

Baudrillard, the criminological shadow, and the risk society

Contributing to the Foucauldian assessment of science's 'panoptic gaze'[142] and his 'hermeneutics of suspicion'[143] – especially given the (criminal justice) academy's inspection and regulation of meritorious research – is Baudrillard's thesis on hyper-reality in ultramodern society. As a social text, the sign-exchange value of the criminological canon is diffuse and manifold. This is because the evolving message about research 'evidence,' offender 'management,' and risk 'control' inundates and engulfs us. Moreover, the logic, language, and labor of science is esteemed in this effusive narrative for its presumed capacity to correct the deviant, diseased, and dangerous elements that populate the social order. This is how Baudrillard's hyper-reality is mobilized and activated. Indeed, at this point, models or replicas of the real (i.e., the criminological canon) are relentlessly and instantaneously disseminated through various media-based outlets with their corresponding effects.

To illustrate, consider the following. Repeated exposure to both print and electronic information about prison privatization as marketed industry; politically charged commercials that insist on three-strikes legislation, mandatory-minimum sentences, or 'get tough on crime' policies; sexually violent predator statutes, serial offenders, or psychotic killers continuously discussed on CNN, C-SPAN, FOX, or other cable stations that ostensibly report the news (read infotainment) for their network; 'reality' television shows that depict police officer practices (e.g., *COPS*) or crime-scene investigation techniques (e.g., *America's Most Wanted, Autopsy:*

Postmortem with Dr. Baden); Nintendo, PlayStation, or Game Cube games that create a violent world in which the participant is the executioner, the punisher (e.g., *Grand Theft Auto*). In instances such as these stylized and mass-marketed images regarding the criminological canon outpace and undo its commodity forms (e.g., research evidence, offender management, and risk control). However, these images captured digitally are *reproductions*; that is, they are simulations of the 'real' phenomenon in question. And, as previously described, given the (criminal justice) academy's mechanism of peer review surveillance what 'counts' as 'truth,' 'knowledge,' and 'progress' is itself a manifestation and incorporation of the micro-physics of power.

For Baudrillard, when facsimiles of authentic experience are rapaciously produced, then their signification is located not in the phenomenon itself and not in the image of the object; rather, their sign-exchange or symbolic value is lodged, temporarily and incompletely, in their representational meanings.[144] In a material culture of mass-mediated conspicuous consumption, what is 'devoured' with respect to the criminological canon are morphing simulacra. Confronted with an insatiable public hungry for more sights, sounds, and pseudo-signs, the commutating message concerning the risk society leaves little room for distinguishing between what is real and what is illusion; between what is authentic and what is representation. Thus, reality implodes and foundations disappear. And with them, the grounding of truth, knowledge, progress, the factual, and, more disturbingly, the social and the self vanish. All that remain are the mutable messages themselves that give us choices about what research evidence is, or what offender management is, or what risk control is, but choices that only the architects of these 'illusions' allow us. The omnipresent criminological shadow endures.

Lacan, the criminological shadow, and the risk society

Another dimension of exclusion that specifies the phenomenology of harm is Lacan's *discourse of the master*. Mindful of the critique thus far concerning the omnipotent criminological canon as well as the omnipresence of this message as expressed through mutating and media-manufactured sign-exchange values, is the nature of desire that speaks the divided self. This is a reference to the circumscribed way of knowing that insists through evidence-based research, actuarial penology, the policing of threat, and the evolving meanings that attach to them all (i.e., the scripted, hyper-real risk society) through the activities of simulation and simulacra.

Harm (i.e., limits on one's being; denials of one's becoming) is embodied in the criminal justice academy's panoptic process of identifying meritorious research. This disciplining is replicated through smartly crafted print and electronic images that showcase, *ad infinitum*, how to correct the deviant, diseased, and dangerous segments of society. Both the micro-physics of institutionalized power and the technologized dissemination of its assorted cultural manifestations constitute the scripted, hyper-real risk society. They emerge from within a commitment to the value of science understood as evidence-based research, actuarial penology, and policing threat or hazard.

Science, as a master signifier, is informed by a chain of related terms and includes such notions as positivism, objectivism, linear causality, equi-librium conditions, theory-testing, the logic of capital, quantification and measurement, and status quo dynamics. These related terms are more con-cealed or covert; they inform what messages are conveyed about the crimi-nological canon and its media-manufactured simulations. However, the scientific knowledge that is received by all conveys circumscribed insights about the scripted, hyper-real risk society. Moreover, the felt exclusion that surfaces (e.g., the desiring subject/researcher who resists and/or opposes panoptic academy disciplining; the desiring subject/citizen who renounces or rebels against technologized and anesthetizing reality con-struction), indicates that something else is missing. In other words, the insights that are communicated remain incomplete.

Thus, the question is what is absent within the scripted, hyper-real risk society? The answer is a more fully developed *philosophy of the subject*.[145] Stated differently, criminology lacks a *theory of the stranger*.[146] As a coun-terpart to the criminological shadow, the development of such a theory questions how positive freedom, individual thought, and personal identity could be promoted, ensuring where possible that automaton conformity is avoided, critiqued, and rejected. Existentially speaking, then, a philosophy of the subject in relation to the phenomenology of harm examines the con-texts in which the flourishing (being) and the transformation (becoming) of the stranger/subject could occur.

Accordingly, it follows that in the Lacanian *discourse of the master*, a theory of the stranger is the *pas tout/e* (the not-all), awaiting articulation, embodiment, and legitimacy. In this respect, then, the stranger as lack is the source of what is needed to address the existential dilemma of exclusion (harms of reduction/repression). Moreover, the stranger's absent but felt suppression is the result of what is communicated from sender to receiver of the scripted, hyper-real risk society message. This is a message that fosters panoptic power, technologized culture, and the divided self. It is here, then, within this Lacanian schematization that we can begin to com-prehend how the omniscience of the shadow endures – from the academy's particularized mechanisms of panoptic surveillance to their subsequent cul-turalized metamorphoses as commutating simulacra of control.[147]

Fromm, the criminological shadow, and the risk society

Understanding the existential dilemma of exclusion in which the criminological shadow's omnipotence, omnipresence, and omniscience endures is incomplete without additional analysis. Specifically, *why* are those forces that discipline the body, implode the reality–appearance divide, and thwart human agency permitted? Stated differently, why do *we* allow the criminological shadow and its felt harms of reduction/repression to remain so all-encompassing in the social order and in our lives? Fromm's thesis on mechanisms of escape is instructive for this purpose. In what follows, both the economy of authoritarianism and automaton conformity are briefly examined.

Criminology and the economy of authoritarianism

As Fromm noted, sadomasochistic tendencies emerge from 'feelings of inferiority, powerlessness, [and] individual insignificance.'[148] Although the person may 'consciously complain about these feelings and want to get rid of them, unconsciously some power within themselves drives them to feel inferior or insignificant.'[149] In the instance of sadism, the person depends on the other (including the state and its system-maintaining institutions) in order to sustain (the illusion of) freedom expressed as domination. In the instance of masochism, the person depends on the other (including the state and its system-endorsing apparatuses) in order to maintain the pretence of freedom expressed as a desire to be dominated. Both are manifestations of authoritarianism. The scripted, hyper-real risk society that renders the subject divided (lack) is rationalized, albeit mostly in unconscious form. Its subtext – understood as fear, isolation, and loneliness – is quelled through sadomasochistic strivings. Indeed, the subject *depends* on the omnipotence, omnipresence, and omniscience of the shadow because it removes the burden of negative freedom that the individual would otherwise profoundly experience.[150] The masochistic researcher/academic as well as the recipient of the ultramodern and digitized social text in which the sign values of research evidence, offender management, and the policing of threat are morphed into hyper-real proportions, submit obediently and docilely to their own exclusion. Under conditions such as these, the subject is territorialized. Indeed, as Fromm noted, explaining masochistic acquiescence,

> They [masochists] tend not to assert themselves, not to do what they want, but to submit to the factual or alleged orders of these outside forces [e.g., government authority; state interests]. Often they are quite incapable of experiencing the feeling 'I want' or 'I am.' Life, as a whole, is felt by them as something overwhelmingly powerful, which they cannot master or control.[151]

Moreover, the sadistic researcher/academic who insists, emphatically, on criminological 'science,' offender 'control' and policed 'threat,' as well as those who endorse/embrace/accept the scripted, hyper-real risk society messages such ideology promulgates, are similarly dependent. However, in these instances, rationalization emerges from the moral entrepreneurship of science,[152] legitimized through state apparatuses of control (the media, education, the law), galvanizing the person's sadistic strivings.[153] Still further, located beneath these destructive inclinations, the sadist *depends* on the 'object of his [or her] sadism.'[154] This is because the individual needs those whom he or she harms in order not to experience the pain of being alone, isolated, or afraid.[155] These feelings of powerlessness are rooted firmly in the condition or quality of freedom that the person would otherwise experience and can best be described as a lack or an absence in identity.[156] Thus, the sadist's insistence on the omnipotent, omnipresent, and omniscient shadow becomes *essential* to the person's identity. Without it, the person would have to confront the quality of his or her humanity in which pervasive feelings of alienation and terror thrived. Indeed, ideological resolve masks the interior self (i.e., the fragile and damaged self) that the subject seeks 'to get rid of' or 'lose.'[157]

Criminology and the economy of automaton conformity

Thus, how can we account for the phenomenology of harm (exclusion) in which the criminological shadow's panoptic power, manufactured hyper-reality, and engulfment of human agency are all sustained, nay, permitted? Consistent with Fromm's analysis on the economy of authoritarianism, what is fundamentally at issue is the complete loss of the self 'traceable to the suppression of critical thinking.'[158] Confronted with the loss of the self, 'pseudo acts' materialize that become a stand-in for the person's own reflection and behaviour, resulting in the emergence of a 'pseudo-self.'[159] Accordingly, this condition produces automaton conformity. As Fromm observed, '[i]n order to overcome the panic resulting from such loss of identity, [the individual] is compelled to conform, to seek ... identity by continuous approval and recognition by others. [The subject] acts according to [the] expectation[s of others].'[160]

Consequently, in order not to experience the increasing aloneness, or insignificance, or emptiness, or insecurity, or dread of one's life stemming from the consumption of a virtual and illusory non-reality that mediates one's thoughts, feelings, and decisions and that disciplines one's corporeal soul, *acquiescence* follows. In other words, the person sacrifices the self (and his/her humanness) at the altar of automaton conformity. This is the 'price' one must pay for displacing the burden of negative freedom; a quality of existence borne out of our relentless commitment to have rather than to be, to conspicuously consume rather than to authentically become.

Indeed, this is the consequence of allowing the existential dilemma of criminological exclusion that is the phenomenology of harm to be seeded, to be nurtured, and to be tolerated.

Conclusion

This chapter suggestively demonstrated how the criminological shadow that fosters harms of reduction/repression represents a profoundly vexing existential dilemma. The subject *of* crime (what transgression is) and the subject *in* crime (who the transgressor is) are not only indistinguishable, they lack tangible foundations. In their place, forms of exclusion (i.e., limits on one's being; denials of one's becoming) persist, especially given the omnipotent, omnipresent, and omniscient criminological message that permeates society and that engulfs the self. Foucault's position on the biophysics of power, Baudrillard's thesis on hyper-reality and technologized culture, Lacan's re-working of the desiring subject as lack, and Fromm's commentary of negative freedom and mechanisms of escape help to conceptually specify the depth and breadth of this ultramodern critique qua crisis.

The reflexive work that remains entails a more thorough assessment of the criminological shadow, the harms that it perpetuates, and those strategies that undo the marginalizing and alienating grip of both. Consistent with these recommendations, attention to a theory of the subject; that is, a 'criminology of the stranger,' is most assuredly warranted.[161] Indeed, the articulation of such a theory may very well be a worthwhile basis by which exclusion as harm is overcome and transcended. Collectively, then, these tasks signal the need for further inquiry into the development of a philosophically informed criminology.

Notes

1 See, e.g., B.A. Arrigo and C.R. Williams (eds.), *Philosophy, Crime, and Criminology*, Urbana and Chicago, IL: University of Illinois Press, 2006; B.A. Arrigo, D. Milovanovic, and R.C. Schehr, *The French Connection in Criminology: Rediscovering Crime, Law, and Social Change*, New York: State University of New York Press, 2005.

2 See, e.g., B. Arrigo, 'Social justice and critical criminology: on integrating knowledge,' *Contemporary Justice Review*, 2000, vol. 3, 7–37; B. Arrigo, 'Critical criminology, existential humanism, and social justice: exploring the contours of conceptual integration,' *Critical Criminology: An International Journal*, 2001, vol. 10, 83–95; B. Arrigo, 'Punishment, freedom, and the culture of control: the case of brain imaging and the law,' *American Journal of Law and Medicine*, 2007, vol. 33, 457–482; K. Anderson and R. Quinney (eds.), *Erich Fromm and Critical Criminology: Beyond the Punitive Society*, Urbana and Chicago, IL: University of Illinois Press, 2000; C. Williams, 'Engaging freedom: toward an ethics of crime and deviance,' in B.A. Arrigo

and C.R. Williams (eds.), *Philosophy, Crime, and Criminology*, Urbana and Chicago, IL: University of Illinois Press, 2006, pp. 167–196.

3 B.A. Arrigo and D. Milovanovic, *Revolution in Penology: Rethinking the Society of Captives*, New York, NY: Rowman & Littlefield, 2009, especially chapter 3.

4 M. Foucault, *Discipline and Punish: The Birth of a Prison*, New York: W.W. Norton, 1977.

5 J. Baudrillard, *Simulations*, New York: Semiotiext(e), 1983.

6 J. Lacan, *Ecrits: A Selection*, New York: W.W. Norton, 1977.

7 E. Fromm, *Escape from Freedom*, New York: Henry Holt and Company, 1994.

8 See also, J. Young, *The Exclusive Society: Social Exclusion, Crime, and Difference in Late Modernity*, London: Sage, 1999. A more complete review of this exclusion; that is, of the denial of being and the possibility of becoming, would necessarily entail a review of several other related strains of theoretical inquiry. Specifically, this would include the contributions of complex systems science, Derrida's deconstruction regarding the metaphysics of presence and logocentrism, and Deleuze's (and Deleuze and Guattari's) position of anti-Oedpius, capital logic, and molar larval forces. For applications of each in the realm of criminology and philosophy, see B.A. Arrigo and D. Milovanovic, *Revolution in Penology: Rethinking the Society of Captives*, New York: Rowman & Littlefield, 2009.

9 S. Maruna, A. Matravers, and A. King, 'Disowning our shadow: a psychoanalytic approach to understanding punitive public attitudes,' *Deviant Behavior*, 2004, vol. 25, 277–299.

10 D. Garland, *The Culture of Control*, Chicago, IL: University of Chicago Press, 2001.

11 A. Matravers and S. Maruna, 'Contemporary penality and psychoanalysis,' *Critical Review of International Social and Political Philosophy*, 2004, vol. 7, 118–144.

12 Arrigo and Milovanovic, *Revolution in Penology*, chapter 3.

13 S. Henry and D. Milovanovic, *Constitutive Criminology: Beyond Postmodernism*, London: Sage, 1996, pp. 115–119.

14 S. Henry and D. Milovanovic, 'Constitutive Criminology,' in M. Schwartz and S. Hatty (eds.), *Controversies in Critical Criminology*, Cincinnati, OH: Anderson, 2003, p. 58.

15 Ibid.

16 J.P. Sartre, *Being and Nothingness*, Hazel Barnes (transl.), New York: Washington Square Press, 1992.

17 Ibid.

18 See also, D. Cooper, *Existentialism*, Oxford: Blackwell, 1999; G. Marcel, *The Philosophy of Existentialism*, New York: Citadel, 1968; C. Taylor, *Sources of the Self: The Making of the Modern Identity*, Cambridge, MA: Harvard University Press, 1989.

19 S. Henry and D. Milovanovic, *Constitutive Criminology*, p. 115.

20 See, e.g., M. Foucault, *Power: Essential Works of Michel Foucault 1954–1984*, New York: The New Press, 1997; M. Foucault, *Power/Knowledge: Selected Interviews and Other Writings 1972–1977*, New York: Pantheon, 1980.

21 Foucault, *Discipline and Punish*, p. 194.

22 Arrigo, 'Punishment, freedom, and the culture of control,' p. 465.

23 D. Garland, *Punishment and Modern Society: A Study in Social Theory*, Chicago, IL: University of Chicago Press, 1990, p. 132.

24 Ibid., at 133–134; Arrigo *et al.*, *The French Connection in Criminology*, pp. 12–13.
25 B.A. Arrigo and C.R. Williams, 'Chaos theory and the social control thesis: a post-Foucauldian analysis of mental illness and involuntary civil confinement,' *Social Justice*, 1999, 26, 179–184.
26 Foucault, *Power/Knowledge*, p. 93.
27 Arrigo, 'Punishment, freedom, and the culture of control,' p. 465.
28 Garland, *Punishment and Modern Society*, p. 132.
29 B. Agger, *Critical Social Theories: An Introduction*, Boulder, CO: Westview Press, 2006, p. 140.
30 Garland, *Punishment and Modern Society*, pp. 137–138.
31 Foucault, *Discipline and Punish*, pp. 192–196; Arrigo *et al.*, *The French Connection in Criminology*, p. 12.
32 Garland, *Punishment and Modern Society*, pp. 137–138.
33 Foucault, *Power/Knowledge*, p. 39.
34 M. Foucault, *Madness and Civilization: A History of Insanity in the Age of Reason*, New York: Pantheon, 1965.
35 M. Foucault, *The Birth of the Clinic: An Archaeology of Medical Perception*, New York: Pantheon, 1973.
36 M. Foucault, *The History of Sexuality: An Introduction Volume I*, New York: Vintage, 1978; M. Foucault, *The History of Sexuality: The Use of Pleasure, Volume II*, New York: Vintage, 1986.
37 Foucault, *Discipline and Punish*.
38 Foucault, *Power/Knowledge*, pp. 39–40.
39 Garland, *Punishment and Modern Society*, p. 138.
40 Ibid., p. 146.
41 Foucault, *Discipline and Punish*, p. 210.
42 Arrigo, 'Punishment, freedom, and the culture of control,' p. 466.
43 Arrigo *et al.*, *The French Connection in Criminology*, p. 12; Garland, *Punishment and Modern Society*, p. 134.
44 Agger, *Critical Social Theory*, p. 140.
45 Ibid.
46 M. Gane, *Baudrillard's Bestiary: Baudrillard and Culture*, New York: Routledge, 1991, p. 94.
47 S. Best and D. Kellner, *The Postmodern Turn*, New York: Guilford Press, 1997, p. 95.
48 D. Kellner, *Jean Baudrillard: From Marxism to Postmodernism and Beyond*, 1989, Stanford, CA: Stanford University Press, pp. 76–84.
49 M. Gane, *French Social Theory*, Thousand Oaks, CA: Sage, 2003, pp. 152–161.
50 J. Baudrillard, *For a Critique of the Political Economy of the Sign*, St. Louis, MO: Telos Press, 1981, pp. 185–186.
51 Agger, *Critical Social Theory*, p. 141; Kellner and Best, *The Postmodern Turn*, pp. 76–84.
52 Gane, *French Social Theory*, pp. 154–155.
53 Arrigo *et al.*, *The French Connection in Criminology*, p. 20; Arrigo, 'Punishment, freedom, and the culture of control,' p. 467.
54 Agger, *Critical Social Theory*, pp. 141–142.
55 G. Ritzer, *The McDonalization of Society*, Thousand Oaks, CA: Pine Forge Press, 2007; G. Ritzer (ed.), *McDonaldization: The Reader*, New York: Pine Forge Press, 2006. For applications in crime and justice, see R.M. Bohm, 'McJustice: on the McDonaldization of criminal justice,' *Justice Quarterly*, vol. 23, 2006, 127–146.

56 Best and Kellner, *The Postmodern Turn*, p. 101.
57 Ibid.
58 Agger, *Critical Social Theory*, p. 140.
59 B.A. Arrigo, 'The ontology of crime: on the construction of the real, the image, and the hyper-real,' in B.A. Arrigo and C.R. Williams (eds.), *Philosophy, Crime, and Criminology*, Urbana and Chicago, IL: University of Illinois Press, pp. 50–51.
60 Kellner, *Jean Baudrillard*, p. 79.
61 Ibid.
62 Best and Kellner, *The Postmodern Turn*, p. 101.
63 Arrigo, 'On the construction of the real, the image, and the hyper-real,' p. 51.
64 Best and Kellner, *The Postmodern Turn*, p. 101.
65 Baudrillard, *Simulation*, pp. 56–57; Arrigo *et al.*, *The French Connection in Criminology*, pp. 20–21.
66 Kellner, *Jean Baudrillard*, pp. 84–89.
67 Best and Kellner, *The Postmodern Turn*, p. 101.
68 Arrigo, 'Punishment, freedom, and the culture of control,' p. 468.
69 Baudrillard, *Simulation*, p. 111.
70 Ibid., p. 3.
71 Ibid., p. 146.
72 Best and Kellner, *The Postmodern Turn*, p. 102.
73 See, e.g., B. Agger, *Fast Capitalism*, Urbana and Chicago, IL: University of Illinois Press, 1989; M. Gottdiener, *The Theming of America: American Dream, Media Fantasizes and Themed Environments*, Boulder, CO: Westview Press, 2001.
74 Kellner, *Jean Baudrillard*, p. 81.
75 Ibid., pp. 80–81.
76 Agger, *Critical Social Theory*, p. 141.
77 Best and Kellner, *The Postmodern Turn*, p. 102.
78 Foucault, *Discipline and Punish*, p. 210.
79 Baudrillard, *Simulation*, pp. 20–21.
80 B. Arrigo *et al.*, *The French Connection in Criminology*, pp. 2–5. For lucid reviews of Lacan's work in criminology and law, see D. Milovanovic, *Critical Criminology at the Edge: Postmodern Perspectives, Integration, and Applications*, Westport, CT: Praeger, 2002; D. Milovanovic, *An Introduction to the Sociology of Law*, Monsey, NY: Criminal Justice Press, 2003, pp. 229–242.
81 S. Freud, *The Interpretations of Dreams*, New York: Avon Books, 1965.
82 Lacan, *Ecrits*, pp. 68–77.
83 Milovanovic, *Sociology of Law*, p. 230.
84 Ibid.
85 Arrigo, *Punishing the Mentally Ill*, p. 133.
86 Lacan, *Ecrits*, p. 75.
87 J. Lacan, *The Four Fundamental Concepts of Psychoanalysis*, New York: W.W. Norton, 1981.
88 Milovanovic, *Sociology of Law*, p. 230.
89 A more complete reading of Lacan here would include his treatment of the *Symbolic Order* (the sphere of the unconscious, nuanced discourse and the 'law-of-the-father'), the *Imaginary Order* (the sphere of imaginary constructions including conceptions of self and others), and the *Real Order* (lived experience beyond accurate symbolization). See Milovanovic, *Critical Criminology at the Edge*, pp. 29–34.
90 Lacan, *Ecrits*, pp. 193–194, 310–316; J. Lacan, *The Seminars of Jacques*

Lacan, Book 2: The Ego in Freud's Theory and in the Techniques of Psycho-analysis, New York: W.W. Norton, 1988, p. 243.

91 R. Descartes, *Discourse on Method and Mediations on First Philosophy*, Indianapolis, IN: Hackett Publishing Company, 1999.

92 In Lacan's *discourse of the master*, the message sent to the other is limited and constrained, yielding circumscribed knowledge. These constrained signifiers stem from what is implicit in the sender (partial truths). The product of the exchange leaves something out; namely, incomplete understanding. This incomplete understanding experienced by the recipient of the message cannot be embodied in the truths that originate from the sender of the message. In the *discourse of the hysteric*, the 'hysteric' – more broadly defined as a person in struggle (including both the clinical, as well as the alienated, oppositional, and revolutionary subject) – communicates her/his suffering to the other who only offers master signifiers (slogans, ideology, dogma, truths, rhetoric) from which a body of knowledge may be constructed. The person in struggle has only a limited range of master signifiers from which to construct a narrative of her/his plight.

93 Foucault's and Baudrillard's respective observations emerge from within the cultural and critical studies tradition of French social theory. See, e.g., Gane, *French Social Theory*, pp. 146–148, 152–161. Fromm's critique is situated mostly within the theorizing of the early Frankfurt School which, at that time, endeavored to construct a brand of Freudian Marxism, mindful of the impact of mass culture and monopoly/late capitalism. See, K. Anderson, 'Erich Fromm and the Frankfurt School critique of criminal justice,' in K. Anderson and R. Quinney (eds.), *Erich Fromm and Critical Criminology: Beyond the Punitive Society*, Urbana and Chicago, IL, University of Illinois Press, 2000, pp. 83–84.

94 E. Fromm, *To Have or to Be?*, New York: HarperCollins, 1976, pp. xxii–xxiii.

95 Ibid., p. 1.

96 Arrigo, 'Punishment, freedom, and the culture of control,' p. 470.

97 Fromm, *Escape from Freedom*, pp. 140–204. Elsewhere, Fromm revisits these themes in which the 'pathology of normalcy,' the 'herd mentality,' and the 'sick society,' are examined. E. Fromm, *Sane Society*, New York: Holt Rinehart, and Co., 1955, pp. 12–21.

98 As Fromm explained, the capitalistic system 'molded the whole personality of man [and woman] and accentuated the contradictions.... [I]t developed the individual – and made [the person] more helpless; it increased freedom – and created dependencies of a new kind.' Fromm, *Escape from Freedom*, p. 104.

99 Ibid., p. 108.

100 Ibid.

101 Ibid.

102 Fromm, *To Have or To Be?*, p. 2.

103 Fromm, *Escape from Freedom*, p. 108.

104 Ibid., p. 111.

105 Ibid., p. 110.

106 Fromm, *To Have or To Be?*, p. 2.

107 Fromm, *Escape from Freedom*, pp. 239–254.

108 Fromm, *Sane Society*, pp. 60–63.

109 Ibid., p. 62.

110 Fromm, *Escape From Freedom*, pp. 255–274.

111 Ibid., p. 257.

112 See, e.g., Fromm, *To Have or To Be?*, pp. 168–202 (describing prospects for human change and prospects for an altered society); Fromm, *Sane Society*, pp. 339–352 (discussing the necessary political and cultural transformations). See also, R. Quinney, 'Socialist humanism and the problem of crime: thinking about Erich Fromm in the development of critical/peacemaking criminology,' in K. Anderson and R. Quinney (eds.), *Beyond the Punitive Society*, pp. 21–30.
113 Fromm, *Escape From Freedom*, p. 240.
114 Ibid., at 135, 140–204.
115 Ibid. (emphasis in the original).
116 M. Heidegger, *Being and Time*, J. MacQuarrie and E. Robinson (transl.), New York: Harper and Row, 1962. See also H. Barnes, *An Existentialist Ethics*, New York: Knopf, 1967.
117 F. Nietzsche, *The Gay Science*, W. Kaufmann (transl.), New York: Vintage, 1974; F. Nietzsche, *Thus Spoke Zarathustra*, W. Kaufmann (transl.), New York: Penguin, 1978; A. Nehamas, *Nietzsche: Life as Literature*, Oxford: Harvard University Press, 2006.
118 Destructiveness is another technique of escape as described by Fromm. Ibid., pp. 177–183. Because it is closely aligned with authoritarianism, expressed through sadistic and/or masochistic inclinations, it will not be discussed here. In brief, however, the aim of destructiveness is 'the elimination of an object.' Ibid., p. 178.
119 Ibid., pp. 162–163.
120 Ibid., pp. 142–144. 'Masochistic dependency is conceived as love, or loyalty, inferiority feelings as an adequate expression of actual shortcomings, and one's suffering as being entirely due to unchangeable circumstances.' Ibid., p. 142. Rationalized sadistic dependency includes such examples as

> 'I rule over you because I know what is best for you, and in your own interest you should follow me without opposition.' Or. 'I am so wonderful and unique, that I have a right to expect that the other people become dependent on me.' [Or], 'I have done so much for you, and now I am entitled to take from you what I want.'
>
> Ibid., p. 143

121 Ibid., p. 150.
122 Ibid., p. 156.
123 Ibid., p. 151 (emphasis in the original).
124 Ibid., p. 184.
125 Ibid., p. 184.
126 R. Burnett and C. Roberts (eds.), *What Works in Probation and Youth Justice: Developing Evidence-Based Practice*, Cullompton: Willan, 200; B.C. Welsh and D.P. Farrington, 'Evidence-based crime prevention: conclusions and directions for a safer society,' *Canadian Journal of Criminology and Criminal Justice*, vol. 47, 2004, 338–355.
127 L. Sherman, *Evidence Based Crime Prevention*, New York: Routledge, 2002.
128 M. Feeley and J. Simon, 'The new penology: notes on the emerging strategy of corrections and its implications,' *Criminology*, vol. 30, 1992, pp. 449–470; M. Feeley and J. Simon, 'The new penology,' in P. Kraska (ed.), *Theorizing Criminal Justice*, Long Grove, IL: Waveland Press, 2004, pp. 302–322.
129 See, e.g., L. Mona 'Waste managers: the new penology, crime fighting, and parole agent identity,' *Law and Society Review*, vol. 32, 1998, pp. 839–869.
130 A. Piquero, D. Farrington and A. Blumstein, *Key Issues in Criminal Career*

Research: New Analyses of the Cambridge Study in Delinquent Development, New York: Cambridge University Press, 2007.

131 R. Loeber and D.P. Farrington (eds.), *Serious and Violent Juvenile Offenders: Risk Factors and Successful Interventions*, Thousand Oaks, CA: Sage, 2002.

132 P. O'Malley, *Crime and the Risk Society*, Aldershot: Ashgate, 1998.

133 B. Hudson, *Justice in the Risk Society: Challenging and Re-affirming Justice in Late Modernity*, London: Sage, 2003.

134 P. Slovic, *The Perception of Risk*, London: Earthscan Publications, 2000.

135 O. Renn, *Risk Governance: Coping with Uncertainty in a Complex World*, London: Earthscan Publications, 2008.

136 U. Beck, *Risk Society: Toward a New Modernity*, London: Sage, 1992; U. Beck, *The World Risk Society*, Cambridge: Polity Press, 1999.

137 C. Shearing, 'Justice in the risk society,' *Australian and New Zealand Journal of Criminology*, vol. 38, 2005, pp. 25–39.

138 See, e.g., B.A. Arrigo, 'Critical criminology's discontent: the perils of publishing and the call to action,' *The Critical Criminologist*, vol. 19, 1999, 10–15.

139 Agger, *Critical Social Theory*, p. 140.

140 This is a reference to Foucault's efforts to 'chart the trajectories of power in contemporary society through studies of hospitals, mental institutions, prisons, and other disciplinary institutions.' Kellner, *Jean Baudrillard*, p. 139. Arguably, the same logic can be applied to the academy.

141 See, e.g., R.F. Almeder, *Harmless Naturalism: The Limits of Science and the Nature of Philosophy*, Chicago, IL: Open Court, 1999; N. Rescher, *The Limits of Science*, Pittsburgh, PA: University of Pittsburgh Press, 2000.

142 Arrigo *et al.*, *The French Connection in Criminology*, p. 36.

143 Ibid.

144 Arrigo, 'The ontology of crime,' pp. 50–51.

145 Arrigo and Milovanovic, *Revolution in Penology*, chapter 3.

146 Ibid.

147 The phenomenology of harm becomes more apparent in the *discourse of the hysteric*. Space limitations do not permit a more detailed assessment of it; however, it can be schematized as follows:

Criminology and the discourse of the hysteric
POSITIVISM   → SCIENCE (e.g., evidence-based research)
THEORY OF THE STRANGER ← SCRIPTED, HYPER-REAL RISK SOCIETY

148 Fromm, *Escape from Freedom*, p. 141.

149 Ibid.

150 Not wanting to deal with one's feelings of terror, given the experience of powerlessness and insignificance, the subject unconsciously submits to the intrusion displacing or removing the burden of freedom (i.e., aloneness, isolation). Ibid.

151 Ibid., pp. 141–142.

152 Arrigo, 'Punishment, freedom, and the culture of control,' p. p. 478.

153 Fromm *Escape from Freedom*, p. 143.

154 Ibid., p. 144.

155 Arrigo, 'Punishment, freedom, and the culture of control,' pp. 478–479.

156 Ibid.

157 Fromm, *Escape from Freedom*, p. 151.

158 Ibid., p. 191. For Fromm, the absence of critical thinking or insight gives rise to 'pseudo thinking.' Ibid., p. 192. However, '[t]he problem is whether the

thought is the result of one's own thinking, that is, of one's own activity.'
Ibid.

159 Ibid., p. 202.

> [P]seudo acts [replace] original acts of thinking, feeling, and willing....
> [They lead] eventually to the replacement of the original self by a pseudo
> self. The original self is the self which *is* the originator of mental activ-
> ities. The pseudo self is only an agent who actually represents the role a
> person is supposed to play but who does so under the name of the self.
>
> Ibid.

160 Ibid., p. 203.

161 The criminology of the stranger appropriates the following notions for theoretical and practical direction: (1) Fromm, on positive freedom and spontaneity; (2) Nietzsche, on a will to power and transpraxis, (3) Derrida, on reversal
of hierarchies, *differance* (with an 'a'), the trace, and arguments that undo
themselves; (4) Lacan on the *discourses of the hysteric/analyst* integrated with
Freire, on dialogical pedagogy; (5) Deleuze and Guattari, on molecular forces,
minor literatures, the perspective of schizoanalysis, and deterritorialization/
reterritorialization; (6) chaos theory, on strange attractors, dissipative structures, and far from equilibrium conditions; and (7) constitutive theory, on
COREL sets that recast the agency/structure duality in non-hierarchical and
non-linear ways. These are strategies for recovering the subject (being) and
transforming the subject (becoming) positionally, provisionally, and relation-
ally. They operate at the micro-, meso-, and macro-levels of analyses. For
more on the criminology of the stranger, see, Arrigo and Milovanovic,
Revolution in Penology, chapter 3 and Conclusion.

Chapter 10

Towards existential hybridization?

A contemplation on the *Being and Nothingness* of critical criminology[1]

Ronnie Lippens

Introduction

In this chapter I intend to revisit and reread the history of critical criminology with an eye on its future. Let me be clear: where critical criminology should be going, or how it should be developing further, are questions that will be answered in practice, by a great number of scholars and researchers who would still call themselves critical criminologists. However, looking back upon the broad trends in critical criminology's twentieth-century history one may perhaps be forgiven for trying to catch a glimpse of what might possibly be lying ahead. Before I begin my argumentation though, allow me to state what I mean by the phrase 'critical criminology'. For the purpose of this chapter I consider critical criminology to be broadly about attempts to critically analyse or assess theories and practices of criminal justice and related social policy, which may then lead to 'negative' reform (to use abolitionist terminology) or to alternatives assumed or claimed to be more 'just'. Such reform or alternatives usually have a pragmatic, moral, aesthetic and even phantasmal aspect to them (I will get back to this later). The language though that tends to be used to express reform or alternatives is often the language of justice, or social justice. Or, to put it slightly differently, the words 'justice' or 'social justice' are often used by critical criminologists in their attempts to assess and evaluate theories and practices of criminal justice.[2] In a Wittgensteinian sense, we might say that the meaning of the words 'justice' and 'social justice' – often left undefined – in much if not most critical criminology, is their use.[3] Whether or not particular visions of social justice – or justice *tout court* – are the starting point for such analyses and assessments, and whether or not such visions remain implicit, is irrelevant for my purposes here. And finally, in this chapter I shall not so much focus on particular policy issues or particular critiques of and alternatives to specific policies, as, rather, on the broad programmatic frameworks within which critical criminologists have produced their *objects of critique*.[4]

Ever since James Inciardi's edited volume on *The Coming Crises* of radical criminology,[5] published in 1980, critical criminology has been said to be in crisis. While the aim of Inciardi and some of his colleagues was limited in scope as they were concerned first and foremost with a slightly conservative critique of some of the flaws of one, albeit the most dominant strand of critical criminology in the 1970s, i.e. Marxist criminology, talk of a crisis in critical criminology never really subsided after the publication of that book. I shall explore this in subsequent sections. By the mid-1990s, after about a decade and a half of unrelenting anti-foundationalism and deconstruction in intellectual culture, and of both punitive emotionality and detached, risk-managing actuarialism in criminal justice, it looked as if critical criminologies and their proposals, those of the *radical* variety in particular, had, within the broader critical criminological community,[6] lost much if not all of their appeal and legitimacy. The aim of this chapter is to have a fresh look at this crisis and its history. In so doing I hope to be able to shed some new light, however weak, on this issue.

By no means am I alone in venturing upon such an undertaking. Recently, a number of essay collections have seen the light in which contributors have made considerable efforts to debate upon the current state and future of critical criminology,[7] and that have used critical thought in order to keep 'expanding the criminological imagination'.[8] I will return to this later. Let me for now focus on one such critical undertaking (arguably one of the most elaborate in recent years) in particular. In his overview and analysis of European critical criminologies, published in 1997, Rene van Swaaningen,[9] inspired by Henry and Milovanovic's[10] notions of *replacement discourse* and *social judo*, argues for a renewed critical criminology. This renewal would aim to 'replace' pervasive risk-management 'discourse' and practice in criminal justice with models that couch earlier abolitionist-inspired forms of conflict resolution in an understanding of current preoccupations with risk and risk management. In an age when, since the 1980s, crime is being taken much more seriously than it used to, van Swaaningen claims, rather than remain wedded to more 'naïve' models of abolitionist informal justice, and reject any kind of formalism out of hand, critical criminologists ought to rethink and if necessary adjust abolitionism. Combined with the necessary formalism that goes with the human rights model, for example, as well as with a decent level of state-directed redistributive social policy, such a renewed and adjusted informal model ought to be achievable. It should be able to accommodate, in the manner of 'judo', quite contradictory late-modern sensibilities about community and cultural diversity on the one hand and hypersensitive risk aversion on the other. Such a renewed and adjusted abolitionism should not only be able to accommodate such sensibilities, it should be able to do so much more effectively and efficiently than law and order policies, punitive models and actuarial managerialism, all of which have a tendency to exacerbate late-modern ills while leading 'into a downward spiral of violent despair, a never-ending penal arms race between "criminals" and law enforcers' (p. 239). In his book – a real *tour de force*, by the way – Van Swaaningen surveys a dizzying amount of materials that he perceives around him (or more precisely perhaps, that he perceives to be lying on his desk): cultural and moral diversity and pluralism, increased emotionality in late-modern times, a strong entrepreneurial ideology, decentralized governance, a pre-occupation with risk and a desire for safety seem to be predominant among them. Each of these materials carries both opportunities and dangers. The trick, Van Swaaningen then chooses to say, is to mobilize the energies in them, 'judo'-wise, towards more social justice. Also lying on this very desk, he notices, is a plethora of often quite contradictory critical criminologies, and models based on them: Dutch and Scandinavian abolitionism, restorative justice, British Left Realism, feminism, John Braithwaite's eclectic *reintegrative shaming*,[11] Willem de Haan's *politics of redress* based on communicative ethics and practical discourse,[12] a Marxist focus on political economy, Southern European human rights legal *guarantismo*, and so on. These too carry opportunities as well as dangers. Taken on their own, each of these theories and models can deliver only part of the promise of social justice. But they are also capable of destroying or precluding any such promise, particularly if their respective proponents, stuck in an ideological rut, refuse to take account of other points of view, or if they stubbornly remain oblivious to late-modern cultural developments. The point is, in van Swaaningen's words, to 'retrieve those elements of critical criminology that are worth saving and to revise those that can no longer be maintained' (p. 1). Van Swaaningen chooses to argue for a renewed critical criminology which, in his words, 'reassess[es] the sociological value of legal safeguards and a culture of human rights, participatory justice, and narrative procedural structures facilitating moral-practical discourse, [and] attempts to formulate a critical, pluriform vision of morality that fits current culture' (p. 250).

Van Swaaningen surveys all sorts of materials which are within his vista, chooses to read them in particular ways, and then chooses to assemble them, again in a particular way, into a renewed critical criminology. His is one of the attempts, quite typical of the 1990s, by critical criminologists to come to grips with a changing world where many beacons of reference and nearly all ultimate foundations seemed to be crumbling away, not just in economics or in political life, but in intellectual life also. Like many other critical criminologists in the 1990s, Van Swaaningen takes stock, makes choices and sets about assembling. I shall return to this later. The reason why I have so far here focused on van Swaaningen's *tour de force* is to do with his taking stock. In his historical overview of European critical criminology van Swaaningen locates its origins in the latter half of the 1960s. In this he does not stray too far from the received wisdom that critical criminology somehow emerged on the crest of the cultural event that we have come to know as May '68. To be fair to van Swaaningen, let me immediately stress here that he *does* make a considerable effort to explicate and situate the thought and work of a number of Dutch inter-war and post-war 'precursors', as he calls them, of critical criminology. Clara Wichmann's 'utopian socialism' and 'proto-abolitionism' of the 1910s and 1920s, Willem Bonger's early Marxist-inspired aetiology of crime, or the immediate post-war Utrecht School of 'ethical humanism', for example, are all rightfully said to prefigure the critical criminologies of the post-1968 era. Van Swaaningen is also at pains to stress the importance of the Second World War for any adequate understanding of the origins of critical, anti-authoritarian thought in criminology. Moreover, van Swaaningen, taking us onto a level of painful concreteness, reminds us of the fact that quite a number of academics and intellectuals in countries like the Netherlands had been imprisoned under Nazi occupation – Bonger committed suicide on the eve of this occupation. This sheer fact had in itself a tremendous impact on legal theory, on criminological thought, and on criminal justice practice. Van Swaaningen is to be credited for bringing all this to our attention. All these materials are on his richly stacked desk. However, on the topic of the overall post-war intellectual climate, and its influence on post-war criminology, van Swaaningen is silent. It is precisely on this issue that I wish to focus in the remainder of this contribution. I hope to be able to show that the period roughly between 1945 and 1965, in Europe, cannot be discarded by anyone who seeks to understand the emergence and development of critical criminology, or who wants to take stock before making a choice of assemblage. I hope to be able to show, quite paradoxically, and quite unfashionably, how one particular strand in immediate post-war thought, existentialism, Sartre's existentialism in particular, may be able to provide us with clues as to a possible re-imagination of critical criminology which, as mentioned above, a number of works have been calling for lately. Allow me to state here that my argumentation, in short, will include the thesis that critical criminology may be able to reinvent itself through Sartre's existentialism – this now nearly forgotten and quite unfashionable source of post-war critical thought – by picking up a particular Nietzschean thread, again, through Sartre, that has hitherto remained largely unexplored by critical criminologists. In what follows I will consider three phases in the development of critical thought in criminology. The first, roughly between 1945 and 1965, I would like to call critical criminology's *zero hour*. The second, between 1965 and 1985, in my view, could be described as the age of spectacular critique in criminology. The last one, stretching from 1985 to about 2005, may perhaps be considered as the age of critical assemblage in criminology. These then will be the materials on my desk. I hope to be able to end this chapter by making a few preliminary choices and suggestions on the topic of critical criminology's future.

Sartre's existentialism

Already during the war and certainly in the immediate post-war period, intellectual life in Europe began to undergo quite considerable shifts. With totalitarianism and authoritarianism, authority as such began to look suspect. Amid the ruins of the war and the shattered fragments of the totalitarian ideologies that had fuelled it, the perception seemed to be growing that authority, in all its moral and legal forms, had lost its ultimate grounds and foundations. Nietzsche's writings on the death of ultimate authority, ultimate law and ultimate morality – the *death of God*, say – were picked up again, particularly in continental Europe. Not just by philosophers; the sense of loss of ultimate foundations was more widespread than that. This was the time when authors such as Albert Camus wrote about the deadly 'plague' of totalitarianism and self-righteousness, whether left or right, that so often hide their judgemental oppressiveness and moral rigidity under names like justice.[13] Camus's non-judgementalism did not stand alone in the French or European literary landscape of the immediate post-war era. In one of the most significant novels of the immediate post-war era, *Mémoires d'Hadrien*, Marguerite Yourcenar, writing immediately after the war, remembers a passage by Gustave Flaubert on the late Roman republic and the early empire, which, in translation, goes like this: 'with the gods having left, and with Christ not having arrived yet, there was, between Cicero and Marcus Aurelius, a unique moment when Man and Man alone was.' It was a time, Yourcenar continues, of the 'last free men'.[14] This may have been the case in the Europe of 1945, in the *twilight of the idols* (Nietzsche again) of totalitarianism, as well. Humanity, once again, had to face itself, alone, in an environment without stable ground and trustworthy foundations. Jeffrey Isaac, writing on the 'modern rebellion', as he calls it, of Hannah Arendt and Albert Camus, terms this predicament *humanity at zero hour*.[15] The moment lasted for only a short period of time, but it produced a wealth of highly influential philosophical reflection, among which Sartre's *Being and Nothingness*, written in 1942, might arguably be said to have taken pride of place.[16] It is to this book that I wish to turn, not just because it had a much more widespread, tangible and indeed popular impact on the intellectual landscape of the 1940s and 1950s than, say, the critical theory of the Frankfurt School, but also because Sartre intervened directly in criminological debates with his follow-up existentialist book on Jean Genet,[17] small time thief turned prostitute turned successful novelist turned international journalist.

Being and Nothingness is actually a critical though sympathetic reading of and elaboration on Heidegger's *Sein und Zeit* which, after the war, had to recede into the background, while Sartre's existentialism, engulfed as it was by an aura of resistance heroics, surged.[18] Through Heidegger, though, Sartre re-awakened the Nietzschean theme of the self-creating *zero hour* Zarathustra,[19] i.e. the subject who *is* not what he is, who is not determined by any essence, whether internal or external, but who creatively and indeed artistically[20] *becomes* what he, or she, is.[21] Sartre also managed, again via Heidegger, to touch upon interactionist themes of Self and Other that, before the war, had been explored, across the Atlantic, by people such as George Herbert Mead. He thus provided the social sciences with a critical space in which some considerable counterweight could be developed against a persisting functionalism, and against newly emerging systems theory and cybernetics. Without wishing to embark upon a full analysis of a massively complex work such as *Being and Nothingness*, I will, however, attempt an outline of its main theses.

At the heart of human being, of human subjectivity, says Sartre, dwell openness and indeterminacy. Human existence is existence that comes into being, indeed that *becomes* through openness and indeterminacy. Without openness and indeterminacy, there is no human existence. Human being is not just 'in-itself', it is, first and foremost, in its capacity of being *human* being, 'for-itself'. The human subject, being human and therefore inescapably 'for-itself', looks at itself. It cannot escape this self-gaze. It cannot escape its human condition. But that means that, within human being, within human beings, at the heart of human subjectivity, is 'a distance', 'a lack', which separates the self from itself. This distance cannot be bridged. The human subject, the human self is thus never only just an 'in-itself'. At its heart, at the heart of the human condition as such, lies, in Sartre's words, a gaping 'hole of being' (p. 637). Human being comes into being, indeed becomes, in and through this hole. This 'hole' is essentially 'negativity', because the very openness of this hole, because the very openness of its distance, always, and inescapably so, is the possibility for human being to come into the world. It is 'pure non-being' or 'nothingness'. 'Nothingness', says Sartre, 'lies coiled in the heart of being, like a worm' (p. 45). Through this 'nothingness' the world, as well as the self, or any subjectivity in it, become. Any such inescapable becoming is essentially negativity, since it takes human being, always and inescapably so, beyond its mere 'in-itself'. Human being *is* not. It *becomes*. Human being is 'being which is what it is not, and which is not what it is' (p. 81). Let us now focus on the self. Positioned in this hole, the human self, in 'anguish', perceives itself in the midst of what it perceives of the world and its materials. It then makes its choice, in 'anguish', before it commits itself to action. The outcome of this choice is not, is never pre-ordained. It is never predetermined. Existence in the 'nothingness' of the 'hole of being' is radically indeterminate. The choice is made in utter, radical freedom. There's no escaping this freedom: 'there is no difference between the being of man' (at the heart of which lies non-being or nothingness) 'and being free' (p. 49). It is this radical freedom that enables the self to creatively *make* itself. This creativity, to a large extent, is spent on the production of a 'life project' which is fundamentally future-oriented, and which is freely chosen by the self which, in all its negativity, decides its own becoming in and through an imaginative projection of its own future. All this has precious little to do with free will. The self may be radically free, it has no free will. The willing self is bound by that which it perceives, that is, by its perception of its own self, by its perception of the world and the materials in it, by its perception of itself and its history in the world, and by its imagined life project, by its imagined future. Any will that is bound in such a way cannot be free. But any decision taken before will emerges and action materializes *is*. All decisions are taken in radical freedom, in utter indeterminacy. The self's perception of itself and its imagined position, current and future, in the world, are certainly important for any understanding of its actions, but, says Sartre, more important is to realize that any perception, any image, any future, any project, is at heart a choice, a decision, and that choice and decisions are radically free. Decisions are taken in the 'hole of being', in utter, indeterminate freedom. There is always another choice possible. Of course we know that human actions and behaviour often follow patterns, structures, routines or tradition. Human beings often will – and the word 'will' needs to be stressed here – conform, or offend, as the case may be, thereby continuing quite stable and more or less predictable patterns and routines. The point is to understand, says Sartre, that any such will is based on a choice, on a decision, which as such, at the time of its making or taking, dwells in sheer indeterminacy, in the utter openness of nothingness. All that we perceive in the world, including our selves, is the result of choices made in radical, inescapable, ineradicable freedom. Even our perceptions are. The most durable – seemingly durable – patterns and structures were born out of nothingness, from 'non-being', the heart of being. This nothingness, this ineradicable indeterminacy remains lurking within each human choice. Without nothingness, without indeterminacy, nothing comes into the world. Without nothingness, without indeterminacy, there simply *is* no human condition. But that means that human existence is inherently *critical*. There is no escaping the *criticality* of human being. Human being comes into the world, *becomes*, in and through free, *critical* choice. Positioned in the *crisis* of the indeterminate nothingness of being, the self surveys the world, makes choices – that is, draws lines and boundaries, criticizes, or acts *critically*[22] – and assembles its own becoming. Human existence *is* ineradicable crisis. Human being *is* inescapable criticality. Most human beings will most of the time choose not to choose. But choice itself, radically free choice, is inescapable. Human freedom, claims Sartre, 'is the freedom of choosing, but not the freedom of not choosing: not to choose is, in fact, to choose not to choose' (p. 503). Elsewhere Sartre wrote about the 'absoluteness of the act of choice'.[23] All denial of this aspect of the human condition, all denial that 'human reality can not receive its ends ... either from outside or from a so-called inner nature' (p. 465), amounts to what Sartre calls 'bad faith'.

One of the most important notions in Sartre's early existentialist thought is *life project*. All human beings choose their project in radical freedom. 'The free project is fundamental', says Sartre, 'for it is my being' (p. 501). An 'original choice' (p. 483) the project includes future projections and future images of the self, and its relations with others. These guide the internal deliberations which the self may have with itself (note the similarities with Mead's symbolic interactionism) and thus somehow do steer perceptions and decisions, but since they too carry nothingness within them, these images and projections, indeed the life project as such, remain themselves *open* to 'abrupt metamorphosis' (p. 486). The self may at any time decide to stray beyond the bounds of its original project. In his *Saint Genet: Actor and Martyr*, published in 1952, Sartre made a tremendous effort to illustrate this point through a reading and interpretation of the minutiae of Jean Genet's life and work and the many creative self-transformations in them. It is important to note that the life project, as well as all the decisions that are taken by the subject within the project's more or less open space, cannot be reduced to mere instrumental, cost–benefit weighing, interest-protecting reasoning, tactics or strategy. Life projects and human decisions are simultaneously and inextricably pragmatic (i.e. problem solving), morally laden, aesthetically coloured and ultimately phantasmal. The subject surveys its world and itself in it, in short, it surveys its 'being-in-situation' (p. 568), it reflects upon its perceptions in the light of its chosen project and the images in it, it defines the situation, it deliberates a decision, and then decides to choose a particular course of action (a spoken word, a gesture, the purchase of an object as an extension of the self, and so on), in short, decides to assemble or reassemble itself and its relations to the world. This choice, made in utter freedom, has, at the same time, a pragmatic, a moral, an aesthetic and a phantasmal quality and finality. It is quite difficult to distinguish these dimensions of choice neatly. In and through existential choice, human being emerges, and *becomes* pragmatically, morally, aesthetically and phantasmally. The mountaineer's decision to either drop on the ground utterly exhausted or to take that one additional step into the infinite expanse of death is a pragmatic, a moral, an aesthetic as well as a phantasmal decision. The choice made by a Parisian waiter to bring a minute variation to his age-old decanting routine, is a pragmatic, a moral, an aesthetic as well as a phantasmal choice.

Being and Nothingness has on occasion been criticized for portraying human existence as solipsistic being. This may be too harsh a verdict. Sartre's point of departure focuses on the distance *within* the surveying, deliberating and choosing self. A good deal of Sartre's efforts, though, are spent on working out how, for example, collectives of resistance emerge, or, in Sartre's words, how 'Us-objects' come to be perceived under the gaze of the authority for whom they are 'Being-for', and how ultimately 'We-subjects' come into the world. They come into the world through the radical freedom of existential choices human beings make. There is a note to be made here on critical criminology's pre-occupation *par excellence*, i.e. social justice. Any such 'We-subject', any such collective of resistance can never encompass universal humanity as such, for it will be the result of decisions, choices, projects made in freedom. There will have been other, alternative choices. Those will have been discarded, or worse, left unperceived, unexplored or not deliberated. Some will have been chosen as the object of critique or resistance. Sartre is quite adamant on this anti-Hegelian issue: 'We should hope in vain for a human "we" in which the intersubjective totality would obtain consciousness of itself as a unified subjectivity' (p. 450). Note the word 'intersubjective' here; it will re-emerge later, in my later section on 'Assembling critical criminologies'. Freedom, nothingness, distance, negativity and indeterminacy: the very elements that together provide the elements of the human condition and that enable human being to become, indeed to come into the world, are the very same that will prevent any closure, or any collapse of 'being-for-itself' into 'being-in-itself' from occurring. Surveying the materials on his desk in front of him, Sartre chooses to assemble the following conclusion: 'the essence of the relation between consciousnesses is not the Mitsein; it is conflict' (p. 451). The radical indeterminacy at the heart of human being cannot be halted. The for-itself that, in the moment of resistance, chooses to make or remake itself in such and such a way by aligning itself with others, does so, in and through its choice, by discarding or confronting others. The distance between any projected future for humanity and its surveyed current state can never be fully bridged in the absence of God, or a God's eye view. It can only be aspired to from the very 'fragmentary ... experiences' (p. 450) of subjects. Any 'We-subject' emerging from the depths of an infinite nothingness does so by carrying this very nothingness, this distance and negativity, in its very core. The project 'humanity' can never be achieved. Nor can any individual's life project. Such 'absurdity', in a way, condemns human beings to the 'eternal recurrence' (to use Nietzsche's words) of negativity and anguish. The subject's 'Present', says Sartre, 'is a perpetual flight in the face of being' (p. 141). The very perception of any overcoming of this absurdity is only the result of a choice, made in conditions of indeterminacy. One does not simply perceive achievement or overcoming; one *chooses* to perceive it.

The *zero hour* of critical criminology (1945–1965)

It may now perhaps become clear how Sartre's existentialism, in the immediate post-war era, became the focal point of much of the intellectual climate in Europe. Sartre's thoughts on openness and indeterminacy, and on self-creation and becoming not only linked up with philosophical themes that before the war had been neglected, they also chimed nicely with the sensibilities of a *zero hour* age. Amid the shattered remains of fallen idols and gods, Man, wavering, without ultimate authority as a guide, had to face humanity, alone. On the eve of reconstruction in Europe, the new Parisian brand of existentialism to some extent captured the forward-looking mood, and the sense of possibility, of the times. Not that it was the only strand of theoretical reflection that managed to do that. Ernst Bloch, to give just one illustration, redirected Marxist thought towards more openness. In his three-volume *The Principle of Hope*, for example, Bloch, who wrote the book at about the same time as Sartre wrote his, theorized the engine of human progress as the open *principle of hope*, through which human beings keep constructing 'forward-dawning' utopias. As 'guiding images', the latter will attract productive energies. Bloch, who had read Nietzsche, Heidegger and Sartre, concludes thus: 'the unfinished world can be brought to its end, the process pending in it can be brought to a result, the incognito of the main matter which is really-cloaked in itself can be revealed', it remains hidden in the 'Not-Yet-Conscious' of matter (a Marxist, Bloch indeed remains a teleological materialist), 'but not by hasty hypostases and by fixed definitions of essence, which block the way'.[24] Sartre's existentialism did more than that. It stirred the intellectual imagination. It freed up space for a critical programme of resistance to authority to gradually unfold during subsequent decades. Dominating significant corners of the European intellectual landscape during the 1940s and 1950s, and, after translation, also penetrating English-speaking academia during the early 1960s, *Being and Nothingness* helped to lay the groundwork for what might perhaps be called a critical attitude and a critical programme in the humanities and social sciences. Having arrived, by 1960 or thereabouts, on the desks of so many theorists, researchers, cultural commentators and teachers,[25] its ideas, concepts and theses entered their surveyed worlds, their projected futures, their deliberations and their choice of critical projects.

If, as Sartre, following Nietzsche, wrote, human being is *becoming*, then very little in human and social existence or in any human being's life, may be predetermined or pre-ordained. Alternatives are then always possible.

If, as Sartre stated, human being comes into the world in and through critical choice born of the unstoppable crisis of indeterminacy, then this goes also for any choice that is presented or accepted as authority. There are then always other choices, other forms of authority, possible.

If, as Sartre says, human choice, any choice, dwells in radical freedom, then precious little in law and morality is based on rock-solid foundations, or on unshakable, divine or ultimate authority. There is then always a way to choose another law, another morality; there is then always the possibility to replace current law and morality with other law and with other morality. Law and morality *are* not. They become.

If, as Sartre wrote, much of what human beings say and do is said and done within the porous parameters and boundaries of an 'original choice' or 'project', then the same might be the case with official discourse and institutional practices. Or, if much of what human beings say and do is said and done within the porous parameters and boundaries of an 'original choice' or 'project', then one might perhaps wonder about the pragmatic, moral and aesthetic dimensions of the projects which will undoubtedly underlie jurisprudence or criminological theories. It may then be worthwhile to unravel the pragmatic, moral, aesthetic and phantasmal dimension of the parameters and boundaries of any such original choice or project. This is what Sartre himself would suggest as existential psychoanalysis. The aim here would be to lay bare their inevitably contingent, partisan, indeed 'absurd' origins. The American philosopher Thomas Nagel, writing in 1970, would analyse such moments of recognition as instances when one suddenly experiences a 'philosophical sense of absurdity'.[26] The absurd, in Nagel's ironic view, shows itself when life's events, and the aims, goals, justifications, indeed judgements made, evoked, or accepted in them, are suddenly seen in all their *particularity* and *circularity*. Such moments of seeing, and, possibly, also of *diagnosis*, occur if and when we make use of our human ability (which we 'have always available', says Nagel) to take 'a point of view outside the *particular* form of our lives, from which the seriousness' of particular life choices suddenly 'appears gratuitous' (p. 14). In *particular* those judgements *in*, and *of* life that claim to rest on the firm ground of transcendent value and foundation, should then appear 'gratuitously' particular.

If indeed, as Sartre tells us, the very 'possibility of a foundation comes to the world' through the indeterminacy of the 'for-itself' (p. 640), or, to put that in more recent terminology, if 'order' comes 'out of chaos', then it may be wise to recognise anti-foundationalism as a crucial element in any critical project of social justice (as perhaps is easier to grasp now than in Sartre's day). 'There are no means of judging', Sartre claims in his 1946 lecture, 'The content [of choice] is always concrete, and therefore unpredictable; it has always to be invented'. He who denies the openness, the eternal becoming of human being risks falling in the trap of fascism, Sartre continues.

If, as Sartre explained, universal humanity is unachievable, and conflict is unavoidable, then the question for anyone interested in issues of social justice becomes the one that was asked by Howard Becker, in 1967: 'Whose side are we on?'.[27]

If, as Sartre's existentialism implies, both oppression and docility are the result of free choice, then the point seems to be to exploit the possibilities in radical human freedom in order to build collectives of resistance.

If Sartre is right in reading human being(s) as becoming, that is, as the result of ineradicable choice, ineradicably unique choices of human beings to be precise, then human diversity comes to be seen in a more positive light. All universalist pretence, particularly the kind that reduces humanity to allegedly universal principles or laws of biology, organic life, systems, cybernetic or machinic processes,[28] becomes suspect and dangerous. Human diversity, indeterminate human diversity, in Sartre's existentialism, appears as the plinth on which any chosen perception of monolithic universal foundations rests. Sartre's humanism is a humanism of insurmountable diversity.

If Sartre is right in recognizing, with Nietzsche, human beings as self-creative and human being as fundamentally creative (albeit often denied as such in 'bad faith'), and if he is right to argue that the results of such creativity invariably end up in the world for human beings to survey and ponder, and in turn to creatively make use of, then it perhaps pays to attempt the invention of new forms of social life, and to experiment with alternatives. Critique in criminology appears here as that which Barbara Hudson has recently called the imaginative effort to 'expand the cultural repertoire' of criminologists, criminal justice practitioners and policy makers.[29] I shall be revisiting this issue later.

Finally, if Sartre's existentialism implies that human life as such *is* critical, that it *is* permanent crisis, then the issue is not to wonder about whether one needs to be critical or not, but rather to ask oneself what kind of critique, what form of criticism, one would wish to pursue. Anyone who realizes this, Sartre admits in his lecture, ought to ask themselves the following Kantian question: 'Am I really a man who has the right to act in such a manner that humanity regulates itself by what I do?'. Such relentless self-criticism would re-emerge after 1985, in the era that I would like to name critical criminology's era of intersubjective assemblage. Here again, allow me to say that I shall be returning to this later.

The above could, arguably, be read as a broad outline of what later became known as critical criminology. A point needs to be made here, though. While Sartre's work did have a very significant impact on the humanities and social sciences more broadly, the same cannot be said about its impact on criminology. This is all the more surprising for in *Saint Genet*, for example, Sartre was not only at pains to apply his insights to the biography of someone he considered to be the prototypical self-creator, Jean Genet, he also rehearsed, as early as 1952, themes that seeped into criminological consciousness only by the early to mid-1960s through the work of the so-called 'labelling' criminologists. In an unparalleled fashion, Sartre for example makes a tremendous effort to paint a detailed picture of the world as he gathers it was perceived by Genet at crucial moments of his life. This world includes that which is said and done by others. It includes institutional practices and 'labels'; it includes legal and moral significations, or, in Sartre's words, 'dizzying words' (p. 17) which it is left to the self to freely ponder, negotiate, deliberate upon, imagine futures around, accept or overcome. However, it should now also be admitted that it was mostly through David Matza's writings, *Becoming Deviant* in particular,[30] that Sartre's existentialism made its way into criminology. A figure towering over what arguably could be called the proto-critical criminology of the early and mid-1960s, Matza, in the book, used Sartre's work, which must have arrived in translation on his desk only after he had completed his earlier work, to reconsider this work in a new light. He also made an effort to survey the state of criminology in the 1960s. He actually apologizes for his attempt, in his 'bringing together or organizing materials', to 'create coherence' in a world which is ineradicable 'disorder' (p. 1). Praising functionalism and ecological theories for having rid criminology of pathologism and correctionalism, he nonetheless berates them for refusing to take account of the radical openness of human and social life. Focusing on the dynamics of 'affinity' (functionalism) or 'affiliation' (ecology) as the fundamental determining principles of social life, Matza goes on to state that these dominant criminological perspectives fail to realize how human beings create themselves in and through negotiations and deliberations between themselves – and within their own selves – and their surrounding world. Nothing in such negotiations and deliberations is predetermined. Only the 'ironic' neo-Chicagoans (Matza refers to symbolic interactionists and 'labelling' criminologists), with their interest in 'signification', begin to understand this. Their focus on the circulation of signs and on the inherent instability of meaning in signification, or, in other words, their understanding of the 'magic of words' (p. 176), makes them aware of the contingency of the human condition. This is why Matza, in the book, makes a considerable effort to also reread and reinterpret the work of the neo-Chicagoans in the light of Sartre's existentialism, using Sartrean categories. 'Capable of creating and assigning meaning, able to contemplate his surroundings and even his own condition, given to anticipation, planning and projection', Matza states, 'man – the subject – stands in a different and more complex relation to circumstance' (p. 92). The task for any critical project in the humanities and social sciences, in Matza's view, is to 'rid the study of man once and for all of the idea of being preordained' (p. 104). It is in this book that Matza also wrote the famous lines on the need for criminologists to study the role of the state ('Leviathan', says Matza) in the production of signs and therefore also in the *becoming* of human being; lines that were noticed with acclaim by eager New Criminologists[31] and other critical criminologists. But here we have arrived at critical criminology's second phase, the one I would like to call *spectacular*.

Spectacular critique in criminology (1965–1985)

The above-mentioned implicit existentialist programme of critique never really materialized, certainly not during the 1940s and 1950s. With hindsight one might perhaps be able to say that much of the phenomenological and ethnomethodological work of the 1950s was, in a way, geared towards a quite relentless exposé of the particular circularities, that is, of the contingent 'absurdity', of cultural and institutional practices, routines and traditions so often taken for granted. Horace Miner's satirical 'Body rituals among the Nacirema', published in 1956, illustrates this perfectly.[32] Within the broader field of criminal justice and criminology we should of course mention work such as Harold Garfinkel's on court trials as 'degradation ceremonies' which also appeared in 1956.[33] Elsewhere, the 1950s saw researchers such as Rijk Rijksen in the Netherlands take the quite revolutionary step to bracket official discourse and officially produced data and instead ask institutionalized people, such as prisoners, how they themselves made sense of their world and their predicament.[34] However, such attempts were few and far between and were unable to loosen the strong grip of neo-functionalism on the social sciences. Only with the second arrival, during the early 1960s, of interactionist-inspired work – Howard Becker's *Outsiders* most notably[35] – did this change. It is tempting to speculate on why it took so long.

One could do worse than recall the immediate post-war period as a time of reconstruction, indeed of creative construction *tout court*. To use Sartrean language here, one might perhaps express it thus: after a survey and contemplation of, and deliberation upon the ruins of totalitarianism and authoritarianism in Western Europe, the choice for a new project emerged out of the indeterminacy of a newly sensed freedom. This new project we now know as the social-democratic welfare state. I shall not here dwell on the strategic dimensions of this project. Let us recall that it did attract a great deal of enthusiasm and that much creative energy went into its construction. One might perhaps be forgiven for saying that during its phase of construction, roughly between 1945 and 1965, this wholly creative process required so much productive attention and energy that the scope for a substantial critical reflection upon its contingent origins and its particular circularities was rather limited. Criminological discourse, as Reece Walters has been able to argue, barely managed to move beyond the doctrine of social defence.[36] By the early 1960s the project, although still expanding, had materialized as the *centripetal* force, or, to paraphrase Jock Young,[37] as the *bulimic* centre of social and political, indeed of everyday life as such, in Western Europe. Young quotes Claude Lévi-Strauss, one of France's foremost representatives of structuralism which, certainly by the 1960s, had managed to dethrone erstwhile paradigmatic existentialism. A strong and centripetal centre seems to have produced a sense of stability and led many academics to choose for structuralism's a-historical determinism. Structuralism was not so much interested in exploring the utter indeterminacy of human existence or the radical freedom of human choice. Quite the opposite was the case. Let us consider the model of human action we introduced earlier: survey of the world and the self in it – internal deliberation – choice and action, and then again survey, and so on. Whereas existentialism would focus on choice, and on the indetermi-nacy and radical freedom underlying it, structuralism would restrict its attention to the structural materials of the world and to their trans-historical, unchanging qualities. Let us have a close look at another bio-graphical work, Michel Foucault's I, Pierre Rivière.[38] Originally published in 1973, this book is situated about halfway between an existentialist reading of self-creation and a pre-occupation with structural determina-tion. Pierre Rivière was a young French peasant who lived in the first half of the nineteenth century, and who, having brutally killed his mother and siblings, wrote a very eloquent explanation of his actions. This explana-tion, at the heart of which Rivière placed his deep compassion for his father who seemed to have suffered terribly, both financially and emotion-ally, at the hands of Pierre's mother and sister. While a number of collaborators to Foucault's Rivière project do make an effort to minutely analyse Rivière's deliberations and his strong will to self-creation, the tone is set on the first pages of the researchers' 'Notes' when they report on a country doctor's 'dismay' and 'astonishment' at the 'shocking ... tranquil-lity' with which Rivière speaks of his crime: 'The fact is that the horrible is the quotidian', they claim,

> In the countryside it has been everyone's lot since time immemorial; ... this family is exemplary in that it so lived as to yell furiously that everything hurts, all the time, and to this one becomes as accustomed as to everything else.[39]

To be more precise though, Rivière's actions are placed squarely in the structural contradiction between on the one hand an emerging contractual culture, and feudal relations persisting in the countryside, on the other. Elsewhere the elite physicians' (the famous Esquirol being among them) elaborate report on the 'mental deficiency' and 'delusion' in Rivière, for example, is explained not just by pointing to the strategic interests of and within a newly emerging institution, i.e. psychiatry (all this with slight inclination to focus on the linear determinations of these institutional interests, rather than on their perceived and deliberated nature). The explanation also reads the 'substance and function' of such reports 'in the context' of an alleged 'logic of medical power'.[40]

This, however, brings us back to the mid-1960s, when the centre was still in place, holding strong. It makes sense, I believe, to notice the centripetal tendencies of this centre. But such tendencies are not the whole of the story. The welfare state, such as it was, also produced centrifugal tendencies. One should keep in mind that the welfare state and its institutions had distributive and redistributive finalities. These generate centrifugal forces which, arguably, became more prominent during the 1960s, i.e. after the completion of the centre's phase of construction. Distribution and redistribution constitute recipients, users, or *consumers*. While production and construction tend to imply and bring forth collaboration and collectives, and possibly an un-reflexive sense of *collectivity* as well, distribution and consumption, on the other hand, tend to lead to separation. One consumes alone.[41] One receives in solitude. Such centrifugal forces, need it be said, were also fuelled by a post-war economy which, to a high extent, was a consumer economy, and which went hand in hand with what would later come to be known as consumer society. There seems to be little fixedness or closed finality in the pragmatics, morals, aesthetics and phantasms of consumptive choice. The centrifugal dynamic and the sense of separateness that it entails therefore also tend to raise critical levels of awareness and self-awareness, of reflection and self-reflection. In the space or distance that opens up between consumers who are drifting apart, and within consumers' selves who are surveying their worlds and contemplating their futures, Sartre's ineradicable freedom re-emerges. From the 'hole' of indeterminacy that suddenly opens up within them, consuming selves are beginning to survey the 'spectacular' materials which are so ostentatiously placed in their worlds. They are gradually beginning to reflect upon them. They are slowly beginning to detect traces of the 'absurd' in the 'spectacles' that unfold in front of their gazing eyes. They are starting to imagine new selves, and new futures. They are also beginning to notice all kinds of hindrances on the road to newly imagined futures. Their 'negativity' – another Sartrean term – becomes more pronounced, more outspoken, and more forceful. It is here, in this centrifugal moment, that academic reflection rediscovers symbolic interaction. It is here that the welfare state and its institutions – any institution, for that matter – are suddenly seen in a new light. It is here that the bureaucratic tendencies of the welfare state – or the state, *tout court* – are recognized as 'absurd', indeed oppressive. It is here that the normalizing tendencies of and the discipline aimed for in or by institutions become a problem. This is the moment when the panoptic gazer *par excellence*, the state, as well as its institutions, and their products, come to be gazed at by the suddenly self-aware consumptive subjects and self-fashioners it has itself produced. It is here, at this conjuncture, that Foucault's genealogies of institutional practice will land on the desk of many a social scientist. In short, it is at this moment in history, say the latter half of the 1960s, when radical freedom, among criminologists and legal scholars, takes the shape of something like a *critical* criminology.

I have above used the word 'spectacular'. That was no mere coincidence. It refers of course to the work of Guy Debord. Published in 1967, Debord's *Society of the Spectacle*[42] paints a gloomy picture of a global society dominated by a mode of regulation and control which seems frighteningly familiar to a twenty-first-century readership. This *society of the spectacle* which, according to Debord, is global and already fully formed in 1967, regulates and controls social life through the cyclical circulation of mediating and mediatized commodities and imagery. The spectacle constitutes subjects as mere consumers of the 'illusions' which, carried by the images and commodities, are circulated within the mediatized circuits of the spectacle. Consumer-subjects live in 'separation perfected'. Not only is there the alienating separation between producer and product; there is also a deep separation between the exchange value of these products as they circulate, as commodity-image, in mediatized circuits, and any possible 'real' use value they may have. In other words, there is a separation between illusion and appearance on the one hand, and 'reality' on the other, with the former having completely destroyed and replaced the latter. The society of the spectacle is one whose reality *is* illusion, mere appearance, mere circulation of commodity-image. It is the 'visual negation of life', to borrow Debord's words. It 'aims at nothing other than itself'. But there is also, and perhaps more importantly, a separation between consuming subjects who, while 'passively' consuming mere illusion in 'perfect' separation, construct their own appearances of selves out of the materials that the spectacle circulates in front of their gaze. 'Separation', writes Debord, 'is the alpha and omega of the spectacle'. With their 'deceived gaze', steeped in 'spectacular separation' and 'false consciousness', and with selves *fashioned* out of illusion and appearance, perfectly separated consumers populate 'the empire of modern passivity'. The latter in turn uses this deep separation between its deceived subjects to feed its regulatory circuits of control with yet more illusion, with yet more cyclic circulations of deceptive commodity-image. A consumer's choice, it must be emphasized here, is not so much an existential and creative choice of becoming as it is one that betrays passive surrender to the spectacle.

This relentless and unstoppable circulation of commodities and images, this 'becoming-commodity of the world', the spectacle in other words, is quite 'dictatorial', and the bureaucratic state is complicit in its organization. There is, in Debord's society of the spectacle, still a Panoptic gaze at its organizing centre. This gaze aims to produce docility, discipline and normality. But it is complemented with that which Thomas Mathiesen was to call, much later, in 1997, the *Synopticon*, i.e. the spectacle gazed at by billions of dazed, passive consumers.[43] Others such as Nathan Moore have meanwhile read 'iconic' control, aimed directly at the senses, as the late modern mode of regulation *par excellence*.[44]

The post-war project of reconstruction, according to Debord, had, by the mid-1960s, produced a monstrously integrated, indeed monolithic machine of illusion and authority, one of global proportions. Its only finality seemed to be the constant and cyclic reproduction of itself, and its logic of operation was built on the circulation of mediatized and mediated illusion, and on the generalization of separation. A new God had arisen. A new Divine Law had been established. Authors such as Jean Baudrillard would, decades after Debord, agree. But while they were quite reluctant to see a way out or beyond this machine of illusion, and would indeed come to acknowledge totalitarian danger in any attempt at arriving at, or even in the mere belief in, an ultimate bed-rock of truth or ultimate foundation,[45] at the time of Debord's writing, a few years before May 1968, it seemed, firm alternatives were still perceived. Through the haze of illusion and appearance, at least some gazing consumers chose to survey and contemplate the society of spectacle, and decided to perceive a way out. Debord himself chose to believe in a kind of authentic, 'real' form of social life which, moreover, would be attainable. Not through theory which, says Debord, is itself caught up in the spectacle's circuits of illusion. And one 'can no longer combat alienation with alienated forms'. Combining Marxist inspiration and Situationist experience, Debord opts for collaborative and creative praxis, where subjects communicate directly, that is, unmediated by circulating, mediatized commodity-image. Producing their own collaborative 'spectacle', their own 'event', rather than consuming illusory and deceptive ones, creative subjects would not only be able to break their suffocating separation, they would also regain their authentic humanity in the process. This, Debord recognizes, is a never-ending process. The destruction of the spectacle, the destruction of authority, the destruction of any God, can only be the 'first condition of critique'; more important is to realize that it is also 'the first obligation of a critique without end'. One cannot allow any spectacular event to dominate all others, as is the danger with God and divine authority, with dictators, with totalitarian icons, or with the absurdity of seductive, numbing deception. Sartre's radical freedom here emerges as the freedom of permanent self-criticism which takes shape – and can only take shape – in and through collective praxis, in and through direct, unmediated communication, in and through the actions of authentic collectives, or 'Councils'. In Debord's words: 'at the revolutionary moment of dissolution of social separation, [the revolutionary organization] must recognize its own dissolution as a separate organization.'

This is not the place to go into the contradictions and paradoxes that seem to be flawing Debord's work. There is much to be gleaned though from Debord's insights for a better understanding of the emergence and subsequent development of a distinct critical criminology in the years roughly between 1965 and 1985. His romantic belief in some kind of human authenticity, for example, seems to have been widely shared. This authenticity was perceived to be a desirable one. It should come about through a thorough critique of and 'combat' against the forces of authority, whether Panoptical or spectacular. Those were assumed to keep this authentic humanity, based on the accommodation of 'real' human needs, from emerging. These inhuman forces had many different names, from the 'centre', the state (including the welfare state, the capitalist state, the bureaucratic state, the authoritarian state, and the seductively illusionist law and order state[46]) to 'capitalism', or even Modernity, with all its modernizing institutions and practices. If, some way or other, these forces could be stopped, and their institutional infrastructure dismantled, then a desirable human authenticity, indeed humanity as such, would flourish. This basic idea seems to have dominated significant sections of the intellectual landscape of the mid-1960s. Another classic, Franz Fanon's third-worldist *The Wretched of the Earth* (in which Sartre wrote the foreword),[47] published originally in 1961, for example, followed the same basic reasoning: if only the colonized could rid themselves of the modernist illusions and indeed the mental and psychosomatic deficiencies which the colonizer causes them, their true and authentic humanity would emerge; and true and authentic humanity would emerge *then and there*. According to the Schwendingers,[48] critical criminologists of the immediate post-1968 moment: if only the dominant forces and systems of order, domination and oppression (the familiar 'isms' such as racism, sexism, imperialism, capitalism) could be peeled away, indeed criminalized, then an authentic humanity would surface where authentic human and social needs and therefore rights would be respected. Much of what went under the name of abolitionist criminology, whose object of critique in many cases was the 'power to criminalize' (I am borrowing the New Criminologists' famous words), did reason along similar lines. This 'power to criminalize', often situated at the heart of the 'capitalist State' (including the capitalist welfare state), with all its spectacular illusions of crime and punishment, with all its 'dizzying words' (in Sartre's words) and images, prevented real human needs from being met. It prevented real human beings from solving real problems. It prevented them from solving, collectively, their real and immediate 'problematic situations'.[49] It was deemed unjust. It prevented real social justice from occurring. By criminalizing particular consumption behaviours, for example, it belittled authentic human beings and prevented them from reaching their full potential through self-expression, hampering their 'quality of life'.[50] The utopian element in those early critical criminological debates, say, broadly between 1965 and 1975, did not so much aim to achieve an organized and organizing, forward-looking and orderly, that is, 'formal' Modernity. Any such modernization was often considered to be the problem, that is, if it hadn't been destroyed, it too, by the cyclic turns of the spectacle already. Utopian alternatives, if any, were often looked for in an 'informal' humanity unspoilt by Modernity, either in a pre-modern past or in a non-Modern otherness.

Critical criminologists did adopt a wide variety of critical 'genres' or styles. There is, indeed, an aesthetic to criticism. George Pavlich has made a serious effort to list some of these styles.[51] One major and related concern that seems to have resurfaced time and again though in the immediate post-1968 period was the one about the purity of the critical alternative, or, in other words, about the boundary between on the one hand the unjust object of critique – Panoptic and/or spectacular domination – and the peripheral, though *just* alternative on the other. This concern manifested itself in debates about 'informal justice', for example, and in the ever-present fear of what some criminologists called the danger of the sapping, by the centre, of resistance and alternatives through the 'net-widening' of formal social control.[52] It also expressed itself in the very frequent use of the word 'counter', as in 'counter-cultural', or 'counter-hegemonic'. This quite pervasive preoccupation with purity and clear boundaries, or, to use Sartrean language again, this will to fix the restless negativity at the heart of the human condition, was expressly contemplated by Thomas Mathiesen. In his *Politics of Abolition*, published in 1974, Mathiesen admits that he has 'gradually acquired the belief that the alternative lies in the unfinished, in the sketch, in what is not yet fully existing'. The 'finished alternative', he continues, 'is finished'.[53] This may sound like Debord's permanent situationist revolution. But Mathiesen clarifies what he means by 'the unfinished'. Critical criminologists, or anyone who strives for social justice, for that matter, and in Mathiesen's view that means abolitionists, should avoid a situation whereby the 'contradiction' of their opposing alternative 'becomes non-competing' with the centre. They should also prevent their 'competition' with the centre from 'becom[ing] agreement'.[54] Critique, in other words, should always make sure to walk the uneasy tightrope between radical contradiction, and therefore ineffective resistance on the one hand, and cooperative competition with the centre – equally ineffective – on the other. Mathiesen's proposed strategy is to keep this tension alive; his tactic is to be 'sketchy', or vague. The clarity of cut-and-dried alternatives and neatly drawn blueprints, according to Mathiesen, is deadly for critical criminology. Any such clarity would allow the fundamentally unjust centre to either reject or adapt the fundamentally just alternative, leaving the latter ineffectual. But all this is only a matter of strategy and tactics. 'What is necessary', claims Mathiesen, is 'to maintain the long-range goal and continually to return to it'.[55] In other words, the notion that there is a fundamentally unjust centre, and that there is a fundamentally just periphery, and that there is a neat boundary between both, in Mathiesen's *Politics*, seems to remain unchallenged. Even though Mathiesen goes on to elaborate that experiments in alternative living – Debord's 'events' – are irrelevant if they are conducted in splendid isolation, and even though he also admits that a revolutionary overhaul of the centre, if such an overhaul is at all possible, would achieve nothing beyond mirrored or inverted forms of domination, there remains this need for critical criminologists to continually go back to *the* long-range goal of a fundamental, unshakeable justice – the justice of an authentic humanity. Mathiesen's permanent revolution remains one that hankers after unspoilt authenticity or, in his words, 'unbuilt ground',[56] i.e. a clearance of real freedom.

However, the centre, so historical experience shows us, is always evolving. So too then must the critical project. Someone like Stanley Cohen would later use the image of the parasite to describe this constant struggle of critical criminology to adapt to, or, to use existentialist phraseology, to negate the absurd. Cohen evokes the image of 'a friendly parasite that grows by turning on itself, constantly reproducing internally but also trying to adapt to changes in its host organism'.[57] Changes in the use of the notion 'human rights' within critical criminology may perhaps illustrate this point. Where the immediate post-1968 critics (like the Schwendingers) tended to suggest human rights models that not only aimed, both negatively as well as normatively, at the destruction of systems of domination – and those often included the state and its 'repressive' and 'ideological' apparatuses – and that, vaguely articulated, or open-ended, promised to go far beyond any existing formal bill, charter, or declaration, this gradually changed. Later, at a time when it was said and heard that 'the centre didn't hold' any longer, critics were more specific and clear in their lists of human rights, more defensive also, and more inclined to argue for the construction or reconstruction of formal structures, including the state, as safeguards for the protection of such precious rights. More recently still, in a risk-obsessed age, when even such defensive hopes have been felt to be problematic, critical sensibilities have gradually shifted[58] towards an acknowledgement of the limitations of human rights discourse and politics. The latter often seem to be underpinned by a view that reduces human existence to legal and moral calculation and exchange while they ignore the critical potential of unresolvable and irreducible ethical encounter and hospitality.[59]

The issue of boundaries brings me to a final point I would like to make here. If Guy Debord's analysis of the spectacle and its MO *par excellence*, separation – non-communicative separation – makes any sense at all, then it may perhaps shed some light on the proliferation of critical criminologies from about 1975 onwards. Not only did the centre no longer hold, neither did critical criminology as a more or less coherent, if not unified, movement. If the spectacle is a predominantly centrifugal force, constituting selves and subjectivities, as it does, by circulating and distributing commodity-image which those selves and subjectivities may then choose to adopt or reject, or partially adopt and partially reject, then this centrifugal dynamic may have had an impact on the post-1968 critical movement and on the development of critical criminology therein. The importance of this process of pragmatic, moral, aesthetic and phantasmal constitution of selves through identification with fragments of circulating commodity-image, and of the consumptive constitution of critical subjectivity, needs to be stressed here. From about 1975 onwards, critical criminology seems to have been caught up in what would later become known as identity politics.[60] The more or less integrated 'isms' of domination which were introduced by the Schwendingers in their seminal paper, set, as they were, against the promise of an authentic humanity, gradually led to the formation of separate 'isms' of liberation,[61] each quite neatly distinct from the others, each producing their own 'events', their own 'spectacle' – which did add a more pronounced aesthetic, indeed artistic dimension to social critique.[62] The liberation and emancipation of humanity were often interpreted as having to pass through the liberation of one's chosen adopted identity first. This led to the proliferation of separated 'We-subjects', to use Sartre's phrase. There may be no mere coincidence in the fact that one of the most iconic philosophical papers of the age, Thomas Nagel's 'What is it like to be a bat?', published originally in 1974,[63] is about the utterly subjective, non-shareable nature of localized experience. In many cases this neatly bordered separateness became institutionalised and in the process all shared ground, all shared objects of critique, to the extent that they *had* been shared before, gradually crumbled away. Not all 'We-subjects', for example, continued to look upon the state as a centre of domination, bureaucratic de-humanization, discipline or control. In some instances the state came to be perceived as the preferred location of protection, if not emancipation and liberation, quite paradoxically so at a time when it was beginning to lose its position as the central hub of regulation. The issue, it now seems, was no longer about the peeling away of an ordering, inauthentic centre, but rather the selective consumption and mobilization of its force and energy.

Let us recall Sartre's words. Universal, authentic humanity is unachievable. The inescapable indeterminacy that dwells at the heart of the human condition, freedom, leads to choice and conflict. It does so inevitably. No centre will hold. No centre will ever be able to hold. Negation is how the human world comes into existence. No critical criminology will ever hold. It will inevitably 'reproduce internally, constantly', to borrow Stan Cohen's words once more. By the mid-1980s this very splintering[64] of critical criminology was itself noticed and contemplated. This renewed self-awareness brought about the third phase in critical criminology's development. This phase, marked by a more entrepreneurial zeal to survey and contemplate the world beyond the confines of previously cherished identities and preferred strategies, I suggest we call the age of critical assemblage.

Assembling critical criminologies (1985–2005)

The historical development of critical criminology, like any other historical development, for that matter, seems to be one of ever-increasing hybridization. Its critical and self-reflexive *zero hour* moment never really disappeared. Its spectacular manifestations of self-righteousness on the other hand never completely dominated the whole critical scenery. And many of its subsequent assemblages, while combining elements of both earlier moments, did try to move beyond the Scylla of radical indeterminacy and the Charybdis of radical foundationalism. It is to those assemblages that I shall now turn. Around the mid-1980s, the broader criminological community witnessed a renewed wave of stock-taking[65] and (self-)reflexivity which was to have a serious impact on the further development of critical criminology. Let us begin this section with a few words on a paper which was published in 1985, and which in a way illustrates or even marks this new wave. In their paper on 'ontological gerrymandering',[66] Steve Woolgar and Dorothy Pawluch developed, as they claim, a 'distanced', or 'anthropologically strange view' of labelling criminologists' work. Still quite dominant at the time, such work, according to Woolgar and Pawluch, was almost invariably self-contradictory. It claimed, on the one hand, that certain 'putative conditions' such as drug abuse or prostitution are or have been labelled deviant or as a social problem in particular ways by particular groups, while, on the other hand, the labelling criminologists explicitly or implicitly assumed that these 'putative conditions' themselves are, and have been, exaggerated by the 'labellers', or have been unproblematic all along. On the one hand, then, it is claimed that social reality is a matter of labels, subjectively applied, while on the other hand it clearly is not, and instead, is about objectively knowable conditions. Labelling criminologists, in other words, reserve the ability, and possibly also the right to access the objective conditions of the world, for themselves – quite self-contradictorily so – and would often deny others such access. This is 'ontological gerrymandering', and in some ways it reflects the often implicitly cultivated assumption that underneath the illusory 'dizzying words' of various authorities and the powerful, there is an authentic, real world to be discovered by the knowledgeable critic. 'One category of claims is laid open to ontological uncertainty and then made the target for explanation in terms of the social circumstances which generated them', Woolgar and Pawluch continue, while 'at the same time, the reader is asked to accept another category of claims in faith'.[67] From their anthropological distance, they then go on to expose the absurdity of this situation. They write about the 'manipulation' and 'management', by labelling criminologists, of their knowledge 'boundary', i.e. the boundary within which ultimate grounds, albeit self-contradictory grounds, of knowledge are assumed and cherished, while any knowledge *without* is then objectively, and again self-contradictorily, defined as subjective, contingent, or simply wrong. Woolgar was, and is, a close colleague of Bruno Latour's, who, from the 1980s onwards,[68] would take up a prominent role in actor–network theory (or ANT). In ANT all strict divisions between object and objectivism, on the one hand, and subject and subjectivism, on the other, collapse. Knowledge there is considered as a subjective assemblage of objects, or fragments of objects, or as an objective assemblage of subjectivities, or fragments of subjectivity.

Woolgar and Pawluch's paper illustrates a growing unease, also within circles of critical criminologists, about the strict policing of boundaries, indeed of separateness. With hindsight one might perhaps argue that this unease was not just about the policing of boundaries of knowledge,[69] but also about the strict policing of social boundaries, geographical boundaries, boundaries of identity, indeed boundaries per se. Writing two decades after his *Society of the Spectacle*, Guy Debord claimed that the centrifugal and separating tendencies of the spectacle had not only continued, but had reached extreme levels to the extent that they had stifled creative, constructive communication. 'Conversation is almost dead', he writes in 1988, 'and soon so too will be those who knew how to speak'.[70] At about the same time, Jürgen Habermas noted the loss or the 'exhaustion of Utopian energies' in the West, and the destruction of an open, public sphere of debate and communication.[71] Closer to the criminological home, Mike Davis, in Los Angeles,[72] excavated the pitiful ruins of collaborative, communicative Utopia in a gloomy cityscape of utter separation, 'gated communities', 'Bantustans', and the harsh policing of boundaries. Jonathan Simon noticed an emerging non-communicative, non-productive, risk-assessing actuarial trend in penology which, he stressed, in its logic of exclusion, seemed to announce the gradual abandonment of notions such as rehabilitation, re-integration, or even mere discipline.[73] Others such as Clifford Shearing and Philip Stenning,[74] they too around the year 1985, detected an emerging society of surveillance where physical control of consumer populations was gradually complementing[75] the morally laden panoptic discipline of individual souls. But if this picture of a very broad and possibly dominant trend of non-communicative social and cultural separation across the West was gaining ground among critics, including critical criminologists, it also rekindled their reflexivity and self-reflexivity. Sartre's 'distance' and 'negativity' welled up once again. If separateness or non-collaborative non-communication together constitute the dominant and therefore problematic force in society, culture, and knowledge, then cooperation and communication may be the critical choice to make. If competition and strict boundary policing and maintenance is the foremost force and problem in society, culture, and knowledge, then perhaps critics ought to opt for open debate, cooperation, and for a kind of hospitality that refuses to remain stuck in the self-righteousness of *particular* identity and difference. If both foundational particularism and foundational universalism have been shown to be unable to ground even their own 'absurd' premises,[76] then critics perhaps should make more of an effort to look beyond the boundaries of their limited views. If the main problem in society, culture, and knowledge is exacerbated, if not underpinned, by a process whereby entrepreneurialism and self-fashioning consumption – the backdrop to this renewed self-reflexivity, after all, *was* the 1980s – tends to get translated into an eternal master–slave dialectic (that is, into an eternal competitive war between 'victims' and 'victors', or between the eternally good and the eternally bad) then perhaps the critical moment lies in renewed attempts to direct creative entrepreneurial energies towards a more nuanced and more democratic politics of citizenship. If that which Foucault once termed[77] 'biopolitics' and 'biopower', that is, the typically Modern ordering and managing of *forms of life*, or, more precisely, the spatial and demographic distribution of populations, their desires, their bio-characteristics[78] (fitness, productivity, self-constraint, etc.), and ultimately, their social forms and subjectivities, is now boiling down to stochastic categorization and control of risk populations, then perhaps encounter across categorical divides ought to be part of any critical project. If those non-communicative forms of control and punishment have themselves in turn come to be perceived by many as just another form of risk to be avoided, confronted, challenged, ridiculed, taunted or even enjoyed, then perhaps more communication is what is called for. If part of today's crisis in society, culture and knowledge production is found in the considerable levels of commodification and instrumentalization of relations and interactions,[79] then perhaps the critical moment is one of ethical communication. If legal pluralism and multiculturalism were once 'cheaply' celebrated, to borrow Craig Calhoun's phrase,[80] then perhaps now is the time, as Jock Young has argued, to attempt a transformation of the public sphere in the direction of the 'dissolution' of dichotomies and bounded identities.[81] If the issue of social justice does now appear to be not so much about the need for peeling back layer upon 'subjective' layer of panoptic gaze and spectacular illusion in the hope of reaching an authentic 'objective' humanity, as it is about trying to mobilize and utilize all available communicative and collaborative energies with a creative eye on the construction of viable alternative ways if life, then perhaps that is what critical criminologists should do. Perhaps they should leave the comfort zone of their home-grown truths and strategies. Perhaps they should cast their net more widely. Perhaps they should sample and assemble a greater diversity of viewpoints. Perhaps they should be more democratic. Perhaps they should be more creative.

This search for a more communicative and creative democratic vision was quite noticeable across the humanities and social sciences. The work of Jürgen Habermas has been instrumental in this process of critical renewal. This should perhaps not come as too big a surprise, since Habermas's critical project[82] addressed all the above-mentioned issues, and quite explicitly aimed at defending and furthering the Modern project, all this in the full glare of deconstructionism. Habermas proposed the regeneration of public debate through 'practical discourse' and 'communicative ethics'. A counterfactual though democratic alternative to both foundationalism (whether in its universalist or particularist guises) and the endless regress of deconstruction, the model combined considerable sensitivity to difference and diversity with a pragmatic interest in the achievement of rational and consensual agreement. Habermas's assemblage, his eclectic 'third way', so to speak, also had a significant impact on critical criminologists, perhaps nowhere more so than in Willem de Haan's *Politics of Redress*.[83] Writing in the 1980s, de Haan, an erstwhile abolitionist, adopted Habermas's model not just as the way forward and out of a theoretical impasse among critical criminologists, but also, and perhaps first and foremost, because the model allowed to think pragmatically about social problems (or 'problematic situations', in abolitionist parlance) and their solution. This pragmatics did not require the critic to bring on board the slightly punitive, state-centred streak of the then quite forceful Left Realists, nor the slight naiveté[84] of abolitionist idealists, nor the slightly desperate and impractical scepticism of revolutionaries, whether Marxist-inspired or other. The model also allowed for a certain combination of formalism and informalism in the resolution of social or community problems, and that in turn prompted de Haan to read it as a possible way out of a conundrum that had been hampering critical criminology for years.

By focusing on the influence of Habermas on critical criminology I certainly do not mean to deny that other influences such as, for example, deconstructionism, post-structuralism, or Lacanian psychoanalysis, were also quite noticeable. Quite the opposite was the case.[85] Habermas's project though was of a more reconstructive (rather than deconstructive) nature, more pragmatic also, more practical indeed, and provided a considerable number of disillusioned and dazed critics with a more or less coherent sense of purpose in a world and in times which, as Jacques Derrida, the deconstructionist *par excellence*, has argued,[86] was growing evermore unhinged, out of joint, without stable foundation, beyond ultimate redemption, beyond the reach of closure, and with many of us now realising this. These are times, to borrow some of Sartre's existentialist phraseology once more, when many have come to realize that negativity, radical indeterminacy and radical freedom lie at the heart of human existence, 'like a worm'. Practical discourse and communicative ethics seemed to offer vistas onto pragmatic and collective endeavours, on communication and democratic debate, on constructive and creative forms of justice and social justice. It is important to note that this model, more procedural and less utopian, more communicative and less fundamentalist, more ethically aware and less self-righteous than earlier models, also invited critical criminologists to be more democratic in thinking about the theory and practice of alternative ways of the just life. It invited them, in short, to venture beyond boundaries previously eagerly policed, in order to assemble more diverse, more sophisticated and therefore also more attractive ideas. This invitation was part of what Peter Dews, in 1987, in his highly sophisticated critical assessment of post-structuralist thought, called the 'move to intersubjectivity'.[87] But such 'intersubjective' venturing and assembling was already ongoing.[88] One could argue that the emergence of British Left Realism, for example, is an illustration of this process.[89] Trying to steer clear from what they called mere control-oriented administrative criminology, whilst also criticizing mere law and order policies, they nevertheless made a strong plea to 'take crime seriously'. Taking on board elements from feminist criminology, and acquiring sensitivity to victims' needs, they argued pragmatically for the reconstruction of the (local) welfare state and for the enhancement of the democratic accountability of police organizations.[90]

I began this chapter by mentioning René van Swaaningen's sophisticated 'social judo' assemblage which is the result of an overview and assessment of a great variety of critical criminologies and what he calls 'visions' of social justice. Others have, more recently, assembled their own models. Assessing injustices in a risk-obsessed culture, and taking account of recent social theories and philosophies, including post-structuralist thought and postmodern anti-foundationalism, Barbara Hudson combined Habermas's procedural and more or less open-ended 'communicative ethics' with a renewed cosmopolitan emphasis on human rights, the latter serving as the more or less stable bed-rock foundation of any critical alternative.[91] But the most elaborate, arguably, is John Braithwaite's model of restorative justice.[92] Combining insights from a wealth of criminological theories (labelling criminology, control theories, left realism, abolitionism and communitarian models), and recognizing the growing importance of emotionality in a de-institutionalizing but still incommunicative society, Braithwaite's highly eclectic and hybrid model of 'pyramidal' or 'responsive' regulation and restorative justice has now probably become, among criminologists, the most ubiquitous model. It has achieved this status precisely because it is so eclectic and hybrid. In Braithwaite's model, the very boundary between critical criminology and mainstream criminology seems to have simply collapsed.

Such venturing beyond the boundaries of the familiar, and such assembling of disparate models into more complex ones, can and probably will continue for quite some time. That should not be too surprising in an age when ideas and models about ways and styles of life have detached themselves from their locality of origin and are now freely whizzing around the globe.[93] It should not come as a surprise in an age when so many have come to sense that any idea, any model, like any culture, or any subject-ivity, is the result of a process of hybridization, and is so inevitably.[94] There is, as I said, probably no limit to the amount of democratic and cre-ative 'border-crossing'[95] that can go on. It looks as if this process has become unstoppable. This constant critical but creative 'negativity' at the heart of human existence which Sartre was talking about is now, it seems, hard at work. Through it, new assemblages emerge, newly assembled models come into the world, none of them able though, it appears, to stem the tide. The very same radical negativity through which new assemblages come into the world is also the radical freedom that will prevent any newly assembled model from achieving complete stability or complete domi-nance. There is probably no mere coincidence – this may sound paradoxi-cal – that chaos theory or complexity theory became such a popular theoretical tool among critical criminologists.[96] If the contingent heart of human existence *has* now spiralled out of institutional control, then things are beginning to become both enabling and complex at the same time, quite indeterminately so.[97] Even Law itself, and morality more broadly, are now being recognised by critical scholars and researchers such as Peter Fitzpatrick as that which emerges through and develops in and through indeterminacy, or, to be more precise, in and through the irresolution between determinacy and indeterminacy.[98]

Many seem to have come to realize that any assemblage of social justice is only just that: an assemblage, the result of inevitable choice made in the midst of disparate materials, and fashioned through the exclusion – through conflict, says Sartre – of that which does not quite fit. That which does not fit then slides back into nothingness. It is nothingness which we try to deny when we fashion assemblages of justice. But it is, as Sartre said, this very nothingness that simultaneously provides us with the conditions for the fashioning of any assemblage whatsoever. It is through this noth-ingness that we are able to critically survey assemblages of social justice, and that we are able to imagine and assemble new ones in hopeful attempts to transcend the absurdity of earlier ones. But whatever we choose to do, whichever road we choose to take, we never seem to be able to halt nothingness; we never seem to be able to tame this heart of indeter-minacy. Many have now come to realize this. Or, as critics such as Zygmunt Bauman have been at pains to argue, between 1985 and 2005: a sense of ambivalence, ineradicable ambivalence (and that includes the ambivalence of critique), has pervaded contemporary culture.[99] Whatever we do, whichever coin we mint, it will have its other, darker side.

Conclusion: towards existential hybridization

Writing in the 1940s, Ernst Bloch seemed irritated by existentialism – Sartre's in particular – when he claimed that the latter's view on progress is that 'all progress is progress into Nothing'.[100] On the eve of European reconstruction one might perhaps have been forgiven for reading existentialism as a form of nihilism. Today's rediscovery of Sartrean existentialism is probably underpinned by a more hopeful attitude.[101] If all progress is progress into nothingness, or if, in other words, human existence, *becoming*, cannot be brought to a standstill, then perhaps this insight today sounds more like good news to those who are theorizing or practising criminal justice with an eye on social justice. If no assemblage is ever going to be able to close the gap of nothingness through which the world becomes, then no assemblage is going to be able to completely dominate all others. If the search for a perfectly just criminal justice is a never-ending one, and we have now come to realize this, then perhaps this bodes well for the future of critical criminology. This brings us to the question that has inspired this contribution: 'whither critical criminology?', or 'whither social justice in criminal justice?'.

I hope I have been able to explore the three broad programmatic stages which, in my view, critical criminology has gone through between 1945 and the present time. The last one has ended in a (still ongoing) proliferation of assemblages of models of, or proposals for social justice. Many of those are the result of what one might perhaps call border-crossing assemblage. Not just boundaries between separate critical criminologies have been crossed in the process. Scholars and researchers have indeed been casting their nets much more widely and have, on many occasions, taken account of that which used to be called, rather dismissively, mainstream criminology. A number of critical criminologists have made some considerable effort to take on board quotidian sentiments and desires that tend to be harboured far beyond the confines of academia. To some extent the very boundary between for example critical criminology and its other, mainstream criminology, once so clear, has collapsed in this process. This may go some way to explaining why a number of prominent voices are now wondering about the meaning of the word 'critical' in critical criminology, and why others are now desperately trying to imagine a new future for critical criminology.

Pat Carlen, for example, has recently been wondering about the word 'critical'.[102] Criminology, she argues, like any other academic endeavour, should always be critical. To be critical is unavoidable if one is engaged in the business of knowledge production. One cannot produce knowledge if one is not critical. Many philosophers would agree. Some would probably go a step further and claim that, since human being is choice, one can not be non-critical. Any denial of this would amount to 'bad faith'. Carlen however proceeds with an outline of a programme for critical criminology. Critical criminology, in Carlen's view, ought to take a stand against a number of isms (theoreticism, politicism, populism), against 'ideological closure', and against academic clubbing, whether of the PC or non-PC kind. It should however also choose *for* a 'moral [and hence communicative] discourse' that acknowledges its particular value-laden origins. Philosophers such as Nagel might say: it should opt for a moral discourse that acknowledges and takes responsibility for its own absurdity. One might be able to read this statement as a firm encouragement of further attempts at border-crossing assemblage.

Jock Young, on the other hand, has recently claimed that ideas and models once introduced by critical criminology are now quite widespread.[103] Again, that should not come as a surprise in an age of constant assembling, disassembling and reassembling. Arguing for a revival of critical criminology, Young makes a plea for 'guiding narratives' that allow for the 'unfinishable' project of critical criminology (i.e. the 'transformation' of strict boundaries of separation[104]) to continue. Young, in my view, need not worry. The unfinishable project of critical criminology is what it is: unstoppable, and fuelled by the radical negativity through which its other (Law – State – Power – Separation – Domination – Rule – Authority – Inequality – Order – Commodification – Categorization – and so on), as well as itself, come into the world. As Michael Hardt and Antonio Negri have argued in their book on *Multitude*,[105] the very same dynamics of immaterial labour and entrepreneurial communication that, in our global age, have produced global Empire, also provide the energy with which restless multitudes construct and circulate alternative ways of life. The very same processes and networks through which 'icons' of consumption (and therefore also of regulation) are circulated, also scatter images of 'integrity' and 'ethical identity' for agents to choose from, that is, to identify with.[106] The task of critical criminologists, writes Young, is to question 'the solidity of the social world and the stated purposes of its institutions'.[107] I don't think we need to worry too much here. The genie of the multitudes is out of the bottle of Imperial institutions. Life as such has become *critical*, and we now know it. That does not mean that critical criminology's programme, as we have sketched it above, is now obsolete. Not at all. It still makes sense to analyse and criticize the absurdity of authorities and their rule. It still makes sense to analyse and criticize the pragmatic origins of policy. It still makes sense to analyse and criticize the moral quality of theories and practices of criminal justice. And I see no reason to stop analysing and criticizing the aesthetic desires in criminological theorizing or in any kind of academic 'clubbing' (to evoke Carlen's image once more) that lacks even a modicum of self-criticism (a lack which Becker, as early as 1967,[108] never tired to expose). It still makes sense, as Jock Young, referring to Mannheim, maintains, to harbour 'dangerous thoughts' that connect problems of crime to 'structural inequalities of wealth and power'.[109] Or, as others have recently argued, it still makes sense, for example, to analyse and criticize the 'utilitarian' and 'servile' attitudes evident in criminological research that remains blind to its complicity in policies that, destructively, combine neo-liberalism and non-communicative exclusion.[110] There is no need to stop analysing and criticizing the phantasms that underlie law and criminal justice and those that fuel the will, *any* will to liberation. An editorial collective summed it up quite forcefully only very recently: critical criminologists need to 'counter the falsehoods and mythical assumptions upon which criminal justice policy is based', and need to criticize criminologies that 'lack[s] the ability to look outside itself'.[111] But all this is now part of the life of 21st century multitudes anyway. The restless worm at the heart of human existence never dies. The issue though which Young rightfully emphasizes, in my view, is the need for 'guiding narratives'. It is on this issue that I should wish to make some concluding remarks.

One might argue that we have now arrived at another *zero hour*. The difference with the immediate post-war period would then be that now there seems to be not so much a dearth of 'guiding narratives', as an over-abundance of circulating, criss-crossing fragments and assemblages. I agree with Young that we do need 'guiding narratives', or, to use Ernst Bloch's words, 'guiding images'. And we could do worse than heed Thomas Mathiesen's call for some necessary vagueness in this respect. Young's call though, as I understand it, invites us to assemble and, if possible, creatively invent – to borrow from the philosopher Gilles Deleuze here[112] – new concepts to think with. It invites us to produce and, if possible, creatively invent new metaphors with which we might perhaps be able not only to express collective aspirations of and efforts made by multitudes, but also to inspire the latter in their ongoing initiatives. As I have tried to argue, the last few decades have been marked by such conceptual or metaphorical assemblages and inventions. 'Restorative Justice' for example has been one of the more successful concepts, albeit it one that is now very much in the process of being analysed and criticized itself. 'Redress' is another one, as we have seen. Many of those conceptual assemblages resulted from surveys of materials that were available quite close to the criminological home. Such assemblages are very likely to continue. Zygmunt Bauman's politics of the 'agora', if picked up and re-assembled, could very well be on its way to becoming yet another one.[113] And so on. The challenge, in my view, is to remain aware of the dangers of circular reasoning in any decision to firmly stick to the safe comfort zone of cherished concepts or metaphors.

Let us now, like Sartre, return to Nietzsche and becoming. Nietzsche's philosophical programme[114] might perhaps be captured, at least in part, in a list of *dos* and *don'ts*. Do not resent; affirm life instead. Do not judge; create instead. Do not take away from life; add to life instead. Do not follow; open up vistas instead. Do not join the herd's resentful struggle for equal rights; practise the noble art of saying Yes to life instead. Do not submit to the good, the true, and the reasonable; be aware of their *human, all too human* origins instead. Don't define human being downwards;

become its future greatness instead. Do not block the energetic potential of life; multiply it instead. We may wish to acknowledge the quite unsettling features of Nietzsche's radical programme. Nietzsche's positive valuation of distance and solitude, for example, may not be to all critics' taste. Also, we do not necessarily have to remain blind to the programme's many contradictions. But its emphasis on creative becoming does seem to chime with our times. Now, it may be impossible to produce utterly novel concepts and metaphors that express, in a thoroughly novel way, new vistas on social justice. We may be less like Nietzsche's Zarathustra than we think. We may not hope to be *that* creative.[115] We may not be that superhumanly artistic. And if someone pretends they are, then a pinch of salt may come in handy, in this weary age of ours. As Craig Calhoun concluded in 1995, referring to Marshall Berman's *All that is Solid Melts into Air*,[116] 'this constant succession of everything by a putatively new successor makes it hard to be challenged by any idea of radical novelty'.[117] But we may try to capture the imagination of collective endeavours. And we may perhaps try to do this more or less imaginatively – if, as we are often told, 'imagination' is what is called for in an age when the obviousness of glaring inequality and separateness goes hand in hand with the complexity of the network of choices which produce them. One way of doing so has been largely underused by critical criminologists. There is something to be said for surveying materials that are available in what some call fictional literature.[118] Like Stephen Dedalus, the great 'artificer',[119] we may choose to venture further afield, beyond the labyrinthine circularities of our particular Dublins. Without Dedalus's eagerness to forget perhaps, but, like Joyce, with an eye firmly cast on what might become. So, if pressed to read the question 'Whither critical criminology?' as requiring a normative answer, I would be inclined to reply by saying that it would probably be a good idea to continue, in theory as in practice, on the road of communicative assemblage. That is the road of further hybridization, if you wish. Nietzsche's creative becoming not so much results from eager isolation (as he seemed to assume) as it develops in and through border-crossing communication. Creative becoming is a matter of communicative assemblage. The object of critique still seems to be non-communicative rigidity, or separateness, both in the theory and practice of criminal and social justice. Separateness is where the choice of identity and hegemony, and where the choice of difference and diversity, block communication.

Such separateness or non-communicativeness has for all too long marked not only the chosen 'logics' of social policy and criminal justice. It has, as I have tried to illustrate above, also been the hallmark of much theoretical reflection about these issues. It is not just social policy and criminal justice that are now undergoing the logic of non-communicative separateness. Critical criminologies too have, between themselves, for far too long, demonstrated too little willingness to overcome the bounds of self-righteousness and dogma. It is not just on the ground that the more or less communicative cosmopolitanism of multiculturalism has given way, in Zygmunt Bauman's words,[120] to the non-communicative rigidity of 'multi-communitarianism'. It is not just on the ground that the competitiveness and consumerism of our age have led many to choose for non-communicative separateness, where it would now appear as vindictiveness and as punitiveness, as anti-social behaviour and as anti-social behaviour orders, as identity politics and as ghettoization. For all too long have similar dynamics coloured developments in critical criminology, or better: between critical criminologies. Such non-communicative separateness – on the ground as well as in theory – tends to be self-reinforcing and is therefore unlikely to foster collective or collaborative efforts to address or perhaps even redress problems related to non-communication. Separateness, however, can only be overcome through genuine communication, and that implies a willingness to transform, a willingness to change.

A final word now is needed on the kind of genuine communication I have in mind here. Let me first return to Bauman's aforementioned notion of the agora. Bauman introduces this notion to describe a model of politics which is all about communication. The agora is not to be confused with the market whose operations are based on abstract and impersonal notions such as exchange value, risk and probability, nor with more tribal forms of community life which are about affinity and emotional proximity. Both the impersonality of exchange value and the desire for proximity emerge jointly in what the French sociologist Michel Maffesoli calls 'neo-tribes', i.e. late modern gatherings of Dionysian, hedonistic consumption.[121] Neo-tribes too are non-communicative and therefore non-transformative (and vice versa). Neither the market nor the tribe involve genuine communication. Nor do impersonal, non-communicative bureaucracies. None of those is very likely to stimulate participants to transform themselves in and through communicative assemblages. None is very likely to encourage participants to join in communicative assemblage and to transform themselves in the process. One does not really communicate with risk, value or probabilities. There is no great need, in tribes, to communicate beyond the bounds of affinity and emotion. In bureaucracies the silence of impersonal non-communication reigns. On the agora though, citizens meet and communicate. They exchange points of view that are open for debate. Points of view change. That which is presented as a private issue suddenly turns out to be of public interest. Solutions to common problems suddenly appear to depend on a wide variety of private concerns. And vice versa. In and through *agoratic* communication, citizens may choose to transform themselves. They may choose change. If they do they are then also likely to dissolve, at least partially, walls of separateness. I believe that Bauman's model of agoratic communication might serve as a 'guiding image' or 'guiding narrative' for efforts toward more creative, indeed transformative social policy and transformative criminal justice. Although there are, as I have explored above, agoratic elements and developments in contemporary society,[122] culture, and knowledge (and as such this proposal does not really fall out of the blue), one could do worse than admit – echoing Habermas – that the image of agoratic communication is largely a counterfactual one. Bauman himself realizes that one important condition needs to be met before anything like a politics of the agora may take shape, i.e. the reduction of existential fear, for it is fear, says Bauman, which prevents citizens from engaging in agoratic, transformative communication.[123]

Let me end with a word on genuine, that is, transformative communication. Genuine, transformative communication is likely to be future-oriented. Future-orientedness brings me to human projects. If human projects as well as the choices upon which they are based, have pragmatic, moral, aesthetic, and phantasmal aspects, then I believe it might be helpful if these aspects too are part of the subject of communication. Whereas Habermas's or de Haan's 'communicative ethics' and 'practical discourse' tend to focus on the rational deliberation of, or the search for the better argument, and whereas the more conservative communitarian ethics of restorative justice tend to emphasize the restoration of communal or emotional bonds, the form of communication which I suggest here entails the voluntary, though critical consideration by participants of each other's projects and choices. I would indeed suggest participants compare the pragmatic, moral, aesthetic and phantasmal aspects of projects and choices. Such comparisons could take place with an eye on possible hybridization, although one would hasten to add that it might be a (totalitarian) bridge too far to require participants – forcefully – to hybridize their projects and futures. But if and when it happens, and if and when it happens under conditions which are as 'power-free'[124] as possible – echoing Habermas's 'ideal speech situations' here – then, I believe, any such communicative process might be worthwhile. One might perhaps call such a process *existential hybridization*. It is this process of hybridization, or creative re-assemblage, if you wish, which in my view constitutes genuine, transformative communication. Such communication would, I hope, carry a promise, however weak and temporary, of overcoming separateness. Rather than focus on identity or community, the communicative process would be about projects. Rather than attempt redress or restoration of past and present, the process would focus on the future. Rather then aim at the exchange of value, participants would aim at the transformation of self and project. Such communicative process could be applied both in the practice of criminal justice and social policy as well as in the theoretical reflections of what I would suggest we continue to call critical criminology. Let me be clear though. This image of transformative communication and existential hybridization is only a 'guiding image', and nothing more.[125] It may be impossible to say how one should choose to put such a proposal into practice. Let me evoke Sartre's words – taken from his 1946 lecture – one last time: 'The content [of choice] is always concrete, and therefore unpredictable; it has always to be invented'. Anyone who would wish to choose to take this road should also realize that it is a never-ending one. The Sartre of *Being and Nothingness* would probably have agreed.

Notes

1 The author wishes to thank the following people for offering highly valued comments on an earlier version of this chapter: Don Crewe, Tim Doyle, Claire Grant, Joe Sim, Philip Stenning, Paul Willis and Majid Yar. All remaining errors are the author's. Sections in this chapter originally appeared as part of another paper on 'Whither critical criminology? A contemplation on existential hybridization', published in *Critical Criminology* (2008) vol. 16, issue 2. The author thanks Springer Publications for allowing him to reproduce said sections here.
2 See, e.g., R. van Swaaningen, *Critical Criminology: Visions from Europe*, London: Sage, 1997, at p. 218 especially.
3 E.g. in L. Wittgenstein, *The Blue and Brown Books*, New York: Harper & Row, 1960 [1958], at p. 69. Underneath the 'use' by critical criminologists of words such as 'social justice', or 'justice', a plethora of (often contradictory) conceptualizations could be distinguished, ranging from human rights, communicative ethics, politics of recognition versus politics of distribution, Marxist radicalism, and so on. However, as I am interested here only in the broad programmatic structures of this body of literature, I shall not pursue this issue further, although, of course, the great variety of critical criminological 'uses' of this terminology will become clear in the many illustrations throughout this chapter.
4 I shall be using the phrase 'critical criminology' in this chapter. I am well aware of the quite staggering diversity of perspectives, theories and models that may be distinguished underneath as broad a banner as 'critical criminology'. Furthermore, many of those often opposing perspectives, theories or models originate in particular legal or political cultures that can not always easily be reduced to a shared common ground (see on this e.g. Rene van Swaaningen's already cited work on critical criminological *Visions from Europe*). However, as I shall here be interested in (1) the broad programmatic structures of a body of literature which, in its institutionalized forms (conferences, journal series, etc.) (2) has, for decades, circulated among members of what one might call a global 'community' of critical criminologists, the undeniable diversity of and between critical *criminologies* may perhaps be bracketed off for the purposes of this chapter. I would like to add one more proviso here. Space and time limitations have obliged me to focus on 'critical criminology' as it has emerged and developed in Western democracies.
5 J. Inciardi (ed.), *Radical Criminology: The Coming Crises*, Beverly Hills, CA: Sage, 1980.
6 Though perhaps not among activists. Thanks to Joe Sim.
7 K. Carrington and R. Hogg (eds), *Critical Criminology: Issues, Debates, Challenges*, Cullompton: Willan, 2002.
8 A. Barton, K. Corteen, D. Scott and D. Whyte (eds), *Expanding the Criminological Imagination. Critical Readings in Criminology*, Cullompton: Willan, 2006.

9 Van Swaaningen, op. cit.
10 S. Henry and D. Milovanovic, *Constitutive Criminology*, London: Sage, 1996.
11 See below, section entitled 'Assembling critical criminologies (1985–2005)'.
12 See below, section entitled 'Assembling critical criminologies (1985–2005)'.
13 E.g. in A. Camus, *The Plague*, London: Penguin, 1960 [1947]; and A. Camus, *The Just*, London: Penguin, 1970 [1949].
14 Translation RL. The novel was later translated into English: M. Yourcenar, *Memoirs of Hadrian*, London: Penguin, 1959 [1951]. On this novel and its place in European post-war intellectual life, see R. Lippens, 'To have done with judgment? Yourcenar's *Hadrian* and the *Crime Against Life*', *International Journal for the Semiotics of Law*, 2006, 2, 153–181.
15 Isaac follows Nichola Chiaromante. J. Isaac, *Arendt, Camus, and Modern Rebellion*, New Haven, CT: Yale University Press, 1992, at p. 21 and p. 266.
16 J.-P. Sartre, *Being and Nothingness*, London: Routledge, 2003 [1942].
17 J.-P. Sartre, *Saint Genet, Actor and Martyr*, New York: George Braziller, 1963 [1952].
18 On Heidegger, see Don Crewe, Chapter 1, this volume.
19 F. Nietzsche, *Thus Spake Zarathustra*, London: Dent & Sons, 1933 [1883–1885].
20 See on this G. Agamben, *The Man Without Content*, Stanford, CA: Stanford University Press, 1999, pp. 85–93 in particular.
21 F. Nietzsche, *Ecce Homo*, London: Penguin, 1992 [1908].
22 The word *critique* is etymologically derived from the ancient Greek *kritein*, meaning to distinguish, to differentiate, or to draw boundaries, or lines of distinction.
23 J.-P. Sartre, 'Existentialism is a humanism', lecture 1946, reproduced at www.marxists.com.
24 E. Bloch, *The Principle of Hope*, Cambridge, MA: MIT Press, 1986 [1947], at p. 1373.
25 One may take this very literally. One of the most popular undergraduate sociology textbooks in the English speaking world of the 1960s, for example, was significantly influenced by Sartre's writings. See: P. Berger, *Invitation to Sociology*, New York: Doubleday, 1963. Richard Eyre captures Sartre's quasi 'poster status' in the early 1960s thus: 'few student bookshelves lacked a (largely) unread copy of *Being and Nothingness*' (cited on p. viii of his preface to the 2003 Routledge re-edition of the book, op. cit.).
26 Reprinted in: T. Nagel, *Mortal Questions*, Cambridge: Cambridge University Press, 1979, at p. 13.
27 H. Becker, 'Whose side are we on?', *Social Problems*, 1967, 14, 239–247.
28 As is the case with reductive, control-crazed 'post-humanism' which, according to Flemish philosopher Eric Rosseel, has, again, been gaining ground and influence rapidly in recent decades; E. Rosseel, *Het Verstomde Spreken. Toekomsten voor Vrijheid en Samenleven*, forthcoming (2009). On post-humanist non-communication, see also infra, in section entitled 'Assembling critical criminologies (1985–2005)' of this chapter.
29 B. Hudson, 'Criminological Theorising: Present and Future', presentation delivered on the occasion of the BSC North West Regional Branch symposium on 'Whose side are we on?', 12 January 2007, Liverpool.
30 D. Matza, *Becoming Deviant*, Englewood Cliffs: Prentice-Hall, 1969.
31 I. Taylor, P. Walton and J. Young, *The New Criminology*, London: Routledge & Kegan Paul, 1973, at p. 268. On this point, see also J. Young,

'Critical criminology in the twenty-first century: critique, irony, and the always unfinished', in Carrington and Hogg, op. cit., pp. 251–274, at p. 270 in particular.

32 H. Miner, 'Body ritual among the Nacirema', *American Anthropologist*, 1956, 58, 503–507.

33 H. Garfinkel, 'Conditions of successful degradation ceremonies', *American Journal of Sociology*, 1956, 61, 420–424.

34 R. Rijksen, *Meningen van Gedetineerden over de Strafrechtspleging* [Inmates on Criminal Justice], Assen: Van Gorcum, 1958.

35 H. Becker, *The Outsiders: Studies in the Sociology of Deviance*, New York: The Free Press, 1963.

36 R. Walters, 'Social defence and international reconstruction: illustrating the governance of post-war criminological discourse', *Theoretical Criminology*, 2001, 2, 203–222.

37 J. Young, *The Exclusive Society*, London: Sage, 1999, at p. 81.

38 M. Foucault (ed.), *I, Pierre Rivière, Having Slaughtered My Mother, My Sister, and My Brother...: A Case of Parricide in the Nineteenth Century*, Lincoln, NE: University of Nebraska Press, 1982 [1973].

39 Ibid., at p. 176.

40 Ibid., at p. 265.

41 On this point, see also: Z. Bauman, *Liquid Modernity*, Cambridge: Polity, 2000, at p. 165 in particular.

42 G. Debord, *Society of the Spectacle*, transl. Black&Red, 1977 [1967], available: www.marxists.org; quotations below are taken from this electronically available text, *partim*.

43 T. Mathiesen, 'The viewer society: Michel Foucault's 'Panopticon' revisited', *Theoretical Criminology*, 1997, 2, 215–234.

44 N. Moore, 'Icons of control: Deleuze, signs, law', *International Journal for the Semiotics of Law*, 2007, 1, 33–54.

45 E.g. in works such as J. Baudrillard, *The Illusion of the End*, Cambridge: Polity, 1994.

46 E.g. S. Hall, C. Critcher, T. Jefferson, J. Clarke and B. Roberts, *Policing the Crisis. Mugging, the State, and Law and Order*, London: Macmillan, 1978.

47 F. Fanon, *The Wretched of the Earth*, London: Penguin, 1967.

48 H. Schwendinger and J. Schwendinger, 'Defenders of order or guardians of human rights', *Issues in Criminology*, 1970, 5, 123–157. It is important to note that 'domination' was not placed in contrast to e.g. 'equality'. One might argue that either too much 'equality' or too little of it *both* tend to reduce levels of 'choice'. Both also tend to imply 'domination' as their *sine qua non*. With regard to the issue of 'equality', one could do worse than consider this: the question seems to be not so much 'Equality or not?', as the one that asks 'Equality of what?'. But see, on precisely this issue, A. Sen, *Inequality Reexamined*, Oxford: Clarendon, 1992.

49 See, e.g., L. Hulsman, 'Critical criminology and the concept of crime', *Contemporary Crises*, 1986, 10, 63–80.

50 Alex Liazos would in 1972 criticize labelling criminologists' focus on, and ephemeral critique of, the criminalization of 'nuts, sluts, and perverts', arguing instead for a more substantial critique of institutional violence; A. Liazos, 'The poverty of the sociology of deviance: nuts, sluts and perverts', *Social Problems*, 1972, 20, 103–120.

51 G. Pavlich, 'Critical genres and radical criminology in Britain', *British Journal of Criminology* 2001, 1, 150–167. Pavlich distinguishes new deviancy

theory's 'subjective problematizations' (paraphrase R.L.); the New Left's 'exposé' criticism; the New Criminologists' immanent critique; and the 'praxis-oriented immanent critique' of post-1975 critical criminology.

52 See, e.g., S. Cohen, 'The punitive city: notes on the dispersal of social control', *Contemporary Crises*, 1979, 3, 339–363.

53 T. Mathiesen, *The Politics of Abolition*, London: Martin Robertson, 1974, at p. 13.

54 Ibid., at p. 14.

55 Ibid., at p. 20.

56 Ibid., at p. 25.

57 S. Cohen, *Against Criminology*, New Brunswick: Transaction, 1988, at p. 16.

58 See, e.g., S. Motha and T. Zartaloudis, 'Law, ethics, and the utopian end of human rights', *Social & Legal Studies*, 2003, 12, 243–268.

59 See, e.g., G. Pavlich, 'Experiencing critique', *Law and Critique*, 2005, 16, 95–112; or J. Chryssostalis, 'The critical instance "after" the critique of the subject', *Law and Critique*, 2005, 16, 3–25.

60 On the phantasmal nature of both law and (critical legal) theory, see D. Caudill, 'Lacan, science, and law', *Law and Critique*, 2003, 14, 123–146.

61 R. Lippens, 'Alternatives to what kind of suffering? Towards a border-crossing criminology', *Theoretical Criminology*, 1998, 3, 311–343. Developments, however, were not as clear-cut as I seem to be suggesting here. To the extent that critical criminologists *did* continue to critically assess, evaluate and react against excessive state power, or lack of democratic accountability, my analysis of a growing separation between critical criminologies stands to be qualified. Thanks to Joe Sim.

62 Not that there was much new under the sun. See, e.g., Q. Bell, *On Human Finery*, London: Allison & Busby, 1992 [1947].

63 Reprinted in Nagel, op. cit., at p. 165.

64 On splinters, see also M. Schwartz, 'Does critical criminology have a core? Or just splinters?', *Critical Criminologist*, 1997, 3, online, available: www.sun.soci.niu.edu/~critcrim.

65 See also this paper, published a few years later: A. Cardarelli and S. Hicks, 'Radicalism in law and criminology: a retrospective view of critical legal studies and radical criminology', *Journal of Criminal Law and Criminology*, 1993, 3, 501–553.

66 S. Woolgar and D. Pawluch, 'Ontological gerrymandering: the anatomy of social problems explanations', *Social Problems*, 1985, 3, 214–227.

67 Ibid., at p. 218.

68 E.g. B. Latour, *We Have Never Been Modern*, Cambridge, MA: Harvard University Press, 1993 [1988]; B. Latour, 'Drawing things together', in M. Lynch and S. Woolgar (eds), *Representation in Scientific Practice*, Cambridge, MA: MIT Press, 1990, pp. 19–68.

69 This was Peter Berger's point when in 1992 he decided to *disinvite* students to a sociology that refused to take account of the contingent nature of the human condition and, in that very refusal, proved to be unable to predict any of the major social and cultural changes of past decades. P. Berger, 'Sociology: a disinvitation?', *Society*, November–December 2002, 12–18.

70 G. Debord, *Comments on the Society of the Spectacle*, London: Verso, 1998 [1988], at p. 29.

71 J. Habermas, 'The new obscurity: the crisis of the welfare state and the exhaustion of utopian energies', in J. Habermas, *The New Conservatism*, Cambridge: Polity, 1989 [1984], pp. 48–70.

72 M. Davis, *City of Quartz. Excavating the Future in Los Angeles*, London: Verso, 1990.

73 J. Simon, *Poor Discipline*, Chicago: University of Chicago Press, 1993.

74 C. Shearing and Ph. Stenning, 'From the Panopticon to Disney World: the development of discipline', in A. Doob and E. Greenspan (eds), *Perspectives in Criminal Law*, Ontario: Canada Law Book, 1985, pp. 335–349.

75 'Complementing', rather than 'replacing'; see, e.g., R. Coleman and J. Sim, 'From the dockyards to the Disney Store. Surveillance, risk and security in Liverpool city centre', *International Review of Law, Computers & Technology*, 1998, 1, 27–45.

76 See on this the hugely influential book, also published in 1985: E. Laclau and Ch. Mouffe, *Hegemony and Socialist Strategy: Towards a Radical Democratic Politics*, London: Verso, 1985.

77 In M. Foucault, *The History of Sexuality*, vol. 1, London: Penguin, 1979 [1976]; and M. Foucault, *Society Must be Defended*, New York: Picador, 2003 [1997] [1975–6], at pp. 239 et seq.

78 See on this N. Rose, 'The biology of culpability: pathological identity and crime control in a biological culture', *Theoretical Criminology*, 2000, 1, 5–34.

79 On this, see S. Hall, S. Winlow and G. Ancrum, 'Radgies, gangsta and mugs: imaginary criminal identities in the twilight of the pseudo-pacification process', *Social Justice*, 2005, 1, 100–112.

80 C. Calhoun, *Critical Social Theory: Culture, History, and the Challenge of Difference*, Oxford: Blackwell, 1995, at p. xv.

81 See Young's *The Exclusive Society*, op. cit., at pp. 167–189 in particular.

82 E.g. in J. Habermas, *Theory of Communicative Action*, Boston, MA: Beacon, 1984 and 1988; and: J. Habermas, *The Philosophical Discourse of Modernity*, Cambridge, MA: MIT Press, 1987.

83 W. de Haan, *The Politics of Redress*, London: Unwin Hyman, 1990.

84 One may want to add here that this 'naiveté' may have been unevenly distributed among abolitionists. Joe Sim for example has been at pains to explain how British abolitionists, without having to renege on their critical stance towards power imbalances, did tend to adopt a certain pragmatism that not only prevented them from getting stuck in strict ideological positions, but actually allowed them to persuade 'mainstream' actors to adopt their 'negative reform' position on issues such as 'deaths in custody, prison conditions, medical power, visiting, censorship and sentencing'. See J. Sim, 'The abolitionist approach: a British perspective', in A. Duff, S. Marshall, R.E. Dobash and R.P. Dobash (eds), *Penal Theory and Practice: Tradition and Innovation in Criminal Justice*, Manchester: Manchester University Press, 1994, pp. 263–284. Unlike Dutch or some Scandinavian-based abolitionisms which had more or less anarchic, anti-authoritarian and indeed anti-statist tendencies, the British variety has focused largely on power imbalances – wherever and whenever manifested – as its favoured object of critique. This focus equipped the latter with more flexibility than the former.

85 For an impressive overview of this influence, see B. Arrigo, D. Milovanovic and R. Schehr, *The French Connection in Criminology: Rediscovering Crime, Law, and Social Change*, New York: SUNY Press, 2005. On deconstruction, see also Pavlich's above-mentioned essay 'Critical genres and radical criminology in Britain', at pp. 161–163 in particular.

86 Particularly in J. Derrida, *Spectres de Marx*, Paris: Galilée, 1993.

87 P. Dews, *Logics of Disintegration. Post-Structuralist Thought and the Claims of Critical Theory*, London: Verso, 1987, pp. 220–244.

88 On criminological knowledge as assemblage and circulation, see also R. Lippens, 'Imagining lines, assembling criminologies, towards negotiation', in K.L. Kunz and C. Besozzi (eds) (transl.), *Social Reflexivity and Qualitative Methods: Toward a Criminological Self-Understanding in Postmodern Society*, Bern: Haupt, 2003, pp. 167–188; R. Lippens, 'Crime, criminology and epistemology: tribal considerations', in B. Arrigo and C. Williams (eds), *Philosophy, Crime, and Criminology*, Chicago, IL: University of Illinois Press, 2006, pp. 103–133; and: R. Lippens, 'Tribal images, fashionable deviance, and cultural distinction: notes on criminological change', in H.-J. Albrecht, T. Serassis and H. Kania (eds), *Images of Crime III*, Freiburg: Edition Iuscrim (forthcoming). On assemblage theory more generally, see M. DeLanda, *A New Philosophy of Society: Assemblage Theory and Social Complexity*, London: Continuum, 2006.

89 E.g. in J. Lea and J. Young, *What is to be Done about Law and Order. Crisis in the Eighties*, Harmondsworth: Penguin, 1984.

90 Looking beyond the strict confines of critical criminology, one might perhaps be able to note, as Joe Sim recently did, that New Labour's ideological universe too does include some fairly contradictory assemblages (e.g. a strong desire for 'modernization' combined with visions of 1950s neighbourhood life). See J. Sim, 'Criminology and the punitive state', presentation delivered on the occasion of the BSC North West Regional Branch symposium on 'Whose side are we on?', 12 January 2007, Liverpool.

91 B. Hudson, *Justice in the Risk Society. Challenging and Re-affirming Justice in Late Modernity*, London: Sage, 2003.

92 E.g. in J. Braithwaite, *Crime, Shame, and Reintegration*, Cambridge: Cambridge University Press, 1989; and J. Braithwaite and Ph. Pettit, *Not Just Deserts: A Republican Theory of Criminal Justice*, Oxford: Clarendon, 1990.

93 See the classic paper A. Appadurai, 'Disjuncture and difference in the global cultural economy', in M. Featherstone (ed.), *Global Culture*, London: Sage, 1990, pp. 295–310.

94 See on this the highly influential H. Bhabha, *The Location of Culture*, London: Routledge, 1994.

95 On 'border crossing', see H. Giroux, *Border Crossings*, London: Routledge, 1992.

96 The work of Dragan Milovanovic has been crucial here. See e.g. D. Milovanovic (ed.), *Chaos, Criminology, and Social Justice. The New Orderly (Dis)Order*, Westport, CT: Praeger, 1997.

97 This may go some way to explain why a number of established as well as emerging scholars in critical criminology are now rediscovering existentialism. See e.g. B. Arrigo, 'Critical criminology, existential humanism, and social justice: exploring the contours of conceptual integration', *Critical Criminology*, 2001, 10, 2, 83–95; D. Crewe, *Will, Power, Constraint & Change: Prolegomena to the Study of Self and the Emergence of Structure in a Young Offender Institution*, Keele: Keele University, 2007, unpublished PhD thesis; S. Mackenzie, 'Situationally edited empathy; an effect of socio-economic structure on individual choice', *Critical Criminology*, 2006, 3, 365–385, but see also the overview in W. Morrison, *Theoretical Criminology: From Modernity to Post-Modernism*, London: Cavendish, 1995, at pp. 349–382.

98 P. Fitzpatrick, *Modernity and the Grounds of Law*, Cambridge: Cambridge University Press, 2001.

99 Bauman's *oeuvre* is vast. But see, e.g., Z. Bauman, *Modernity and Ambiva-*

lence, Ithaca: Cornell University Press, 1991; Z. Bauman, *Postmodern Ethics*, Oxford: Blackwell, 1993.

100 Op. cit., at p. 433.

101 E.g. C. Williams, 'Engaging freedom: toward an ethics of crime and deviance', in B. Arrigo and C. Williams (eds), *Philosophy, Crime, and Criminology*, Chicago, IL: University of Illinois Press, 2006, pp. 167–196.

102 P. Carlen, 'Critical criminology? In praise of an oxymoron and its enemies', in Carrington and Hogg (eds), op. cit., pp. 243–250.

103 In the already cited essay on 'Critical criminology in the twenty-first century: critique, irony, and the always unfinished', at p. 255.

104 But see also, from Deleuzoguattarian inspiration, D. Milovanovic, 'Diversity, law and justice: A Deleuzian semiotic view of "criminal justice"', *International Journal for the Semiotics of Law*, 2007, 1, 55–79.

105 M. Hardt and A. Negri, *Multitude. War and Democracy in the Age of Empire*, London: Penguin, 2004. See also R. Lippens, 'Tracing the legal boundary between Empire and multitude. Wavering with Hardt and Negri (2000–2005)', *Leiden Journal of International Law*, 2005, 3, 389–402.

106 For an interesting illustration of such images as tools in a more 'responsive' regulation of financial markets, see J. Braithwaite and V. Braithwaite, 'Democratic sentiment and cyclical markets in vice', *British Journal of Criminology*, 2006, 46, 6, 1110–1127.

107 Again in 'Critical criminology in the twenty-first century: critique, irony, and the always unfinished', at p. 271.

108 See again his paper on 'Whose side are we on?', at p. 107 in particular.

109 J. Young, 'In praise of dangerous thoughts', *Punishment & Society*, 2003, 5, 97–107, at p. 105.

110 P. Hillyard, J. Sim, S. Tombs and D. Whyte, 'Leaving a stain upon the silence: contemporary criminology and the politics of dissent', *British Journal of Criminology*, 2004, 3, 369–390.

111 A. Barton, K. Corteen, D. Scott and D. Whyte (eds), op. cit., at p. 2.

112 G. Deleuze and F. Guattari, *What is Philosophy?*, New York: Columbia University Press, 1994.

113 Z. Bauman, *In Search of Politics*, Cambridge: Polity, 1999.

114 Expressed most forcefully in F. Nietzsche, *Twilight of the Idols. The Anti-Christ*, London: Penguin, 1990 [1889–1895].

115 For slightly more positive or optimistic argumentation though, see G. Pavlich, 'Nietzsche, critique and the promise of not being thus...', *International Journal for the Semiotics of Law*, 2000, 13, 357–375.

116 See the classic work M. Berman, *All that is Solid Melts into Air: The Experience of Modernity*, New York: Penguin, 1982.

117 C. Calhoun, op. cit., at p. 290.

118 G. Deleuze, *Essays Critical and Clinical*, Minneapolis, MN: University of Minnesota Press, 1997.

119 The young Joyce, in other words; J. Joyce, *A Portrait of the Artist as a Young Man*, London: Penguin, 1992.

120 In *In Search of Politics*, op. cit., pp. 197–202.

121 See M. Maffesoli, *The Time of the Tribes: The Decline of Individualism in Mass Society*, London: Sage, 1996.

122 E.g. the need for consumers to orient themselves towards the exterior; the unrelenting demand of self-fashioning placed on current day consumers; the wandering, 'nomadic' character of consumers' life trajectories; the ongoing hybridization of contemporary cultures; the relentless scepticism of our age;

the emerging collaborative and communicative dimensions of post-Fordist, immaterial labour (Hardt and Negri), etc.

123 Bauman suggests the guarantee of a basic income as the means *par excellence* to reduce existential fear; see *In Search of Politics*, op. cit., pp. 180–190.

124 It might of course be objected that 'freedom' from power imbalances can only be established (in both senses of the term) in and through the very process of transformative communication and, as I shall call it, existential hybridization itself. I would not be inclined to disagree.

125 It might also be objected that any process of communicative existential hybridization of projects that takes no account of the possibility that much, if not most, suffering might be the unintentional result of action, is a seriously flawed one. Again I would be inclined to agree. However, levels of possible non-intentionality, and of possible remedial action, have to be debated and hopefully agreed, in my view, in and through a communicative process such as the one expounded here.

Index

abolitionism 287n84
absolutes, collapse of 96–100
academic publication process 235–6
action 149
actor–network theory 41, 272
actuarial penology 234–5
Adler, P. 176
agency: and free will 14–16; and structure continuum 12–13
Agger, B. 226
angst 26, 46n44
Anthony, Donna 187, 195n163
appearance 34–5
Aristotle 20
Arrigo, B. 222
aspect: of objects 72–3, 75; of violence, changing 76–9
assumptive world 177–9, 185–6
Attig, T. 179
authenticity 26; and conformity to norms 22–3; and death 24–5; Ultimate Fighting 116
authoritarianism 233, 239–40
autobiographies: Angela Cannings' 175; issues in studying 154; as research tool 145, 152–4; stigma of white-collar ex-offenders 156–8; study of 175; study of in criminology 154–5; of white-collar offenders 155
automaton conformity as mechanism of escape 233, 240–1

Balke, F. 59–60, 61
Barak, G. 82
Baudrillard, Jean 97–8, 226–8, 236–7
Bauman, Zygmunt 70, 86, 87, 112, 279, 281
Beauvoir, Simone de 201–2
Beck, U. 98, 100, 105, 109, 110
Becker, Howard 262
becoming: crime as 63–4; social conditioning of 33–41

Becoming Deviant (Matza) 6, 261
Beder, J. 177
Being: for-itself/of-itself 4; as fundamental theme 2–5; Heidegger on previous views of 20–1; as idea in social sciences 5; social conditioning of 33–41; violence as reduction of 71–81; and will 19
Being and Nothingness (Sartre) 253–7, 258
Being-in-time 25–7
Being-with-one-another 21–2
beliefs and values 150–1, 174
biaphobia 82–3
biopower 60, 224–5
Bloch, Ernst 258, 276–7, 279
Braithwaite, John 275
Brandom, Robert 32–3
British Left Realism 275
Bull, J. 177

Calhoun, Craig 280
Calverley, A. 146
Campbell, K. 171
Cannings, Angela 175, 179–85, 186, 189
capitalism, effects of 230–3
care 25–6
Carlen, Pat 277–8
Carlsson, Chris 132
Castells, Manuel 99
choices and reference groups 36–7
Christianity as herd morality 3
Chtcheglov, Ivan 138
civility 199–201, 210–13
Clark, C. 151
Clark, Sally 186
classicist criminology 12–13
classification schemas 234
cognitive transformation, theory of 176–7
Cohen, Stanley 269
collapse of absolutes 96–100
communication 280–3
community activation: and crime control 200–1; and exchange 207–9

completeness 28, 29–31
conformity: automaton 240–1; as mechanism of escape 233; to norms 22–3, 203–4
consciousness: as intentional 72–3; and language 229–30; reflexive 98
consumer culture 131–3, 213–16, 264
consumer nihilists 102–3
consummation by adoption of supplements 29
contingency in Ultimate Fighting 112–16, 117–18
contractual governance by the state 211–13
contribution, social inclusion by 213–16
controls and crime 17–18
Corporeal Transaction (TCT), Theory of 104–6
crime: as becoming 63–4; compared to scrounging 140; and controls 17–18; as default behaviour of humans 18; genealogy of 58–62; seduction of 203–4; will to 42–4; and will to power 53–5
crime control and community activation 200–1
criminal motivation: agency–structure continuum 12–13; will as tool for analysing 13–14
criminals, pale/great 54, 60, 61
criminology: current interest in existentialism 7–8; early application of existentialism 5–7; existentialism in 176–7; hybridization of 271, 276–83; impact of Sartre 260–1; and phenomenology of reciprocal exchange 209–13; and philosophy 222; of the shadow 223, 225, 228, 229, 230, 233; study of autobiographies in 154–5; *see also* critical criminology
critical criminology 1965–1985 262–70, 1985–2005 271–6; crisis of 250; defined 249; historical overview 251–2; renewal of 250–1
Critical Mass 138
Culler, J. 28, 47n56
cultural criminology 7
culture, technologized and hyper-real 226–8, 236–7
Cusson, M. 177

das Man 21–2, 45n38
Dasein 2, 21–6, 74
de Certeau, Michel 137, 142n15
de Haan, Willem 274
death: and authenticity 24–5; of God 96–8; and making choices 27; of the social 97–100
Debord, Guy 265–7
decisions as oriented towards the future 27

Dedalus, Stephen 280
Deleuze, Gilles 279
Delinquency and Drift (Matza) 16–18
Denov, M. 171
Denzin, N. 173
dérive 138
Derrida, J. 28–30, 40, 47n74
détournement 137–8, 139
Dewey, J. 104
Dews, Peter 275
disciplined body in Ultimate Fighting 118–21
discourse of the master 237–8, 245n92
distantiality 22–3
dominating body in Ultimate Fighting 116–18
Douglas, J.D. 5, 149–50, 151, 174
Durkheim, E. 81

Ebaugh, E. 172, 173, 174, 175
Edelhertz, H. 147
edgework 108–11; Ultimate Fighting as 112–16; and violent street crime 122–3
ego in Ultimate Fighting 115–16
Elias, N. 86
Elster, J. 200
emotions 148–9, 151–2, 173–4, 204–9
escape, mechanisms of 232–3
Essay on the Origin of Languages (Rousseau) 28–9
ethics and God 3
Ethics of Ambiguity, The (de Beauvoir) 202
ethnomethodology 135–6, 143n13
Europe post WWII 253
Evasion (Anon.) 131, 139, 142n3
evidence-based research 234–5
exchange: and emotions 204–9; reciprocal, and criminology 209–13; theory of 206–7
exclusion, forms of 234–5
existence as preceding essence: as idea in social sciences 5; as theme in existentialism 2, 4
existential criminology 7
existential sociology 149–52, 172–5
existentialism: Being as fundamental theme 2–5; characteristics of 148–9; contemporary relevance 95–6; criminologist's current interest in 7–8; in criminology 176–7; defined 2, 172; early application to criminology 5–7; Heidegger 2–3, 4; hybridization 276–83; impact of Sartre post WWII 258–61; Kierkegaard 2–3; methodological stance 174–5; and reciprocity 201–4; Sartre 4–5; use of by writers 1–2
ex-offenders, resettlement of: blocked paths faced by white-collar ex-offenders 158–61; issues and concepts 146–7;

return to previous life by white-collar ex-offenders 161–3; stigma of white-collar ex-offenders 147–8, 150, 156–8, 160–1; white-collar offenders 147–8
extension 39–41

Fanon, Franz 267
Farrall, S. 146, 154
Fear and Trembling (Kierkegaard) 3
feelings *see* emotions
Ferris, Julie 187, 195n162
Fight Club (Palahniuk) 94, 100
flâneur 136
Flint, J. 212
flows, logic of 99–100
Fontana, A. 174, 175
Foucault, M. 13, 85, 86, 110, 224–5, 235–6, 263
Frank, A. 105, 117
Franks, D. 104, 117, 119
Franks, R.H. 206
free will 14–16, 19
freedom: of choice 148; existentialists' interest in 51; as idea in social sciences 5; man as condemned to 4–5; positive/negative 231–3; and will 19
Fromm, Erich 230–3, 239–41
fundamentalism 101
future: decisions as oriented towards 27; primacy of existence as 26–7

Galtung, Johan 71
Gane, M. 226
Garfinkel, H. 42, 135, 142n13, 262
Garland, D. 223, 225
genealogy: of crime 58–62; of morality 55–6
Genet, Jean 5–6, 256, 260–1
Gewalt 84
Giddens, A. 12, 15, 100, 101, 105, 109, 110
gift-society 214–15
Giordano, P.C. 147, 176–7
God: death of 96–8; and meaningfulness of life 2–3
Goffman, Erving 37–9, 216
Gorz, André 209
Gouldner, A.W. 200
great/pale criminals 54, 60, 61
Grounds, A. 171–2
Guignon, C. 97
guilt 26, 46n52, 148–9, 174

Habermas, Jurgen 104, 106–7, 108, 272, 273–4
Hardt, Michael 278
harm 223
Heidegger, Martin 2–3, 4, 228, 253–4; Being-in-time 25–7, 46n54; Being-with-one-another 21–2; care 25–6; Dasein 21,

26; death and authenticity 24–5; inauthenticity 22–3; ontological definition of violence 73–6; on past views of Being 20–1
Henry, S. 223
Hirschi, T. 208
Hochstetler, N. 147, 154
Hope, Tim 199
Hudson, Barbara 275
Huff, C.R. 170
human agency, critique of 228–30
human rights 269
humans: crime as default behaviour of 18; existence of 254–6; self-interest of 197–8
Hume, D. 197
Husserl, E. 72–3, 204–5
hybridization 271, 276–83
hyper-real culture 226–8, 236–7

I, Pierre Rivière (Foucault) 263
identity: after wrongful convictions 185; search for 172–3
importance of self 149–50
inauthenticity 22–4
Inciardi, James 249–50
incivility, regulation of 210–13
indeterminacy in Ultimate Fighting 112–16
institutions, regulatory 235–6
intellectual life in Europe post-WWII 253
intentionality 31
interactionism, symbolic 6, 34–9, 264

Jackman, Mary 71
James, William 45n32
Jarvis, Simon 215
Jewkes, Yvonne 49
Johnson, M. 5
Joyce, James 280

Kahan, D.M. 198
Kane, Stephanie 138–9, 143n15
Kant, I. 20
Katz, Jack 7, 113, 117, 154, 176
Kauffman, J. 178
Kaufman, W. 57
Kazantzakis, N. 62–3
Keith, Michael 136
Kellner, D. 228
Kerouac, J. 142n8
Kierkegaard, Søren 2–3

Lacan, Jacques 228–30, 237–8, 245n92
language 229–30
Lash, Scott 98, 99, 100, 105, 109, 110
Latour, Bruno 41, 272
law and will to power 53–5
Lawler, E.J. 205–8
Lee, Nick 29–30, 47n74

Lejeune, P. 152
Lévi-Strauss, C. 29, 262
life narratives *see* autobiographies
life projects 255, 256
life-world 104–7
Loader, I. 187
logic of flows 99–100
logocentrism 28
Luhmann, Niklas 71
Lyng, S. 104, 109, 114, 117, 119

McAdams, D.P. 152
McIver, R. 17
McQuarrie, J. 148, 173
Making it Explicit: Reasoning, Representing, and Discursive Commitment (Brandom) 32–3
Manning, P. 172
mapping when scrounging 134–6
Martin, D.L. 170
Maruna, S. 147, 154, 177, 188, 189
Mathiesen, Thomas 265, 268–9, 279
Matza, David 6, 16–18, 42–3, 261
Mauss, M. 214–15
Mead, G.H. 88
meaningfulness of life and God 2–3
mechanisms of escape 232–3
Mehan, Hugh 136
Meisenhelder, T. 177
methodology, existentialist 174–5
Milovanovic, D. 222, 223
Miner, Horace 262
Mixed Martial Arts *see* Ultimate Fighting
modernization 96–100, 105
Moore, Nathan 265
morality: and God 3; slave 101
morality, genealogy of 55–6
Morgan, S. 154–5
Morrison, W. 176
Multitude (Hardt and Negri) 278
music, origins of 40–1

Nagel, Thomas 16n15, 31n76, 270
negative freedom 231–3
Negri, Antonio 278
Neimeyer, R.A. 178
neo-conservatism 101
Nietzsche, Friedrich 2, 3, 96–8, 279–80; biopower 60; and contemporary nihilism 101–2; and criminology 62–5; and existentialism 51–2; genealogy of crime 58–62; genealogy of morality 55–6; pale/great criminals 54, 60, 61; political and legal theory 57–8; slave morality 101; will to power 111; will to power and crime 53–5
nihilism, contemporary 101–3
Nixon, J. 212

No Holds Barred (NHB) Fighting *see* Ultimate Fighting
non-linear reflexivity 99
norms: civility and reciprocity 199–201; conformity to 22–3, 203–4; and crime 17–18

objects: perception of spatial 72–3; social conditioning of 31–3
observation 75
Oleson, J.C. 155
Olson, Mancur 197
Olson, R.G. 46n44
On Cooling the Mark Out (Goffman) 38
On Face Work (Goffman) 38–9
On the Genealogy of Morals (Nietzsche) 3
Outsiders (Becker) 262

Palahniuk, Chuck 94, 100
pale/great criminals 54, 60, 61
Parkes, C.M. 177
Pasteur, Louis 41
Patel, Tripti 187, 195n160
Pawluch, Dorothy 271, 272
peacemaking criminology 6
perception of spatial objects 72–3
Pereboom, D. 97
performance 37–9, 49n95
phenomenology 20, 72–3, 75, 204–5, 205, 209–13
philosophy and criminology 222
Pinsonneault, P. 177
Plummer, K. 153
policing of risk 234–5
politics, Nietzsche on 57–8
Politics of Abolition (Mathiesen) 268–9
Politics of Redress (de Haan) 274
Ponse, B. 175
positive freedom 231, 232
positivist criminology 12–13, 23
power: and completeness 29–31; Foucauldian construct of 224–5
Presentation of Self in Everyday Life, The (Goffman) 39
Principle of Hope, The (Bloch) 258
prisoners, resettlement of: blocked paths faced by white-collar ex-offenders 158–61; issues and concepts 146–7; return to previous life by white-collar ex-offenders 147–8, 161–3; stigma of white-collar ex-offenders 147–8, 150, 156–8, 160–1; white-collar offenders 147–8
productivity of violence 81–4
profiles of aspects of objects 72–3
punishment 58–9, 61, 224–5

Radelet, M. 170

Radical Criminology: The Coming Crises (Inciardi) 249–50
rationality 106–7
reality as rich and cluttered 75
reason 106–7
reciprocity: and civility 199–201; and existentialism 201–4; and self-interest 198
reduction, harms of 223
reference group theory 35–7
reflexivity 98–9, 105, 109–10
regulation of incivility 210–13
relational cohesion, theory of 205–6
resettlement of ex-offenders: issues and concepts 146–7; lessons from wrongful convictions 188–9; *see also* white-collar offenders
rhythm and scrounging 130–1
Rijksen, Rijk 262
risk, policing of 234–5
risk consciousness 107
risk society: and the criminological shadow 235–41; emancipatory experience in 106; responses to 100–3; Theory of Corporeal Transaction (TCT) 105; and violent street crime 122–3
risk-taking 108–9
Roberts, B. 152
role taking/making 35
Rose, Nikolas 215
Rousseau, Jean-Jacques 27, 28–9, 40–1
Runciman, W.G. 36

Saint Genet: Actor and Martyr (Sartre) 5–6, 256
Sartre, Jean-Paul 4–5, 5–6, 228; existentialism of 253–7; impact of post-WWII 258–61; reciprocity and existentialism 201–2
scale of violence 79–81
Schopenhauer, A. 16
Schwendingers, H. and J. 267
scientism, dominance of 235–6
scrounging: and mapping 134–6; and rhythm 130–1; and space 133–41; subversion through 127–8; and time 128–33
Seductions of Crime (Katz) 7
self: evolution of a moral 56–7; importance of 149–50; as performance 49n95; as a social product 37–9; transformations in 173; and values and beliefs 150–1
self-actualization during Ultimate Fighting 114, 120
self-interest of humans 197–8
self-presence 30
self-reflexivity 109–10
shadow, criminology of the 223, 225, 228, 229, 230, 233

Sheridan, S. 120, 153
Shover, N. 147, 154, 177
sign-exchange value 226–7
Sim, Joe 287n84
simulations, society of 226–8, 236–7
Situationists 137–8
slave morality 101
Smith, Adam 197, 215
Smith, Margaret 187, 195n161
Smith, S. 152
Snyder, Gary 142n9
social, death of the 97–100
social conditioning: of being and becoming 33–41; of objects 31–3
social inclusion by contribution 213–16
social sciences, existentialist ideas in 5
sociality and violence 82–3
society and states, violent tautology of 87–90
Society of the Spectacle (Debord) 265
sociology, existential 149–52, 172–5
Sociology of Translation 41
Sofsky, Wolfgang 85
soft determinism 17
Sparks, J.R. 187
sparring sessions in Ultimate Fighting 114–15
states: contractual governance by 211–13; relationship with following wrongful conviction 186–7; and society, violent tautology of 87–90; violence of 84–90; welfare 262, 264
stigma: after wrongful convictions 156–8, 160–1, 185; of white-collar ex-offenders 147–8
Stouffer, S.A. 36
structuration theory 12–13
structure and agency continuum 12–13
subversion: temporal, and scrounging 132; through scrounging 127–8; of urban space 136–9
supplementation 29, 30, 40–1
Swaaningen, Rene van 250–2
symbolic interactionism 6, 34–9, 264
Synopticon (Mathiesen) 265
system colonization of the life-world 105–6

tapout 115, 126n74
tautology of state and society 87–90
technologized culture 226–8, 236–7
theories: actor–network 41, 272; choice process 208; cognitive transformation 176–7; Corporeal Transaction (TCT) 104–6; exchange 206–7; reference group 35–7; relational cohesion 205–6; structuration 12–13
there-being 2, 21–6
Thompson, Hunter S. 111

time and scrounging 128–33
Tiryakian, E. 5
tradition: breakdown of 96–100; desire to
 reclaim 101
transaction 104–6
transformative communication 282–3
transgression, will to 42–4
typification 34–7

Ultimate Fighting: authenticity in 116;
 contingency in 112–16; disciplined body
 118–21; dominating body in 116–18; and
 ego 115–16; indeterminacy in 112–16;
 reason for focussing on 111–12; rise of
 94–5; self-actualization during 114, 120;
 sparring sessions 114–15; tapout 115,
 126n74
uncertainty: modern condition of 96–100; in
 Ultimate Fighting 112–16
United States, wrongful convictions in
 170–1

values and beliefs 150–1, 174
Veneigem, R. 142n3, 142n4, 144n23
violence: changing the aspect of 76–9;
 definition problems 70–1; elements of
 definition of 72–6; ontological definition
 of 73–6; productivity of 81–4; as
 reduction of being 71–81, 83–4; scale of
 79–81; and sociality 82–3; of the state
 84–90; street crime and the risk society
 122–3

Wacquant, L. 114, 119
Warnock, Mary 51
Warren, C. 175
Watson, J. 152
Wealth of Nations (Smith) 197
Weisburd, D. 147
Weisman, R. 171
welfare state 262, 264
What is a Bat? (Nagel) 31n76, 270
white-collar offenders: blocked paths faced
 by 158–61; resettlement of 147–8; return
 to previous life by 161–3; stigma faced by
 147–8, 150, 156–8, 160–1
will 12–44; and freedom 19; to power 53–5,
 111; to self-consummation 41–2; as tool
 for analysing criminal motivation 13–14;
 will to crime 18–19
Wood, Houston 136
Woolgar, Steve 271, 272
work, commitment to 102
Wretched of the Earth, The (Fanon) 267
writing 29, 40, 47n74
wrongful convictions: Angela Cannings
 179–85, 186; defining 169–70; impact on
 convictees 171–2; lessons for
 rehabilitation and resettlement 188–9;
 number of cases 170–1; relationship with
 the state following 186–7; Sally Clark
 186; wider context of Cannings' case
 187–8

Young, Jock 262, 278